FAMOUS EPOCH=MAKERS

AUTHENTIC BIOGRAPHIES OF THE WORLD'S
GREATEST CHARACTERS

ROBERT E. LEE

BY

HENRY ALEXANDER WHITE, M.A., Ph.D., D.D.

PROFESSOR OF HISTORY IN THE WASHINGTON AND LEE
UNIVERSITY

GREENWOOD PRESS, PUBLISHERS
NEW YORK

Originally published in 1897
by G. P. Putnam's Sons

First Greenwood Reprinting 1969

Library of Congress Catalogue Card Number 69-14148

SBN 8371-1864-6

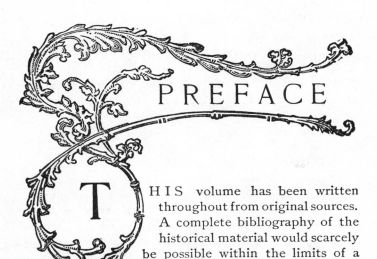

PREFACE

THIS volume has been written throughout from original sources. A complete bibliography of the historical material would scarcely be possible within the limits of a preface.

The statements concerning the English ancestry of General Robert E. Lee are based upon researches made by members of the Lee family, and set forth in various recent publications. The story of colonial and Revolutionary days has been found in a mass of material extending from the writings of John Smith, founder of Virginia, to the editorial labours of Justin Winsor, librarian of the Harvard University. The Journals of Congress and of various State legislatures, Force's *American Archives*, the publications of various State historical societies, the Johns Hopkins University Studies, the letters and works of Washington, Henry, Jefferson, Madison, Mason, Franklin, Hamilton, and John Adams have been used. I desire to add a word of special thanks for the aid derived from the valuable publications of the

Virginia Historical Society, and from the *Quarterly Magazine* issued by the William and Mary College. The debates in the Federal Convention, in the State Conventions that adopted the Constitution, and speeches in Congress extend the list.

The subsequent social and political history of our country, down to the year 1870, has been drawn chiefly from the speeches delivered in Congress, from party platforms, and from the biographies and letters of American statesmen. I must acknowledge my indebtedness for much collateral material set forth in the series, *American Commonwealths*, and in the series, *American Statesmen*, and in the general and special works of Story, Curtis, Schouler, Mc-Master, Henry Adams, Roosevelt, John Fiske, Von Holst, Rhodes, Benton, Blaine, Cox, Greeley, A. H. Stephens, and Jefferson Davis.

With reference to slavery, I may say that I have read nearly all the literature, from *Uncle Tom's Cabin* and Wilson's *Slave Power* to the most recent biography of William Lloyd Garrison.

In the discussion of the campaigns of the Army of Northern Virginia, the basis of my work has been the *Official Records* of the war. In addition to these reports, a large mass of testimony from participants and eye-witnesses is contained in the *Southern Historical Society Papers* and in the four volumes entitled *Battles and Leaders of the Civil War* (Century Company). *The Campaigns of the Civil War* (Scribners) contain excellent special studies by Federal officers. I have consulted the voluminous work of the Comte de Paris and also

the biographies of Lincoln, Davis, Seward, J. E.
Johnston, Stuart, Jackson, Hancock, and other
Federal and Confederate leaders; likewise the *Memoirs* of Grant, Sherman, and Sheridan, and military histories of different Federal *corps d'armée*.
Of special importance among these are the various
biographies of General Robert E. Lee.

I desire to express my great appreciation of the
courtesy of General G. W. Custis Lee, President of
the Washington and Lee University for valuable
items of information, and also for permission to use
the letters and papers of his illustrious father.

I wish to acknowledge my indebtedness to Major
Jed Hotchkiss, of Staunton, Virginia, of the Engineer Company, Second Corps, Army of Northern
Virginia, a member of the personal staff of both
Jackson and Lee. Major Hotchkiss is now engaged in the work of collecting from veterans of
the war their personal testimony concerning important events in the campaigns. This information he
has generously placed at my disposal, and has also
rendered assistance in reading the proof-sheets. I
desire also to make acknowledgment of assistance
rendered by my father-in-law, Judge Beverley Randolph Wellford, Jr., of Richmond, Virginia, formerly
connected with the War Department of the Southern
Confederacy. Judge Wellford has furnished valuable suggestions and historical facts, and has also assisted in the work of examining the proof-sheets. I
regret that I cannot here mention a host of other
friends, veterans of the war, who have given me the
benefit of their personal testimony as eye-witnesses.

The account herein given concerning the campaign in the Wilderness is, for the most part, a paper which I had the honour to read before the Military Historical Society of Massachusetts.

HENRY ALEXANDER WHITE.

WASHINGTON AND LEE UNIVERSITY,
August 23, 1897.

CONTENTS.

ILLUSTRATIONS.

ROBERT E. LEE.

CHAPTER I.

BIRTH—FAMILY.

1642–1807.

OBERT EDWARD LEE was born at Stratford on the Potomac, in Westmoreland County, Virginia, January 19, 1807. This eighth year after the passing of Washington saw new fierceness added to the commercial warfare between England and Napoleon. It witnessed also the rise of the war-spirit in the United States in connection with President Jefferson's struggle to maintain the honour of his Administration against British seizure of American seamen.

Robert Edward was the third son of Colonel Henry Lee and Anne Hill Carter, his second wife; the baptismal name of the child was bestowed in honour of two scions of the house of Carter. " Light-Horse Harry " Lee, as a Federalist of the

school of General Washington, held himself aloof
from political affiliation with the sage of Monticello.
When Jefferson assumed the robes of office as Chief
Magistrate in Washington, Lee withdrew himself
from the halls of Congress to the shade of his own
maple-grove in the country of his fathers, where,
during the first decade of the new century, he bore
mild sway as the patriarch of a Virginian household.
There did he often repeat and then make careful
record of the story of marches and fields of war in
the Revolutionary days when he himself was the
chief leader of horse in Washington's armies.

Stratford, the stately dwelling-place, had become
the property of Colonel Lee through his marriage
with the daughter of Philip Ludwell Lee in 1782;
about 1790 she had passed away, leaving behind her
a daughter and one son, who bore his father's name,
Henry Lee.   From Thomas Lee, of the third generation of Lees in Virginia, this mansion had
descended to the succeeding heirs in the days of
King George II.   The tradition runs that Queen
Caroline's admiration for the colonial officer led her
to send a private gift of money to Thomas Lee for
the construction of a mansion befitting the dignity
of the President of the colonial Council.   Spacious
were the rooms, and lofty was the ceiling of this
dwelling of brick; from the platforms laid between
the chimney towers, the promenader could catch
glimpses of Virginia's broadest and deepest river.

Since the early reign of Governor Berkeley, the
family of Lee had become native to the soil of the
Old Dominion.   Richard Lee, first of his line to

cross the seas, was a landholder of Stratford-Langton, in the county of Essex, England. According to his own claim, this founder of the Virginian house sprang from that line of knights and gentlemen bearing the name of Lee who dwelt originally in Shropshire. By King James I., in 1620, a member of this Shropshire family was honoured with a baronetcy; but, in 1660, the title passed away on the death of the second baronet. The Virginian emigrant did not claim descent from these two baronets of the Langley branch, but from the collateral and younger branch, the Lees of Coton Hall. With the Lees of Ditchley he had no affinity; but a daughter of the latter house, Eleanor Calvert, became the wife of John Parke Custis, and thus unto the wife of Robert Edward was transmitted the blood of a separate and distinct family of Lees.

In the portrait handed down to us, the face of the first Richard Lee of Virginia, framed in the official wig of the colonial Councillor, is marked with the lines of benevolence and vigour. The earliest land-grant recorded in his name, bearing the date, August 10, 1642, gave him title to one thousand acres of territory in Yorke County. To this farm on Poropotank Creek he gave the name "Paradise." In November, 1647, as member from the county of Yorke, Richard Lee took his seat in the House of Burgesses at Jamestown. Richard Lee was loyal to the family of Stuart; for, in 1650, he sailed across the sea to Breda as member of a commission to invite the second Charles to wear the crown in Virginia; and, in 1651, he was styled by

Berkeley, Colonel Richard Lee, Esquire, Secretary
of State for this Colony. But he was also loyal to
the young democracy cradled in the arms of the
noble rivers that seek the Chesapeake, for, in 1654,
when a Dissenter sat in the Governor's chair, Lee
was described as " faithful and useful to the interests of the Commonwealth." At the time of his
death, about the year 1663, he held the office of
Lieutenant, or Master of the Militia, of the county
of Westmoreland. Unto his two daughters and five
sons, then living, this head of the Virginian line
devised vast tracts of that sun-smitten soil on both
banks of the Potomac, described by Captain John
Smith as " lusty and very rich."

Before death claimed him, the father had seen
two sons, John and Richard, bear away the seals of
graduation from Oxford University. The mantle of
family patriarch soon fell to Richard, the second
son, a diligent reader of books, a busy planter, and
man of affairs. " Mt. Pleasant " on the Potomac
was his home; there he dwelt in the midst of an
estate of two thousand acres inherited from his
father and elder brother John. In 1676, this second Richard was called to fill his father's former
position of Councillor, and henceforth he bore the
title Colonel Richard Lee. When he donned the
official wig, the smoke was just clearing away from
that summer of strife known as Bacon's Rebellion.
It may have been, in part, his personal friendship
for Berkeley that led Lee to support the Governor
in the day of his warfare with Nathaniel Bacon, who
played the noble role of patriot while Berkeley at-

tempted the part of despot. During seven weeks
Bacon kept Lee shut up in prison. In 1691, Lee's
attachment to the house of Stuart held him back,
for a time, from taking the oath of allegiance to
William and Mary. Not many years passed, however, until Governor Spotswood spoke of Colonel
Lee as " a gentleman of as fair character as any in
the country for his exact justice, honesty, and unex-
ceptional loyalty."

Fifth in order among the sons of the second
Richard and Lætitia Corbin, his wife, was Thomas
Lee. The year that saw the birth of George Washington, 1732, brought to Thomas the seals of office
as colonial Councillor. Thomas was not educated
in England, but received his scholastic training at
home, under the care of tutors.

He afterwards became a proficient in the classics
through his own unaided researches in the library
at Stratford. In the Council, Thomas Lee was ever
a stout upholder of the Established Church of the
colony; his voice was against the wide extension of
the privileges of public worship to the religious Dissenters. In the home of wealth and intellectual
cultivation maintained at Stratford by Thomas Lee
and his wife, Hannah Ludwell, six sons were trained
for large service unto their commonwealth and
country. Foremost among these was that quartet
of patriot brothers, Richard Henry, Thomas Ludwell, Francis Lightfoot, and Arthur Lee. The
spirit of democracy was not completely banished
from the fireside of this Virginian royalist and
Churchman, who could bequeath to his sons two

hundred and twenty adult negro servants and at the same time lay the command upon his executors to educate his children " in such manner as they think fitt, religiously and virtuously, and, if necessary, to bind them to any profession or trade, soe that they may learn to get their living honestly."

A younger brother of Thomas Lee bore the name Henry. This Henry Lee was sixth in order among the sons of the second Richard. Upon a plantation in Westmoreland, adjoining his father's estate, he built Lee Hall, and there by the Potomac, in ease and quietness, did he dwell with his wife, Mary Bland. Three sons blessed this marriage, and to the third son were bequeathed the father's name, Henry, and large estates in Prince William and Fairfax counties. Concerning this son Henry, the patriarch of Lee Hall left behind him this injunction: " My Will and desire is that my son Henry be continued at the College two years from the date hereof [1746], and afterwards to be a writer in the Secretary's Office, till he be twenty-one years of age." From William and Mary College this scion of Lee Hall betook himself to Prince William County, and there, at Leesylvania, in 1756, was born the eldest son of Henry Lee and Lucy Grymes, his wife. This heir-at-law, christened with the name of his parent, was afterwards to become famous as " Light-Horse Harry," the father of Robert E. Lee.

The hour of separation from the mother-country was now drawing nigh. When the Revolutionary programme was outlined by Patrick Henry in " The Parsons' Cause," in 1763, wherein he denounced

the Establishment as an incumbrance, and denied
the King's authority to veto a statute of the colonial
Assembly, a full-fledged republican party already
stood behind him, composed of the Dissenters of the
upland counties of Virginia   The rifles of these Ulstermen had enabled Washington to win the Ohio
Valley from the French and Indians, and the same
guns were still primed on the mountain-top, ready
to resist the aggressions of King George III.   As
opposed to Grenville's imperial theory that the colonies were mere trading corporations, to be taxed
by the English Parliament, this republican party
advanced the home-rule view that the colonies
were political communities, self-governing commonwealths from their origin, controlled and taxed by
local parliaments.

When Patrick Henry's voice rang out in opposition to the Stamp Act in 1765, claiming for the
Assembly the charter-right to supreme authority in
Virginia, his resolutions were passed through the
House of Burgesses by the republican party against
the votes of the conservatives from the tide-water
section.   With these stern Calvinists, who held
that government must be based on compact, many
of the Potomac planters were in full accord.   Among
the latter were Washington, Mason, Madison, and
several members of the house of Lee.

From his early studies in law and government,
Richard Henry Lee had come forth an ardent republican of the type of Hampden and Sidney.   This
son of the royalist, Thomas Lee, stood side by side
with Patrick Henry in the leadership of the Vir-

ginian republicans against the party of the Establishment. It was not to William and Mary, the stronghold of the Establishment, but to Princeton College, the academic centre of the Revolutionary party, that Henry Lee of Leesylvania sent the vigorous young horseman of the household.

One glimpse of the young Henry Lee, in 1770, at the feet of Witherspoon, reveals him thus: " He is more than strict in his morality, has a fine genius, and is diligent." In 1773, he bore away the seal of graduation from Nassau Hall, and returned to Prince William in time to see his father, the County Burgess for many years past, depart as delegate to the Convention, a body that afterwards presided at the birth of the independent Commonwealth of Virginia.

The younger Henry Lee soon laid aside the law books which he had set himself to study, and in the summer of 1775 began to assist in the work of organising and drilling the militia of the colony. This preparation for warfare was due to the resolution pressed through the Convention of March, 1775, by Patrick Henry, with the assistance of Richard Henry Lee and other republican leaders. In July, 1775, the Committee of Safety, appointed by the Convention, assumed complete executive control of the colony; a prominent member of that committee was Thomas Ludwell Lee. Virginia was absolutely independent now of all external authority. Representatives elected by the people exercised complete legislative, judicial, and executive functions. May, 1776, marked the assembling of the fifth and last colonial Convention that gave permanence to the republican

form of government. In this Convention sat three
members of the Lee family, Henry of Prince William,
his brother Richard of Westmoreland, and Thomas
Ludwell of Stafford. June 29, 1776, was the birthday of the Commonwealth of Virginia, for that day
added George Mason's Constitution to his previous
Bill of Rights. The adoption of these instruments
by the Convention, in the name of the sovereign
people, constituted their formal separation from the
English Crown. This written Constitution of Virginia was, in large part, the model followed by the
other colonies in the formation of permanent state
governments.

At the same time with this Virginia Convention,
another assembly of delegates from all the colonies
was in session in Philadelphia. This Congress of
deputies was clothed only with advisory powers. It
formed a central committee whose business it was to
secure concert of action among the colonies through
a series of recommendations to the different colonial
legislatures. Among the Virginia deputies were the
brothers Richard Henry and Francis Lightfoot Lee.
May 15, 1776, the Williamsburg Convention sent
commands to the Virginia representatives to secure
from the Congress a formal announcement of the
already existing fact that the thirteen colonies were
independent States. When Richard Henry Lee, on
June 7, offered a resolution to that effect, every royal
governor had fled, and the thirteen commonwealths
were each as sovereign and independent as ever were
the kingdoms of Holland, Denmark, or Portugal.
Lee's resolution was adopted by the Congress, July 2,

and, two days later, delegates from twelve of the thirteen colonies agreed to Jefferson's formal Declaration of Independence. Authority to vote for the Declaration had been forwarded to their delegates by all the colonial conventions and legislatures, except the legislature of New York. Back to those legislatures was the Declaration sent for ratification; the formal sanction thereof by the thirteen law-making bodies at last gave legal character to this great document and transformed a committee's work into a colonial compact.

Wearing a captain's sword, as the leader of a band of volunteer horsemen, Henry Lee the younger entered the field of war at the call of the Commonwealth of Virginia. In April, 1777, Lee presented himself for orders at Washington's headquarters in Morristown, New Jersey. The flower of the American army at that point was composed of riflemen from Virginia and Maryland. These patriots, one hundred days before Lee's arrival, had enabled Washington to save the cause of the Revolution at Trenton and Princeton. Upon the arduous service of scouting and foraging for Washington's army did Lee now enter. Not long did he wait to secure the commander's commendation for " gallant behaviour " and for " conduct of exemplary zeal, prudence, and bravery." Lee kept his men at hot work in the days of Brandywine and Germantown. During the winter of suffering at Valley Forge he was continually astir in bringing bread and beef to the starving soldiers. Early in 1778, he was promoted to the rank of major, and placed in command

of a corps of light-armed horsemen. Lee now became the eye and the ear of the army; the daring
courage which marked the man of swift vigilance
soon fastened upon him the name of " Light-Horse
Harry " Lee. It was Lee who suggested the capture of Stony Point, and it was a band of North
Carolinians who formed Wayne's head of column in
the assault upon that fortress. Three hundred Virginians followed Lee in his successful dash against
Paulus Hook on the Jersey coast, August, 1779.
In honour of Lee and his Legion in this enterprise,
the Congress bestowed a medal with warm commendation of his " remarkable prudence, address,
and bravery."

The summer of 1780 brought the darkest hour of
the Revolution. Cornwallis was sweeping northward through the Carolinas in order to end the war
by the subjugation of the South. The people of
New England were now mending their fishing-nets
and unfurling the sails of their trading-vessels.
Virginia was girding herself for the combat; her
sons stood behind Washington as he watched New
York; they withstood the British in Carolina, and
they made ready to keep back the invader from
their own soil. The victory of King's Mountain in
October scattered the cloud of gloom. In December came Greene to take command of the Southern
army, and with him came Lieutenant-Colonel Lee
with his Legion.

Washington's opinion of the cavalry leader was set
forth in the declaration that Lee had "great resources
of genius." Under Greene served Morgan, Will-

iam Washington, Marion, Pickens, Sumter, and
Lee; of the latter Greene declared, " No man in the
progress of the campaign had equal merit." In the
course of that masterly strategy whereby Greene drew
Cornwallis away from his base into the mountains of
North Carolina, Lee's Legion formed the American
rear-guard. More than a match for the British cavalry leader, Tarleton, was Lee in this long running-
fight. The skill and daring of the Virginian horseman enabled Greene to unite his two wings for the
battle at Guilford. In September, 1781, when Washington was hurling his army like a thunderbolt from
the Hudson to the York to secure Cornwallis in the
toils, Lee and Marion had already led Greene's
advance southward, and were now making hot pursuit after Rawdon's recruits as they scampered into
Charleston from the last battle in Carolina, at
Eutaw Springs. The famous trooper celebrated his
own victories by coming to witness the surrender of
Cornwallis at Yorktown, and by his marriage to the
heiress of Stratford the following year.

Colonel Lee's ardent support was accorded to the
Federal Constitution when it was presented to the
separate States for ratification. His career in the
field of war had revealed to him the necessity for a
governmental compact more binding than the old
Articles of Confederation; his admiration for Washington made him desirous of giving sanction to that
leader's work as President of the Convention of
1787. Richard Henry Lee, made cautious by his
experience in the Continental Congress, stood in
the forefront of the opposition to the compact. He

affirmed that the proposed Constitution was "dangerously oligarchic " in its " blending of the legislative powers with the executive." But Colonel Henry Lee spoke and voted in the Convention of 1788 in company with Madison; the latter won Virginia's sanction for the Constitution on the ground that it was only a compact wherein the contracting parties were " the people—but not the people as composing one great body, but the people as composing thirteen sovereignties." This was the view held in all the commonwealths by the Federalists, who triumphantly established the new league among the States.

As member of the Virginia Legislature, Colonel Lee watched the early sessions of the Federal Congress. When that body adopted Hamilton's scheme for centralising in Congress the management of the finances of the States, the Virginia Assembly made protest. Lee was on the committee that formulated the following declaration: " Your memorialists can find no clause in the Constitution authorizing Congress to assume the debts of the States." In this juncture of affairs Lee wrote to Madison: " To disunite is dreadful to my mind; but, dreadful as it is, I consider it a lesser evil than Union on the present conditions."

In 1792, when Lee entered upon his three years' tenure of office as Governor of Virginia, the political differences between Hamilton and Jefferson in the Cabinet had assumed the form of personal hostility. As Jefferson withdrew to wave the magician's wand from Monticello and call into existence the Republican-Democratic party, Colonel Lee drew himself into closer political sympathy with the Federalists. When the farmers of Western Pennsylvania raised an insurrection against Hamilton's direct tax on whiskey, it was Lee whom Washington sent against them as commander of the militia; but the rioters were suppressed without the shedding of blood.

In the crisis of party warfare that marked the close of the century, Lee played his part as a zealous Federalist. Talleyrand's insult to the envoys of President Adams in 1798 aroused the wrath of the American people and swept the Federal Administration into active preparations for war with France. Lee was given commission in the army as Major-General. Adams and his Federalist followers rode upon the whirlwind and directed the storm. Against the foreigners who held positions as editors and leaders of the republican party, they passed through Congress the Alien and Sedition laws. In opposition to these two measures that lodged great personal power in the hands of the President, vigorous protests came from the legislatures of Kentucky and Virginia, drafted by Jefferson and Madison. They declared the Constitution to be a compact formed by the different States as integral parties; they further denounced the Alien and Sedition laws as violations of the compact, with a dangerous tendency toward consolidation. The Virginia resolutions, however, were passed against the voice of Colonel Henry Lee, who denied that these Congressional statutes were breaches of the Constitution. In

1799, Lee was elected to Congress on the Federalist platform. His friendship for Washington rendered him hostile to Jefferson, and the only ground on which the enemies of Jefferson could stand was Federalism. Washington made use of his own great personal influence among the Potomac planters to secure Lee's election as their representative. When the news reached Congress that the sage of Mount Vernon had passed away, it was Lee who prepared the resolution referring to him as " The man first in war, first in peace, and first in the hearts of his fellow-citizens." Upon Colonel Lee was laid the task of delivering before Congress a formal oration on the character of Washington, and in the performance of this labour of love he manifested " distinguished powers of eloquence."

But the doom of Federalism was at hand. The Virginia and Kentucky resolutions became the slogan of the democracy. The Federalists had sought to concentrate authority in the hands of an oligarchy, and now the masses of the people began flocking to Jefferson's standard. Dissensions split the Federalist party in twain; the Presidential election in 1800 was thrown into the House of Representatives, where the votes of ten States out of sixteen gave the office to Jefferson. So intense was Lee's antipathy to the republican leader that he cast his vote from beginning to end of the contest for Aaron Burr. When Jefferson and his party, in 1801, entered upon their long voyage of supremacy, with the compact theory nailed to the masthead as the rule of Constitutional interpretation, Colonel Lee retired from the field of politics, and sought repose beneath the trees, by the still waters of Stratford on the Potomac.

The planting of fields and the gathering of harvests were engaging the warrior's care when the home was made glad in 1807 by the birth of the soldier-child, Robert. From Shirley, on the lower James River, to Stratford had Colonel Lee brought as wife the eldest daughter of Charles Carter and Anne Moore Carter. The eldest male heir of the fourth generation of the house of Carter in Virginia was this Charles Carter of Shirley. He passed from earth in the summer before the advent of his illustrious grandchild, Robert E. Lee.

Among the papers of his daughter, the wife of Colonel Henry Lee, was found this obituary testimonial to Charles Carter: " His long life was spent in the tranquillity of domestic enjoyments. From the mansion of hospitality his immense wealth flowed like silent streams, enlivening and refreshing every object around. In fulfilling the duties of his station, he proved himself to be an Israelite indeed, in whom there was no guile."

When we trace the Carter line backward from Charles of the fourth generation, we find his father, John Carter, eldest son of the house, becoming the master of the Shirley plantation through marriage with the heiress, Elizabeth Hill. This John was son of Robert Carter of Lancaster, familiarly known as " King Carter " of the realm of the upper Rappahannock River; Robert's father was the emigrant

John who sat as member of the Virginia House of
Burgesses as early as 1649. " King Carter " played
his part in the public service as Speaker of the Burgesses, Rector of William and Mary College, and
Governor of the Colony of Virginia.   A large stone
in former time stood at the east end of Christ
Church in Lancaster County to speak of him as
" An honourable man, who by noble endowments
and pure morals gave lustre to his gentle birth
.   .   .   Possessed of ample wealth, blamelessly
acquired, he built and endowed, at his own expense, this sacred edifice,—a signal monument of
his piety toward God.   He furnished it richly.
Entertaining his friends kindly, he was neither a
prodigal nor a parsimonious host."   It was the
daughter of this house of Carter who became the
mother of Robert E. Lee, and her prayers with her
tender admonitions were the forces that cast his
growing character in that mould of noble self-control
that made the child the father of the man.

In the days of Robert E. Lee's early childhood
the leadership among all the States of the Federal
Union was held by Virginia.   In population, in
wealth, and in political prestige she stood like a
tower above the other commonwealths; in law and
in politics she was furnishing leaders to other States;
new commonwealths were growing up within her
former domain, and the Ulstermen from her Alleghanies, a race regarded by Jefferson as the basis of
an everlasting democracy, were reaching out brawny
arms to conquer and organise the Southwest.   In
Virginia was intrenched the Jeffersonian Democracy

that was now shaping the home and foreign policy
of the United States. But ere the child at Stratford had learned the art of speech, the sky grew
dark with the cloud of approaching war with England. Little more than five months had passed over
his head, when his opening ears may have heard,
perhaps, the sound of heavy guns rolling up the
Potomac from the capes that form the gateway to
the Chesapeake. The wrath of the people of the
United States was kindled into flame by the broad-
sides poured from the guns of the British frigate
Leopard, without provocation, into the American
vessel *Chesapeake*, June 22, 1807. When Jefferson's
party in the following December passed the Embargo Act, cutting off all commercial intercourse
with foreign ports, as the only mode of public defence, short of war, against English aggression, the
New England Federalists at once rushed into fiercer
opposition to Jefferson's Administration. The Federalists of Virginia and South Carolina cast themselves into the bosom of the Republican-Democratic
party, or like " Light-Horse Harry " Lee, retired to
the quietude of plantation-life. But Lee was not
ready to join the active Opposition party. While he
busied himself in writing, *Memoirs of the War in the
Southern Department of the United States*, that campaign which brought independence to all the States
nearly three decades before, Lee kept watch upon
the course of public events, and was ready to buckle
on the sword and take his place among his own
people. Long before had Colonel Lee given expression to the following sentiment, which con-

tinued to glow within him to the end of life: " No consideration on earth could induce me to act a part, however gratifying to me, which could be construed into disregard or forgetfulness of this Commonwealth."

CHAPTER II.

1811–1846.

O the quiet town of Alexandria, Virginia, in the year 1811, came Colonel Lee with his family. The schools there available for the children drew the old soldier away from the scenes of plantation life at Stratford. An epoch-making scene in the governmental drama was soon to burst upon his view. The child of four years, Robert, in the house on Cameron Street, near Christ Church, could not yet understand the political situation, but with eager interest did the father keep watch upon events in the Capital.

Just across the Potomac from Alexandria sat James Madison in the President's chair. Into the Capitol in the autumn of the year 1811 came the Twelfth Congress to consider the grievances against England, grievances that had burdened the people of our country for twenty years. At the head of

the Republican-Democratic party in the House
stood now two young men from the South, John
C. Calhoun and Henry Clay. They were filled with
the spirit of patriotism; they were burning with the
desire to maintain the honour of the United States
against foreign aggression. These leaders inaugurated a vigorous policy toward the haughty mistress
of the sea, and succeeded in carrying a declaration
of war against England, June 18, 1812. The Opposition was composed of the ancient Federalists,
assisted by John Randolph of Virginia. The news
of war was greeted in New England with the tolling of bells, despite the fact that England had
forcibly impressed into her navy more than four
thousand American seamen. Some of the Eastern
States carried their Opposition policy to the extent
of nullifying the Acts of Congress, and, in 1814,
delegates from these commonwealths assembled in
the Hartford Convention to give serious consideration to the policy of secession from the Federal
Union.

But the Federalism of " Light-Horse Harry "
Lee was not of this extreme Opposition type.
The friend of Washington could not bestow his
sympathies upon England in the day of her attack
upon our merchant-marine. Nor could Lee forget
the battle in behalf of the Federal Constitution,
wherein he had touched elbows with Madison.
" Our friendly sympathies never lost their force,"
said Madison afterwards concerning Lee. A commission as Major-General in the army in Canada was
the President's tribute to Lee's skill and loyalty.

The latter prepared to draw sword in his country's behalf, but grievous disaster came to him through chivalrous aid offered in defence of a personal friend. Hanson, the editor of a Federalist paper in Baltimore, had heaped bitter words upon the Administration and the war-measure of Congress. His attacks stirred up the Republicans of Baltimore to fierce anger. The evening of June 20, 1812, saw Hanson's press and printing-house destroyed by a mob. Lee made a journey to Baltimore and there found Hanson preparing to issue the paper, printed now in Georgetown and forwarded. Hanson made a fortress of his house, and boldly announced that he would assert the freedom of the press. About twenty friends stood with him as garrison to the stronghold. Among these were General Lingan and Colonel Lee. July 27th, the mob stationed a cannon in front of the building, and the beleaguered garrison surrendered to the Mayor. The jail building wherein they took refuge was attacked the following night; the doors were beaten down in the fierce struggle that ensued. General Lingan was slain and Colonel Lee received the wounds that, six years later, terminated his life. Through the agency of President Madison, he was enabled to reach Barbadoes in the summer of 1813, and in the West Indies he lingered until February, 1818. The climate of these islands revived his waning strength. In the midst of great sufferings he continued to write with regularity to his son Charles Carter Lee, then at Harvard. These letters are full of tender affection for his wife and children; they contain repeated injunctions to his eldest son to " cherish truth and abhor deception." He advised the reading of " history and ethical authors of unrivalled character." Of John Locke he said: " Do not only study, but consult him as the Grecians did the Delphic oracle." Francis Bacon he described as " wonderfully instructive; though of cowardly, despicable character." Among the English poets, he gave the palm to Pope: " He is worthy of universal applause, far superior to Milton, as his *Iliad* compared with *Paradise Lost* evinces."

As a writer of tragedy, Lee placed Sophocles upon the same plane with Shakespeare. Of Lucretius, the Roman poet, he made this affirmation: " If I had not partly read him, I never could have believed there ever lived a man who was in judgment an atheist."

The military hero he termed the " most useless " member of the human race, " except when the safety of a nation demands his saving arm." Such heroes as Alexander and Cæsar he admired for " mental excellency," but could not " applaud the object for which they wasted human life." Hence, his three heroes were Hannibal, Frederick the Great, Wellington; Hannibal he described as " first of antiquity in cabinet and field."

In the last letter of all, he thus summed up his creed:

" My dear Carter, what is happiness? *Hoc opus, hic labor est?* Peace of mind based on piety to Almighty God, unconscious innocence of conduct, with good-will to man ; health of body, health of mind, with prosperity in our vocation ; a sweet, affectionate wife ;

mens sana in corpore sano ; children devoted to truth, honour, right,
and utility, with love and respect to their parents ; and faithful and
warm-hearted friends, in a country politically and religiously free ;—
this is my definition."

After long suffering the dying man turned his
face homeward. But his strength bore him up only
until he reached Cumberland Island on the coast of
Georgia. There were his last hours soothed by the
daughter of his old commander, General Greene;
there did he enter into rest, March 25, 1818, and there
do the magnolias still stand guard over his grave.

The love of the father in affliction turned often
to his son Robert. To Carter he wrote a year before his death : " Robert was always good, and will
be confirmed in his happy turn of mind by his
ever-watchful and affectionate mother. Does he
strengthen his native tendency ?'' To that mother,
now an invalid in Alexandria, was Robert left as the
only guardian. Full of all gentleness and tenderness was Anne Carter Lee; full of all thoughtful-
ness and devotion was the young son of eleven
summers, who became the head of the household
when his father died. The elder brother Carter
was still at Harvard; Sidney Smith Lee had entered
the navy; one sister was an invalid in Philadelphia,
and the other was younger still than Robert. A
man's part in life was thus assigned to the boy, and
nobly did he bear himself. The Alexandria Academy
furnished ample instruction for mind and morals.
But the moulding hand of the mother was giving
shape to that moral character which stands yet in
our annals unrivalled for earnestness and self-sacri-

fice. The domestic duties connected with the house
were laid upon him; the office of chief nurse was
his. Thus did the lives of mother and son approach
the parting of the ways, when they might no longer
meet their duties with hand resting in hand. The
young man's heart turned toward his father's calling, and it was decided that he should seek admit-
tance to the Military Academy at West Point.

To acquire the necessary mathematical training
he spent one winter at the school of Benjamin Hallowell in Alexandria. Concerning those days of
preparation, Mr. Hallowell has thus left testimony:

" He was a most exemplary student in every respect. He was
never behind-time at his studies ; never failed in a single recitation ;
was perfectly observant of the rules and regulations of the institution ; was gentlemanly, unobtrusive, and respectful in all his deportment to teachers and his fellow-students. His specialty was
finishing up. He imparted a finish and a neatness, as he proceeded,
to everything he undertook."

The diagrams which he drew on a slate in the
study of conic sections were made " each one with as
much accuracy and finish, lettering and all, as if it
were to be engraved and printed." Another side
of his character is revealed to us in the home-life of
those last months with his mother. At twelve
o'clock each day he hastened from the school-room
to her side. In his arms he bore her to the cush-
ions of the carriage, and sought ever to cheer her
during the drive. " He nursed her night and day.
If Robert left the room, she kept her eyes on the
door till he returned." The hours of watching

grew longer after he entered West Point in 1825.
Each summer he hastened from the Hudson to
Alexandria, in the uniform of grey adorned with
white bullet-buttons. During his entire cadet life
the mother was still spared to watch his growth in
beauty of person and in winsomeness of manner, as
he continued to increase, if possible, in depth of
moral character.

No breach of discipline nor any neglect of duty
was ever charged against him during his years of study
in the Academy. No unbecoming word ever fell
from his lips; but speech and action indicated always
that he lived as under his great Taskmaster's eye. He
attained the position of adjutant of battalion, and
was graduated second in his class. Manliness, true
and noble, was stamped upon the form and the face of
the second lieutenant of engineers who hastened to
the waiting mother at the close of his four years'
course. She was granted only time to smile upon
him with a mother's pride in her best-beloved child.
In July, 1829, she passed away.

On Virginia's coast, in the construction of the
military defences of Hampton Roads was Lieutenant Lee's first service rendered to the Federal Government. It was fitting that Virginia should receive
benefit from his first labours, for more than their
due share had the people of the Southern States
contributed to furnish Lee the training offered at
the Military Academy. For the most part, it was
tax-money from the South that had reared and
equipped the halls at West Point; even in the third
decade of this century Southern commerce was fur-

nishing sixteen and a half millions of the twenty-
three million dollars revenue gathered for the use of
the Federal Government.

The evening of June 30, 1831, marked the union
in marriage of Robert E. Lee with Mary Randolph
Custis, daughter of George Washington Parke Custis, and great-granddaughter of Martha Custis, the
wife of General Washington. On the Virginia bank
of the Potomac stood Arlington, the home of the
Custis household, uplifted on stately Doric pillars.
At the base of the lofty bluff in front of the mansion swept the broad river; from the porch could
the observer watch the stream disappear toward
Alexandria in the distance, while just across the
water could one look down upon the city of Washington and her massive Hall of Legislation. Unto
this home had Mr. Custis removed his family from
Mount Vernon in 1802. As the seat of generous
hospitality was Arlington known under the *régime*
established by the heads of the Custis line. Mary
Custis was the only surviving child when she
gave her hand to the talented young lieutenant.
The wedding-scene was enacted before the household altar. The portraits and relics brought as a
heritage from Mount Vernon bore witness from the
walls to the sacred ceremonial in the right-hand
drawing-room. Never upon any man of spirit more
high and rare, "and true to truth and brave for
truth," nor upon a woman of queenlier grace, of
loftier mould, had those Washington memorials
looked down, than the bridal pair which they saw
that night in June at Arlington.

Six fair bridesmaids and attendant groomsmen formed the inner circle around the contracting pair. A band of relatives and friends looked on while the ritual of the Episcopal Church declared them man and wife. Then followed the festivities, in which the colony of Africans had bountiful share. Faithful to every vow in the coming days of peace did this couple remain; faithful throughout the time of terror from war, and faithful even unto death.

Through the marriage with the heiress of Arlington was Robert E. Lee ultimately ushered into the position of patriarch over Virginian plantations and their adherent servants, Arlington itself and the White House farms on the Pamunkey River. This same year, 1831, saw the beginning of the Abolitionist assault, under Garrison's leadership, against the institution of slavery in the Southern States. Mr. Custis himself was a believer in gradual emancipation, and left provision in his will that his servants should become freedmen a certain number of years after his own demise. As executor, Robert E. Lee carried out that provision to the very letter, and, in 1862, sent these manumitted servants with passes through his own military lines into the Northern States. Throughout life he was the gentlest and most indulgent of masters to his African retainers. We are told that one of the earliest duties laid upon himself by the young commissioned officer was to take his mother's negro coachman, a consumptive, to the mild climate of Georgia, and there to provide tender nursing until the end came.

From 1829 until the outbreak of the Mexican War

in 1846, Lee passed his days in the quiet labours that fall to the lot of an army engineer. When we look into the details of his work and the faithfulness shown in its performance, we see the growing greatness of the man. Devotion to his public duties was the foremost characteristic of the official; strong affection for his family shone in all his words and deeds. The care and exactness of the early school-days marked his attention to the minute and seemingly unessential parts of his labour. He loved children and young people; he was modest and unaffected in forming estimates of his own capacity. A quiet humour and hidden satire gave zest and colouring to his correspondence and familiar intercourse with friends.

Until 1834, Lee remained at Hampton Roads. Then, as assistant to the chief engineer of the army, he was busy with office-work in Washington until 1837. During this period he dwelt at Arlington, and his handsome figure drew much attention as the gallant horseman passed daily along Pennsylvania Avenue. In the summer of 1837, Lee was placed in charge of the work of improving the navigation of the Mississippi River at St. Louis. In the following year he was advanced to the grade of Captain of Engineers. In this first period of prolonged absence from his family and his Virginia friends, we find him beginning to write those letters that lay bare the deep affection burning in the heart of the husband, the father, and the friend. To a cousin, in 1838, he wrote concerning the coat-of-arms of the Lee family, and assigned as reason for

the inquiry: " I begin in my old age to feel a little
curiosity relative to my forefathers." At the same
time he declared that he was " on the lookout for
that stream of gold that was to ascend the Mississippi, tied up in silk-net purses ! It would be a
pretty sight, but the tide has not yet made up
here."

To his wife, then at Arlington with her three
children, George W. Custis, Mary Custis, and William Henry Fitzhugh, he wrote as follows in 1839:

"You do not know how much I have missed you and the dear
children, my dear Mary. To be alone in a crowd is very solitary.
In the woods I feel sympathy with the trees and birds, in whose
company I take delight, but experience no interest in a strange
crowd. I hope you are all well and will continue so, and therefore
must again urge upon you to be very prudent and careful of those
dear children. If I could only get a squeeze at that little fellow
turning up his sweet mouth to ' Keese Baba.' You must not let him
run wild in my absence, and will have to exercise firm authority over
all of them. This will not require severity or even strictness, but
constant attention and an unwavering course. Mildness and forbearance, tempered by firmness and judgment, will strengthen their
affection for you, while it will maintain your control over them."

In 1839, the chief engineer offered Lee a position
as instructor at West Point in the proposed work of
building up a skilled corps of sappers and miners for
the army. But Lee, in a most courteous reply,
begged permission to leave the position " to abler
hands " because of " an apprehension of being unable to realise your expectations." To a friend
concerning the same theme he confesses his lack of

" The taste and peculiar zeal which the situation requires ; nor can
I see what qualifications I possess that render me more fit for this

duty than others, or that in the least would counterbalance the want of those that I have mentioned. My attention has never been directly given to this branch of the profession, though I presume (unless I am too old to learn) a sufficient knowledge of it might in a short time be attained, and the opportunity which you hint at of becoming acquainted with the practice of the European schools, besides that of learning other matters, I confess, would be very agreeable. But there is an *art* in imparting this knowledge, and in making a subject agreeable to those that learn, which I have never found that I possessed."

In 1841, we find Captain Lee in military charge of New York Harbour, with headquarters at Fort Hamilton. There he remained until the war with Mexico, in 1846, called him to the field of battle. His work in the harbour kept him continuously busy. He declined to act as executor of the Carter estate because lack of time would render him " guilty of injustice to the legatees." Further he said : " My private affairs have suffered ever since I have been in the army from the impracticability of my attending to them. I am at no time master of my movements, and my whole time is engrossed by my duties." General Henry J. Hunt has borne testimony that Lee was then " as fine-looking a man as one would wish to see, of perfect figure and strikingly handsome. Quiet and dignified in manner, of cheerful disposition, always pleasant and considerate, he seemed to me the perfect type of a gentleman."

To his brother Carter, August 17, 1843, he sent this message : " . . . I can be content to be poor with the knowledge of being able to pay my debts and that no one has a just claim upon me that I cannot meet. But I cannot bear to enter into en-

gagements without the certainty of being able to
fulfil them." Concerning the proposed increase of
the army, he thus expressed himself in June, 1845:

"In the event of war with any foreign government I would desire
to be brought into active service in the field with as high a rank in
the regular army as I could obtain, and if that could not be accomplished without leaving the Corps of Engineers I should then desire
a transfer to some other branch of the service and would prefer the
artillery. I would, however, accept no situation under the rank of
field-officer."

Crowded with high purposes, with work and with
study were these early years of Robert E. Lee. A
grave dignity marked his bearing. Strong passion
dwelt within him, but it was kept well under control; humour would ofttimes break through the outward reserve, and then was the soldier genial and
his conversation charming. General Meigs gives us
a glimpse of Lee during the engineering days on the
Mississippi as " A man then in the vigour of youth-
ful strength, with a noble and commanding presence,
and an admirable, graceful, and athletic figure. He
was one with whom nobody ever wished or ventured
to take a liberty, though kind and generous to his
subordinates, admired by all women and respected
by all men. He was the model of a soldier and the
beau ideal of a Christian man."

CHAPTER III.

N the year 1845, the Commonwealth
of Texas brought into the Federal
Union her dispute with Mexico concerning the true western boundary of
the Lone Star State. In 1821,
Mexico had revolted from Spain and organised a
republic; Texas was one of the provinces of this
confederation. The great multitude of home-build-
ers moving westward from the Ohio and Mississippi
valleys, composed chiefly of Ulstermen, at once
swarmed into the Texan plains, and established
themselves upon lands granted by the Mexican government. Under the leadership of Houston, the
Virginian, these colonists threw off the sovereignty
of Mexico by the victory of San Jacinto, and formed
the independent Republic of Texas in 1836. The
following year saw the recognition of this Republic
by the United States, and some European king-

doms.   A treaty proposing the annexation of Texas
to the Federal Union was rejected by the United
States Senate in 1844.   In the Presidential campaign
of that year, the leading issue between the Democratic and Whig parties was the admission of Texas
into the Union.   The Democrats secured the victory
on the platform of annexation, and a joint resolution
of both houses of Congress ushered Texas into the
Federal household.

The United States supported the State of Texas
in the claim that her true western boundary was the
Rio Grande.   This river formed the limit of the
district named Texas, as a part of the Louisiana territory sold by Spain in 1800 and by France in 1803.
But Mexico warned the United States not to attempt
to establish jurisdiction west of the Nueces River.
This stream marked the limit of actual American
occupation.

Without consulting Congress, President Polk
ordered General Taylor to lead an army across the
Nueces to hold the country as far as the Rio Grande.
The Mexicans crossed this river and attacked Taylor
at Palo Alto and at Resaca de la Palma.   Taylor
drove the Mexicans in rout, followed in pursuit and
captured Matamoras, a town on the western bank of
the Rio Grande.   Polk then declared to Congress,
May 11, 1846, that a state of war already existed
" by the act of Mexico herself."   Congress was in
sympathy with the President's action, and war was
formally recognised.

This action was a response to the war-spirit ablaze
in the West, which was due to the lust for land that

characterised the Western colonists of that heroic
age, and to race hatred against the Mexicans. This
hatred was deepened by the cry of the Texans for
help against their oppressors. A desire to thwart
England in her supposed design of gaining control of
Texas led many to demand the invasion of the region
west of the Nueces. Some of the Southern leaders
were anxious to secure prospective States in order to
maintain Democratic control of the Senate, although
Calhoun was stoutly opposed to all aggression.
These various motives brought about the popular
clamour for war. Roosevelt declares (*Life of Benton*,
p. 174) that " slavery had very little to do with the
Western aggressions on Mexican territory." Far
less had it to do with the invasion of 1846, but to
this matter we shall refer again. As leaders of the
demand for battle on Mexican soil, the people of
the West were far in advance of the people of the
Southern Atlantic States. From these two parts
of our country, the greater part of the volunteer
army was enlisted. Two-thirds of all the American
soldiers engaged came from the Southern States.

In September, 1846, General Taylor planted his
flag on the fortifications of Monterey, nineteen miles
south-west of the Rio Grande. On the plateau of
Buena Vista, February 22 and 23, 1847, Santa
Anna with twelve thousand soldiers assailed Taylor's army of fifty-two hundred. All of Taylor's
infantry and four-fifths of his cavalry were volunteers and most of them had never been under fire.
The splendid courage of the men from the Mississippi valley gave Taylor complete victory. Santa

Anna withdrew to the defence of his Capital which was now threatened from the direction of Vera Cruz by General Scott.

In the band of twelve thousand American soldiers who gathered around the old Spanish walled town of Vera Cruz in March, 1847, was Robert E. Lee, Captain of Engineers. He was a member of General Scott's military staff. At Arlington he had left the beloved wife and seven children with his prayers and blessings. " I, therefore, trust . . . that this is the last time I shall be absent from you during my life," was a message sent back to the home-circle. Before the arrival in front of Vera Cruz, Lee sent these injunctions to his two eldest sons:

" I was much gratified to hear of your progress at school, and hope that you will continue to advance, and that I shall have the happiness of finding you much improved in all your studies on my return. I shall not feel my long separation from you, if I find that my absence has been of no injury to you, and that you have both grown in goodness and knowledge, as well as stature. But, ah! how much I will suffer on my return if the reverse has occurred. You enter all my thoughts, into all my prayers ; and on you, in part, will depend whether I shall be happy or miserable, as you know how much I love you. You must do all in your power to save me from pain. . . . Tell Rob he must think of me very often, be a good boy, and always love papa."

With the assistance of Lieutenants Beauregard and Tower, Captain Lee arranged the batteries whose firing compelled the surrender of Vera Cruz within seven days. One of the American guns was served by Captain Lee's brother, Lieutenant Sydney Smith Lee, of the navy: " No matter where I

turned," wrote Lee, "my eyes reverted to him,
and I stood by his gun whenever I was not wanted
elsewhere. Oh! I felt awfully, and am at a loss
what I should have done had he been cut down
before me. I thank God that he was saved. He
preserved his usual cheerfulness, and I could see his
white teeth through all the smoke and din of the
fire." Concerning the firing against the fortress,
Lee wrote: "The shells thrown from our battery
were constant and regular discharges, so beautiful
in their flight and so destructive in their fall. It
was awful! My heart bled for the inhabitants.
The soldiers I did not care so much for, but it was
terrible to think of the women and children."

The middle of April, 1847, saw General Scott's
army upon the march of over two hundred miles
north-westward to the city of Mexico. In the pass
of Cerro Gordo, Santa Anna .massed his army to
give battle. Lee was sent forward by General Scott
to make reconnaissances along the front and around
the left of the Mexican position as far as the Jalapa
road. Upon the report made by Lee, Scott's plan
of battle was based. Lee in person guided the
storming party under Riley and Shields that turned
and routed the Mexican left, cut off the Mexican
right from retreat and compelled its surrender.
General Scott thus made mention of Captain Lee:
"This officer was again indefatigable during these
operations, in reconnaissances as daring as laborious,
and of the utmost value. Nor was he less conspicuous in planting batteries and in conducting columns
to their stations under the heavy fire of the enemy."

To his eldest son, Lee wrote as follows after the battle:

"I thought of you, my dear Custis, on the 18th, in the battle, and wondered, when the musket balls and grape were whistling over my head in a perfect shower, where I could put you, if with me, to be safe.   I was truly thankful that you were at school, I hope learning to be good and wise.   You have no idea what a horrible sight a battlefield is."

The fearful sights and sounds of the place of carnage lingered in Lee's memory as the source of a personal grief.   The one note of the after-scene that continued to sound in his ear was the plaintive tone of a little Mexican girl whom he found bending over a wounded drummer-boy.   Lee longed to escape these horrors.   From the next camp he wrote to his wife concerning Jalapa as "the most beautiful country I have seen in Mexico, and will compare with any I have seen elsewhere.   I wish it was in the United States, and that I was located with you and the children around me in one of its rich bright valleys."

Early in August, Scott's army of ten thousand effectives advanced from Puebla upon Mexico, with the engineer company at the head of the column. At Ayotla, near the northern shore of Lake Chalco, Scott's camp was pitched, and reconnaissance was begun.   Lee was the leader of the band of enginneers who made investigation of the Mexican position.   It was at length decided to turn the right flank of the Mexican defences.   Therefore, the American army was moved along the highway skirt-

ing the southern shore of Chalco until it reached
San Augustin.   This town was at the foot of the
mountains, twelve miles south of the city of Mexico,
and it now became the base of operations in the
attempt to take the Capital.   The strategic movement by which the Mexican line of defences were
thus assailed on the right flank and overwhelmed,
was very largely due to the advice offered to the
commanding general by Captain Lee.

The city of Mexico rests in a valley of elliptical
shape, seven thousand five hundred feet above the
sea level.   In the valley are five lakes.   The two
smallest lie north of the city; Texcoco is east of the
city; Xochimilco and Chalco lie toward the south-
east.   During the winter months, the valley is
partly submerged by water; hence the approach to
the city is made on seven high causeways bordered
by deep ditches.   Toward the east and south the
Mexicans had erected strong fortifications commanding these narrow approaches.   The causeway
from San Augustin to Mexico was high and broad,
and, three miles in advance, was fortified at San
Antonio.   West of the San Augustin causeway two
parallel roads ran toward Mexico.   Padierna, or
Contreras, four miles due west of San Augustin, was
the key to these two highways.

Lee and Beauregard were sent, August 18th, to
reconnoitre the position of Contreras.   They had to
cross a vast field of lava or volcanic rock, of broken
and uneven surface, called the Pedrigal.   A few
footpaths were the only roads over this rough field
of sharp ridges and deep fissures.   The movement

of the next day upon Contreras was under Lee's personal direction. It was he who planned the attack and guided the troops to victory.

From San Augustin, on the morning of August 19th, Lee hastened westward in charge of a pioneer corps. At the end of a mile's marching, the workmen began the construction of a road across the lava ridge that barred the way. By noon-day Lee had brought up the divisions of Pillow and Twiggs to assail the guns of Valencia posted in the edge of the lava field beyond the ridge. Concerning the attack made by Twiggs's column under Lee's guidance, the latter thus made report: " I advanced with the rifle regiment deployed as skirmishers, and selected the best route for the artillery through the impracticable fields of lava. . . . The enemy was intrenched behind the San Angel road on the hills of Contreras."

Against the fortified hill a flank movement was at once set in operation. Lee led Smith's brigade toward his right in order to turn the Mexican left and rear. But darkness checked this movement, and, upon Lee's advice, it was decided to bring up reinforcements from San Augustin. This perilous mission over the dangerous Pedrigal was entrusted to Lee himself. Through the darkness and the rain he groped his way across the lava wilderness, and midnight found him making report to General Scott. Before dawn he was on the return journey, leading Ransom's command to make assault in front of the Mexican position. Over the ridge and field of lava, Lee guided this force to the attack, just as the flanking columns were rushing upon Valencia's rear. The Mexicans fled in every direction, and twenty-two heavy guns were left behind as the spoil of war.

The daring courage of Lee, so signally shown at Contreras, was melted into tenderness when he saw in J. E. Johnston's face the grief caused by the death of a relative in the battle. To his old friend, through the gathering tears, Lee "expressed his deep sympathy as tenderly in words as his lovely wife would have done."

"The gallant and indefatigable Captain Lee" was accorded by General Scott the chief credit for securing the victory of Contreras. Concerning Lee's night journeys across the Pedrigal and its dangerous pitfalls, General Scott made this declaration: "He, having passed over the difficult ground by daylight, found it just possible to return to San Augustin in the dark,—the greatest feat of physical and moral courage performed by any individual in my knowledge, pending the campaign." When Scott reached the field of Contreras he found his troops already moving, under Lee's advice, toward San Antonio. At once Scott sent Lee to make reconnaissance toward the rear of that place. Scott was now advancing directly towards Mexico. The highways leading to that city from Contreras and San Augustin were found to converge in the village of Churubusco. The Mexican army was there concentrated to resist the American advance over both roads. Direct assault upon the village was made in front; Lee led a turning column under Shields and

Pierce across the Churubusco Bridge toward the Mexican right and rear.

" Advancing from Coyoacan," says Lee, " toward the city of Mexico until I had crossed the stream over which the bridge of Churubusco is thrown, I crossed the field obliquely to the rear, towards the road from Churubusco to Mexico. Discovering a large mass of infantry on the Churubusco bridge, and apprehending a fire from batteries to defend the rear, I drew out towards the city of Mexico until I reached the large hamlet on the Mexican road about three fourths of a mile in the rear of the bridge of Churubusco. Throwing the left of his brigade upon this building which offered protection against the mass of cavalry stretching towards the gates of Mexico, and his right upon the building in the field in rear of which we had approached, General Shields formed his line obliquely to that of the enemy, who, not to be outflanked, had drawn out from his entrenchments and extended his line from the bridge to nearly opposite our left. General Pierce's brigade coming up just after General Shields's brigade had commenced the attack, took position to his right, enveloping the building in the field. Our troops being now hotly engaged and somewhat pressed, I urged forward the Howitzer battery under Lt. Reno, who very promptly brought the pieces to bear upon the head of their column with good effect. Perceiving that the enemy's cavalry were showing themselves on our left, and that our force was greatly outnumbered, I hastened back to the General-in-chief, who directed Major Sumner to take the Rifle regiment and a squadron to the support of that wing. About the time this force reached the open country in rear of Churubusco, the enemy began to give way, and before they had reached the position occupied by General Shields, had broken in all directions. Their front forced by General Worth's division, and the main body driven into the main road to Mexico by our infantry and cavalry, I joined the troops in pursuit."

After an unsuccessful attempt to negotiate a peace, the two combatants girded themselves for the final struggle. Across the highway leading into the city from the south-west the Mexicans concen-

trated their troops for defence. In front they presented a fortified line five hundred yards in length.
At the left of this line was Molinos-del-Rey, the
Mills of the King, and at the right stood a fort,
within which was a large building termed the Casa
Mata. Along the front of this entire line extended
a deep ditch. On a height, in rear of the line,
towered the fortified Castle of Chapultepec. Hovering on the right wing were the Mexican cavalry.

Early on the morning of September 8th, Worth
made a gallant assault that continued two hours,
and carried by storm the Casa Mata and Molinos-
del-Rey. Behind the second line of defences, whose
centre bristled with the guns of Chapultepec, Santa
Anna's troops were now massed. Lee and other
engineers advised a flank movement to the right of
Chapultepec, and an assault on the San Antonio
gate, south of the city. Beauregard was the only
engineer who favoured a direct attack upon the fortress of Chapultepec. This plan was adopted. An
isolated mound of rock, one hundred and fifty feet
high, surmounted by a large building, constituted
the castle; a solid wall enclosed the building and
grounds. Breastworks added strength to the hill,
and heavy batteries commanded the approaches.
Along the steep western slope were a series of
mines. This strong tower, the key to the city,
loomed up two miles in front of the gates of·
Mexico.

Four batteries were established and a hot fire
maintained upon the Castle during fourteen hours
of September 12th. The early morning of Septem-

ber 13th saw two columns advancing to the assault
under Quitman of Mississippi and Pillow of Tennessee. The batteries continued their fire, while up
the steep ascent with scaling ladders the two bands
moved. Southern soldiers were the chief leaders in
this bold dash through the storm of shells and bullets. Many of the most prominent officers who stood
arrayed against each other nearly two decades later
in the war between the States, marched side by side
up the steeps of Chapultepec. Up the western slope
marched Pillow's column, J. E. Johnston leading
the advance; Lewis A. Armistead was first to leap
into the great ditch, and the wall itself was captured
and held. A little later, the South Carolina regiment, leading Quitman's advance, reached the south-
eastern summit, and broke through the fortifications.
Longstreet fell wounded on the side of the hill;
Geo. E. Pickett led the charge which carried the
flag of the 8th Regiment through the works and
planted it on the Castle's summit. Shields and
Casey were wounded; Beauregard was a member of
Pillow's column, and G. B. McClellan was directing
the artillery fire. Around the left base of the fortress a section of Magruder's artillery was advanced
under T. J. Jackson. Steadily onward went Jackson until he reached the point-blank range of the
Mexican batteries intrenched across the road immediately in the rear of Chapultepec; away from these
guns he drove the enemy, held the position, and
with the additional guns brought up as reinforcement, kept back the Mexican soldiery who were
coming from Mexico to help maintain the Castle.

For his effective management of batteries at Contreras, Churubusco, and Chapultepec, Jackson was
brevetted captain and major of artillery.

Through the hottest firing that day, Lee galloped
as Scott's chief aide, bearing orders to the attacking
columns. Scott thus made mention of Lee in his
report: " Captain Lee, so constantly distinguished,
also bore important orders from me (September
13th), until he fainted from a wound and the loss of
two nights' sleep at the batteries." For his gallantry at Chapultepec, Lee was advanced to the
brevet rank of colonel; he had already been brevetted
as major after Cerro Gordo, and as lieutenant-colonel
for daring and skill at Contreras and Churubusco.

Close upon the retreating Mexicans, the American
army moved toward the Belen and San Cosme gates.
Quitman's column was first at the goal, and announced its success by waving from the wall, above
the Belen gate, the flag of the Palmetto regiment of
South Carolina. Worth's division fastened its grasp
upon the San Cosme gate about nightfall. The
hours of darkness were seized upon by Santa Anna
as an opportunity for the evacuation of the city of
Mexico. The hour of sunrise, September 14th,
found Lee bearing Scott's orders to Quitman to
occupy the city. Lee was with the squadron that
advanced to the Grand Plaza and took possession of
the halls of the Montezumas.

While the army was awaiting the conclusion of
the treaty of peace, the engineer officers were engaged in making surveys and drawings of the city of
Mexico and its defences. In addition to these

labours, Lee took upon himself the work of re-
establishing peaceable relations between General
Scott and some of his subordinate officers. " He
was a peacemaker by nature," says Henry J. Hunt,
who has told us of this work of conciliation on the
part of Lee.

Lee took great interest in the making of the
treaty with Mexico. " I would not exact now," he
wrote in February, 1848, " more than I would have
taken before the commencement of hostilities, as I
should wish nothing but what was just, and that I
would have sooner or later." Concerning Mexico
in the war, he wrote, with a touch of humour: " It
is true we bullied her. For that I am ashamed, for
she was the weaker party, but we have since, by
way of set-off, drubbed her handsomely and in a
manner no man might be ashamed of. They begin
to be aware how entirely they are beaten, and are
willing to acknowledge it." As to the official recognition of his own services by the President of the
United States, he had only this to say:

" I hope my friends will give themselves no annoyance on my account, or any concern about the distribution of favours. I know how
those things are awarded at Washington and how the President will
be besieged by clamourous claimants. I do not wish to be numbered
among them. Such as he can conscientiously bestow, I shall grate-
fully receive, and have no doubt that those will exceed my deserts."

In the early days of April, 1848, we find him
sending description of the Romish Church, situated
on the mountain to the west of Mexico, and at the
same time giving a young friend in Alexandria the

advice that " you had better dismiss that young
divine, and marry a soldier.   There is some chance
of the latter being shot, but it requires a particular
dispensation of Providence to rid you of the former."
While the Mexican Government was making delay
in the completion of the treaty, Lee expressed the
view that a display of force would bring these shrewd
people to terms; " I might make a rough diploma-
tist, but a tolerably quick one."

To spare his war-horse from fatigue, Lee made
the slow journey homeward up the Mississippi River
by steamer.   Wilcox has declared that Lee was then
" the handsomest man in the army."   The last
hours of June, 1848, closed upon him at Arlington,
sending this despatch to his brother:

> " Here I am once again, my dear Smith, perfectly surrounded by
> Mary and her precious children, who seem to devote themselves to
> staring at the furrows in my face and the white hairs in my head.
> It is not surprising that I am hardly recognisable to some of the
> young eyes around me and perfectly unknown to the youngest, but
> some of the older ones gaze with astonishment and wonder at me,
> and seem at a loss to reconcile what they see and what was pictured
> in their imaginations.   I find them, too, much grown, and all well,
> and I have much cause for thankfulness and gratitude to that good
> God who has once more united us."

Lee was now entrusted with engineering work in
constructing the defences of the city of Baltimore.
When the order of the Secretary of War in 1852
assigned him to the position of Superintendent of
the Military Academy at West Point, he made
protest, as follows, to the Chief Engineer:

> " I learn with much regret the determination of the Secretary of
> War to assign me to that duty, and I fear I cannot realise his expec-

tations in the management of an Institution requiring more skill and more experience than I command.

"Although fully appreciating the honour of the station, and extremely reluctant to oppose my wishes to the orders of the Department, yet if I be allowed any option in the matter, I would respectfully ask that some other successor than myself be appointed to the present able Superintendent."

In spite of these objections, he was assigned to the position, and all of its duties he discharged with signal success. Lee found his eldest son, Custis, a cadet in the Academy. J. E. B. Stuart was a class-mate of Custis Lee. The latter stood at the head of his class when his father came, and he maintained himself in that grade until his graduation in 1854. Painstaking care and attention to all the details of official business marked Lee's administration of three years. The discipline of the Academy was made more efficient, the course of study was extended to five years, and a spacious riding-hall was constructed.

In 1855, Captain Lee was promoted to the rank of lieutenant-colonel of the 2d Cavalry, and sent to the scene of Indian troubles in western Texas. He spent the summer of 1856 in parleying with the Comanche chief, Catumseh, and in pursuing his marauding bands. Under the scorching suns of the Wachita and Brazos River valleys he rode eight hundred miles in forty days. The fourth day of July he celebrated by an early march of thirty miles, and during the rest of the day he sought refuge from the fierce heat by lying under his blanket, " which was elevated on four sticks driven in the ground as a sunshade.'' When his wife wrote him of a possible vacancy in the list of brigadier-generals in the army, he sent this answer: '' Do not give yourself any anxiety about the appointment of the brigadier. If it is on my account that you feel an interest in it, I beg you will discard it from your thoughts. You will be sure to be disappointed; nor is it right to indulge improper and useless hopes. It, besides, looks like presumption to expect it.''

The month of December, 1856, found him enjoying garrison life on the Rio Grande, yet longing to be with the loved ones at Arlington during Christmas-tide. In daily walks he passed alone up and down the banks of the river, and there found pleasure, as he declared, in his own thoughts, in the varied plumage of the birds and in the beauty of the vines and flowers. Lee's character breathes in the following injunctions to his son, written about the time that the father began service with the 2d Cavalry:

"You must study to be frank with the world. Frankness is the child of honesty and courage. Say just what you mean to do on every occasion, and take it for granted you mean to do right. . . . Never do a wrong thing to make a friend or to keep one. . . . Above all, do not appear to others what you are not. . . . We should live, act, and say nothing to the injury of anyone."

In closing this letter of counsel, Lee told his son of the Connecticut legislator who desired lights to be brought during the darkness of an eclipse that the House might proceed with its duty, even though the day of judgment were at hand:

" There was quietness in that man's mind—the quietness of heavenly wisdom and inflexible willingness to obey present duty. Duty, then, is the sublimest word in our language. Do your duty in all things, like the old Puritan. You cannot do more ; you should never wish to do less. Never let me or your mother wear one grey hair for any lack of duty on your part."

But the shadow of approaching war between the States grew darker during these brief years of Lee's training as a frontier cavalry officer. In the discussion of political affairs he had taken no part. From the Rio Grande, December 27, 1856, he despatched the following letter, as his earliest extended reference to the social problem that had already sundered the States of the Federal Union into two separate and distinct sections:

" I was much pleased with the President's message. His [Pierce's] views of the systematic and progressive efforts of certain people at the North to interfere with and change the domestic institutions of the South are truthfully and faithfully expressed. The consequences of their plans and purposes are also clearly set forth. These people must be aware that their object is both unlawful and foreign to them and to their duty, and that this institution, for which they are irresponsible and unaccountable, can only be changed by *them* through the agency of a civil and servile war.

" There are few, I believe, in this enlightened age, who will not acknowledge that slavery as an institution is a moral and political evil in any country. It is useless to expatiate on its disadvantages. I think it a greater evil to the white than to the black race. While my feelings are strongly enlisted in behalf of the latter, my sympathies are more strong for the former. The blacks are immeasurably better off here than in Africa, morally, physically, and socially. The painful discipline they are undergoing is necessary for their further instruction as a race, and I hope will prepare them for better things. How long their servitude may be necessary is known and ordered by a merciful Providence. Their emancipation will sooner result from the mild and melting influences of Christianity, than from the storms and tempests of fiery controversy. This influence, though slow, is sure. The docrines and miracles of our Saviour have required nearly two thousand years to convert but a small portion of the human race, and even among Christian nations what gross errors still exist. While we see the course of the *final* abolition of human slavery is still onward, and give it the aid of our prayers, and all justifiable means in our power, we must leave the progress as well as the result in His hands who sees the end ; Who chooses to work by slow influences ; with whom two thousand years are but as a single day. Although the Abolitionist must know this, must know that he has neither the right nor the power of operating, except by moral means, and that, to benefit the slave, he must incite angry feelings in the master ; that, although *he* may not approve the mode by which Providence accomplishes its purpose, the result will still be the same ; that the reasons he gives for interference in what he has no concern with, hold good with every kind of interference with our neighbour ; still I fear he will persevere in his evil course. . . . Is it not strange that the descendants of those Pilgrim Fathers who crossed the Atlantic to preserve their freedom have always proved the most intolerant of the spiritual liberty of others ? "

CHAPTER IV.

SECESSION AND SLAVERY.

1860.

HE hour was now at hand which compelled Robert E. Lee to resign his commission in the army of the United States. The public and private reasons that controlled him in this withdrawal from a service of thirty-two years can be clearly stated only in a review of the political theory of secession and the social problems connected with the institution of slavery. The beginning of this long story, which shall here be made brief, calls us back again to the era of the first war with England.

In the prosecution of active warfare during the Revolution, the legislatures of the thirteen individual colonies furnished the men and the revenue necessary to organise the American armies. Delegates from each colonial legislature were sent to Philadelphia as members of the central advisory committee, known as the Continental Congress; this Congress had no general authority to make laws, but, as a

ARLINGTON IN 1860.

diplomatic body, it made recommendations to the legislative bodies in the separate colonies. The war itself was inaugurated for the maintenance of the sovereign authority of the thirteen separate colonial legislatures against the assumed authority of the British Parliament.* A legal bond was at length formulated, organising the thirteen States into a confederacy styled " The United States of America." It was expressly stipulated in Article II. that " Each State retains its sovereignty, freedom, and independence." Article III. specified that " the said States hereby severally enter into a firm league of friendship with each other," while Article IV. spoke of perpetuating " mutual friendship and intercourse among *the people of the different States."* In the determination of questions in the Congress of the League, it was provided that " each State shall have one vote." These Articles of Confederation were not adopted by all the States until the year of Cornwallis's surrender at Yorktown, 1781. Two years later, 1783, peace was established with England through a Treaty which began as follows: " His Britannic Majesty acknowledges the said United States, viz., New-Hampshire, Massachusetts-Bay, Rhode-Island and Providence Plantations, Connecticut, New-York, New-Jersey, Pennsylvania, Delaware, Maryland, Virginia, North-Carolina, South-Carolina, and Georgia, to be *free, sovereign, and independent*

---

* The Declaration of Independence did not assert independence for the colonies as a unit. Under special authority from their legislatures, the delegates from twelve colonies concurred in pledging mutual suppo t in maintaining separate independence.

States." The fifth article of this Treaty of Peace contained the agreement, " that the Congress shall earnestly recommend it to the legislatures of the respective States to provide for the restitution " of all property confiscated from the Tories. This recommendation was made by the Congress, and flatly rejected by the legislatures of the States. The Tories did not receive the stipulated compensation, because of the sovereign authority asserted and exercised by the people of the individual Commonwealths.

The binding force of the Articles of Confederation grew weaker by degrees. When the common enemy had been overthrown, the separate States became more jealous than ever of their individual sovereignty. Adjoining States collected customhouse duties from one another, and began fierce quarrels about boundary lines. In 1786, loud threats of secession from the League were made in New England and in the South. In the same year Rhode Island did actually secede from the Confederacy, and withdrew her delegates from the Congress. Delegates from the other twelve States met at Philadelphia in 1787 and drew up a new series of Articles which were submitted to the separate States upon the basis specified in Article VII. : " The ratification of the Conventions of nine States shall be sufficient for the establishment of this Constitution between the States so ratifying the same." Legislative powers were granted in this Constitution to a Congress consisting of a House of Representatives chosen proportionately by " the people of the sev-

eral States," and a Senate composed of "two
Senators from each State." The executive power
was vested in a President to be chosen by electors
appointed, proportionately, by "each State"; each
separate body of electors was directed to meet and
cast ballot " in their respective States."

The year 1788 saw these Articles ratified by
eleven States, and in the following year the Federal
Government began to operate throughout these
States upon the basis of a secession from the Articles of Confederation of 1781. Virginia distinctly
reserved the right to withdraw from the new league,
if the compact should be perverted to her injury;
this same reservation was implied in the method of
ratification followed by the other Commonwealths.
The first Federal Congress decided that the duties
levied on imports from foreign countries must be
imposed on goods from North Carolina and Rhode
Island. In the seventh month after the inauguration of the Federal Union, North Carolina voluntarily entered the compact as the twelfth State,
November 21, 1789. Just at the close of Washington's first year as President, Rhode Island sought
admission to the Federal household, May 29, 1790.
This little Commonwealth had held herself entirely
aloof from the other States since her secession in
1786. The political sentiment of this entire period
of the establishment of the Federal Constitution,
held each State to be the self-governing member of
a league of Commonwealths organised for the purposes of mutual defence and mutual intercourse.

The first serious attempt to fasten a different

construction upon the Constitution was made by
the Federalist party about ten years after the inauguration of the Federal Government.   In 1798, the
Administration of John Adams followed the example offered by England, and passed the Alien and
Sedition laws.   The Sedition Law declared it a
punishable crime to publish any malicious charge
against the Federal Government or any part thereof.   The Alien Law gave authority to the President
to arrest or exile any alien whom he should consider
dangerous to the country.   These laws lodged great
power in the hands of Congress and the President,
and they were executed after the manner of political
persecution.   Legitimate pamphlets of the political
sort were adjudged by Federal officials to be criminal
libels.   In the same year, 1798, were issued the
resolutions of the Virginia and Kentucky legislatures, prepared respectively by Madison and Jefferson, denouncing these laws as contrary to the letter
and spirit of the Constitution.   Both resolutions
affirmed that the Constitution was a " compact "
between the States; that these sovereign Commonwealths had reserved the right to restrain the creat-
ure of the compact, the Federal Government, from
assuming any powers not expressly granted to it.
In the election of the year 1800, a great wave of
popular approval swept Jefferson's party into power;
the effort at centralisation had thus far met naught
but disaster.

When Jefferson made the purchase of Louisiana
from Napoleon in 1803, in the form of a treaty ratified by the Senate, a clearly developed spirit of sec-

tionalism at once manifested itself. The people of
the Southern States believed that the development
of the western territory both north and south depended upon the free navigation of the Mississippi.
Immediate action was necessary; there was not time
to follow Jefferson's suggestion of an amendment
to the Constitution; they therefore supported the
treaty that secured the western bank of the great
river. On the other hand, the Federalists of New
England opposed the treaty, not merely on Constitutional grounds, but on the further ground
expressed by Tracy of Connecticut, that the admission of prospective States from the Louisiana territory would result in " absorbing the Northern States
and rendering them insignificant in the Union."
This Eastern opposition to the treaty grew into a
strong spirit of separatism, and in 1804 the air was
full of serious threats from the New England Federalists that they would secede from the Federal
Union and organise a Northern Confederacy. When
Jefferson's Administration passed the Embargo Act
in 1807, it proved a failure because of the refusal of
the people east of the Hudson River to obey its
provisions. This resistance went to such length
that the Massachusetts Legislature, February 1,
1809, issued an official call of the commercial States
to send delegates to a convention to consider the
union of the Eastern Commonwealths against the
Federal Government. The movement was checked
by the repeal of the Embargo.

The opposition party became more determined
under Madison's régime. A few months before the

declaration of war against England, Josiah Quincy on the floor of Congress, thus made resistance to the bill granting statehood to Louisiana: " If this bill passes, it is my deliberate opinion that it is virtually a dissolution of this Union; that it will free the States from their moral obligation; and, *as it will be the right of all*, so it will be the duty of some, definitely to prepare for a separation, amicably if they can, violently if they must." Not from any quarter was denial made of the right of secession thus boldly announced. The war-measure of 1812 added fuel to the flame, and New England proceeded to carry threats into active resistance to the Federal Government.

The call of the Secretary of War for the militia of the States met blunt refusal from the Governors of Massachusetts, Rhode Island, and Connecticut. The Assembly of the latter State sustained its Executive in a formal address which denounced the war and declared Connecticut to be a free, sovereign, and independent State, and that the United States was not a national but a confederated republic. President Madison was held up as an invader of the State's authority over her militia. The highest court of Massachusetts gave sanction to this view, and the three States furnished none of the sinews of war. The burden of public defence fell upon the South and West. The campaigns in Canada failed, but New England did not come to Madison's help. While the mounted riflemen of Kentucky were assembling for the onset which gained the victory of the Thames in the North-west; while the

fierce soldiery of Tennessee were burnishing their
mountain rifles to teach Packenham's veterans their
first lesson of defeat at New Orleans, the people of
New England were permitting a British force to
hold without resistance the territory of Maine.   In
the very midst of the deadly struggle, while the
Southern States were voting men and money for
the war, Vermont's Executive was recalling troops
sent by his predecessor, and the Massachusetts lawmakers were holding aloof with the declaration that
New England had been totally excluded from a
share in the Federal Government.   From the mountains of New Hampshire there came also to President
Madison, a memorial which ran, in part, as follows:
" If a separation of the States ever should take
place, it will be on some occasion when some portion
of the country undertakes to control, to regulate,
and to sacrifice the interest of another."

Secession became the sentiment of the hour in
the East as the war dragged itself onward.   " The
flag of five stripes " was the cry that arose in New
England when the stars and stripes were going down
before the colours of Britain.   The Federalists of
New York made response to this call by offering as
a toast, the Northern Confederacy, with its boundary " the Delaware, the Susquehanna, or the
Potomac."

As the year 1814 drew near its end, with the
Federal Government on the verge of bankruptcy
and the flames enkindled by the British consuming
the Capitol at Washington, delegates from the New
England States were assembling in the Hartford

Convention. Nullification had not brought satisfaction to the Federalists. Secession must be formally considered. The scheme that had now grown
ripe presented two alternative courses; either the
long-cherished Northern Confederacy must be established, or, as the Massachusetts legislature suggested, there must be made " a radical reform in
the national compact " by a convention representing
all the States in the Union. At Hartford, December 15, 1814, the ablest and most influential men of
New England met together to express their hostility to Madison's Administration. The resolutions
passed by the Hartford Convention asserted the
State's right of " interposition " against the Federal
Government, and " were so framed," says Roosevelt, " as to justify seceding, or not seceding, as
events turned out." Harrison Gray Otis at once
proceeded toward Washington to take note of times
and seasons, whether the hour had yet come for
leading New England out of the Union. News of
the treaty of peace with England turned Otis back,
and the attempt was made to draw a veil over the
proceedings at Hartford.

The decade following the peace of 1814 saw the
widening of the gulf between the agricultural and
commercial sections of the Federal Union. The
next issue which thrust itself between them was the
question of a tax on imported merchandise.

The South from the first paid the largest share of
the expenses of the Federal Government, because
she sent out the great bulk of American exports.
After 1824, the protective tariff-law aided in binding

a yet heavier public burden upon her. In that year the wool-growers of the West joined hands with the wool-workers of the Middle and Northern States to fasten Henry Clay's protective system upon foreign traffic. At once New England, whose representatives had opposed the earlier tariffs, left her ships on the sand, to begin the work of multiplying looms and spindles, and to advocate a heavier tax on foreign goods in the interest of home manufactures. In 1828, the West cast her vote with the North to pass a tariff-law still more burdensome to the South, but in the same year the West supported the South in giving more than two thirds of the electoral vote to the hero of New Orleans. In 1830 the West drew further apart from the North in regard to the sale of public lands, and in a moment the halls of Congress were ablaze with the debate over the tariff, the building of new States, and nullification.

The sectional wrestle began in the Senate over Foot's [Connecticut] resolutions, December, 1829, to abridge the sale of public lands in the West. Benton of Missouri leaped to his feet to charge New England with long-continued hostility toward the West, and declared this measure a blow aimed against the growth of that section. Hayne of South Carolina came to Benton's aid by holding up the second resolution of the Hartford Convention, which demanded some provision " for restraining Congress in the exercise of an unlimited power to make new States." Hayne charged New England with the design of consolidating the Government in order to administer public affairs in the sole interest

of the North.   He claimed that the South was con-
tending for the true intent of the Federal Constitution, in her opposition to the unjust tariff of 1828,
and that she might desire to practice the theory of
nullification so often exhibited in the conduct of
New England.   Webster, in reply, laboured long to
show that nullification had never found foothold in
New England!   " No public man of reputation
ever advanced it in Massachusetts," cried Webster,
in utter forgetfulness of the formal action of the
Massachusetts legislature.   In opposition to nullification as a governmental theory, he brought forward the claim of *original consolidation.*   He affirmed
that the Federal Constitution of 1787 was not a
compact between the States, but an instrument
adopted by the American people as one great body-
politic.   Webster's address was a master-piece of
fervid eloquence.   The spirit of the man himself
was aglow with patriotic earnestness, but his biographer, Henry Cabot Lodge, makes the following
admissions concerning the two lines of argument:

" Unfortunately the facts were against him [Webster] in both instances.   When the Constitution was adopted by the votes of the
states at Philadelphia and accepted by the votes of States in popular
Conventions, it is safe to say that there was not a man in the country
from Washington and Hamilton on the one side, to George Clinton
and George Mason on the other, who regarded the new system as anything but an experiment entered upon by the States and from which
each and every State had the right peaceably to withdraw ; a right
which was very likely to be exercised."

Against the recent tariff-statutes the people of
South Carolina entered solemn protest in the form

of an ordinance of nullification, November, 1832. Before the ordinance became operative, the tariff was reduced by Clay's compromise measure. The fierce commercial wrestle, however, indicated the complete separation of the old Federal Union into two hostile sections. Into the arena of debate between the two divided peoples was thrust the question of slavery in this same year, 1832.

The institution of slavery in the South was a vast labour-system. Under that system, the negro was registered as a member of a patriarchal household; day by day the habits of African savagery were purged from his life by the power of law, represented in the will of his master. The State laws were severe on crimes committed by negroes; but any abuse of servants was prohibited by statute. Self-interest restrained harsh masters from cruelty, and a wholesome public sentiment enforced the practice of kindness toward the quiet wards of the plantation. Cruelty was the exception. Not often was the lash used; not often were negro families separated by sale, except as penalty for misdemeanor, or in the distribution of estates to heirs or to creditors. The system produced no paupers and no orphans; food and clothing the negro did not lack; careful attention he received in sickness, and, without a burden the aged servants spent their closing days. The plantation was an industrial school where the negro gradually acquired skill in the use of tools. A bond of affection was woven between Southern masters and servants which proved strong enough in 1861–'65 to keep the negroes at voluntary labour to furnish food for the armies that contended against military emancipation. In the planter's home the African learned to set a higher value upon the domestic virtues which he saw illustrated in the lives of Christian men and women; for, be it remembered, the great body of the slaveholders of the South were devotees of the religious faith handed down through pious ancestors from Knox, Cranmer, Wesley, and Bunyan. With truth, perhaps, it may be said than none other economic system before or since that time has engendered a bond of personal affection between capital and labour so strong as that established by the institution of slavery.

Slowly upward toward a fitness for citizenship this mild servitude was lifting the negro, but only at the expense of Southern prosperity. Slavery was a blight upon the economic development of the South; it repressed inventive talent, it paralysed Anglo-Saxon energy, and it left hidden in the earth the South's material resources. As a system of labour, slavery secured slight service; harvests were not abundant in proportion to the vast acreage, mines were not opened, forests were not felled, railroads were not constructed, and factories were not established. From an early date a large proportion of the Southern slave-holders desired to cast off the burden, but the problem ever arose: " What shall be done with the emancipated serf ? "

It must not be forgotten that the commercial greed of England fastened the black race upon the American colonies against the vigorous protests of

the colonial assemblies.   Many of the English sov-
ereigns made investments in slave-ships.   John Wesley advocated the purchase of slaves for the colony
of Georgia, in order that they might there hear the
Gospel.   In 1776, slavery existed in all the thirteen
commonwealths, and at the close of the Revolution
more than half a million Africans were dwelling side
by side with three million Americans.   The Virginia
statesmen saw danger in this juxtaposition of two
diverse races, and they led a crusade against the
foreign slave-traffic.   Into the Federal Convention
this war was carried, but there New England voted
with South Carolina and Georgia to leave the African trade as a stain upon the country for twenty
years longer.   The Constitution further recognised
the institution by adding three fifths of the number
of slaves to the white population as the basis of
each State's representation in Congress, and by the
provision for the return of fugitive slaves.

Unto the ships of New England the slave-carry-
ing trade was transferred after the Revolution.
Even before that war, her skippers had taken car-
goes of rum from Cape Cod and Narragansett to
exchange for flesh and blood on the coast of Africa.
Fresh impetus was now given to this kind of barter.
Wealth was rapidly heaped up in Rhode Island
through the traffic of her fleet of slave vessels.
Gradually the negroes of Northern masters were
sent to the Southern markets, and thus were the
Southern States filled up with the alien race.

From the beginning, the Virginians had scented
danger.   In the opening years of the new century,

they began to look with alarm upon the increasing
multitude of unenlightened negroes. To them it
was a colossal race-problem; not the mere question
of the patriarchal relation of master and servant,
but the presence of a barbarous race in the heart of
Anglo-Saxon commonwealths. Mere emancipation
from serfdom did not seem to these statesmen an
adequate remedy; emancipation on a small scale
was attempted by individuals, but the last state of
the free negroes in the South, as well as in the
North, was worse than the first state. The complete removal of the negroes appeared to them the
only course of treatment that could touch the
sources of the malady; they feared even greater
evils from the tribes of emancipated Africans
within the States. It was Patrick Henry who said,
" Much as I deplore slavery, I see that prudence
forbids its abolition." Marshall declared that abolition would not remove the evils caused by the
negro's presence. Jefferson deplored the danger to
the stability of the Republic, and advocated the
foreign colonisation of the African. The views of
all these Southern leaders were set forth by Henry
Clay in 1829 as follows: " If we were to invoke the
greatest blessing on earth which Heaven, in its
mercy, could now bestow on this nation, it would
be the separation of the two most numerous races
of its population, and their comfortable establishment in distinct and distant countries." Again, he
said, " The evils of slavery are absolutely nothing
in comparison with the far greater evils which would
inevitably follow from a sudden, general, and indis-

criminate emancipation." The Virginia legislature in 1832 made long debate over a proposition to emancipate the slaves of the Commonwealth; but the bill was defeated because of the dread of more difficult race-problems after emancipation.

In spite of these Southern views, in spite of the fact that the English Government, in 1833, made liberal payment for all the slaves set free on her West Indian plantations, the Abolitionists began the work of crying death to the Federal Constitution for sheltering the alleged crime of slavery. They flooded the mails with publications intended to incite the negroes to rise in insurrection against their masters; they denounced slave-holders as out-laws, and besieged Congress with petitions that it should step beyond the pale of Federal authority and begin the destruction of the institution.

In 1790, the Congress of the United States had declared that it possessed " no power to interfere with slavery or the treatment of the slaves within the States." For thirty years this remained the policy of Congress. But in 1820 the country was swept by the hot fever-blast of contention over the admission of Missouri as a State. The ancient hostility of the East against the extension of the Union toward the south-west, in that year forced the concession from the South that henceforth slavery should not be recognised as legal in the territories north of the parallel 36° 30'. This early assault upon the system of slavery was clearly due to political and not to humanitarian motives. But it was aggressive warfare upon slavery itself that John Quincy Adams

waged in the House of Representatives under the
guise of upholding the right of petition.   Bundles
of denunciatory petitions he continued to present,
even after the House, in 1836, reaffirmed the declaration of 1790, asserting lack of jurisdiction over
slavery, and after the House had also passed a rule
against receiving these documents.

From his seat in the Senate, February, 1839,
Henry Clay thus laid bare the real aim of the agi-
tators :

> " Civil war, a dissolution of the Union.   .   .   .   are nothing [with
> the Abolitionists].   .   .   .   In all their leading prints and publica-
> tions, the alleged horrors of slavery are depicted in the most glowing
> and exaggerated colours, to excite the imaginations and stimulate the
> rage of the people in the free States against the people in the slave
> States.   The slave-holder is held up and represented as the most
> atrocious of human beings.   Advertisements of fugitive slaves are
> carefully collected and blazoned forth to infuse a spirit of detestation
> and hatred against one entire and the largest section of the Union.
> .   .   .   To the agency of their powers of persuasion they now pro-
> pose to substitute the powers of the ballot box ; and he must be blind
> to what is passing before us who does not perceive that the inevitable
> tendency of their proceedings is, if these should be found insufficient,
> *to invoke, finally, the more potent powers of the bayonet.*"

When the old question of territorial expansion
toward the south-west lifted up its head in the proposition to admit Texas into the league of American
States, the Abolitionists made resistance.   Although
the settlement of Texas was only an incident in the
great westward migration of home-seekers from the
Alleghanies and the Mississippi Valley, yet the
Abolitionists made the charge that the presence of
African servants in these new frontier households

indicated a gigantic scheme to construct a slave-empire. In 1842–1843, therefore, Adams and Giddings presented petitions from citizens of Massachusetts and Ohio, asking Congress at once to take steps toward " the peaceable dissolution of the Union." Adams, Giddings, and other Congressmen issued a public address, in March, 1843, declaring that the annexation of Texas would be " so injurious to the interests of the Northern States as not only inevitably to result in a dissolution of the Union, but fully to justify it." The month of August, 1843, saw a National Convention of the Liberty Party binding itself by formal resolution " to regard and treat the third clause of the Constitution whenever applied to the case of a fugitive slave, as utterly null and void." Formal announcement was made in May, 1844, by the American Anti-Slavery Society that they rejected the entire Federal Constitution as " a covenant with death and an agreement with hell." They further declared that " secession from the Government " was the duty of every Abolitionist. Two weeks later the Society issued an address to the country with the formal summons: " Up with the banner of revolution!" More than sixty thousand voters abandoned the Whig Party to render support to this dis-union banner; this defection caused the defeat of the Whig, Henry Clay, by Polk, the Democratic candidate for the Presidency.

In the year 1845, in protest against denunciations of slavery by Northern pulpits, the Southern Baptists withdrew themselves into a separate organisa-

tion. The year 1846 saw the formation of the
Southern Methodist Church upon the same basis,
and the new Constitution of Kentucky, in 1849,
was more rigid than the old in maintaining the relation of master and servant. But these protests only
served to redouble the vigour of the Abolitionists.
Against slavery in the territories secured from Mexico they now concentrated their assaults. In the
Congressional struggle of 1850 over the organisation of these lands, Webster united with Clay and
Calhoun in condemning the aggressions of abolition-
ism. In February, Clay said, " Upon this subject I
do think that we have just and serious cause of com-
plaint against the free States." In May he further
declared, " The body-politic cannot be preserved
unless this agitation, this distraction, this exaspera-
tion, which is going on between the two sections of
the country, shall cease." March 4th found Calhoun in the Senate, pale from the weakness of
approaching death, while Mason read his last appeal
for the cessation of Abolitionist attacks upon the
old Federal Constitution. Calhoun declared that
the existing relation between master and servant
" Cannot be destroyed without subjecting the two
races to the greatest calamity and the section to
poverty, desolation, and wretchedness."

Concerning the Abolition movement Webster declared, March 7th, "The South, in my judgment,
is right, and the North is wrong." Again, in July,
1850, Webster asserted that Northern prejudice
against the Southern labour-system " all originates
in misinformation, false representations, and misap-

WASHINGTON MONUMENT AND CAPITOL, RICHMOND, VIRGINIA.

prehensions arising from the laborious efforts that
have been made for the last twenty years to pervert
the public judgment and irritate the public feeling.''

But other voices were heard in this senatorial
battle. W. H. Seward, of New York, disciple of
the school of J. Q. Adams, made announcement of
a '' Higher Law,'' above the Constitution, and, for
himself, foreshadowed, a readiness for the programme of immediate emancipation by violence, if
necessary. Chase of Ohio made zealous proclamation of the same creed. The '' Higher Law '' thus
brought forward was merely the conscience of the
Abolitionists. Side by side with Seward's announcement must we place the matured judgment
of Clay, Calhoun, and Webster, sustained by the
entire people of the Southern States, that the conscience of the Abolitionists was wrong—that the
Higher Law was without foundation.

The fugitive-slave enactment of 1850 was the
issue made prominent now by the anti-slavery revo-
lutionists, and this issue gave them great advantage
before the new generation of immigrants and citizens in the North. The law itself was a strategical
mistake on the part of the Southern people; they
had sought to emphasise a constitutional right for
the sake of the few servants who were persuaded
to flee across the border. The crusade against
slavery rapidly gained strength. The Free-Soil
Convention of 1852 openly denied the '' binding
force '' of the fugitive-slave law, and Sumner, in the
Senate, declared it a '' dead letter '' in the public
conscience of the Free States. The legislatures of

some of these States passed "personal liberty" laws practically nullifying the Congressional statute. Into a whirlwind of passion against slavery did the erroneous portraiture in *Uncle Tom's Cabin* begin to sweep the people of the North. The incidents of this story were altogether exceptional, but the dearth of accurate information in the North gave this volume wide acceptance as a realistic sketch of the alleged barbaric civilisation of the South! The anti-slavery war increased in fierceness, although the supposed basis for such hostility was scarcely greater in 1854 than it had been in 1850, when Webster expressed himself as follows:

" No seizure of an alleged fugitive slave has ever been made in Maine . . . New Hampshire . . . Vermont. No seizure of an alleged fugitive slave has been made in Rhode Island within the last thirty years.—No seizure of an alleged fugitive slave is known to have been made in Connecticut, except one, about twenty-five years ago ; and in that case the negro was immediately discharged for want of proof of identity. Some instances of the seizure of alleged fugitives slaves are known to have occurred, in this genera- tion, in Massachusetts ; but except one, their number and their history are uncertain. . . . What is there to justify the passionate appeals, the vehement and empty declamations, the wild and fanat- ical conduct of both men and women which have so long disturbed and so much disgraced, the Commonwealth and the country ? "

The year 1854 marked the passage of the Kansas- Nebraska Bill, and the formal repeal of the Missouri Compromise of 1820. It was asserted by Senator Douglass that the Compromise of 1850 had already repealed the earlier compromise by the prohibition of slavery in California, south of 36° 30'; at the same time, Douglass further declared, the legislation of 1850 had inaugurated a new method of organising the territories. Therefore, in 1854, the two territories, Kansas and Nebraska, lying north of 36° 30', were established without any prohibition of slavery, inviting immigration upon the pledge that the people of the territories themselves were left " perfectly free to form and regulate their domestic institutions in their own way, subject only to the Constitution of the United States."

A. H. Stephens of Georgia affirmed that the Southern people gave their support to this measure, not for the purpose of forcing slavery upon the territories, " but to let free emigrants to our vast public domain, in every part and parcel of it, settle this question for themselves, with all the experience, intelligence, virtue, and patriotism they may carry with them."

A race for the possession of the soil of Kansas began at once between bands of armed men from the North and from the South. Fierce and open warfare ere long was raging upon these Western plains over the question of recognising or prohibiting slavery in the new State Constitution.

The Democratic platform of 1856 endorsed the Kansas-Nebraska Bill, and reaffirmed the " compact " theory of the Constitution as " laid down in the Kentucky and Virginia resolutions," and further declared that the agitations of the slavery question by the Abolitionists " endanger the stability and permanency of the Union."

June 17, 1856, marked the consolidation of the

clans opposed to the Kansas-Nebraska Bill into a
new party. These opponents of slavery hitherto
classed under various names as Abolitionists, Free-
Soilers, and Whigs, came together and, in Convention assembled, rebaptised themselves as The
Republican Party. Representatives were present
from all the Northern States, and from Maryland,
Delaware, and Kentucky. No voice from the other
States was heard in this Philadelphia Council, which
closed its third resolution with the claim that " It
is both the right and the imperative duty of Congress to prohibit in the territories those twin relics
of barbarism—polygamy and slavery."

Before the close of the month of June, ex-Presi-
dent Fillmore at Albany denounced the new party
as distinctly sectional, organised for the avowed
purpose of electing its candidates " by suffrages of
one part of the Union only, to rule over the whole
United States. . . . Can they have the mad-
ness or folly to believe that our Southern brethren
would submit to be governed by such a chief magistrate ? " Rufus Choate described it as " The new
geographical party calling itself Republican . . .
which knows one half of America only to hate and
dread it." He added further :

" The triumph of such a party puts the Union in danger. . . .
If the Republican party accomplishes its objects and gives the
government to the North, I turn my eyes from the consequences.
To the fifteen States of the South that government will appear an
alien government. It will appear a hostile government. It will
represent to their eye a vast region of States organised upon Anti-
slavery."

In this Presidential campaign of 1856, the warning note emphasised in the Democratic canvass in the Southern States was the necessity of secession from the Federal Union, if the Republican party should carry the election. The Border States and the Cotton States alike were ready to withdraw themselves in a body for the organisation of a Southern Confederacy in the event of Fremont's accession to the Presidency. But in the political battle the victory was adjudged to Buchanan. The Democratic platform interpreting the Constitution to be a " compact " between sovereign States, received overwhelming popular sanction at the polls.

For this reason alone the Southern States remained as yet within the Federal League. But the critical four-year period now opening did not seem luminous with approaching peace in view of the following deliverance on the part of the Disunion Convention at Worcester, Massachusetts, January 15, 1857: " Resolved, that the sooner the separation takes place, the more peaceful it will be; but that peace or war is a secondary consideration in view of our present perils. Slavery must be conquered, ' peaceably if we can, forcibly if we must.' "

Two days after Buchanan's inauguration, the Dred Scott decision was handed down by the Supreme Court of the United States. This decision affirmed that the mere fact of Dred Scott's temporary residence in a territory organised from the Louisiana purchase north of 36° 30' did not bring freedom to an African slave. First of all did the Court declare that a slave was not a citizen under the Constitution; in assigning the reason for this interpretation, the Court affirmed that the Louisiana domain " was acquired by the general government as the representative and trustee of the people of the United States, and it must, therefore, be held in that character for their common and equal benefit." Beyond this the Court advanced to say that Congress, the trustee acting for the States, had no authority to pass the Missouri Compromise in 1820, invalidating the rights established by the Constitution. Thus was the Constitution by the highest legal tribunal interpreted as sanctioning the full claims of the Southern people concerning slavery. Justice Curtis's dissenting opinion was merely the republication of the theory of the original consolidation of the thirteen States.

The case was now made up on both sides, and the lines of battle were clearly drawn. The people of the South were of one mind still in denying the alleged barbarity of their labour-system. Moreover, they began to draw attention to the tribe of emancipated negroes in the United States as more debased than their brethren in bonds. At the same time they could point to the dismal failure of emancipation in the English West Indies.

In 1860, Dr. Charles Hodge, the Princeton theologian, wrote as follows:

" When Southern Christians are told that they are guilty of a heinous crime, worse than piracy, robbery or murder, because they hold slaves, when they know that Christ and His Apostles never denounced slave-holding as a crime, never called upon men to renounce it as a condition of admission to the Church, they are shocked and offended without being convinced. . . . The argument from the conduct of Christ and his immediate followers, seems to us decisive on the point, that slave-holding in itself considered is not a crime."

Like an echo of Southern opinion in 1860 sounds the following, written twenty years after Mr. Lincoln's Emancipation Proclamation:

" Emancipation without any training for freedom could not be a blessing. . . . The Christianity and the philanthropy of this age have before them a task that is far more serious, more weighty and more difficult than it would have been, if the emancipation had been a regulated process, *even if its final consummation had been postponed for generations.*"—G. T. Curtis's *Life of Buchanan.*

The echo is redoubled in force when we read the following, of a date still more recent:

" It was perfectly possible and reasonable for enlightened and virtuous men, who fully recognised it [slavery] as an evil, yet to prefer its continuance to having it interfered with in a way that would produce even worse results. Black slavery in Hayti was characterised by worse abuse than ever was the case in the United States ; yet looking at the condition of that republic now, it may well be questioned whether it would not have been greatly to her benefit in the end to have had slavery continue a century or so longer."—Theodore Roosevelt's *Life of Benton.*

CHAPTER V.

1859–1861.

HE Autumn of 1859 witnessed the attack of John Brown upon the town
of Harper's Ferry in Virginia. From
the field of blood in Kansas, Brown
had recently fled eastward. In con-
cert with prominent Abolitionists, he made preparation to incite the slaves in Virginia to rise in
insurrection against their masters. More than four
thousand dollars were furnished to Brown for the
prosecution of the campaign.* Two hundred

---

* It was the belief of the Virginians, and of the Southerners generally, that the negroes were being organised for the purpose of
attacking their masters. It was the contention, on the other hand,
of men like Gerrit Smith, Thomas Wentworth Higginson, and others,
through whom these moneys were raised, or who had personal knowledge of the instructions given for their use, that the negroes were
expected merely to maintain their organisation in a defensive campaign, in the hope that public opinion in both North and South,
would be aroused in the end, on behalf of their cause.

Sharpe's rifles, two hundred revolvers, and nine hundred and fifty iron-pointed pikes he collected in his arsenal at the Kennedy farm in Maryland, four miles from Harper's Ferry. The pikes were manufactured especially for the purpose of arming the slaves whom he expected to flock to the standard of revolt.   On the night of October 18 Brown entered Harper's Ferry with eighteen followers, each man armed with a rifle and revolvers.   By midnight the conspirators were masters of the village, and had intrenched themselves in the United States arsenal.   Their leader sent out a party to begin the work of emancipating the slaves; one negro man was shot down in cold blood, and two prominent citizens, with a number of slaves, were seized and carried into the arsenal.   After sunrise, the citizens and militia came together, and, during the firing that followed, men were slain on both sides, among them the Mayor of the town, and also a prominent land-holder of the vicinity.   At mid-day, Brown betook himself to the engine-house in the armory yard; there he barred the doors and windows, cut portholes through the brick walls, and prepared to maintain his position.   Already he had failed in the chief aim of his attack; not a single slave had volunteered to assist him.   Late in the evening of the 19th came Colonel Robert E. Lee, with a company of United States Marines.   He had returned from Texas to Arlington on brief leave of absence, and was at once ordered from Washington to the scene of action.

Lee's memorandum-book states that he found the

railroad at Harper's Ferry " blocked with arrested trains." He hurried his soldiers across the Potomac, and " posted them," the memorandum continues,

" in the United States armory which was held by a party of banditti that had taken refuge in the engine-house, where they had been driven by the troops and citizens from Virginia. All retreat of the insurgents being cut off, I determined to wait for daylight, as I learned that a number of citizens were held as hostages by the robbers, whose lives were threatened if they should be attacked. . . . Tuesday about sunrise, with twelve marines under the command of Lieutenant Green [accompanied by J. E. B. Stuart], broke in the door of the engine-house, secured the robbers and released the prisoners unhurt. All were killed or mortally wounded but four, John Brown, Aaron Stevens, Edwin Coppie, and Green Shields (black). Had the prisoners removed to a place of safety and their wounds dressed,"

Five men killed and nine wounded was the substance of the crime charged against Brown and his companions at the bar of the Circuit Court in Charlestown, Virginia. After a fair and lengthy trial, in which they were defended by able counsel, Brown and his accomplices were found guilty of murder and executed, December 2, 1859. Before this, application for appeal was made through counsellors of the highest ability. The Supreme Court heard the case, and refused the application for appeal. After this manner, the sentence of Brown was affirmed by the highest legal tribunal in Virginia.

To the Southern people, the real significance of John Brown's attack appeared not alone in the bloodshed caused by a band of nineteen men; not merely in the purpose of Brown, according to their belief, to stir up servile war and to repeat in the

Southern States the horrors of San Domingo. They knew that he could not succeed in this purpose.

The real meaning of the assault was unveiled to the world, on the day of Brown's execution, by the tolling of funeral bells and the firing of minute-guns in many parts of the North. It was revealed by the Church services and the public mass-meetings held for the purpose of glorifying the cause of immediate abolition, and for enrolling Brown's name in the calendar of martyrs. John Brown was merely a narrow-minded fanatic who assumed for himself the right to carry to a logical conclusion the teachings of the Abolitionists. For almost three decades, the latter had made increasing strides in popularity by denouncing slavery as a crime, and the slave-holder as criminal and outlaw. It was only natural that a stern, unsympathetic spirit like that of John Brown should use this moral code to justify his inauguration of a programme of blood-shed. It was his opinion, revealed, as the Southern people believed, by his deeds, that the slave-holder had forfeited all right to life, and Brown supposed that he did service unto God by attempting to incite the slaves to take arms and slay their masters.

John Brown's raid startled the South, for it suddenly revealed the width of the social chasm between the two sections of the Federal Union. A blow was struck, and slave-holding citizens were slain; the scaffold of the slayer was compared to the cross on Calvary. Reputable persons made this latter assertion in various forms, and went un-rebuked. " Saint John the Just " was the verdict of the Concord philosophers concerning John Brown. '' The new Saint . . . will make the gallows glorious like the Cross '' was the sentiment of Emerson that drew applause from a vast assemblage in Boston. In the Senate, January, 1860, Douglas declared that the responsibility for John Brown's attack must be laid upon Lincoln's doctrine that the Union could not endure half-slave and half-free, and upon Seward's theory of '' irrepressible conflict '' between the North and the South.

In May, 1860, Abraham Lincoln was nominated for the Presidency by the Republican Convention in Chicago. Mr. Lincoln had won this position of party-leader by his speeches in the campaign of 1858 in the State of Illinois. In the joint debates with Stephen A. Douglas, Lincoln's central theme was that the slavery of the South was wrong; and that the Federal Union must be made all slave or all free territory. At Alton, October 15, Mr. Lincoln declared that nothing had '' ever threatened the existence of this Union save and except this very institution of slavery! '' At the same time he announced the existence of an '' eternal struggle '' between Northern and Southern principles—declaring that the North was the champion of '' the common right of humanity,'' while the South was defending the old principle of '' the divine right of Kings! '' Douglas charged Lincoln with thus announcing the policy of open warfare against the institution of slavery; the Southern people believed this to be the creed of the Republican standard-bearer of 1860.

The Chicago platform upon which Mr. Lincoln presented himself to the country contained the declaration that " the normal condition of all the territory of the United States is that of freedom.''

This doctrine was based upon the claim that the founders of the Federal Government were emancipationists who had " abolished slavery in all our national territory.'' The platform further declared that no legislative body, Federal or territorial, could " give legal existence to slavery in any territory of the United States.'' This view set at naught the decision of the Supreme Court in the case of Dred Scott, and only represented a more advanced stage in the evolution of the consolidation theory.

In the prosecution of the political campaign of 1860, the supporters of the Chicago platform while disclaiming the purpose to interfere with slavery in the States, made the key-note of the canvass violent denunciation of the inhumanity of American slavery and the iniquity of its extension into any of the territories. In this crisis the Democratic party presented a divided front. John C. Breckinridge was the leader of the Southern Democrats who upheld the full text of the Dred Scott decision that slavery had legal existence in the territories under the Constitution. Douglas was nominated by the Northern wing of the Democratic Party; Bell and Everett were leaders of those who spoke, indefinitely, of preserving the Union. At the polls the eighteen Northern States held together, and gave Mr. Lincoln a majority of the electoral vote; of the popular vote he failed to receive a majority by about one million ballots. In the entire block of the Southern States, only about twenty-six thousand ballots were cast for the Republican candidate.

A majority of the Southern people looked upon the Federal Union as substantially broken and divided by the election of a sectional candidate upon a platform which they declared to be revolutionary and hostile to the South. There was no practical division of sentiment as to the obligation of the citizen to obey the mandate of his State. But there was difference of opinion concerning the proper time to withdraw from the Federal compact. One party now advocated *immediate* secession, while the other desired to *postpone* secession until compromise between the sections of the Union should be attempted. In the Cotton States the people decided for immediate withdrawal as the only legal, and therefore, peaceable remedy for sectional differences. Between December 20, 1860, and February 1, 1861, these seven Commonwealths summoned conventions in accordance with the precedent of 1787 in the adoption of the Federal Constitution, and, through these bodies as the incarnation of the sovereignty of the people, revoked each Commonwealth's assent to the Federal compact. As sovereign Commonwealths they stood now, even as they stood before the organisation of the Federal league. Not for a moment did they think to remain isolated from one another as separate States. The experiment of 1787 had proved a failure, and these seven Commonwealths, with kindred sympathies and similar ideals, formed a new Federal compact among themselves in February, 1861, as the Southern Confederacy.

It was not conspiracy among a few malcontent slave-holders that carried these States out of the old Union. There was not and had never been any practical division of sentiment between slave-holders and non-slave-holders, and a wave of popular enthusiasm swept both classes alike as one mass of people into the movement, and the leaders were compelled to yield to their practically unanimous demand for secession. Nor did these people take action as the enemies of the black race. They were the benefactors of the African serfs. But the Anti-slavery crusaders had stirred up a race-war of that anomalous sort wherein the negro was ready to take sides with his alleged oppressor against his self-appointed champion. Although the African did not greatly desire emancipation, and was loyal to his master, yet the Southern people had endured denunciation as a race of outlaws because of negro servitude. Against these charges the resentment of the non-slave-holding class was perhaps greater than that of the owners of slaves. In behalf of racial dignity and racial solidarity did these Southern Commonwealths prepare to assert their legal rights, in much the same spirit in which the people of Poland had opposed dismemberment. " The maintenance of the honour, the rights, the equality, the security, and the glory of my native State in the Union, if possible; but if these cannot be maintained in the Union, then I am for their *maintenance at all hazards, out of it.*" Thus spoke A. H. Stephens, of

Georgia, a member of the postponement wing of
the secessionists. But when the voice of the people
of Georgia hurried the convention into immediate
withdrawal, then all the members of that body took
pledges of loyalty to the Commonwealth, and thus
was the Convention " unanimously committed to
the maintenance of the sovereignty of Georgia."
Even so stood as one man the people of all the
seven States who, in March, 1861, adopted a Constitution like the old Federal Constitution, except,
among other features, in the forbidding of bounties
and of protection in the tariff, and in imposing on
the Confederate Congress the duty of passing pre-
ventive and punitive laws to prohibit the importa-
tion of slaves from Africa.

The attitude of the Federal Administration toward
this Confederacy was based upon the written opinion
of the Attorney-General, J. S. Black, concerning the
power granted to Congress to control the militia:
"All these provisions are made to protect the States,
not to authorise an attack by one part of the country upon another; to preserve the peace, and not
to plunge them into civil war. . . .   The Union
must utterly perish at the moment when Congress
shall arm one part of the people against another."
The views of President Buchanan were the same,
as thus expressed in his Annual Message: " The
long-continued and intemperate interference of the
Northern people with the question of slavery in the
Southern States has at length produced its natural
effects.   The different sections of the Union are
now arrayed against each other."   While Buchanan

refused to concede the legality of secession, he acknowledged that an attempt to coerce a seceded State would be only a gratuitous act of war against her.

The postponement party of secessionists held sway in the Border States. In 1856, these States were ready to secede, but now in 1860 they wished to continue discussion in the halls of legislation and establish a compromise measure. Crittenden of Kentucky brought before the Senate a proposition to amend the Constitution by extending the old 36° 30' line to the westward. This amendment would have recognised territorial slavery only in New Mexico and the Indian Reservations, where the nature of the country itself forbade the employment of African labour. Virginia called a Peace Convention, and submitted to Congress practically the same compromise. The advantage in the territories was thus offered to the Anti-slavery party. Both schemes were buried, as S. S. Cox, an actor in the drama, has declared, under the solid Republican vote in both Houses.

The Border States now awaited the policy of President Lincoln. The Virginia Convention was still in session with the postponement wing in supremacy. They desired to know if the intent of the new Administration was peaceable. Peaceable it professed to be. The President entered office with the claim that he desired harmony between the sections; he claimed to offer peace upon a Constitutional basis. Webster's great speech in reply to Hayne gave colour to the President's views; its

historical inaccuracies were accepted by Lincoln as
veritable history.   Want of accurate knowledge
concerning the origin of the Federal Union inspired
the historical errors of the Inaugural Address of
March 4, 1861, which was merely the untenable
theory of original consolidation:

> " The Union," said President Lincoln, " is much older than the
> States.   It was formed in fact by the Articles of Association in 1774.
> It was matured and continued in the Declaration of Independence
> in 1776.   It was further matured, and the faith of all the thirteen
> States expressly plighted and engaged that it should be perpetual by
> the Articles of Confederation in 1778."

President Lincoln ventured to designate a committee's recommendation in 1774 as a legal instrument establishing a government!   The olive-branch
proffered in this Inaugural was interpreted in the
South as a virtual declaration of war, and the party
advocating immediate secession grew stronger in
the Border States.

President Lincoln refused to recognise the Commissioners sent by the seven Commonwealths to ask
" peaceful solution " of all matters in dispute.   The
most pressing issue had reference to the control of
Forts Sumter and Pickens, in the harbours of
Charleston and Pensacola, then occupied by Federal troops.   The foundation of these forts was
originally the property of the States of South Carolina and Florida, and these Commonwealths, having
withdrawn from the Union, claimed that the island-
fortresses had reverted to the original owners as
military posts.   There was complete willingness to

make compensation to the Federal Government for the property value of the forts.

Since the closing days of 1860 many Republicans had advocated the policy of non-coercion in the case of the seceded States. Greeley's paper, *The Tribune*, made this declaration on November 9

"If the Cotton States shall decide that they can do better out of the Union than in it, we insist on letting them go in peace. The right to secede may be a revolutionary one, but it exists nevertheless. . . . Whenever a considerable section of our Union shall deliberately resolve to go out, we shall resist all coercive measures designed to keep it in. We hope never to live in a republic, whereof one section is pinned to the residue by bayonets."

" It will be an advantage for the South to go off," said H. W. Beecher. After the inauguration of Mr. Lincoln there was a strong current of opinion in the North that the Federal troops should be withdrawn from the Southern forts. President Lincoln's " organ," the *National Republican,* announced that the Cabinet meeting of March 9 had determined to surrender both Sumter and Pickens. That Anderson would be withdrawn from Sumter " was the universal impression in Washington " (Rhodes, *U. S.,* vol. iii., p. 332). Welling, of the *National Intelligencer,* was requested by Seward to communicate the Cabinet's purpose to George W. Summers, member of the Virginia Convention (*The Nation,* Dec. 4, 1879). March 15 Secretary Seward unofficially notified the Confederate Commissioners, through Justice Campbell of the Supreme Court, that Sumter would be yielded at once to the Southern Confederacy. Meanwhile, Captain G. V. Fox

had suggested a plan for throwing reinforcements
into Sumter.   On this same fifteenth day of March,
Fox was sent by Mr. Lincoln to obtain " accurate
information in regard to the command of Major
Anderson."   March 21, after dark, upon the parapet of Fort Sumter, Fox held a private conversation
with Anderson.   The latter

" at once earnestly condemned any proposal to send him reinforcements.   He asserted that it was too late ; he agreed with General
Scott that an entrance by sea was impossible ; and he impressed upon
Captain Fox his belief that any reinforcements coming would at
once precipitate a collision and inaugurate civil war, and to this
he manifested the most earnest opposition." (*Genesis of the Civil
War*, pp. 369–371.   By Major-General S. W. Crawford who, in
1861, was an officer under Major Anderson in Fort Sumter.   The
above statements are based upon Fox's personal letters to Crawford.)

" Every hour now tended to strengthen the belief that the garrison
was to be withdrawn, and the preliminary steps to be taken were
considered upon both sides.   The public press as well as private advices from Washington, all seemed to place the fact of withdrawal
beyond doubt.   The engineer officer had made his arrangements and
had reported to his chief [Major Anderson] his intentions, and had
received from that official his instructions as to the disposition to be
made of the property." (Crawford's *Genesis of the Civil War*, p.
373.)

March 25 brought Colonel Ward H. Lamon of
Washington to Fort Sumter.   He obtained permission from Governor Pickens to visit Major Anderson
upon the representation that he had come as " con-
fidential agent of the President," to make arrangements for *the removal of the garrison.*   " The
impression produced upon Major Anderson [by
Lamon] as well as upon the officers and men of the
garrison, was that the command was to be with-

drawn." Lamon informed Governor Pickens " that
the President professed a desire to evacuate the
work." After Lamon's return to Washington he
sent a written message to Pickens, that he " hoped
to return in a very few days to withdraw the command." *

Meanwhile, the radical Republican leaders began
to make protest against the surrender of Sumter. After the Cabinet meeting of March 29 Mr.
Lincoln ordered a naval expedition to be in readiness to move by the 6th of April; at the same time
he disavowed the promise of withdrawal made by
Lamon. Nevertheless, on April 7 Seward made
written renewal of his assurance, as follows : " Faith
as to Sumter fully kept—wait and see." On that
same day, April 7 a courier was already drawing
nigh to Charleston with a message from President
Lincoln himself, announcing to Governor Pickens
that an effort would be made to throw supplies
into Sumter, and that " if such attempt be not resisted, no effort to throw in men, arms, or ammunition will be made without further notice, or in case
of an attack upon the fort." †

Pickens soon received advices that the naval flo-
tilla was steaming southward to enforce President
Lincoln's policy. At once the cry was raised in the
South that the Federal Administration had been
guilty of equivocating conduct; that negotiation
had been flung aside, and war declared, in sending
the naval armaments to relieve Forts Sumter and

---

* Crawford's *Genesis*, pp. 373, 374.
† *Ibid.* 340, 394–396.

Pickens.   When Beauregard, in obedience to orders
from Montgomery, Alabama, opened fire on Sumter
in the early morning of April 12, 1861, the Federal
war vessels, with provisions, troops, and arms aboard,
were just reaching the outer bar of Charleston harbour.   In the opinion of the people of the South,
Beauregard's guns expressed nothing more than
the defensive attitude of the Southern Confederacy
against the approach of actual armed invasion.

Meanwhile, the Border States were playing the
part of peacemakers.   An ordinance of secession
submitted to the Virginia Convention, March 17
was rejected by a vote of ninety to forty-five.   Mr.
Lincoln at once requested an interview with a representative of the Convention, and the fourth day
of April found J. B. Baldwin in conference with the
President.   Baldwin has stated under oath that Mr.
Lincoln greeted him with the assertion that he had
come too late.   The President was deaf to Baldwin's
entreaties that he should yield the Southern forts,
and thus maintain peace.   Another committee from
the Convention arrived in Washington April 12
Their mission was to ascertain, definitely, the policy
proposed by the President.   Mr. Lincoln's written
answer to the committee, April 14 was " distinctly
pacific, and he expressly disclaimed all purpose of
war."   The railway train which bore the committee
to Richmond the following day carried the President's proclamation asking the various Governors
for an army of men.*   April 15, 1861, Mr. Lincoln
issued an official call to the States for seventy-five

* Crawford's *Genesis*, pp. 310–312.

thousand volunteers to overcome " combinations
too powerful to be suppressed by the ordinary
course of judicial proceedings." Immediately the
Border States flamed up in wrath; they declared
that Mr. Lincoln had inveigled them into the policy
of inaction, and had then inaugurated a war of invasion. The Virginia Convention at once passed the
ordinance of secession, April 17 North Carolina,
Tennessee, and Arkansas followed Virginia's example, and a few weeks saw the people of eleven States
fused together in the Southern Confederacy, ready,
they declared, to wage only a war of defence. At
the same time, the people of the Northern States
sprang to arms to " save the Union." The North
and the South stood opposed in deadly hostility,
each charging the other with the guilt of aggression.

War had arisen at the last, from certain misunder-
standings as to questions of fact. One of these was
centred about President Lincoln's governmental theory of original consolidation. In the Inaugural Ad
dress this view made its first appearance; and again
in the message to Congress, July 4, 1861, it was
expanded in these terms:

" The States have their status in the Union; and they have no
other legal status. If they break from this, they can only do so
against law and by revolution. The Union, and not themselves
separately, procured their independence and their liberty. By conquest or purchase, the Union gave each of them whatever of independence and liberty it has. The Union is older than any of the
States, and, in fact, it created them *as* States. Originally, some independent Colonies made the Union; and, in turn, the Union threw
off their old dependence for them and made them States, such as
they are. Not one of them ever had a State Constitution independent of the Union."

It is scarcely necessary to say again that this consolidation theory cannot stand for one moment in
the light of the actual historical facts.   When Mr.
Lincoln proposed this view of the origin of the Federal Government as the basis of his alleged " war
power," the difference between him and the people
of the Southern States was far more hopeless than
that between Charles Stuart and his Parliament.
When Mr. Lincoln offered peace on the basis of
this theory, the Southern people with one voice
interpreted that peace to mean their submission to
an unprecedented form of centralised government.

A second misunderstanding was concerned with
the extent and character of the secession movement
in the South.   Among the Republican officials and
legislators in Washington, it was maintained that
the withdrawal of the Southern States was due to a
few *conspirators*, who had used trickery in securing
the passage of the secession ordinances in opposition to the will of the majority of the people.   Davis
and Toombs, who were in fact adherents of the
postponement wing of secessionists until late in
December, 1860, were pointed out as the arch-
conspirators who had stirred up " rebellion " on the
part of the slave-holding minority in each seceding
State.   In the message of July 4, 1861, President
Lincoln said: " It may well be questioned whether
there is to-day a majority of the legally qualified
voters of any State, except, perhaps, South Carolina, in favour of disunion.   There is much reason
to believe that the Union men are in the majority
in many, if not in every other one, of the so-called
seceding States."

JEFFERSON DAVIS,
PRESIDENT OF THE SOUTHERN CONFEDERACY.

Mr. Lincoln totally misunderstood the attitude of
the *postponement* party among the secessionists.
This explains his attitude during the month of
March, 1861. When the Virginia Convention voted
largely against immediate secession, he supposed
that the majority gave complete acquiescence in the
theory of Federal consolidation announced in the
Inaugural Address. Whereas, these Virginians were
only awaiting the President's policy with reference
to the Confederate Government at Montgomery.
When he called for volunteers to suppress sovereign
States designated as unlawful " combinations," the
former Union men of Virginia were enraged. The
delegates yielded at once to the unanimous demand
of the people of the State, and secession was immediate. John B. Baldwin, an Ulsterman, representing the Valley of Virginia, where few slaves were
held, and who voted against secession on April 17,
at once signed the ordinance, and, later, wrote these
words: " There are now no Union men in Virginia.
But those who *were* Union men will stand to their
arms and make a fight which shall go down in history as an illustration of what a brave people will do
in defence of their liberties, after having exhausted
every means of pacification." In the four States of
Virginia, North Carolina, Tennessee, and Arkansas,
with the sole exception of the districts of western
Virginia and eastern Tennessee, there was but one
heart and one voice among slave-holders and non-
slave-holders alike; as one man, they were ready for
battle against the invasion threatened by President
Lincoln. The adherence of the entire mass of the
Southern people was accorded to their State gov-

ernments and to the government of the Confederacy
at Montgomery, with an enthusiasm not excelled by
that of the Swiss Cantons in the hour of Austrian
invasion, nor by the Highland clans at the call of
Roderick Dhu.   With reference to the unanimity
existing among the people of the South, we quote
the recent words of Mr. J. F. Rhodes:

> " Had the North thoroughly understood the problem ; had it
> known that the people in the Cotton States were practically unani-
> mous ; that the action of Virginia and North Carolina and Tennes-
> see was backed by a large and genuine majority, it might have
> refused to undertake the seemingly unachievable task.   .   .   .   It
> is impossible to escape the conviction that the action of the North
> was largely based on a *misconception* of the strength of the disunion
> sentiment in the Confederate States.   The Northern people accepted
> the gage of war and came to the support of the President on the
> theory that a majority in all of the Southern States, except South
> Carolina, were at heart for the Union." (*History of the United States,*
> iii. 404–5.)

The censure heaped upon Buchanan for failing to
imitate the " Jacksonian policy " of coercion, indicates that this misapprehension continues to exist.
It is beyond doubt that an army or a fleet from
Washington sent to subdue Charleston during the
last days of Buchanan's Administration would have
driven the entire brotherhood of Southern States
into immediate secession.

President Lincoln's call for an army to subdue
the Southern States found Colonel R. E. Lee at
Arlington.   After the execution of John Brown,
he had remained in Washington until midwinter.
On January 15, 1860, by permission of the War
Department he was hurrying away to Richmond at

the request of a legislative committee to throw the
light of his experience on the matter of organising
and arming the Virginia militia, although he had
already written the protest, " My limited knowledge
can be of little avail." From army headquarters,
February 9, came the order assigning him to the command of the Military Department of Texas. The
entry in his diary for February 10, is thus briefly
made: " At 6 A.M., left Arlington and its dear inhabitants for Texas." From February 20, 1860,
the day when he assumed command at San Antonio,
until February 13, 1861, the day when he laid down
his authority at Fort Mason and repaired to Washington at the call of the Secretary of War, Lee was
occupied with the passing excitements and monotony of frontier garrison life. The early part of these
twelve months was spent in pursuit of the brigand
Cortinas, who would steal across the Rio Grande,
burn the homes and drive off the horses of the
ranchmen, and then retire to his lair in Mexico.
Lee manifested great energy in pushing across the
wastes of western Texas; his chief daily concern
was the search for grass and water, and he spent
some time, also, in a fruitless correspondence with
the authorities in certain Mexican towns. The
summer months from June to December, 1860,
were spent in San Antonio. He was always alert
and busy. The Episcopal Church building in the
town was hurried forward by liberal contributions
from Lee; his private business in Virginia was at
the same time receiving due attention through correspondence.

Lee's political views began to find expression, January 23, 1861, as follows:

" I received from Major Nicholl, Everett's *Life of Washington* . . . and enjoyed its perusal very much. How his spirit would be grieved, could he see the wreck of his mighty labours. I will not, however, permit myself to believe, until all the ground for hope has gone, that the fruit of his noble deeds will be destroyed and that his precious advice and virtuous example will so soon be forgotten by his countrymen. As far as I can judge from the papers, we are between a state of anarchy and civil war. May God avert both of these evils from us. I fear that mankind for years will not be sufficiently Christianised to bear the absence of restraint and force. I see that four States have declared themselves out of the Union ; four more apparently will follow their example. Then, if the Border States are dragged into the gulf of revolution, one half of the country will be arrayed against the other. I must try and be patient and await the end, for I can do nothing to hasten or retard it."

On the same day he wrote in these terms to his son :

" The South, in my opinion, has been aggrieved by the acts of the North, as you say. I feel the aggression, and am willing to take every proper step for redress. It is the principle I contend for, not individual or private benefit. As an American citizen I take great pride in my country, her prosperity, and her institutions, and would defend any State if her rights were invaded. But I can anticipate no greater calamity for the country than a dissolution of the Union. It would be an accumulation of all the evils we complain of, and I am willing to sacrifice everything but honour for its preservation. I hope therefore, that all Constitutional means will be exhausted before there is a resort to force. Secession is nothing but revolution. The framers of our Constitution never exhausted so much labour, wisdom and forbearance in its formation, and surrounded it with so many guards and securities, if it was intended to be broken by every member of the Confederacy at will. It is intended for ' perpetual Union,' so expressed in the preamble,* and for the establishment of a govern-

* Lee was mistaken in this statement. The term " perpetual Union " does not occur in the preamble to the Constitution nor any-

ment, not a compact, which can only be dissolved by revolution, or the consent of all the people in Convention assembled. It is idle to talk of secession ; anarchy would [otherwise ?] have been established, and not a government, by Washington, Hamilton, Jefferson, Madison and all the other patriots of the Revolution. . . . Still, a Union that can only be maintained by swords and bayonets and in which strife and civil war are to take the place of brotherly love and kindness, has no charm for me. I shall mourn for my country and for the welfare and progress of mankind. If the Union is dissolved and the Government disrupted, I shall return to my native State and share the miseries of my people, and save in defence will draw my sword on none."

After the withdrawal of Texas from the Union, Lee was recalled to Washington. As he passed through San Antonio, February 16, he saw the Federal troops marched out of the place, and the public property handed over to the commissioners representing the Convention of the people of Texas. As the shades of evening were gathering about Arlington, March 1, he alighted at the gate from the carriage that had borne him from Alexandria.

As Lee entered his home, his heart was full of love for the old Union which his father had helped to establish. He did not believe in secession as a legal method for the redress of grievances. As to slavery, he said that " if he owned all the negroes in the South, he would gladly yield them up for the preservation of the Union." But he also loved his own people and his native State, and for Virginia, first and last, he was ready to sacrifice property and life itself. At Arlington, therefore, he

where in the Constitution itself. It did occur in the Articles of Confederation which were annulled by the secession of eleven States in 1787.

kept anxious watch during the first forty days of President Lincoln's Administration.

April 18, Francis P. Blair, at the suggestion of Mr. Lincoln, came to offer Lee the command of the proposed army of invasion. Afterwards (February 25, 1868) Lee thus described the interview:

" After listening to his remarks, I declined the offer he made me to take command of the army that was to be brought into the field, stating, as candidly and courteously as I could, that though opposed to secession and deprecating war *I could take no part in an invasion of the Southern States.*

" I went directly from the interview with Mr. Blair to the office of General Scott,—told him of the proposition that had been made to me and my decision. Upon reflection after returning home, I concluded that I ought no longer to retain any commission I held in the United States army, and on the second morning thereafter I forwarded my resignation to General Scott.

" At the time I hoped that peace would have been preserved— that some way would be found to save the country from the calamities of war; and I then had no other intention than to pass the remainder of my life as a private citizen.

" Two days afterward, on the invitation of the Governor of Virginia, I repaired to Richmond, found that the Convention then in session had passed the ordinance withdrawing the State from the Union, and accepted the commission of commander of its forces, which was tendered me. These are the simple facts of the case."

That which drove Lee from the United States army was President Lincoln's preparation to invade the South. The service required of him he declared unworthy, and at once resigned his office and retired to his own home. From that home, as a citizen, he was summoned by the voice of the people of his native State to lead them on the field of battle.

April 20, Colonel Lee sent to General Scott his official resignation, adding that

"It would have been presented at once but for the struggle it has cost me to separate myself from a service to which I have devoted the best years of my life, and all the ability I possessed. During the whole of that time—more than a quarter of a century—I have experienced nothing but kindness from my superiors and a most cordial friendship from my comrades. To no one, General, have I been as much indebted as to yourself for uniform kindness and consideration, and it has always been my ardent desire to merit your approbation. I shall carry to the grave the most grateful recollections of your kind consideration, and your name and fame will always be dear to me."

To his sister in Baltimore, on the same day, Lee expressed these sentiments:

"The whole South is in a state of revolution, into which Virginia, after a long struggle, has been drawn; and though I recognise no necessity for this state of things, and would have forborne and pleaded, to the end, for redress of grievances real or supposed, yet in my own person I had to meet the question whether I should take part against my native State. With all my devotion to the Union, and the feeling of loyalty and duty of an American citizen, I have not been able to make up my mind to raise my hand against my relatives, my children, my home. I have therefore resigned my commission in the army."

To his brother, Sidney Smith Lee, he sent a message, April 20, as follows:

"The question which was the subject of my earnest consultation with you on the 18th inst. has in my own mind been decided. After the most anxious inquiry as to the correct course for me to pursue, I concluded to resign, and sent in my resignation this morning. I wished to wait till the ordinance of secession should be acted on by the people of Virginia; but *war seems to have commenced and I am liable at any time to be ordered on duty which I could not conscientiously perform.* To save me from such a position, and to prevent the necessity of resigning under orders, I had to act at once, and before I could see you again on the subject, as I had wished. *I am now a private citizen* and have no other ambition than to remain at home. Save in the defence of my native State, I have no desire ever again to draw my sword."

What were the events characterised by Lee as war already commenced ? They were the armament sent by sea to relieve Sumter and Pickens; President Lincoln's call for the militia to move against the Southern States; the encampment around the Federal Capitol, April 18, of a regiment from Pennsylvania; the invasion of Maryland, April 19, by a regiment from Massachusetts, and the President's proclamation, April 19, declaring the ports of seven Southern States in a state of blockade and closed against the commerce of the world. The President of a league government had assumed the functions of the Congress of lawmakers, under the alleged military necessity which he had himself created, and the bayonets of his army were already gleaming about the Capitol, when Lee resigned on the morning of April 20.

When Lee reached Richmond, April 22, the Convention placed him in command of the military forces of Virginia. The twenty-third day of April, 1861, saw Major-General Lee introduced to the Convention. The weight of fifty-four years had not bent the tall, well-knit frame, nor had they engraved any lines in the handsome features. Lee's manner was grave; a great modesty tempered all his words and all his actions. The admiration that fell upon him from every eye in that standing throng of Virginians was more trying to the quiet officer than the fire from a battery of guns. President John Janney stood with Governor Letcher and Vice-President A. H. Stephens at his right hand, and expressed to General Lee the welcome accorded to him by the Convention. After references to the patriotic sons of Westmoreland County and to Lee's own achievements in Mexico, Janney thus concluded:

" Sir, we have by this unanimous vote expressed our convictions that you are at this time among the living citizens of Virginia ' first in war.' We pray to God most fervently that you may [so] conduct the operations committed to your charge, that it will soon be said of you that you are the ' first in peace,' and when that time comes you will have earned the still prouder distinction of being ' first in the hearts of your countrymen.' When the Father of his country made his last will and testament, he gave his swords to his favorite nephews, with the injunction that they should never be drawn from their scabbards except in self-defence, or in defence of the rights and principles of their country, and that, if drawn for the latter purpose, that should fall with them in their hands rather than relinquish them. Yesterday, your mother, Virginia, placed her sword in your hand upon the implied condition that in all things you will keep it to the letter and spirit, *that you will draw it only in defence*, and that you will fall with it in your hand rather than that the object for which it is placed there should fail."

To this address, General Lee made reply in these terms:

" Mr. President and Gentlemen of the Convention : Deeply impressed with the solemnity of the occasion on which I appear before you, and profoundly grateful for the honour conferred upon me, I accept the position your partiality has assigned me, though I would greatly have preferred that your choice should have fallen on one more capable. Trusting to Almighty God, an approving conscience, and the aid of my fellow-citizens, I will devote myself to the defence and service of my native State, in whose behalf alone would I have ever drawn my sword."

CHAPTER VI.

1861–1862.

IN COMMAND OF THE FORCES OF VIRGINIA—THE
CAMPAIGN IN WESTERN VIRGINIA—CONSTRUC-
TION OF ATLANTIC COAST DEFENCES.

HE military forces of the Commonwealth of Virginia were under the
control of Major-General R. E. Lee
from April 23 until May 10, 1861.
Thereafter, until June 8, he was assigned to the command of the forces of the Southern Confederacy operating in Virginia. May 25
marked the change in his military rank from the
position of Major-General in the State militia to
that of Brigadier-General in the army of the Southern Confederacy. The Confederate Government
had not yet created a military rank in the field service higher than the grade of brigade-commander;
it was Lee's indifference to the mere insignia of
office that prevented friction in the matter of lowering his rank.

When Vice-President Stephens, in the month of

April, saw the admiration poured out upon Lee by the Virginia Convention, and saw him created Major-General, he scented danger. He perceived that the Convention of Virginia would not unite with the Confederacy if General Lee should refuse to step down to the grade of brigadier. He sought Lee on the evening of April 23.

" I unfolded to him," writes Stephens, " with perfect candour the object of my mission [alliance of Virginia with the Confederacy], the nature of the alliance I should propose, and particularly the effect it might have upon his official rank and position. There was on his part equal candour and frankness—no reserve whatever. He understood the situation fully. With a clear understanding of its bearing upon himself individually, he expressed himself as perfectly satisfied, and as being very desirous to have the alliance formed. He stated in words which produced thorough conviction in my mind of their perfect sincerity, that he did not wish anything connected with himself individually, or his official rank or *personal* position, to interfere in the slightest degree with the immediate consummation of that measure."

The Convention soon discovered the omission of any provision for General Lee's permanent rank in the new alliance. They were ready to withhold Virginia from the Confederacy upon this single issue, but Lee's own solicitations led to the union with the other States. Stephens adds this word: " The truth is, a look, or an intonation of voice, even, at this time, which would have indicated that his professed satisfaction was not the real and unaffected feeling of his heart, would have defeated that measure."

Twelve hours after the interview with Stephens,

Lee was at work preparing Virginia to meet war with war. To Cocke in Alexandria he thus gave instructions, April 24: " Let it be known that you intend no attack; but invasion of our soil will be considered an act of war."

Until June 8, when President Davis, as Commander-in-chief of the Confederate army and navy, assumed the direction of all movements in the field, General Lee was setting in order the defences of Virginia. He foresaw that the Old Dominion would be the main theatre of strife, and Richmond the objective point of Northern invasion. He clearly perceived also the magnitude of the task involved in defending the South from the Northern onset. President Davis, as late as the month of May, despatched an agent to England to purchase ten thousand Enfield rifles to arm the Confederacy. More than a month before this, Lee had written to his wife: " The war may last ten years. . . . Make your plans for several years of war." At the same time he wrote this: " Tell Custis [Lieutenant in the U. S. Army] he must consult his own judgment, reason, and conscience as to the course he may take. I do not wish him to be guided by my wishes or example. If I have done wrong, let him do better. The present is a momentuous question which every man must settle for himself and upon principle."

Lee's eye rested now upon the approaches to Virginia's borders. He set himself to the task of erecting fortifications and batteries for the defence of the Potomac, Rappahannock, York, James, and Elizabeth rivers. Forty thousand Virginia volunteers were armed by June 15, and sent to watch the outposts. Already in April, the State government had seized the military posts at Harper's Ferry and Norfolk, located on Virginia's soil. About one hundred and fifteen cannon were thus furnished to Lee. The machinery at Harper's Ferry for the manufacture of arms and munitions was transplanted to Richmond and Fayetteville, North Carolina. Only fifty-six thousand stand of small arms, of inferior quality, were available. Secretary Floyd's alleged removal of Federal cannon and muskets southward, had failed to furnish the Southern States with their just share of serviceable arms and munitions. With the equipment of a few war vessels and the construction of various field works this part of Lee's task was completed.

The strictly defensive policy of the Confederacy prevented the effective protection of the lower Valley of Virginia. Upon that lion of war, Colonel T. J. Jackson, who was straining at the leash and anxious to make ready for the maintenance of Harper's Ferry by planting heavy guns on Maryland Heights, Lee laid mild restraint by suggesting, May 9, that it was not yet advisable to "intrude upon the soil of Maryland." To a restless officer, May 13, he gave his opinion concerning the relation of rank to honour: "I do not consider that either rank or position are necessary to bestow upon you honour, but believe that you will confer honour on the position."

On June 8, President Davis assumed the practical management of the great military game. To his wife, then at the White House on the Pamunkey, Lee thus expressed himself:

" You may be aware that the Confederate Government is established here. Yesterday I turned over to it the command of the military and naval forces of the State . . . I do not know what my position will be. I should like to retire to private life, so that I could be with you and the children, but if I can be of service to the State or her cause, I must continue."

Mrs. Lee had led her daughters in flight from Arlington, and her stately mansion was occupied as Federal headquarters in Virginia, May 24. Furniture, portraits, chinaware, and other property, brought as heirlooms from the house of Washington, were left to become the spoil of the Federal soldiery. Lee's words of comfort were these: " I grieve at the anxiety that drives you from your home. I can appreciate your feelings on the occasion, and pray that you may receive comfort and strength in the difficulties that surround you. When I reflect upon the calamity pending over the country my own sorrows sink into insignificance."

Nominally as military adviser of President Davis, Lee remained in official connection with the Confederate Cabinet. The war-cloud was now about to burst in two quarters: in the mountains of western Virginia, and on the banks of the Potomac. We find no record of a formal division of executive labours, but, in fact, President Davis did take entire charge of the larger movements in the Valley and around Manassas, while Lee busied himself with the fortunes of the Confederacy in north-western Vir-

ginia and on the Chesapeake Bay. Lee's usual
term for Davis was, " The commanding General."

At Philippi, June 3, three thousand Federal soldiers surprised eight hundred Confederates and put
them to flight.   To Colonel Porterfield, Lee sent
swift words of sympathy concerning " the unfor-
tunate circumstances " with which that Confederate
officer had been beset.   In sending R. S. Garnett
to supersede Porterfield, he broke that news to the
latter in the most delicate and courteous terms:

> " It is hoped that he [Garnett] will soon reach the scene of action,
> that a more agreeable state of things will be inaugurated, and that
> loyal-spirited citizens of the country will be encouraged and enabled
> to put down the revolution which you mention.   Your services will
> be very valuable to General Garnett in giving him information as to
> the state of affairs in the country under his command, and in aiding
> him to achieve the object of his campaign."

By the first of July, Lee had concentrated beyond
Beverly forty-five hundred men under Garnett.   By
July 18, he had placed thirty-eight hundred muskets and ten field guns under Henry A. Wise on the
Kanawha below Charleston.   In these operations,
or in some active field-work, Lee desired to share,
but was prevented.   On June 24, he wrote: " My
movements are very uncertain, and I wish to take
the field as soon as certain arrangements can be
made."

Up into those western mountains General Mc-
Clellan led twenty thousand soldiers from Ohio and
Indiana, in search of Garnett's band.   In imitation
of the Emperor Napoleon, McClellan issued a proc-

lamation from Grafton, dated June 23. He heaped
withering scorn upon the Confederates. He urged
his men forward to victory with the cheering intelligence: " Your enemies have violated every moral
law; neither God nor man can sustain them!" Garnett stationed his men in two detachments on Rich
Mountain and Laurel Hill in advance of Beverly.
A flank movement enabled McClellan to capture a
part of Pegram's detachment on Rich Mountain
and to cut off Garnett at Laurel Hill. The pursuit
beyond Carrick's Ford resulted in the death of the
brave Garnett, on July 13.

McClellan supposed that the two fragments of
Garnett's command were two large separate forces,
and hence his next proclamation announced that
he had " annihilated two armies." While he was
glorying in the title accorded him of the " Young
Napoleon," Lee, on the other hand, was bending
every energy to collect the scattered Confederates,
and to bring additional forces into the mountains.
How tender his sympathy for the defeated, as expressed to H. R. Jackson, the next officer sent to
command them: " Our brave troops must bear up
against misfortune. Reverses must happen, but
they ought only to stimulate us to greater efforts."

Before the advance of J. D. Cox as far as Gauley
Bridge, Wise retreated entirely from the Kanawha
Valley, and the trans-Appalachian regions seemed
lost to the Confederacy. But before this, the victory at Manassas brought great hope to the Southern people. In the movements on the latter field,
Lee had no share. But he was full of eagerness to

GENERAL JOSEPH E. JOHNSTON.

join his brethren in arms.   On July 12, he unbur-
dened himself to his wife in these terms:

> " I am very anxious to get into the field, but I am detained by
> matters beyond my control.   I have never heard of the assignment
> to which you allude—of Commander-in-chief of the Southern army—
> nor have I any expectation nor wish for it.   President Davis holds
> that position.   I have been labouring to prepare and get into the field
> the Virginia troops."

The military game against General Scott was
played by President Davis.   Four of the seven
military bands in Virginia he left to the control of
General Lee: Wise and Garnett in the mountains of
western Virginia, Huger at Norfolk, and Magruder
at Yorktown.   Davis himself directed the movements of the other three.

J. E. Johnston was withdrawn from Harper's
Ferry to Winchester; his force there, July 1, was
eleven thousand men and twenty guns.   Later in
the month, Holmes was moved across from Aquia
on the Potomac to unite with Beauregard at Manassas, and thus were concentrated behind the Bull
Run, twenty-two thousand men with twenty-nine
guns.   The railroad from Manassas to Strasburg
was now to be used in combining these two armies,
either in the Valley, or at Manassas, according to
General Scott's choice of routes in making the grand
Federal assault.   But President Davis had no carefully arranged plan for the rapid shifting of soldiers
soon to be necessary, and Lee was not ordered to
prepare such a plan, although Beauregard asked that
one should be adopted.   Johnston and Beauregard

were left almost entirely to their own devices in mapping out a method of combination against the enemy. This message passed from Beauregard to Johnston eight days before the battle: " Oh, that we had but one good head to conduct all our operations! We are labouring, unfortunately, under the disadvantage of having about seven armies in the field, under as many independent commanders, which is contrary to the first principles of the art of war." As late as July 9, however, each of these officers was convinced that his own position would be assailed, and each demanded assistance from the other.

July 16, saw McDowell moving upon Manassas with thirty thousand men; two days later, Johnston eluded Patterson in the Valley, and sped across the Blue Ridge Pass. On July 21, an army of twenty-nine thousand under Johnston and Beauregard stood on the southern bank of Bull Run to withstand the Federal advance. The miscarriage of an order to Ewell withheld the proposed movement of the Confederate right wing across Bull Run and against the heights of Centreville; the delay gave McDowell opportunity to throw his own right over the stream, and to fall upon the Confederate left flank. It was the eagle eye of General T. J. Jackson that found the key-point of defence on the field that was well-nigh lost. His brigade formed the rallying-centre for the Confederate left; his advance pierced the Federal centre, just as Kirby Smith and Early came from afar to strike the Federal right flank, and McDowell fled to Washington. The victory thus won brought over-confidence to the South. Manassas was ultimately disastrous by reason of the resultant inactivity in the Confederacy. No advance across the Potomac was attempted; the politicians began to discuss the possible successor of President Davis, six years hence, and the different States made rival offers to secure the position of permanent capital of the Southern Confederacy.

The army at Manassas soon proceeded to battalion drill and the construction of log-tents, while Davis, Johnston, and Beauregard entered into a three-cornered discussion concerning the responsibility for the management of the recent campaign.

In Richmond, General Lee's heart was swelling with joy for his country's victory. To Beauregard, three days after the battle, he wrote: " I cannot express the joy I feel at the brilliant victory of the 21st. The skill, courage, and endurance displayed by yourself excite my highest admiration. You and your troops have the gratitude of the whole country." To Johnston, also, Lee wrote: " I almost wept for joy at the glorious victory achieved by our brave troops. The feeling of my heart could hardly be repressed on learning the brilliant share you had in its achievement."

To his wife, July 27, he thus poured out his sentiments:

" That, indeed, was a glorious victory and has lightened the pressure upon us amazingly. Do not grieve for the brave dead, but sorrow for those they left behind—friends, relatives, and families. The former are at rest; the latter must suffer. The battle will be repeated there in great force. I hope God will again smile on us, and strengthen our hearts and arms. I wished to partake in the former struggle and am mortified at my absence. But the President thought it more important that I should be here. I could not have done as well as has been done, but I could have helped and taken part in a struggle for my home and neighbourhood. So the work is done, I care not by whom it is done. I leave to-morrow for the army in western Virginia."

Lee was definitely asked for an opinion in connection with the controversy between the two Generals and the President. But he would say only this (November 24): " The successful combination of the armies was made, and the glorious victory of July 21 followed."

August 1, 1861, dawned upon General Lee as he rode through the rain from Monterey towards Huntersville in the mountains of western Virginia. He had been placed in command of all the Confederate troops in this American Switzerland of steep ridges and narrow valleys. The magnificence of the wooded heights, in parallel lines, " covered with the richest sward of blue-grass and white clover " caught the eye of the soldier every hour of the three days' journey. August 8 found General Lee at the Confederate outpost known as Valley Mountain, on the road from Huntersville to Huttonsville. There he enjoyed the company of his son, Major W. H. F. Lee, who commanded the cavalry on that mountain-top. Through the pouring rain, Lee now looked westward over the regions sloping toward the Ohio. In that land of hills and swift streams the forces of the foe were marshalled under General Rosecrans. By August 15, Rosecrans had stretched a chain of fortified posts

parallel to the Ohio, extending from Clarksburg and
Weston through Bulltown, Sutton, and Summers-
ville to Gauley Bridge. At the latter point, Cox
had charge of the Federal guns that were pointing
up the valleys of the New River and the Gauley.
A large Federal force under Reynolds had pushed
forward from Buckhannon to hold Tygart's Valley.
Reynolds left reserves at Huttonsville, and planted
two thousand men on Cheat Mountain, guarding
the Staunton and Parkersburg road, and three thousand at Elkwater on the Huntersville road.   These
two posts were seven miles apart in a bee-line course.
Meanwhile, Rosecrans was busy in recruiting a
larger force from these mountainous counties that
were soon afterward knocking for admission into the
Federal Union as the new State of West Virginia.

The element of politics played a controlling part
in Lee's campaign in the mountains.   Four brigadiers were subject to his orders.   On the Staunton
turnpike, in Camp Bartow, facing Cheat Mountain,
were twenty-five hundred muskets under H. R.
Jackson; on the Huntersville road, threatening Elkwater, were Loring's thirty-five hundred.   Along
the highway from Lewisburg toward Gauley Bridge
and the Kanawha Valley, marched John B. Floyd
and Henry A. Wise, two former Governors of Virginia.   They had received military commands because of their political influence in the western and
south-western parts of the ancient Commonwealth.

In the closing days of July, Wise had retreated
from the Kanawha across the Alleghanies to the
Greenbrier River.   Again, in August, Wise was sent

westward under Floyd as his superior in command.
Both were expected to use their personal influence
in gathering recruits, and their swords in driving
Cox from Gauley Bridge. As a political expedient
the appointment of Floyd and Wise may have been
well advised; as a military measure, it proved disastrous. An angry contention arose between these
two brigadiers, and a large part of Lee's time was
spent in pouring oil upon troubled waters that
should have dashed their united volume against the
enemy.

Just as Lee at Valley Mountain began to spy out
Reynolds's position, he heard the first gun in the
Wise-Floyd warfare, in the form of a message from
Wise, dated August 7, asking " special orders,
separating the command of General Floyd from
mine." This request for distinct fields of operation
was the result of the first personal interview between
the two brigadiers. In reply, Lee kindly advised a
concentration of forces. August 15 found Wise
convinced by Floyd's orders that the latter wished
to " mutilate " Wise's legion in order to augment
Floyd's brigade; two days later, Wise set himself in
bold opposition to Floyd on the ground that he was
" bound to maintain the integrity " of his legion.
From the summit of Big Sewell Mountain, August
18, Wise declared the firm purpose, never to permit his own subordinate officers to take orders
directly from Floyd. The two lines of riflemen,
five thousand six hundred under Floyd, and two
thousand two hundred under Wise, now moved
westward toward the Gauley. To Wise, Lee sent

a message appealing to " patriotism and zeal " in rendering due obedience to his legal superior, Floyd.

Wise wrote to Lee, August 24, as follows: " I am compelled to inform you expressly that every order I have received from General Floyd, indicates a purpose to merge my command in his own, and to destroy the distinct organisation of my legion." Moreover, Wise criticised the wisdom of Floyd's movements, and made this request: " Send me anywhere, so I am from under the orders of General Floyd." Two days later Floyd floated a force across the Gauley at Carnifex Ferry, and drove back Tyler's Ohio regiment. This river now separated the two Confederate brigadiers. Since all appointments were made by the administration in Richmond, Lee felt constrained to limit the exercise of his authority to a simple appeal " for the sake of the cause " that there should be no "division of sentiment or action " in the Army of the Kanawha.

Thus in slowness of military movement did the August days wear themselves away. As September began to tell off the hours, Rosecrans was marching with three heavy brigades from Clarksburg to bring assistance to Cox. September 9 found Wise and Floyd sending hot words back and forth across the river, in a dispute over the ownership of a certain brass six-pound gun. The daybreak of September 10 marked the advance of Rosecrans's column upon Floyd at Carnifex Ferry. Wise sent not a man to aid the latter. But Floyd's men knew how to fight; they wrapped their breastworks in a

flame of musketry, and the Federal assault was soon
rolled back with severe loss to Rosecrans. But
unity of action now seemed impossible to Floyd
and Wise. No further advance was made toward
the Kanawha; and the two forces retired again
toward the mountain-tops. Rosecrans followed the
retreating Confederates, and on September 23 his
flag was planted on Big Sewell Mountain, and his
supplies furnished by waggons that passed over a
road sixty miles in length. While the Kanawha
expedition was thus dragging out its course in complete failure and permitting Rosecrans to threaten
the flank of Lee's own columns, the latter was confronted by other difficulties on the ridges overhang-
ing the head waters of the Cheat River.

Of the two brigadiers in this field, Loring out-
ranked H. R. Jackson; it was Loring, therefore,
who had made the preliminary movements. At
Huntersville, Lee found Loring busied in planning
an advance against the Federal forces under Reynolds. The latter had only a small body of soldiers
in the early days of August, and most of these he
planted in a fort in the Cheat Mountain Pass, overlooking Cheat River. Along the Parkersburg road
Jackson was sent forward against Reynolds. Loring betook himself to Huntersville, and there began
preparations to move around the south-western end
of Cheat Mountain to the right and rear of the
main Federal position. Loring's men were eager to
move; the way to Huttonsville and Beverly was
practically undefended. Success depended upon
immediate advance. But Loring's scheme de-

manded a transportation train with large stores concentrated at Huntersville for the forty-mile march
to Beverly! For seven days Lee awaited the completion of Loring's battalion of waggons. He rode
forward and stationed himself at Valley Mountain;
while Federal reinforcements were pouring into
Tygart's Valley beyond him, he still awaited
anxiously the advance of Loring. Loring had out-
ranked Lee in the old army. Upon the latter
modesty and courtesy were so visibly stamped, that
he would not exercise his authority. Lee did not
assume formal command, nor would he order Loring
forward, so long as Loring protested that he was un-
prepared. The rain continued to fall; measles and
typhoid fever invaded the ranks. Loring's army
soon became a multitude of sick and dying, encamped in the mud. When Loring did move his
waggons and his men to Valley Mountain the enemy
outnumbered the Confederates on both roads, and
were strongly fortified in the valley at Elkwater and
on the central ridge of Cheat Mountain. The hour
for an opportune flank attack had passed. Lee was
now in charge of two small columns which must
drive superior forces out of mountain strongholds,
or retire. When this task fell upon him, he was at
the same time bearing the burden of anxiety concerning the soldiers led by the quarrelling brigadiers
on the Kanawha turnpike. It was not encouraging,
just as he pressed forward to feel the position of
Reynolds, to receive from Wise this message, written September 5: " Let us [Floyd and Wise]
divide the balance of State forces, and then let us

part in peace. I feel, if we remain together, we will unite in more wars than one.''

It was determined to attack, simultaneously, the two Federal fortifications. Eastward from Huttonsville the Cheat Mountain lifts itself in three parallel ridges, and upon the second or central height, Reynolds had placed about two thousand men behind the walls of a log fort. At Elkwater he had three thousand men behind breastworks, while five thousand waited at Huttonsville to bring succour to either outpost. Colonel Rust, of H. R. Jackson's band, reconnoitered the Federal fortress on the Cheat Mountain, and declared his ability to flank the post and capture it. Upon this representation, Lee decided to make the double assault on the mountain-top and at Elkwater. The march was to begin under cover of darkness, and the blows were to fall in the early morning twilight of September 12.

From Jackson's column of twenty-five hundred, the two regiments of Taliaferro and Fulkerson were assigned to Rust for the flank attack on the (Federal) right and rear of the Cheat Mountain fortress. Jackson was ordered to lead the rest of his men boldly in front along the turnpike against this post.

From Loring's column of thirty-five hundred, three regiments under S. R. Anderson were ordered to gain the roadway between the Cheat Mountain fort and Huttonsville, and likewise keep in touch with the two flanking regiments under Rust. Two regiments under Donaldson were to seek the (Federal) left and rear of the Elkwater works, and hold the roadway in their rear. The remainder under Loring were to move forward along the highway against Elkwater. The troops were to move in silence during the night, and Loring's bands were to await, as the signal for attack, the guns of Rust's regiments on the mountain ridge. To encourage the troops, Lee published the following order:

" The forward movement . . . gives the General commanding the opportunity of exhorting the troops to keep steadily in view the great principles for which they contend, and to manifest to the world their determination to maintain them. The eyes of the country are upon you. The safety of your homes and the lives of all you hold dear, depend upon your courage and exertions. Let each man resolve to be victorious, and that the right of self-government, liberty, and peace shall in him find a defender. The progress of this army must be forward."

The initial steps in the movement were completed with great spirit. Through the heavy rain and the darkness, marching partly in Cheat River itself and then through the dense forest, over boulders and up steep ascents, the soldiers hurried with noiseless tread. The dawn found each column at the appointed place. Anderson and Donaldson reached the rear of the two Federal positions; Loring and Jackson advanced to threaten each position in front. Rust succeeded in placing his band to the (Federal) right and rear of the mountain intrenchment. Muskets were loaded and bayonets fixed for the assault. But the signal sounded not.

Unfortunately, Rust captured some pickets, who made him believe that five thousand Federal troops were fortified on the mountain summit awaiting his onset.   As the morning dawned, he saw before him heavy abatis and, beyond these, intrenchments, and, within the intrenchments, he saw the soldiers with ready guns.   He gave no signal except the signal to retreat.   The other columns grew impatient and strained their ears to catch the sound of the musketry-fire on the ridge.   Rust withdrew and acknowledged his failure; two days later all the bands were withdrawn to their former camping-places.   Let it be remembered that widely separated bodies of soldiery usually fail to make simultaneous attacks.   In this case, the movement under Lee's own eye at Elkwater was a complete success—but no communication was possible between the wings of his army.   In an order of September 14, Lee spoke of the movement as a " forced reconnaisance," and commended " the cheerfulness and alacrity displayed by the troops in this arduous operation."

Lee had no words of blame to lay upon his subordinates.   To his wife he wrote: " I cannot tell you my regret and mortification at the untoward events that caused the failure of the plan.   I had taken every precaution to insure success, and counted on it; but the Ruler of the Universe willed otherwise, and sent a storm to disconcert the well-laid plan."

To Governor Letcher he thus expressed himself:

" I was very sanguine of taking the enemy's works on last Thursday morning.   I had considered the subject well.   With great effort the troops intended for the surprise had reached their destination, having traversed twenty miles of steep, rugged mountain-paths, and the last day through a terrible storm, which lasted all night, and in which they had to stand drenched to the skin in the cold rain. Still, their spirits were good. When the morning broke, I could see the enemy's tents on [Tygart's] Valley River at the point on the Huttonsville road just below me. It was a tempting sight. We waited for the attack on Cheat Mountain which was to be the signal, till 10 A.M.; the men [Federals] were cleaning their unserviceable arms. But the signal did not come. All chance for surprise was gone. The provisions of the men had been destroyed the preceding day by the storm. They had nothing to eat that morning, could not hold out another day and were obliged to be withdrawn. The party sent to Cheat Mountain to take that in the rear had also to be withdrawn. The attack to come off from the east side failed from the difficulties in the way ; the opportunity was lost and our plan discovered.

" It is a grievous disappointment to me, I assure you. But for the rain-storm I have no doubt it would have succeeded. This, Governor, is for your own eyes. Please do not speak of it. We must try again. Our greatest loss is the death of my dear friend, Colonel [John A.] Washington . . . Our greatest difficulty is the roads. It has been raining in these mountains about six weeks. It is impossible to get along. It is that which has paralysed all our efforts."

Time was not given Lee to devise another plan against Reynolds. He was compelled to bring a portion of Loring's command to aid Floyd and Wise in checking the advance of Rosecrans toward Lewisburg. The two retreating columns of Confederates he succeeded in concentrating in a fortified position on Big Sewell Mountain. With the addition of Loring's troops, Lee had now about eight thousand men. Upon a parallel ridge one mile distant, Rosecrans was established behind stout breastworks, with probably a larger force than that of Lee. Each commander waited for the other to attack. Before September closed, an order from Richmond relieved Wise of his command.

In the midst of great labours and still greater anxieties, Lee had time to cherish great sympathy for the suffering soldiers. He wrote to his wife: " We are without tents, and for two nights I have lain buttoned up in my overcoat. To-day my tent came up, and I am in it, yet I fear I shall not sleep for thinking of the poor men." Until October 6, both armies continued to look defiance at each other across the narrow valley. It was clear to see that the attacking party, from either side, would probably be defeated. During the night of October 6, Rosecrans retreated toward the Kanawha. Lee was not adequately equipped for pursuit. Three days before this, on October 3, Reynolds had led five thousand men from Cheat Mountain to test the strength of H. R. Jackson's eighteen hundred posted on the banks of the Greenbrier. The latter played a gallant part, and hurled back every assault until Reynolds was glad to retire. On October 7, Lee wrote as follows to his wife:

" I am sorry, as you say, that the movements of our armies cannot keep pace with the expectations of the editors of the papers. I know they can regulate matters satisfactory to themselves on paper. I wish they could do so in the field. No one wishes them more success than I do, and would be happy to see them have full swing. General Floyd has three editors on his staff. I hope something will be done to please them."

The approach of winter closed the campaign, and left the Federal forces in possession of the western slopes of Virginia. They had failed to pass the summit of the Alleghanies. The golden moments of autumn, however, had passed away, and the Confederacy had wasted time and men in a vain attempt to defend the Kanawha Valley and adjacent regions. The point open to attack and offering fruitful results to a strong invading force was the State of Maryland. But the Confederate Administration let slip the opportunity. While Lee was attempting to maintain the Confederate flag in the midst of the bleak regions that slope toward the Ohio River, Federal troops and munitions were pouring into Washington, and the spring of 1862 found that city completely fortified against attack.

Gallant and obedient to his superiors, and modest as to his own abilities, Lee had done his best to carry out the orders given him. Failure had been the result, chiefly because the campaign in that quarter was ill-advised from the beginning, and because the inefficiency of some of the brigadiers had foredoomed every plan before Lee assumed active control. In perfect silence, however, Lee bore the blame which public clamour laid upon him for defeat, and not one word of criticism fell from his lips nor from his pen concerning his superiors or his subordinates in office.

During the autumn of 1861, the Federal Administration was gathering at Washington a vast armament of land and naval forces to be sent against Virginia and the other Atlantic States of the Confederacy. President Lincoln had proclaimed a blockade of all the Southern ports, and now sought to enforce it by sending expeditions against the forts and batteries planted at the water's edge along the coasts of the Carolinas, Georgia, and Florida.

The cannon of the Confederates were of small calibre, and could make only a feeble defence against heavy naval guns. August 28 saw the reduction of the Confederate forts guarding Hatteras Inlet. The broad waters of Pamlico Sound, formerly the refuge of blockade-runners, were thus opened to the Federal war-vessels. The chain of islands along the coast of each State could, very evidently, not be held by means of light shore-batteries against the Federal men-of-war. General Lee was sent to render more efficient the defences of the entire Southern seaboard.

On the evening of November 7, as Lee drew near the entrance to Port Royal Harbour he was met by the intelligence that the Federal fleet during the day had passed the Confederate batteries. Lee looked anxiously about for men and weapons to offer resistance. There were neither batteries nor guns in front of Beaufort; only three thousand soldiers were available to meet the thirteen thousand men set ashore on Hilton Head. The Federal vessels now held the key of inland navigation, commanded all the islands between Charleston and Savannah, threatened the connecting railway, and menaced those two great cities themselves. Two days after reaching his field, Lee made this report:

"The enemy, having complete possession of the water and inland navigation, commands all the islands on this coast, and threatens both Savannah and Charleston and can come in his boats within four miles of this place [Coosawhatchie]. His sloops of war and large steamers can come up Broad River to Mackay's Point, the mouth of the Pocotaligo, and his gunboats can ascend some distance up the Coosawhatchie and Tulifiny. We have no guns that can resist their batteries and have no resource but to prepare to meet them in the field."

Lee's call for men was heard by the Carolinians and Georgians. But arms there were none. November 13 brought the steamer *Fingal* through the blockade with the ten thousand Enfield rifles ordered from England by President Davis. Four rifled cannon likewise came aboard the runner. Only half of these were assigned to Lee; the other half went to the Tennessee army under A. S. Johnston, although the Governors of Florida, South Carolina, and Georgia clamoured for a share.

By November 21 Lee had glanced along the coast as far ·south as Fernandina, and he was now ready with the general plan of defence: " The entrance to Cumberland Sound and Brunswick, and the water approaches to Savannah and Charleston, are the only points which it is proposed to defend." While engrossed in these larger cares, Lee could yet find time, as he always did find time, to consider more trivial matters affecting the interests of the citizens. On the same day when he reported to Richmond his scheme for defending the entire coast, he caused the issue of the order forbidding " the evil practice of tearing down fences and other private property for firewood and other purposes. . . . The General hopes that it will only be necessary to remind the troops that they are citizens as well as soldiers."

In a private letter he said of the existing means of defence along the coast : " They are poor indeed, and I have laid off work to employ our people a month. I hope our enemy will be polite enough to wait for us. It is difficult to get our people to realise their position."

The skill of Lee had blocked the further encroachment of the hostile fleet. November 24, five Federal vessels crossed Savannah Bar, and Tybee Island was occupied. Lee, however, had strengthened Forts Pulaski and Jackson, and Savannah was safe.

As December came on, the Federal fleet increased in numbers. The twelfth day of the month saw eighty prows in Port Royal Harbour. Slowly were heavy guns added to the Confederate equipment. The land force was strengthened as fast as arms and munitions could be procured. So strong by this time were the harbour defences of Charleston, that no effort was made to capture the city. On the contrary, the Federal fleet sought to do the city permanent injury by attempting to close up the ship-channel, an act certainly not in accordance with the laws of nations. At this the spirit of Lee blazed out :

" It has been reported to me by General Ripley that the enemy brought his stone fleet to the entrance of Charleston Harbour to-day [December 20], and sunk between thirteen and seventeen vessels in the main ship channel. The North Channel and Maffit's Channel are still open. This achievement, so unworthy any nation, is the abortive expression of the malice and revenge of a people which it wishes to perpetuate by rendering more memorable a day hateful in their calendar [secession of South Carolina]. It is also indicative of their despair of ever capturing a city they design to ruin, for they can

never expect to possess what they labour so hard to reduce to a condition not to be enjoyed. I think, therefore, it is certain that an
attack on the city of Charleston is not contemplated, and we must endeavour to be prepared against assaults elsewhere on the Southern
Coast."

From this matter he turned away to make suggestion to the South Carolina Convention to replace
the twelve-months men by soldiers enlisted for the
war. " The Confederate States," he wrote, " have
now but one great object in view, the successful
issue of their war for independence. Everything
worth their possessing depends on that. Everything should yield to its accomplishment." The
following letter of this period gives further expression of opinion :

" Among the calamities of war, the hardest to bear, perhaps, is
the separation of families and friends. Yet all must be endured to
accomplish our independence, and maintain our self-government.
.   .   .   Your old home [Arlington], if not destroyed by our enemies,
has been so desecrated that I cannot bear to think of it. I should
have preferred it to have been wiped from the earth, its beautiful hill
sunk, and its sacred trees buried, rather than to have been degraded
by the presence of those who revel in the ill they do for their own
selfish purposes. You see what a poor sinner I am, and how unworthy to possess what has been given me ; for that reason it has
been taken away. I pray for a better spirit, and that the hearts of
our enemies may be changed."

Concerning Arlington, he wrote as follows to his
wife, December 25 :

" They cannot take away the remembrances of the spot and the
memories of those that to us rendered it sacred. That will remain
to us as long as life will last, and that we can preserve. In the absence of a home, I wish I could purchase Stratford. It is the only

place I could go to now acceptable to us, that would inspire me with pleasure and local love. You and the girls could remain there in quiet. It is a poor place, but we could make enough corn-bread and bacon for our support and the girls could weave us clothes."

A month before, his thoughts had been carried back to his birthplace, as the following indicates:

" It [Stratford] is endeared to me by many recollections and it has always been the desire of my life to be able to purchase it. Now that we have no other home, and the one we so loved has been forever desecrated, that desire is stronger with me than ever. The horse-chestnut you mention in the garden was planted by my mother. I am sorry the vault is so dilapidated. You do not mention the spring, one of the objects of my earliest recollections. How my heart goes back to those happy days."

A visit to Cumberland Island on the coast gave him the first sight of his father's tomb: " The garden was beautifully enclosed by the finest hedge of wild olive I have ever seen." As the Federal fleets began to make attack, he said: " The contest must be long, and the whole country has to go through much suffering."

In the midst of multiplied labours and anxieties, there was restiveness, and, perhaps, jealousy among some of his subordinate officers. Yet Lee preserved his calm, dignified bearing throughout, so that Governor Pickens was led to say, " General Lee is a perfect head, quiet and retiring. His reserve is construed disadvantageously."

Early in February the Federal movements were more aggressive. Burnside passed inside Pamlico Sound with a fleet and an army of twelve thousand, and captured Roanoke Island. New Berne was in their hands by the 14th, and Fort Macon by the 26th. On February 11 a Federal force was established on Edisto Island. But the mainland was not reached in any vital point. Success had crowned Lee's policy of " abandoning all exposed points as far as possible within reach of the enemy's fleet of gunboats, and of *taking interior positions* where we can meet on more equal terms."

With an utterly inadequate force and poor equipments, Lee had neutralised the operations of a large Federal armament on land and sea. His works continued to stand the test of every assault. His inner lines were never shaken. But now the cloud of war was growing dark around Richmond, and a hasty message from President Davis, March 2, hurried him back to Virginia. On March 13, 1862, to General Lee was assigned the task of superintending, under the direction of President Davis, all military operations connected with the defence of the Southern Confederacy.

CHAPTER VII.

THE PENINSULAR CAMPAIGN—LEE IN COMMAND
OF THE ARMY OF NORTHERN VIRGINIA—THE
SEVEN DAYS' BATTLES IN DEFENCE OF RICH-
MOND.

1862.

THE day that saw General Lee's assumption of authority over all the
forces of the Southern Confederacy
marked also the final adoption of
General McClellan's plan for the
capture of Richmond. March 13, 1862, while Lee
was casting his first official glance over the entire field of war, McClellan was holding a council at
Fairfax Court-House with the corps-commanders of
the Army of the Potomac. These officers ratified
the Federal leader's plan to menace the Confederate
capital with a land and naval force moving from
Fort Monroe as a base, through Yorktown and West
Point as the line of operations. McClellan's well-
drilled host of one hundred and forty thousand men
was to be transferred by water from Alexandria to
Fort Monroe. From the latter point the army was
to force passage up the Peninsula between the

James and the York.   The Federal fleet was expected to sail past the Confederate defences at
Yorktown, and bring supplies up the York River to
furnish the land force as it advanced on Richmond
from West Point.

In the forts around Washington, McClellan proposed to leave eighteen thousand men under Wadsworth; about seven thousand were to plunge through
the mud as far as Manassas, and over thirty-five
thousand under Banks were to cross the Potomac
and hold Winchester.   On the southern branch of
the Potomac in western Virginia were massed the
fragments of the army of Rosecrans, soon afterwards increased to sixteen thousand six hundred
men, and placed under the direction of Frémont.
On the Gauley River were eight thousand Federal
soldiers commanded by Cox; some reserves under
arms in Pennsylvania were directed to march to
Manassas.   These different bands of armed men,
with complete equipments and vast stores of supplies, received orders to press toward the city of
Richmond from three points of the compass.

The prospects of the Confederacy in March, 1862,
were overcast with clouds.   Roanoke Island and
New Berne had just fallen, and twelve thousand
men under Burnside were on the soil of North Carolina; Fort Pulaski, defending Savannah, was threatened.   The coasts of Florida were lost.   Farragut
with his men-of-war was approaching the Lower
Mississippi and New Orleans.   In February, Forts
Henry and Donelson had surrendered, and along
with them passed the military control of Kentucky

and a part of Tennessee; Nashville and Island No. 10, soon likewise became Federal spoil. The Confederacy was surrounded by a wall of fire. Every point was assailed by strong forces. The devoted men of the South stood at bay at the threshold of nearly every State.

To meet McClellan's multitude in Virginia, Lee could muster only a few scattered bands. Magruder held the lower Peninsula with eleven thousand muskets. Huger was on guard at Norfolk with some heavy guns and seven thousand infantry. In Hampton Roads were the Confederate ironclad, *Merrimac*, and the Federal ironclad, *Monitor*. Since the struggle of March 8, these two naval giants had been glaring at each other, neither of them confident of victory; but the *Merrimac* held the *Monitor* and the Federal fleet at bay, and the James River was safe as yet from hostile prows. Johnston had withdrawn from Manassas his army of about forty-seven thousand behind the Rappahannock and Rapidan. Holmes commanded a brigade of two thousand at Fredericksburg. Edward Johnson near Staunton had thirty-five hundred, and Stonewall Jackson was watching Winchester with five thousand men. Lee could marshal only about seventy-five thousand men along the line of defence threatened by the Federal force of two hundred thousand.

Thus far in Virginia, however, the prestige of success had remained with the small battalions. The Federal retreat from Manassas in July, 1861, had been followed by the disaster at Ball's Bluff on the Potomac, wherein Evans, the Confederate hero of the Stone Bridge visited destruction upon a strong Federal column under Baker, Senator from Oregon. Moreover, J. E. Johnston's army of less than fifty thousand on the plains of Manassas was supposed by McClellan to be a host more than double that number, and during the long winter weeks kept the Federal Administration in constant fear of the capture of Washington. President Lincoln desired to celebrate Washington's Birthday by a general advance and ordered all his armies forward on that day. But February 22 dawned and closed upon his inactive regiments. With redoubled energy, again the cry was raised, "On to Richmond," and the closing days of March saw the Federal brigades floating down the Potomac to gain a foothold at Fort Monroe.

Lee found the Confederate army organised into separate divisons, and at once began the work of securing arms and supplies, and of concentrating his forces to meet threatened assaults. We find him writing in one direction to quiet the murmurings among a group of captains in garrison: "This is not a time to squabble about rank; every one must work, and do what he can to promote the cause." In another direction he was compelled to deny a request for artillery because there were no guns available, and, moreover, organised companies "all through the Confederacy" were waiting to be supplied.

The twenty-first day of March brought some revelation of McClellan's plan of operation. Magruder reported the landing of large bodies of Federal troops at Fort Monroe, and asked for thirty thousand men to withstand their advance. Lee then began to fortify the water-approach to Richmond by obstructions in the James and batteries at Drewry's Bluff; at the same time he called back the troops from the line of the Rappahannock to Richmond. The daring attack of Stonewall Jackson against Shields at Kernstown, March 23, put a new face upon affairs in northern Virginia. Banks had sent one division east of the Blue Ridge to take possession of Manassas and rebuild the railroad; the division of Shields he retained at Winchester. With three thousand men Jackson assaulted the seven thousand of Shields; during three hours the scale of battle wavered, and in the gathering darkness Jackson withdrew from the field. He maintained ever afterward that the result would have been a Confederate victory if Garnett had not retired his brigade when their ammunition failed. But the results of Jackson's attack were of great value to the Confederacy. The other forces of Banks were hastened westward from Manassas and also up the valley from the Potomac to Winchester. Moreover, the Federal Administration began at once with anxious care to count the soldiers in the defences of Washington, and Blenker's division of ten thousand men brought additional trouble by failing to find the direct route to the Valley of Virginia. In the face of increasing foes, Jackson suggested the idea underlying his subsequent Valley campaign. On April 5, he wrote this: " If Banks is defeated,

it may greatly retard McClellan's movements.''
'' Stonewall '' sheltered his little band in the Swift
Run Pass, and established communication across the
Blue Ridge with Ewell at Gordonsville.

The early morning of April 4 found McClellan
directing two columns from Fort Monroe against
Magruder. The latter had six thousand men for
the defence of Mulberry Island and Yorktown, and
in addition he had arrayed five thousand between
these two points in breastworks behind the Warwick
River. To force a passage toward Richmond, Mc-
Clellan's scheme was as follows: A column of
assault under Heintzelman was to move against
Yorktown; a column of advance under Keyes was
to brush aside Magruder's infantry and press up
the Peninsula; the Federal navy was to co-operate
in the demolition of Yorktown, and McDowell's
corps was to sail up the York to some point offering
a favorable flank movement on the Confederate
Capital. First among the disappointments met by
McClellan was the information that the entire fleet
of Federal war-ships must continue to keep watch
over the Merrimac, then floating in front of Norfolk. Only a few gunboats were sent to co-operate
in the assaults upon Yorktown and Gloucester-
Point. Nevertheless, he put his columns in motion.
Through the mud and rain of the 4th day of April,
they left twelve miles of the journey behind them.
The morning of April 5 dawned upon the column
of Keyes as it was peering through the rain and mist
across the twenty-foot stream of waist-deep water at
Lee's Mills. Through the tangled underbrush

across the Warwick were seen the cannon and the rifle-pits of the Confederates.   In the presence of this barrier, peopled, as McClellan supposed, by a great host of soldiery, the column of Keyes tarried for one month!   Ten o'clock of the same day found the column of Heintzelman receiving a salutation of shells from the guns of Yorktown.   As McClellan stood thus, on the afternoon of April 5, with both columns halted, chagrined at the absence of the Federal fleet, which was kept on guard before the Merrimac, he was handed a telegram announcing that McDowell's corps had been separated from his army and retained as a bulwark to withstand Jackson's entrance into Washington.   The flanking column, intended for the upper York, was thus withheld and McClellan now began to concentrate his force for the beleaguerment of Yorktown.

Not long was Lee occupied in discerning McClellan's plan.   The Confederate commander spent the remaining days of April in arraying Johnston's army across the Peninsula, and in uniting Jackson and Ewell for the movement against Banks.   Jackson's suggestion of April 5 was now developed.   To his lieutenant Lee wrote, in these terms, on April 25: "I have hoped in the present divided condition of the enemy's forces that a successful blow may be dealt them by a rapid combination of our troops."   Four days later, Jackson mapped out to Lee the main campaign itself; first the blow against Milroy and McDowell, and then the assault upon Banks at Winchester.   "You must use your judgment and discretion," Lee wrote in assent to the plan, May 1.

Johnston was now in control of the Peninsular field. He advised a retreat to the works in front of Richmond. Lee opposed the withdrawal of troops from the Southern seaports to assist in defending Richmond, and Johnston was ordered to meet McClellan in the trenches prepared by Magruder. But McClellan's heavy guns were soon in readiness to pour their fire upon Yorktown. Johnston did not consider his fifty-five thousand strong enough to march out of the rifle-pits and assail McClellan's eighty-five thousand. During the night of May 3, Johnston withdrew his forces toward Richmond. On May 5, Longstreet arrayed his division with that of D. H. Hill athwart the path of McClellan's advance at Williamsburg. Hooker's division advanced against Longstreet's right wing, but the Confederate fire sadly thinned his ranks, and compelled him to leave his artillery on the field. D. H. Hill held the Confederate left firm against Hancock. Time for the withdrawal of the Confederate army was gained by the repulse of the Federal attack at Williamsburg, and Johnston now arranged his forces in line of battle between Richmond and the Chickahominy. Huger evacuated Norfolk and the *Merrimac* was given to the flames. Franklin's Federal division had been moved up the York to Eltham, above West Point, in order to strike Johnston's line in flank. But McClellan was compelled now to draw up his forces behind the Chickahominy, facing Richmond at a distance of from seven to twelve miles. He still expected aid from McDowell, who had pressed forward from Manassas to

Fredericksburg with forty-one thousand men. A union of McDowell with the right wing of his own army was urged by McClellan. But the movements of Jackson in the valley again frustrated the Federal plan of campaign.

Early in May, Jackson was able to count six thousand muskets in his own army. Opposed to him were six thousand six hundred, under Milroy, threatening Staunton from the westward. Ten thousand more were marching with Frémont to unite with Milroy. Banks held twenty thousand in the lower valley, and McDowell's forty-one thousand tarried at Fredericksburg. May 8 saw Jackson, at the close of a swift march, crushing Milroy near the village of McDowell, and pursuing him to Franklin. Thence he turned eastward to the valley and united his force with Ewell's division. Shields had now been sent to add strength to McDowell at Fredericksburg, and with only one division Banks received Jackson's sudden onset at Winchester, May 23. " Stonewall " pursued the flight of Banks to the Potomac, and added the huge Federal supply train to his own meagre equipment.

The vain dream of taking Jackson in the toils now entered the mind of President Lincoln. Orders were sent to Frémont to hasten eastward across the mountain to Strasburg; McDowell was directed to make speed from Fredericksburg back to Front Royal with twenty thousand men. Moreover, McDowell's advance toward Richmond was checked, and McClellan's assault on Richmond was thus delayed until a quietus should be administered to Jackson.

On May 25, while Jackson was chasing Banks,
McClellan was completing the movement of his
Third and Fourth *corps d'armée* to the southern
bank of the Chickahominy. There they were fortified in position across the turnpike leading to Richmond. McClellan's other corps, three in number,
remained still on the northern bank of the stream,
pushing out their right toward Fredericksburg to
grasp McDowell's friendly hand. But May 30
found McDowell at Front Royal, the companion of
Frémont in watching the passage of Jackson's rearguard up the valley. The fox had escaped from
Lincoln's trap. As Frémont and Shields both
started in pursuit only to meet disaster from the
strong arm of "Stonewall" a few days later at Cross
Keys and Port Republic, on that same thirtieth
day of May, Johnston was ordering his line of battle
to assault the two advanced corps of McClellan's
army. May 31 saw this assault delivered at Seven
Pines. The advanced Federal left wing was driven
back against the Chickahominy, but delays on the
part of the Confederate officers gave time for the
passage of Sumner's corps across the swollen river,
and thus prevented the probable destruction of the
two corps of Keyes and Heintzelman. June 1 witnessed some additional Confederate assaults and
then the two antagonists secured themselves behind
intrenchments.

General J. E. Johnston received a severe wound
on the field of May 31, and President Davis at
once directed General Robert E. Lee to take control of the Army of Northern Virginia. June 1

found Lee riding to the front at Seven Pines to assume that active leadership in the field which he retained until the close of the bloody drama. Concerning his new duties Lee thus wrote: "I wish his [Johnston's] mantle had fallen upon an abler man, or that I were able to drive our enemies back to their homes. I have no ambition and no desire but for the attainment of this object." In the first general order issued by Lee occurs this appeal to the Confederate army:

"The presence of the enemy in front of the Capital, the great interests involved, and the existence of all that is dear to us, appeal in terms too strong to be unheard, and he [Lee] feels assured that every man has resolved to maintain the ancient fame of the Army of Northern Virginia, and the reputation of its general [Johnston] and to conquer or die in the approaching contest."

Every day Lee was seen riding along the Confederate lines, while he kept watch over McClellan's men working like beavers. An eye-witness thus speaks of him:

"Calm, dignified and commanding in his bearing, a countenance strikingly benevolent and self-possessed, a clear honest eye, that could look friend or enemy in the face; clean-shaven, except a closely trimmed moustache which gave a touch of firmness to the well-shaped mouth; simply and neatly dressed in the uniform of his rank; felt hat, and top-boots reaching to the knee; sitting his horse as if his home was in the saddle: such was Robert E. Lee as he appeared when he assumed command of the Army of Northern Virginia." The following is Lee's description of himself: "My coat is of gray, of the regulation style and pattern, and my pants of dark blue, as is also prescribed, partly hid by my long boots. I have the same handsome hat which surmounts my gray head (the latter is *not* prescribed in the regulations), and shields my ugly face, which is masked by a white beard as stiff and wiry as the teeth of a card. In fact, an uglier person you have never seen, and so unatractive is it to our enemies that they shoot at it whenever visible to them."

During the first half of the month of June, 1862, McClellan was massing four of his corps on the southern bank of the Chickahominy, near Seven Pines, for the advance against Richmond. Porter's corps was fortified on the northern bank of the river. This separation of the wings of his army was caused by McClellan's expectation that McDowell would march southward from Fredericksburg to lend aid to his right wing. The York River railroad furnished supplies to the Army of the Potomac from the wharf at the White House on the Pamunkey. June 13 brought to Porter's assistance McCall's division of McDowell's corps; Jackson's victories at Cross Keys and Port Republic kept McDowell's remaining divisions on the alert along the northern borders of Virginia. June 20 found one hundred and fifteen thousand men arrayed under McClellan's battle flag, ready for the struggle with Lee. Lee could, at first, muster only fifty-seven thousand men against McClellan. From the coast of the Carolinas he brought forward about fifteen thousand more. On June 6 Jackson sent the following suggestion: "Should my command be required at Richmond, I can be at Mechum's River depot, on the Central railroad, the second day's march." This letter was based upon a previous exchange of views. Just after the defeat of Banks at Winchester, Jackson sent word to Richmond that if reinforced, he would capture Washington. "Tell General Jackson," replied Lee, "that he must first help me to drive these people

away from Richmond." June 8, while Jackson was
defeating Frémont at Cross Keys, Lee was thus
writing to his lieutenant: " Should there be nothing
requiring your attention in the Valley, so as to prevent your leaving it for a few days, and you can
make arrangements to deceive the enemy and im-
press him with the idea of your presence, please let
me know, that you may unite at the decisive moment with the army near Richmond." When
Jackson received this, he had already routed Shields
at Port Republic, June 9, and was now watching
Frémont and Shields retire down the valley. From
the generous commander-in-chief he soon read this
despatch of June 11:

" Your recent successes have been the cause of the liveliest joy in
this army as well as in the country. The admiration excited by your
skill and boldness has been constantly mingled with solicitude for
your situation. The practicability of reinforcing you has been the
subject of earnest consideration. It has been determined to do so at
the expense of weakening this army. Brigadier-General Lawton
with six regiments from Georgia is on the way to you ; and Brigadier-
General Whiting with eight veteran regiments leaves here to-day.
The object is to enable you to crush the forces opposed to you. . . .
With your main body, including Ewell's division and Lawton's and
Whiting's commands, move rapidly to Ashland by rail or otherwise
—and sweep down between the Chickahominy and Pamunkey,
cutting up the enemy's communications, while this army attacks
General McClellan in front."

With banners waving and drums beating, the
brigades of Lawton and Whiting departed from
Richmond. Lee took measures to convey to Mc-
Clellan the news of this reinforcement of Jackson.
The Federal commander thus remained under the

impression that Jackson would continue in the
valley.   Lawton proceeded to Port Republic, but
Whiting was turned back at Staunton.   On June
12, Lee despatched Stuart, with twelve hundred
horsemen, to reconnoitre McClellan's rear.   This
daring trooper passed through Hanover Court
House to Tunstall's Station on the York River
railroad; across this road he pressed southward,
passed the swollen Chickahominy, and by moving
night and day reached the James River and rode
thence to Richmond.   Stuart cut a pathway entirely
around McClellan's army in forty-eight hours and
brought to Lee information concerning the Federal
position.   Lee's plan was finally arranged by the
16th, as he announced it to Jackson in a letter of
that date:

" Frémont and Shields are apparently retrograding, their troops
shaken and disorganised, and some time will be required to set them
again in the field.   If this is so, the sooner you unite with this army
the better.   McClellan is being strengthened. . . . The present, therefore, seems favourable for a junction of your army and this.
If you agree with me, the sooner you can make arrangements to do
so the better.   In moving your troops, you could let it be understood
that it was to pursue the enemy in your front.   Dispose those to hold
the Valley, so as to deceive the enemy, keeping your cavalry well in
their front, and at the proper time suddenly descending upon the
Pamunkey.   To be efficacious, the movement must be secret.   Let
me know the force you can bring, and be careful to guard from
friends and foes your purpose and your intention of personally leaving the Valley.   The country is full of spies and our plans are immediately carried to the enemy."

The second day after this letter left Richmond
Jackson began the march from the valley.   His

footsore men trudged from Port Republic to Gordonsville between June 18 and June 21, inclusive. Sunday, June 22, was spent in camp. Since McClellan held a portion of the railroad, the hour of one o'clock, Monday morning, found Jackson galloping towards Richmond with a single companion. He left fifty-two miles behind him by noon, and at 3 P.M. began the conference with Lee concerning the movement against McClellan's right wing. At early dawn of this same day, June 23, Jackson's men formed column for the march to the Chickahominy.

Bewilderment now prevailed in the Federal councils. June 24, McClellan telegraphed the rumour concerning Jackson's approach and then asked for " the most exact information you have as to the position and movements of Jackson." Stanton forwarded to McClellan, June 25, the various reports that located Jackson at many points from Gordonsville to Luray, and the mountains of western Virginia. Sixty thousand Federal troops were on the alert guarding the mouth of the valley, and the city of Washington against " Stonewall." The late afternoon of June 25 brought convincing news to McClellan, who thus announced the situation: " I incline to think that Jackson will attack my right and rear. The rebel force is stated at two hundred thousand, including Jackson and Beauregard. I shall have to contend against vastly superior odds if these reports be true! "

Lee's plan of attack against McClellan's right, on the northern bank of the Chickahominy, was outlined as follows: Jackson was to lead his sixteen thousand from Ashland, on June 25, to an encampment west of the Central railway. Thursday morning, June 26, at 3 A.M., he was to advance across the railway toward Pole Green Church, a point in the rear of Porter's right flank. As Jackson crossed the railway, he was to inform Branch, who held one of A. P. Hill's brigades on the Brook road; Branch had orders then to cross the Chickahominy and move down the northern bank upon Mechanicsville. The next step in the movement was to be taken by A. P. Hill's eleven thousand men, as thus ordered: " As soon as the movements of these columns [Jackson and Branch] are discovered, General A. P. Hill, with the rest of his division, will cross the Chickahominy near Meadow Bridge [Central railway] and move direct upon Mechanicsville." After that, in succession, Longstreet was to move his nine thousand, and D. H. Hill his ten thousand, across the Mechanicsville bridge and unite with the general flank movement down the northern bank of the river. Stuart's cavalry was sent to guide Jackson's column. These fifty thousand men were to strike the flank and the rear of McClellan's right wing. They moved in four divisions *en échelon.* D. H. Hill was expected to support Jackson's rear attack, and Longstreet to support A. P. Hill's attack at Mechanicsville. It was prescribed that Jackson's column should be in advance of the others, " bearing well to his left, turning Beaver Dam Creek and taking the direction towards Cold Harbor." From Cold Harbor,

Jackson and D. H. Hill were to "press forward towards the York River railroad, closing upon the enemy's rear and forcing him down the Chickahominy." In this order Lee arrayed his own left wing, and moved it into action. His right wing, thirty thousand strong, was left in the line of fortifications covering the eastern and southern approaches to Richmond. Holmes held three brigades at Drewry's Bluff and Chaffin's Bluff. Magruder and Huger, with twenty-five thousand men, confronted the four advanced Federal corps of nearly eighty thousand. It was a dangerous movement for Lee thus to divide his forces in the face of the foe. But Lee knew McClellan's extreme caution, and he ordered Magruder and Huger to impose upon him with great demonstrations in his front, and, if need be, to hold their own trenches at the point of the bayonet.

Jackson was ordered to set the pace. By the night of June 25, he had pushed his column only as far as Ashland. The footsore and weary veterans passed over the distance of fifty miles from Gordonsville in three days. June 26, at 3 A.M., Whiting led the advance from Ashland on the Ashcake road; the head of his column began to cross the Central railway at 9 A.M., and at 10 A.M. Branch was reading Jackson's announcement of progress. The columns of Jackson and Branch were just six hours later in advancing than had been expected. This delay was due to the fatigue of Jackson's men incurred in the long march, and to the tardiness of the arrival of the provisions sent him from Richmond. It was not due to his own weariness from the ride of Monday morning. "Stonewall's" vigour was unabated and his spirit was aglow with the ardour of battle.

In accordance with instructions, Jackson kept well to the left and pressed toward Cold Harbor, with Stuart's cavalry guarding his flank. At 3 P.M., Hood's Texans were engaged in a hot skirmish across the Totopotomoy Creek, where the bridge had to be rebuilt. Darkness fell upon Jackson at Hundley's Corner, six or eight miles to the rear of the Federal position. He was not within reach of the battle prematurely commenced by A. P. Hill at Mechanicsville, and his orders bound him to an eastward course.

Branch's advance down the northern bank of the stream was delayed by Federal skirmishers, and at Atlee's Station he found serious battle. When the hour of 3 P.M. brought neither Jackson nor Branch, A. P. Hill feared that the delay might " hazard the failure of the whole plan." He therefore crossed the river, drove the Federal soldiers from Mechanicsville and drew up his lines before McClellan's fortress on the bank of Beaver Dam Creek. D. H. Hill and Longstreet moved across their bridge to Hill's support.

A. P. Hill's advance was daring but imprudent. Lee's plan was seriously embarrassed. Jackson was marching toward Porter's rear; he had almost obtained a vantage point when Hill's forward movement brought three of Lee's four flanking divisions face to face with the shotted guns frowning from the Federal fortifications. Beaver Dam Creek was waist-deep and bordered by swamps. Trees had been

felled along the steep ascent and their branches
sharpened to resist the assailants. The artillery
posted on the eastern bank could sweep every approach. Five brigades of riflemen under McCall
stood ready behind breastworks of logs. It was to
flank this force that Lee sent Jackson to strike
Porter's rear. Now that A. P. Hill's passage had
divulged his plan, Lee rode forward from his headquarters on the Mechanicsville turnpike and pressed
the attack. At 5 P.M., while Jackson was still north
of the Totopotomoy, engaged in bridging that
stream, A. P. Hill was ordering Archer, Anderson
and Field into active battle along the Bethesda
road, at Beaver Dam Creek. D. H. Hill sent
Ripley to support Pender at Ellison's Mill. This
disposition was made in obedience to Lee's order to
assail both flanks of the Federal line. But the Confederate brigades were torn and shattered by the
storm of iron poured upon them from guns in position and infantry intrenched.

June 27 dawned upon Ewell leading Jackson's
advance eastward from Hundley's. Porter's five
brigades under McCall had scented danger from the
rear, and were falling back to Porter's central position near Cold Harbor. Jackson's flank movement
thus accomplished what A. P. Hill's assault failed
to do.

A difficulty of fearful significance now began to
disturb the movements of the Confederate divisions.
This difficulty was ignorance of the country. The
Confederate maps were of little value. The corps
of engineers selected by President Davis had not

discovered the exact location of the Federal defences. Jackson's guide led him south-eastward to Walnut Grove Church until Ewell's division stood face to face with A. P. Hill's division. The latter was moving from Ellison's Mill toward New Cold Harbor, while Longstreet was pursuing the river road to the Gaines House. While Jackson's advance column was jammed into a narrow cross-road, and Ewell was reversing his guns, D. H. Hill hastened from Beaver Dam Creek and led the march eastward along the Bethesda road towards Porter's right rear. At the same time A. P. Hill started on the two-mile journey to find Porter's left flank at Gaines Mill.

Porter had intrenched himself east of Powhite Swamp, with his back turned to the Chickahominy bridges. His line of battle formed a semicircle upon the bluffs within the curve of Boatswain's Swamp. Through tangled underbrush, boggy swamps, and felled trees, the Confederates must advance to meet the plunging fire of a park of artillery and of twenty-five thousand muskets, increased in the evening to more than thirty-five thousand.

At 2 P.M., Jackson was passing Old Cold Harbor with D. H. Hill's division; he had pressed forward against sharp-shooters and through fallen trees, and was closing in upon Porter's right flank. General Lee, at the Walnut Grove Church, had directed Jackson to hold the eastward course until he should strike Porter in reverse and threaten his communication with York River, while A. P. Hill and Longstreet should drive him down the Chickahominy. At Old Cold Harbor, Jackson sent forward a battery

to test the Federal position.   Fierce was the artillery
fire poured upon Bondurant, and Jackson knew at
once that he stood in Porter's front.   Just as Jackson, with the head of his column was locating Porter's line, at 2.30 P.M., A. P. Hill was ordering his
entire division into assault at New Cold Harbor.
Away from Gaines Mill, he had before this driven
Porter's strong skirmish line.   When he learned that
Longstreet was at his right hand, Hill dashed
through the tangled brushwood of the swamps
against the strong batteries of the Federal centre.
Gallant and fierce was this attack, and for two hours
the roar of Hill's battle continued to summon the
other Confederate divisions to his field.   He forced
Porter to ask aid, and at 3.30 P.M. Slocum's five
thousand came to give strength to the Federal defence.

The force of Hill's attack gradually abated; his
line of riflemen could not drive three lines of muskets from rifle-pits and barricades one above another
on the steep wooded slope, while the plateau above
was studded with heavy guns that rained an iron
storm upon the devoted Southerners.   At four
o'clock, Lee ordered Longstreet to relieve the
pressure on Hill by making a feint against Porter's
left wing.   Sixty feet above the plateau where
Longstreet's brigades formed their line of assault,
the guns of Morell frowned from the crest of Turkey
Hill.   Rifle-pits and fallen trees gave protection to
the Federal infantry.   Moreover, the approaches towards the Federal left wing were swept by the fire
of the heavy siege guns that McClellan was operat-

ing from the southern bank of the Chickahominy. Longstreet sent his men forward. The fire which they provoked revealed a foe so strong that the full vigour of Longstreet's entire division would be required for the blow. The hour of seven had come when Longstreet was ready to strike.

The Confederate left wing, however, was the first to beard Porter in his lair on the crest of the hill. When the roar of the battle against the Federal left wing called Jackson into the field at Old Cold Harbor, no time remained for outflanking Porter's right wing. Jackson supposed that Hill and Longstreet had found the Federal left flank, and that they were driving Porter sidewise into his own corps. Jackson, therefore, drew up his men in the edge of the field at Old Cold Harbor. Across the open space in his front he expected Porter to be driven toward the York. But the sound of the firing taught him that his comrades on the right were assailing fortifications. He sent a staff-officer to bring his men forward. The officer misunderstood the command and left the brigades at rest. But R. L. Dabney, chief of staff, had heard Jackson's order in detail and he now hurried the troops into battle. As they entered the forest a wild yell rang around the Confederate semicircle, " Jackson 's come ! " D. H. Hill formed the left of Jackson's attacking column. To the right of Hill was Ewell, and to his right, *en échelon*, advanced the old division of Jackson and then the division of Whiting. The lack of guides even yet prevented unity of action. Jackson's brigades moved obliquely into the tangled swamp toward the

sound of A. P. Hill's musketry. They enveloped
Porter's entire right and centre, and took the place
of Hill's exhausted troops against a portion of the
Federal left. The Confederate cannon could not be
moved through the dense brushwood. With bayonets fixed, "Stonewall's" soldiers dashed forward
through the wilderness of obstructions against the
hail of lead and iron. Lee now sent orders to his
entire line to press forward in the Wellington style
of "up and at them."

Porter's hours of successful defence were numbered. He had sent urgent demands for aid to
McClellan across the Chickahominy. But apprehension for the safety of the four corps filled the
mind of McClellan and his subordinates on the
southern bank of the river. The gallant Magruder
did admirable work with his twenty-five thousand.
The Confederate artillery under General Pendleton
in different places blazed forth with furious bursts
of fire; the infantry marched and counter-marched,
and seemed ever on the point of making fierce assault against the lines of Franklin and Sumner.
When McClellan made requisition upon these two
commanders for some brigades in Porter's behalf,
Franklin replied, "not prudent," and Sumner said
"hazardous." Only the brigades of French and
Meagher were sent. These five thousand men
reached the rear crest of Porter's fortress in the
evening twilight, in time to receive into their arms
the routed and fleeing fugitives of Porter's defeated
corps.

The Confederate battle-storm fell most heavily

upon Porter's right flank.   D. H. Hill was the first
to gain a foothold beyond the swamp to confront
his old West Point room-mate, Sykes.   The latter
was fortified behind fence, ditch, and hill-top, and
his heavy guns made the steep ascent appear like
a tower of fire.   The McGehee knoll, held by Sykes,
was the key to this part of the field.   The keen vision
of Hill's brigadiers, Garland and G. B. Anderson,
caught sight of the right end of Sykes's line.   With
Hill's permission, the men of North Carolina began
to swing around against the Federal right flank.
With a wild yell they touched the vital point in the
Federal defence and began to roll back the line of
regulars.   At the same moment with this flank attack, against the front of Sykes's line glittered the
bayonets of the " Stonewall " brigade under Winder.
The latter had moved obliquely across the path of
Ewell to D. H. Hill's support.   The impact of
Carolinians and Virginians against flank and front,
scattered the men of Sykes in rout.   Lawton's Georgians swept forward on Winder's right and made
another gap in Porter's line.

While Jackson was thus crushing the Federal
right wing, the Federal centre and left wing still
made obstinate defence.   The hill's crest was
crowned with Federal guns.   Here was the key-
stone of Porter's arch.   Jackson sent Whiting to
carry these central works at the point of four thousand bayonets.   More than this number of Federal
troops held the defences in Whiting's immediate
front.   He ordered his two brigades under Hood
and Law to move down the long slope to the foot

of the Federal fortress in double-quick time, with
trailed arms and without firing a shot. A withering
storm of balls and shell began to beat into the faces
of the Confederates as they advanced. Federal
cannon from the sixty-foot plateau volleyed and
thundered; muskets blazed from the trenches on
the steep ascent, and from the log breastworks at its
base. Into the jaws of death dashed Hood and
Law without a pause. Hood led the right with
the 4th Texas; Law led the left with the 11th
Mississippi and the 4th Alabama. In silence and
swiftness advanced the two lines of grey; not a
shot did they fire. A thousand men fell, but the
lines closed up where the cannon tore gaps in the
ranks, and the pace was quickened to a run. As
the Confederates rushed against the very muzzles of
the enemy's rifles, the Federal soldiers turned and
fled up the hill. With a fierce yell the men of
Hood and Law leaped the ravine and the breastworks, and poured a close fire into the mass of
fugitives. Up the steep ascent the Confederates
clambered, in pursuit, and drove the Federal line in
confusion across the plateau. Thus in quick succession, after the rout of Sykes, Jackson's line under
Whiting crushed Porter's centre and captured two
regiments and fourteen guns. As Whiting's brigades
reached the hill's crest, they heard the cheers of
Jackson's left wing already sweeping in victory
across the McGehee ridge toward the Chickaham-
iny; at the same moment the brigades of R. H.
Anderson and Pickett led the advance of Longstreet's division against the Federal left wing.

But the victory snatched by Longstreet's gallant battalions from the brow of Turkey Hill, was shared by two of the brigades (Cunningham and Fulkerson) of Jackson's old division. These had pressed far to the right, and furnished aid in breaking through the line opposed to Longstreet.

Behind the Adams House in the edge of the Chickahominy swamps, Porter's men found shelter within the new line of battle formed by the brigades of French and Meagher. More than thirty-five thousand men, in all, thus faced the Confederate advance on the north bank of the Chickahominy. The Federal soldiers held their lines with great obstinacy, and Porter conducted his battle with coolness and ability. But the Confederate soldiers out-fought their opponents. It is true that Lee sent fifty thousand to drive Porter from his lair. But the unsupported attack of A. P. Hill, at 2.30 P.M. threw the Confederate battle out of balance, until Jackson brought his entire line into action near the close of the day. Even then, the Federal line was out-numbered at scarcely a single point of attack, while against Whiting's column Porter presented a more numerous front. Tangled swamps, ravines, heaps of logs and fallen trees, trenches, earthworks, and blazing cannon had not kept back the rush of Jackson's men, although they could not make use of their own heavy guns and were resisted at most points by equal numbers, and in some places by a more numerous foe. The mantle of complete darkness fell upon the Confederate advance as they reached the summit of Porter's fortress. Confederate ignorance of the roads and bridges across the Chickahominy prevented the complete destruction of Porter's corps.   Porter lost about seven thousand men and twenty-two guns.   The Confederate loss was about six thousand.   When the sun first beamed across the field of blood on the morning of June 28, he found the troops of Porter on the southern bank of the Chickahominy.   Under cover of darkness they had crept across the stream, and the axe and the torch removed every plank and trestle.   The swamp and the river were unbridged between McClellan and Lee's main army.

Lee's plan, thus far successful, contemplated the capture of the York River railroad, and the severance of McClellan's communication with the Pamunkey; this was to be followed by the destruction or capture of the Federal army.   This plan was in part frustrated by McClellan's decision to cut loose from the Pamunkey as a base, and to move his army into vital connection with his war vessels on the James River.   Such a change of base he had anticipated some days before by sending a fleet of supply-boats up the James to Westover.   At the midnight hour following the disaster of Cold Harbor, McClellan gave his five corps leaders instructions for the flight across White Oak Swamp to the James.   No other favourable course was open to him.

The morning of June 28 saw McClellan's hundred and five thousand men massed on the Richmond side of the river.   Between him and the Confederate capital was a force one-fourth the size of his own, under Magruder and Huger.   Lee's army was cut in twain; two-thirds of his force were on the northern bank of the unfordable swamp. What an opportunity for a vigorous leader to lay the hand on Richmond! But McClellan already sought escape, and it seems that none of his subordinates urged an assault against Magruder's thin line. Porter's corps faced northward, and with a vast array of heavy guns guarded the Chickahominy against Lee's advance. Four corps held the line facing Richmond, stretching from the Golding farm to the brink of the White Oak Swamp. Between these two lines of bristling bayonets, McClellan made ready his five thousand waggons and started them toward the James. A herd of lowing cattle followed the waggons. Great columns of smoke marked the destruction of stores that could not be moved. Along the single roadway that traverses the Swamp, marched the corps of Keyes in advance to force the way for the supply train. Noonday, June 28, found Keyes's corps guarding the cross-road four miles southward from the Swamp bridge. All day the waggons and the cattle were crawling through the wilderness, concealed by the dense forests and the walls of living men.

Twenty-four hours passed away from the beginning of the Federal retreat until Lee discovered the intention of McClellan. Early on the 28th, Lee sent Stuart and Ewell to Dispatch Station. The railway was seized, part of the track torn up, and Stuart spread destruction as far as the White House. The Federal troops withdrew to the southern side of the river, burned the railway bridge, and ran entire ammunition trains with their engines into the Chicka-

hominy.   Lee then knew that McClellan must seek
another base than the Pamunkey.   But what base ?
The James was open to him across White Oak
Swamp.   The Peninsular route was also accessible
across the lower fords of the Chickahominy.   If
McClellan should retreat down the Peninsula, Lee's
army must remain where it was on the northern
bank of the Chickahominy.   It was impossible to
follow McClellan's rear in the face of Porter's batteries on the bluff.   Ewell was therefore sent to
hold Bottom's Bridge, and Stuart's cavalry moved
down to guard the Peninsular route to Williamsburg.
But the Federal retreat troubled not again the waters
of the Chickahominy.   The clouds of dust arising
from the march of the Federal host warned Lee in
the evening twilight of June 28 that his foe was
seeking the James.   The assault of two of Magruder's regiments against Franklin at Golding's, revealed the fact that this wing of the Federal force
was withdrawing from the Chickahominy.

Lee's orders were at once given for pursuit to
begin at the dawning of June 29.   Longstreet and
A. P. Hill were ordered to move across the river at
the New Bridge and to follow the Darbytown route
to the Long Bridge road until they should strike the
Federal flank.   Magruder was sent in pursuit down
the Williamsburg road, and Huger moved along the
parallel Charles City road.   Holmes led six thousand
men down the River road to intercept the retreat at
Malvern Hill.   Jackson was commanded to rebuild
the Grape Vine Bridge and to follow McClellan's
rear through the Swamp.

The afternoon of Sunday, June 29, offered Lee an opportunity for striking a blow, and he bent all his energies toward bringing his columns into action. McClellan's army was then outstretched over the long roadway from Savage's Station to Malvern Hill. The corps of Keyes was in advance, supported by the shattered brigades of Porter; these watched the waggons on the Quaker road and were feeling their way across the Malvern slopes toward the James. The broken divisions of McCall and Slocum had just emerged from the Swamp road and were in camp near the Willis Church. Heintzelman's advance was crossing at Brackett's ford at 6.30 P.M., and going into bivouac just south of the Swamp at 10 P.M. About the hour of four in the afternoon, Sumner's corps and Smith's division of Franklin's corps, were resisting the onslaught of Magruder at Savage's Station. The vulnerable part of this long, creeping serpent was the middle part of his body, at the southern edge of the Swamp. Toward this point Lee urged Huger forward by the Charles City road, Longstreet and A. P. Hill by the Darbytown road, and Holmes on the River road. Much now depended on the vigour of Huger and the celerity of Longstreet. Huger was held back by the trees felled across his path, while Longstreet marched only twelve miles from the Chickahominy to Atlee's farm on the Darbytown road, and went into camp some miles from McClellan's retreating line. Jackson spent the day in bridging the Chickahominy, while Magruder sent only a part of his men into battle under McLaws at Savage's Station.

Moreover, Holmes failed to strike the serpent's head on Malvern Hill, and McClellan's movement continued.   With a more rapid march by Longstreet and Hill, Lee might have cut the long line in twain at the Willis Church and thus have forced the Federal commander to attack the Confederates in position.

The early dawn of June 30, found the situation completely changed.   Success had crowned McClellan's retreat across the Swamp.   His trains had all made the passage, and his rearguard, Richardson's division, was destroying the Swamp bridge at 10 A.M.   The main body of the Federal army, over sixty thousand men, was now concentrated south of the Swamp in defence of the line of retreat.   At the edge of the Swamp, facing northward and commanding the roadway by a park of artillery, stood the rearguard of twenty thousand men under Franklin. Encircling the Charles City cross-roads, in front of Frayser's farm, were arrayed over forty thousand men under Sumner and Heintzelman with their cannon and muskets commanding the two Richmond approaches.

McClellan's position was strong; he occupied a compact defensive stronghold on the edge of the Swamp, his right and his left within supporting distance of each other on inner lines.

At eleven o'clock, the head of Jackson's column in pursuit ran against Franklin's heavy guns in position to defend the road across the unbridged Swamp. Crutchfield's batteries, twenty-eight guns, opened fire on Franklin and drove back his artillery; Jackson then made an attempt to cross, but the effort only revealed Franklin's strength in cannon and muskets. Two brigades of Sedgwick's division moved rapidly to Franklin's aid to repulse Jackson's advance at Brackett's ford. Franklin thus arrayed twenty-five thousand men against Jackson's twenty-one thousand. The latter saw the odds against him and wisely held back his wearied veterans from a costly charge against the intrenched foe.

While Jackson sent a storm of shells across the Swamp, Huger began an exchange of cannon-shot with Slocum at 3 P.M. Slocum's guns were planted on the Charles City road behind dense masses of fallen trees, and Huger could not advance. At 4 P.M., Longstreet's battle began against McCall at Glendale or Frayser's farm. General Lee in person moved the Confederate column of less than twenty thousand along the New Market road against the Federal host of twice that number. Longstreet directed the operations on the field. The Confederates had to advance through tangled underbrush over uneven ground on their left, and on their right the foe had to be sought behind a marsh. With the spring of the tiger, Longstreet leaped through the jungle upon McCall's left flank, and routed him from the field. Hooker saw McCall's panic-stricken regiments follow their own colours in a wild rush backward through his line of battle. Randol's battery, guarding the gap between McCall and Kearney, became Confederate spoil. Against Kearney's left rushed the Confederates, but Kearney was aided by Slocum; two brigades returned from Franklin's field to strengthen Sedgwick's part of the battle, while Hooker made assault against Longstreet's flank. A. P. Hill's men now rushed into the fight, but the Confederates could only hold the ground from which McCall's men had fled. McCall himself remained behind as Longstreet's prisoner, in company with fourteen Federal field-guns.

While the battle raged at Frayser's farm, Holmes led his six thousand and a six-gun battery over the slopes of the Malvern Hill to Turkey Island Bridge. But Warren's brigade of fifteen hundred men and thirty guns, assisted by the formidable shells from the gunboats, drove Holmes back. In answer to his call for help, Magruder's column was deflected from the edge of Longstreet's battle and sent to Malvern Hill, but that conflict was concluded before he reached the field.

The result of this day's struggle was to leave McClellan in possession of his line of retreat. Gladly did his corps-commanders avail themselves of it without specific directions from McClellan, and in the hours of darkness his column was withdrawn along the Quaker road to the crest of Malvern Hill. As night settled down upon the carnage of June 30, McClellan was thus telegraphing Stanton: " Another day of desperate fighting. We are hard pressed by superior numbers. I fear I shall be forced to abandon my material to save my men under cover of the gunboats. You must send us very large reinforcements."

Sixty feet above the James stand the Malvern bluffs. Northward to the distance of nearly two miles, the Malvern plateau falls away in a gradual slope until it enters the swamps of upper West Run. Across this plateau, along the crest of the hill, commanding the approach by the Quaker road-way, McClellan massed his guns and his infantry. In an arc from Crew's house to Binford's were planted the corps of Porter and the division of Couch. McCall stood in Porter's rear; to Couch's right and rear were stationed the three corps of Heintzelman, Sumner and Franklin. The corps of Keyes linked this fortress with the Federal gun-boats; the declivities on each flank were made strong with cannon and men.

Noonday of July 1 found Lee marshalling a part of the forces of Jackson and Huger across the Quaker road in front of McClellan's stronghold. Ignorance of the fact that two different roadways were called the Quaker road caused Magruder several miles of counter-marching, and kept him away from the field until the day was waning. Longstreet and A. P. Hill were not ordered into the battle; Holmes, on the River road, faced the Malvern bluff, but made no assault.

The Confederate artillery could not all be moved through the dense thickets into action against the Federal guns. A few of Lee's batteries for a time withstood the fury of the iron storm. On the Confederate left, the batteries of Balthis, Poague, and Carpenter, held their position; on the Confederate right, Davidson and Pegram faced the Federal guns after the repulse of Grimes and Moorman. As the Confederate infantrymen aligned themselves in the edge of the swamp, they saw the Federal cannon stationed in their front tier above tier. Sixty field-pieces swept the meadows and the slope in front of Porter's position at the Crew house. Behind this line were ten heavy siege guns. Moreover, the crest of the slope was swarming with riflemen and Couch at the West house stood behind heavy ordnance. Lee ordered an attack by his front line under Huger, Magruder, D. H. Hill, and Whiting. Armistead's brigade on the right was to give the signal for the assault by advancing with a yell. A yell was heard, but not from Armistead, and Hill attacked alone; afterwards, Armistead gave the signal, but no concert of action followed. Later, Magruder fought his way toward the Crew house, but Huger failed to render adequate support. Porter's line was shaken, and he called for aid; the additional canister and musketry at last forced Magruder to retire.

D. H. Hill made gallant assault upon the Federal centre and left centre in front of West's. Whiting on the left heard not Hill's signal and made no advance. Hill's blow caused the Federal centre to waver; but reinforcements swarmed to the aid of Couch, and Hill's battle proved to be only the slaughter of his brave soldiers. The reinforcements hurried forward by Lee were checked by the falling darkness. Five thousand Confederates paid the tribute of wounds and death to their zeal and devotion. The lateness of the hour, the misunderstanding of orders, and the impossibility of forming line of battle in the edge of a dense wilderness, resulted in bringing only fourteen Confederate brigades into the assault. Against the irregular charge of this small body, two or three brigades at a time, McClellan's position was impregnable. But the Federal commander had no heart to hold his ground; silence had scarcely fallen on the field when McClellan ordered Porter to start the whole army " at once " towards Harrison's on the James, with this specific injunction: " In case you should find it impossible to move your heavy artillery, you are to spike the guns and destroy the carriages." The order to Porter contained this final suggestion: " Stimulate your men by informing them that reinforcements, etc., have arrived at our new base." This night retreat toward the river bore the semblance of a rout. Waggons and equipage were abandoned and rifles by the thousand were thrown away by the disheartened Federal soldiers. Hooker thus describes the flight: " It was like the retreat of a whipped army. We retreated like a parcel of sheep; everybody on the road at the same time, and a few shots from the rebels would have panic-stricken the whole command."

Lee ordered Longstreet to lead the Confederate advance to the left of Malvern Hill. But Longstreet marched only two miles through the rain of July 2, and halted for the night on the River road. On Thursday, July 3, the army was counter-marched to Willis Church to seek the Charles City roadway, but incompetent guides again retarded the advance of Longstreet. When Lee presented his army in front of McClellan's camp at Westover, at noon, on Friday, July 4, the Federal host was safe behind strong defensive works. Failure had fallen upon the entire Federal campaign for the capture of Richmond. Disaster in the valley had been followed by disaster on the James. Eighty thousand Confederates, directed by the skill of Lee and of Jackson, had paralysed the movements of two hundred thousand Federal soldiers. McClellan now called for " more than one hundred thousand " fresh troops, and Mr. Lincoln actually ordered Halleck to send him a strong band from the western army near Corinth. McClellan's artillery had saved him from destruction. In each battle the Federal hosts held strong positions, in most cases fortified. The Confederates moved across open fields, and by sheer courage carried these intrenchments. They had literally driven McClellan to the James. The result of these bold assaults was a Confederate loss of twenty thousand men, while the Federal loss was sixteen thousand men. But the war-cloud lowered no longer near the capital of the Confederacy.

" Under ordinary circumstances, the Federal army should have been destroyed." Thus spake Lee of the Seven Days. The chief reason for McClellan's escape, said Lee, was

"the want of correct and timely information. This fact, attributable chiefly to the character of the country, enabled General McClellan skilfully to conceal his retreat, and to add much to the obstructions with which nature had beset the way of our pursuing columns ; but regret that more was not accomplished gives way to gratitude to the sovereign Ruler of the Universe for the results achieved."

In his tender of thanks to the army, July 7, Lee

summed up the results of the struggle in these terms:

" The immediate fruits of our success are the relief of Richmond from a state of siege ; the rout of the great army that so long menaced its safety ; many thousand prisoners, including officers of high rank ; the capture or destruction of stores to the value of millions, and the acquisition of thousands of arms and forty pieces of superior artillery.

"The service rendered to the country in this short but eventful period can scarcely be estimated, and the General commanding cannot adequately express his admiration of the courage, endurance and soldierly conduct of the officers and men engaged. These brilliant results have cost us many brave men ; but while we mourn the loss of our gallant dead, let us not forget that they died nobly in defence of their country's freedom, and have linked their memory with an event that will live forever in the hearts of a grateful people.

" Soldiers, your country will thank you for the heroic conduct you have displayed, conduct worthy of men engaged in a cause so just and sacred, and deserving a nation's gratitude and praise."

General Lee now possessed the full confidence of his soldiers. Every day during this struggle they had seen his eyes flash with fire as he urged the lines into battle. Under heavy fire from the enemy's guns he rode in person to direct the assaults. Reconnaissances to points of danger he made alone in person. His own fierce determination moved Hill and Magruder against the artillery at Malvern Hill, yet not one word of censure did he have for his officers and men when he saw McClellan's escape. Even amidst the heat of battle he could attribute this to the difficulties of the field itself. At Willis Church, during the stir and bustle of pursuit, D. H. Hill saw Lee calm and cool: " He bore grandly his terrible disappointment of the day before [Frayser's farm], and made no allusion to it.'' A tower of strength had Lee made himself by one month's service in the field with this army of heroes. Soldiers looked with devotion upon a leader who dared to give battle against heavy odds, and who showed, also, the generous daring to shoulder the responsibility for every movement.

CHAPTER VIII.

LEE'S ADVANCE INTO NORTHERN VIRGINIA—SECOND MANASSAS.

1862.

HE disaster incurred in the Chickahominy swamps at the hand of Lee, induced the Federal Administration to attempt the capture of Richmond from the direction of the upper Rappahannock. June 26 had seen the organisation of the Army of Virginia, under John Pope, who had recently attained some success in front of Corinth. Pope's force was made up of the three corps of Frémont, Banks, and McDowell. Burnside's thirteen thousand were ordered to hasten from North Carolina up the Potomac to Aquia, and preparations were made to withdraw McClellan's ninety thousand from the James to the plains of northern Virginia, to add strength to Pope.

To facilitate McClellan's retreat from the eastern front of Richmond was Pope's first business. He was ordered to plant himself at the eastern base of the Blue Ridge in order to menace Charlottesville,

Gordonsville, and the line of the Central railroad.
It was expected that Lee would divide his Richmond forces to make resistance against Pope; thus
McClellan could move down the James in safety.
McClellan made strenuous opposition to the entire
plan; he demanded reinforcements for another
advance against Richmond. But the Administration overruled the young Napoleon, and the army
under Pope became now the Federal advance guard
in the movement toward the Confederate capital.

Early in July, Sigel led Frémont's corps from the
lower Valley to Sperryville; Banks likewise moved
his force across the Ridge to Little Washington.
Ricketts's division of McDowell's corps advanced
from Manassas to Waterloo Bridge on the Rappahannock, and King's division remained in camp at
Fredericksburg. With his standard thus unfurled
in the Piedmont region, Pope sought by means of a
formal address, July 14, to reanimate the brigades
whom Jackson had left demoralised in the valley:

"I have come to you from the West, where we have always seen
the backs of our enemies,—from an army whose business it has been
to seek the adversary, and beat him when found,—whose policy has
been attack, not defence. . . . I desire you to dismiss from your
minds certain phrases, which I am sorry to find much in vogue
amongst you. I hear constantly of taking strong positions and holding them,—of lines of retreat and of bases of supplies. Let us discard such ideas. The strongest position a soldier should desire to
occupy is one from which he can most easily advance against the
enemy. Let us study the probable lines of retreat of our opponents,
and leave our own to take care of themselves. Let us look before us
and not behind. Success and glory are in the advance. Disaster
and shame lurk in the rear."

Pope also issued certain orders directed against

the unarmed citizens of this section. Private property was appropriated by roaming bands of soldiers; citizens were held personally accountable for attacks made upon the Federal trains and troops by guerillas and partisan bands; all male citizens, in case of refusal to swear allegiance to the Federal Government, were to be driven beyond the Federal lines and "notified that if found again anywhere within our lines, or at any point in rear, they will be considered spies, and subjected to the extreme rigour of military law."

Lee saw the danger to Richmond, with Pope in the Piedmont section and McClellan still encamped on the James. But the Federal plans were not yet apparent. On July 13, Jackson was sent to Gordonsville, with the divisions of Winder and Ewell, and Robertson's cavalry, twelve thousand men. Soon thereafter were published Pope's unprecedented orders, which Lee characterised as "atrocities" threatened against "defenceless citizens." By direction of the Confederate authorities, Lee sent to Halleck a note protesting against Pope's orders as a violation of the recent agreement for the exchange of prisoners, and as inaugurating "a savage war in which no quarter is to be given." Halleck refused to consider the protest, but Pope abandoned his proposed policy. A week before sending the protest, Lee wrote this to his wife:

"In the prospect before me I cannot see a single ray of pleasure during this war; but so long as I can perform any service to the country I am content.

"When you write to Rob [of Jackson's artillery] again, tell him to catch Pope for me, and also to bring in his cousin Louis Marshall, who, I am told, is on his staff. I could forgive the latter fighting against us, but not his joining Pope."

On July 27, Lee sent forward twelve thousand additional troops under A. P. Hill, to aid Jackson in opposing the advance of Pope.

Before the gates of Richmond, Lee retained only about fifty thousand muskets. D. H. Hill was sent secretly to the southern bank of the James, and from Coggins Point, under cover of darkness, he suddenly poured the fire of forty-three guns upon McClellan's shipping and his city of tents. Hill's assault stirred McClellan into activity. August 5 saw him advance from Westover to his former field of Malvern Hill. Lee moved to meet him as far as the Long Bridge road. The Confederate left wing was pushed out to the Willis Church with orders to threaten McClellan's rear; at the same time the brigades of Evans and Cobb, on the right, drove the Federal advance behind the Malvern guns.

When Lee advanced his line of battle against the heights held by the Army of the Potomac, the morning light revealed the fact that McClellan had again retired under cover of darkness. While Lee thus held McClellan in ward behind his Westover fortifications and Stuart guarded the line between Richmond and Gordonsville, Jackson was preparing to spring across the Rapidan upon his old antagonist, Banks, who was now under Pope's orders. Lee's strong desire was to send part of his own force to assist Jackson. He regarded McClellan's movement to Malvern Hill as merely a demonstration, but held it prudent to retain his full line near Richmond. The manage-

ment of the Rapidan campaign he entrusted to his
lieutenant, and encouraged Jackson on the eve of
battle in these terms: " Relying upon your judgment, courage, and discretion, and trusting to the
continued blessing of an ever-kind Providence, I
hope for victory."

Jackson was watching Pope's effort to concentrate
his army at Culpeper. On August 7, the Federal
forces, to the number of thirty-six thousand five
hundred, were arrayed along the turnpike from
Sperryville to Culpeper, while the Federal cavalry
kept watch near the Rapidan. Jackson marched
across the Rapidan against Culpeper Court House.
Banks led eight thousand men southward to oppose Jackson's advance across Cedar Run. Ricketts's division of nearly ten thousand, likewise moved
from Culpeper to sustain Banks. Across the roadway, Jackson drew up the heads of his columns,
to meet the assault delivered by Banks; the six
brigades forming the Confederate front line of battle
numbered eight thousand, seven hundred muskets.
Upon the plain south of Cedar Run, the eight thousand of Banks rushed to the attack. Jackson's front
line held the field until three brigades from the rearguard made him strong for the forward movement.
From the northern slope of Cedar Mountain, Jackson's guns rained their heavy shot upon the plains
below; along the Culpeper road rushed Jackson's
left wing; their bayonets completed the work of
Jackson's batteries in routing Banks across Cedar
Run to the refuge offered by the darkness and by
the ten thousand men under Ricketts.

The sunrise of August 10 revealed over thirty thousand Federal troops concentrated behind Cedar Run on the Culpeper road, ten thousand more under King at the distance of one day's march, and eight thousand of Burnside's contingent only three marches distant under the leadership of Reno. Jackson therefore drew back to keep in touch with Lee, and the morning of August 12 dawned upon him near Gordonsville, while Pope remained at Culpeper to make conjectures concerning "Stonewall's" movements. Jackson thus made report to Lee: "On the evening of the 9th instant, God blessed our arms with another victory." Immediately in reply Lee sent Jackson this generous commendation: "I congratulate you most heartily on the victory which God has granted you over our enemies at Cedar Run. The country owes you and your brave officers and soldiers a deep debt of gratitude."

Pope now advanced his batteries to the northern bank of the Rapidan, and McClellan showed signs of final flight down the Peninsula. Lee at once divined the plan to concentrate the entire Federal force under Pope's banner, and thus to strike Richmond from the north. Even before McClellan folded his Westover tents, Lee began to move. His aim now was to hurl his entire army against Pope before the army of the Potomac could transplant itself from the James to the Rappahannock. Longstreet's corps was set in motion from Richmond toward Gordonsville, on August 13; not until the following morning, August 14, did McClellan begin to move his army from Westover in the direction of

Fortress Monroe. Into Gordonsville itself marched the head of Longstreet's column, August 15, at an hour when McClellan's rearguard had not yet broken camp to retreat from Westover. Lee's strategy was thus making rapid progress toward success.

The Confederate scouts brought news from the summit of Clarke's Mountain of a vast city of Federal tents pitched in the plains about Cedar Mountain and guarded by cavalry outposts at the Locustdale and Raccoon fords. By the addition of Reno and King, Pope's muskets now numbered beyond fifty thousand. Longstreet counselled a flank movement toward the Confederate left, in order to seek battle on the Blue Ridge slopes. But to Lee and Jackson it seemed wiser to press rapidly toward the Confederate right and to thrust the Confederate army between Pope and Washington.

Jackson moved with rapid step, and August 16 found his corps in camp at Pisgah Church, ready to leave the Somerville ford behind them at the dawning of the 18th. On the same day, August 16, Lee ordered Longstreet forward from Gordonsville as far as this same Pisgah Church, with his tents pitched toward the Raccoon ford, where Lafayette crossed with his battalions in Revolutionary days. Longstreet made objection to the movement on the ground that his men were without provisions. Jackson offered to furnish bread to Longstreet's men, and pleaded for immediate advance against Pope's flank. Lee yielded to Longstreet's obstinacy and postponed the attack, and with characteristic mag-

12

nanimity assumed entire responsibility for the delay,
as may be seen from the following report:

" It was determined with the cavalry to destroy the railroad bridge
over the Rappahannock in rear of the enemy, while Longstreet and
Jackson crossed the Rapidan and attacked his left flank. The movement, as explained in the accompanying order, was appointed for
August 18th, but the necessary preparations not having been completed, its execution was postponed to the 20th."

The calmness of Lee while planning this bold
flank movement may be seen in the following letter,
dated August 17:

" Here I am in a tent instead of my comfortable quarters at
Dobbs's. The tent, however, is very comfortable and of that I have
nothing to complain. General Pope says he is very strong, and
seems to feel so, for he is moving apparently up to the Rapidan. I
hope he will not prove stronger than we are. I learn since I have
left that General McClellan has moved down the James River with
his whole army. I suppose he is coming here too, so we shall have
a busy time. Burnside and King from Fredericksburg have joined
Pope, which, from their own report, has swelled Pope to ninety-two
thousand. I do not believe it, though I believe he is very big.
Johnny Lee saw Louis Marshall [General Lee's nephew on Pope's
staff] after Jackson's last battle, who asked him kindly after his old
uncle, and said his mother was well. Johnny said Louis looked
wretchedly himself. I am sorry he is in such bad company, but I
suppose he could not help it."

August 19 found both Confederate corps massed
near the Rapidan ready to strike Pope's left and rear
the following day. But Fitz Lee had led his brigade
too far afield, because of Stuart's indefinite orders,
and failed to reach the appointed rendezvous. The
entire cavalry corps was thus delayed twenty-four
hours; the delay, moreover, resulted in the capture

of Stuart's adjutant on outpost duty. A paper on the person of this adjutant revealed to Pope the entire Confederate plan.

From the summit of Clarke's Mountain, that same nineteenth day of August, Lee looked across the Rapidan in sorrow upon the Federal army moving back toward the Rappahannock. He was disappointed to see that Pope was turning toward his own rear. Lee was full of the spirit of combativeness. But his eagerness for battle was not greater than that of his own soldiers. Although their only habitation was the bare ground with the covering of a single blanket, their only food " now and then an ear of corn, fried apples, or a bit of ham broiled on a stick, but quite frequently [they] do without either from morning until night," yet with cheers and burning zeal did Lee's veterans leap forward in pursuit of Pope.

August 21 found Lee's fifty thousand confronting Pope's fifty-five thousand along the Rappahannock River from Kelley's ford to Beverley ford. Across the stream the artillery continued to play a furious game and cavalry assaults were made by both commanders. The advance corps of McClellan's army were in rapid approach from Alexandria and Fredericksburg. The plains of Virginia, as far north as Washington, were rapidly filling up with the Federal hosts.

Lee now decided to move up-stream, to swing Jackson's corps across the river, around the Federal right flank, and thus to cut off Pope from his line of communication with Washington. Jackson's move-

ment began to the sound of Longstreet's guns; the
latter kept Banks and McDowell under arms to oppose the feigned advance of Lee's right wing across
the river.   At swift pace Jackson moved northward
and threw Early across the stream at the Sulphur
Springs.   Stuart led fifteen hundred horsemen across
Waterloo Bridge through Warrenton as far as Cat-
lett's Station on the Orange and Alexandria railway.
Pope's official papers became Stuart's spoil, but tor-
rents of rain prevented the daring trooper from in-
flicting further damage.   The swollen river checked
the progress of Jackson's rearguard, and Stuart and
Early recrossed the river and bivouacked once more
on the southern bank.   Pope had kept his brigades
busy in zigzag movements to meet the threatened
advance of the Confederate columns.   Utter bewilderment had already settled like a cloud over
the mind of the Federal commander.

Lee summoned forward from Richmond the divisions of D. H. Hill, J. G. Walker, and McLaws, and
made ready for an assault upon Pope's rear.   He
sought conference with Jackson.   Eye-witnesses of
this conference report Lee as listening while Jackson
made boot-marks in the sand and gesticulated with
his hands.   The decision was made to send Jackson
around Pope's right flank, to cut his communications
and then to hold him at bay until Lee could bring
forward Longstreet's corps and deliver battle with
his entire army on the plains beyond the Rappahannock.

Jackson's corps of twenty-two thousand men
stripped themselves of every encumbrance, and

MAJOR-GENERAL J. E. B. STUART.

girded their loins for the conflict. Ammunition only was to be conveyed on wheels. Some tough biscuits and a handful of salt formed the contents of the haversacks. Green corn from the fields, and apples from the trees, were to supply food until these heroes could draw rations from the vast store-houses located on the railway in the rear of Pope's army. The sun of August 25 arose in midsummer glory upon Jackson's march. Enthusiasm and fierce courage flashed from every eye as these raw-boned, half-clad athletes pressed onward after their beloved leader. As sunset fell upon the weary column, the barefooted veterans with swinging caps and sup-pressed cheers filed past Jackson in the roadway at Salem. Not a soldier nor an officer knew his plans. Twenty-five miles had been left behind them during the single day. A radiance lit up Jackson's face as he said, " Who would not conquer with such men as these! " From morning until afternoon they had listened to the sound of Longstreet's artillery as he kept Pope at bay below Waterloo Bridge. Those guns spoke of another corps as brave and as true as the men under Jackson; they spoke of Lee's stern courage, and of his sublime confidence in his lieu-tenant, now entrusted with full authority and dis-cretion to strike the chief blow of the campaign. Lee was violating a fundamental principle of mili-tary strategy in dividing his own forces before the very face of the enemy; but this act of splendid daring reveals the perfect harmony that bound to-gether the two chief Confederate leaders. It shows Lee's quick knowledge of the temper and intrepid valour of his citizen-soldiers, that he could swing his army in separate columns from the Rappahannock to Manassas, and there deliver the aggressive battle that forced a more numerous foe from the soil of Virginia into the defences around Washington.

August 26 found Jackson hastening from Salem forward through the narrow gorge in Bull Run Mountain called Thoroughfare Gap. As the darkness fell upon his swift-foooted veterans at the end of a twenty-four-mile march, their banner was unfurled at Bristoe Station, Alexandria railway, and at midnight Trimble's bayonets and Stuart's sabres were in possession of Manassas Junction, four miles to the eastward. Sunset of this same day saw Longstreet's head of column going into camp at Orleans; Lee had left six thousand men to watch the river at Waterloo and was pushing his main column forward in Jackson's footsteps. The latter had now planted himself directly between Pope and Washington. Pope's army had been augmented by the arrival of Porter's ten thousand men at Bealeton, Heintzelman's ten thousand at Warrenton Junction, while Sumner, Franklin, and Cox were approaching from Alexandria. The morning of August 27 dawned upon Pope's vast Federal host with face turned to the rear, and under orders to march toward Gainesville in search of Jackson.

The early hours of August 27 witnessed great commotion on the plains between the Rappahannock and Bull Run. The waters of the former stream heard not the sound of a gun, but flowed unvexed toward the Bay. The rumble of cannon carriages and the tramp of heavy columns drew near the Bull Run bluffs. Behind the mountain chain to the north, the veterans of Longstreet, accompanied by Lee in person, were pressing forward at steady pace from Orleans through Salem to White Plains. The disturbing cause of all this hasty marching by Federal and Confederate forces was enjoying in quietness the spoil of war at Manassas. Jackson's corps held high carnival all day long amid the wealth of Pope's store of supplies. Bare feet were shod and naked bodies were clad, but first of all were Jackson's starved heroes fed upon the abundance of Manassas.

Ewell, behind Broad Run, held Hooker at bay; but Sigel and McDowell in Gainesville, and Kearney and Reno at Greenwich, were, at sunset between Jackson and Lee. The march of Longstreet's corps on the 27th carried him over the fifteen miles from Orleans to White Plains. Lee rode in advance and left the control of the corps entirely to his lieutenant. Longstreet states that because couriers from Jackson affirmed all to be well, he did not urge his men to a swift pace. The gallant brigades under his banner, not aware that speed was necessary, did not make a forced march. As Lee was moving onward far in front with his staff, he narrowly escaped capture near Salem by a squadron of Federal cavalry. A large body of Federal horsemen were hovering near the Confederate column. More than an hour's delay in the march of the corps was caused by the sending of infantry to drive them away.

At the dawn of the 28th, the corps was moving out of White Plains, but Longstreet did not bring the

head of his column to the mouth of Thoroughfare
Gap, seven miles away, until three o'clock in the
afternoon. The pass was gleaming with Federal
bayonets entering from the east. Across the Bull
Run Mountain rolled the booming sound of distant
cannon, telling of Jackson standing like a lion at
bay. To the right and to the left Lee sent scouting
parties in search of a path across the steep cliffs.
His features were calm, and courtesy and geniality
marked his manner in this hour of impending battle.
Lee sent D. R. Jones's Georgians straight through
the pass; at the eastern gateway they grappled with
the Federal muskets and cannon under Ricketts.
Three brigades under Wilcox were sent three miles
to the northward to cross at Hopewell Gap and turn
the Federal position. Over the steep rocky crest
that immediately overlooks Thoroughfare Gap clambered Law with one of Hood's brigades. Down the
eastern slope of the mountain rushed Law's men
in the gathering darkness. As they fell upon the
Federal flank Ricketts drew his troops away. Lee's
brigades began to pour through the gap and their
campfires were lighted at the eastern base of the
mountain within eight miles of the field of Groveton, where Jackson was delivering fierce battle and
awaiting the coming of Lee.

During the twenty-four hours preceding this
bivouac of Lee on the Manassas side of the Bull
Run Mountain, Jackson had wrought vast changes
in the great field of war. As the darkness of the
27th fell upon him at Manassas, Jackson set torch to
the spoil that could not be removed, and behind the

curtain of the night began the game of deluding Pope. The latter had begun to dream of " bagging the whole crowd," and now changed the direction of his marching columns and urged all his brigades upon Manassas Junction. But the fox was escaping even while Pope was preparing the toils. Jackson sent Taliaferro with the trains directly to Sudley. Due eastward toward Washington he despatched A. P. Hill and Ewell; Hill moved beyond Bull Run to Centreville. This night march of Jackson was made through darkness so dense that Porter with lighted candles failed to track his way in pursuit from Warrenton Junction to Manassas. The morning of the 28th gave Hill and Ewell time to move southwestward across the Stone Bridge to Sudley Church. Noonday saw Jackson's bayonets all in line on the southern bank of Bull Run. His shotted guns were ready behind the Warrenton turnpike looking downstream toward the field of their former victory of July, 1861.

Far afield were Pope's brigades on this momentous morning. Amidst the smoking embers of his burnt supplies at noonday he heard rumours of war from Centreville, and from the line of railway beyond. The movement of Hill's division and of Fitz Lee's horsemen toward Washington gave indications to Pope that the fox might yet be ensnared on the northern bank of the Bull Run. The third time a change was made in his proposed point of concentration. Gainesville and Manassas in turn had been assigned as the goal for his converging battalions; the waning hours of the 28th saw them all dragging weary feet toward Centreville. While Pope thus deluded himself with the vain idea that he was in hot pursuit of a defeated foe, the object of his pursuit, Jackson, stood defiantly at the edge of the Warrenton roadway on the left flank of the eastward-moving Federal columns. With tardy step the division of King, McDowell's corps, was passing along this highway from Gainesville toward Centreville in the late afternoon. With the spring of the lion two of Jackson's three divisions leaped upon King's column. The sun had disappeared when the assault began; short and fierce was the encounter, and Taliaferro and Ewell, the division commanders, were both disabled. King's line was forced backward, and under cover of darkness he withdrew from the field of blood. During the night, King was overtaken by the division of Ricketts in full retreat from Lee's vanguard at Thoroughfare Gap. Both Federal divisions fled from Jackson's front, and the morning of the 29th dawned upon them near Manassas. Lee's strategy was now practically a success. No Federal force opposed the union of the two wings of his army. Sunrise of the 29th saw Longstreet's brigades starting upon the eight-mile journey to Jackson's right at Groveton; at the same hour were the troops of Pope scattered through the fields and along the highway from Bristoe and Manassas even to Centreville. From the latter place Pope began to issue his morning orders for a fourth rendezvous, reversing the direction of his columns and calling all his men toward "Stonewall's" field near Groveton.

The corps of Longstreet moved leisurely eastward from Thoroughfare Gap.   But the morning's early hours brought them the sounds of Jackson's renewed conflict; like war-horses, these gallant soldiers snuffed the battle from afar and voluntarily quickened their pace.   Under Lee in person they filed through Gainesville down the turnpike to the left, and at ten o'clock they were taking position in front of that village upon the right flank of Jackson's line. As Lee stood near Groveton, he saw toward his left a great battle in full progress.   The roar of heavy guns and the crash of musketry told him where Jackson's men were arrayed in a line of two and one half miles from Groveton to Sudley Church. Behind the embankments and excavations of an unfinished railroad, and in the midst of heavy woods, stood "Stonewall's" veterans fighting their second day's battle on the same field.   Since early morning, the storm of battle had lowered heavily against Jackson's left, under A. P. Hill.   Sigel's entire corps, from 6.30 to 10.30, had there attempted to push its way up the southern bank of the Bull Run, but had met severe repulse at the hands of Gregg's brigade of South Carolinians, assisted by Thomas's Georgians.   Just as Lee was planting Longstreet in front of Gainesville, Heintzelman and Reno were leading up their two corps, eighteen thousand five hundred men, to Sigel's aid against Jackson's left.   Moreover, the clouds of dust, the waving banners, the varied sounds of war that were manifest upon the knolls and plains that stretched away toward Manassas and Bull Run, told Lee

where the Federal host was assembling for a grand
assault.

Pope's troops were wearied by the protracted
marchings in quest of Jackson. From far Centreville rode Pope himself that morning of the 29th,
and at noonday he took position on Buck Hill near
the Warrenton turnpike. Deployed in his front,
and holding the triangle between the Warrenton
and Sudley roads, Pope found the corps of Heintzelman, Reno, and Sigel, and the division of Reynolds.
These thirty-five thousand stood at last face to face
with Jackson. Pope urged them against "Stonewall's" left where Sigel had already suffered defeat.
The two corps of McDowell and Porter, nearly
thirty thousand strong, Pope ordered to advance
from Manassas upon Gainesville. Banks, with
eight thousand, was yet absent from the scene.
The Federal cavalry were hovering about the flanks
of the army. Pope refused to believe that Lee had
reached the field and proposed to hurl his seventy-
five thousand against Jackson's line of about twenty
thousand.

Lee stationed himself between the Meadowville
and Pageland lanes, near the southern edge of the
Warrenton highway. Even farther to the front he
rode to watch the movements of his foe. He found
himself in close proximity to the Federal left flank.
As the Federal line moved forward again to assail
Jackson's left, Lee urged Longstreet to assail the
Federal left. After reconnaissance, Longstreet reported that the position " was not inviting."

" General Lee was quite disappointed," says

Longstreet, " by my report against immediate attack along the turnpike, and insisted that by throwing some of the brigades beyond the Federal left, their position would be broken up and a favourable field gained." At this moment came Stuart with news of the approach of McDowell and Porter from Manassas. This force, however, failed to attack. Lee urged Longstreet to attack Porter, but Longstreet watched and waited. When McDowell soon afterward turned to his right and marched by the Sudley road to Pope's battle against Jackson, leaving Porter alone near Manassas, Lee " again became anxious to bring on the battle by attacking down the Groveton pike." But Longstreet pleaded the near approach of darkness as an objection, and suggested a forced reconnaissance. " To this he reluctantly gave consent," says Longstreet.

With this repeated urgency did Lee seek to deliver assault against Pope's centre and left during the afternoon hours when the battle waxed fierce and fiercer in the woods near Sudley. Six successive waves of attack surged against Jackson's left during the day. After 10.30 A.M., additional brigades moved forward, but Gregg and Thomas drove them back. At 3 o'clock P.M., another Federal column essayed to break the Confederate line, but Johnson and Starke rushed to aid the brigades of Hill, and a fearful slaughter was visited upon Pope's divisions. After 5 P.M. were the divisions of Kearney and Stevens massed for a final assault. During ten hours of almost continuous battle against an increasing foe, the same small Confederate brigades held the field.   The gallant and modest Gregg now sent this message: " Tell General Hill that my ammunition is exhausted but that I will hold my position with the bayonet." As his Carolinians were forced backward, Thomas's Georgians and Branch's North Carolinians came to their aid. From rock to rock, from tree to tree, they retired, still offering courageous battle.   The Virginians under Field and Early, the Georgians under Lawton, and the Louisianians under Hays, rushed to the rescue and turned the Federal tide backward in complete defeat.   During a portion of the time, the majority of the Confederates engaged in this struggle were without a cartridge.   Pope's brigades on this flank were completely shattered.   In the centre, Lee defended his position against the power of Reynolds by a hot fire from Hood's batteries, and at sunset he turned loose the war-dogs of Hood's division in a forced reconnaissance against the Federal centre.   King was driven back and Hood retained as battle-trophies one heavy gun and three flags.

The night of the 29th closed down upon the Confederate army in the position selected at midday. Defeat had been visited upon every assault made by Federal arms.   While Pope telegraphed to Washington his claim of victory, Lee awaited the dawning of Saturday, August 30, in the full confidence of driving his foe across Bull Run.   With absolute truth it may be asserted that Lee's banner now floated over an army whose fighting qualities have never yet been surpassed on any field of war. Cæsar's Tenth Legion and Napoleon's Guard were more than matched by the heroes who rested where they had fought, and at any moment were ready to spring to arms to beat back the foe. Pale with hunger and worn with long marching, the Confederate soldiers were still practically invincible. The two chief leaders, Lee and Jackson, had inspired their men to trust in the God of battles. As both chieftains closed their eyes that night in slumber, the whispered prayer was yet upon their lips. Along the Confederate line of battle, but chiefly in Jackson's corps, when night had closed the strife, groups of veterans gathered themselves for united prayer.

By the chaplains, or by some ragged soldier, were these midnight devotions led. With the last petition to Heaven, the men betook themselves to their allotted posts ready for the battle of the morrow. Like Bruce's men at Bannockburn, these embattled patriots were ready to give life for home and country:

> " Upon the spot where they have kneeled,
> These men will die or win the field."

As brilliant as the sun of Austerlitz arose the sun of the Second Manassas, August 30, 1862. Lee stood defiant near the Warrenton road, one half-mile west of Groveton, within the angle formed by his two wings. Across the rolling country to the left, as far as Sudley Church, the forests and uplands behind the unfinished railway were held by Jackson's guns and muskets under A. P. Hill, Lawton, and Starke. Almost at a right angle to this left wing was Lee's right wing, drawn out across the

Warrenton turnpike and across the Manassas railroad as far as Dawkins's Branch.   Behind the heavy
forests, Lee had here arrayed the brigades of Longstreet under Wilcox, Hood, Kemper, and D. R.
Jones.   R. H. Anderson's six thousand muskets
stood in the roadway as a reserve behind the Confederate centre.   Nearly fifty thousand men stood
ready to obey his orders, as Lee measured with his
eye the triangular field of war.   Eastward along
the turnpike which equally divided the battle-terri-
tory, he saw the forest and the open ground separated into ridges and plateaus by the winding tribu-
taries of Young's Branch.   Behind this screen of
trees and hills he could hear the early rumþling of
the enemy's gun-carriages.   Upon a ridge that
marked the angle made by his two converging
wings, Lee placed thirty-six guns under S. D. Lee
to sweep the plains and the heights in front of Jackson's line.

Strange to record, Pope noticed the absence of
Lee's advanced skirmishers of the day before, and
conceived the idea that the Confederate army was
in full retreat toward the Bull Run Mountain.   He
therefore ordered his columns " in pursuit " along
the Warrenton and Haymarket roads.   Porter's
corps had been drawn from Dawkins's Branch to
Pope's centre and was now thrust forward to lead
the Federal advance.   The defeat of Cold Harbor
was fresh in Porter's memory, and he did not believe in Lee's retreat.   Instead of hurrying forward
in column, Porter formed his own corps in threefold
line of battle; King's division he arrayed on his right

in seven lines of attack; the division of Reynolds
was to render support at Porter's left.   Behind this
host under Porter, the corps of Sigel and half the
corps of Reno stood ready.   In the dense wood that
lies east of Groveton, and north of the Warrenton
turnpike, Porter stationed this thunderbolt of war
for an assault upon Lee's left centre.   Against the
extreme Confederate left were massed the corps of
Heintzelman and half of the two corps of McDowell
and Reno.   Pope was ready to throw his entire force
against Lee's left wing.   In two lines of battle stood
Jackson's Ironsides ready for the attack.

Noonday looked down upon the brigades that
were still moving forward to take position under
Porter's banner.   The early morning had witnessed
Heintzelman's advance against the extreme Confederate left; A. P. Hill's guns roared defiance, and
Ricketts drew back.   Against the Confederate centre Reynolds's skirmishers had felt their way, and
Federal artillery had volleyed and thundered, but
Lee's thirty-six guns visited severe repulse on all
such distant advances.   At 3 P.M. Porter sounded
the signal to charge.   Through the dense wood his
men pressed forward; then across the open field,
from the Dogan house to the railway cut, rushed
Porter's first blue-coated line.   The old " Stonewall "
division under Starke, and the division of Lawton
were first to greet the Federal troops with the
leaden messengers of death; heavy guns from the
rearward heights poured their weight of iron upon
Porter's brave men.   In Starke's immediate front
the conflict was fierce and almost hand to hand.

The two Confederate lines were merged into one, and with tenacious grasp held the edge of the railroad excavation. Two flags waved defiance for thirty minutes within ten paces of each other; men were strewn upon the ground like leaves in autumn. Ammunition failed with a part of Jackson's line, but these men of Virginia and of Louisiana, Johnson's and Stafford's brigades, gathered stones from the ground and flung them with deadly effect. Porter's charge was checked by these stone missiles. Through the forest, farther to the Confederate left, stood the lines of Lawton and A. P. Hill engaged in similar fierce conflict.

While thus the storm of battle surged and roared, Porter's reserve lines essayed to cross the open field to bring their comrades aid. Now it was that Lee's central battalion of thirty-six guns with enfilading fire, carried death across the treeless plain in front of his left wing. Porter's assault was visibly shaken by these guns. Bayonets, stones, and musket-balls, still preserved an impregnable front along Jackson's line. Longstreet replied to Lee's command to advance by opening an additional artillery fire upon Porter's left rear. These cannon-shot had just begun to play when the Federal troops fell back in routed masses from the fire of Jackson and S. D. Lee. " Stonewall's " brigades sprang to the charge in hot pursuit. Lee's eye had already discerned the crisis of battle, and his order had gone to Longstreet to dash upon the Federal left. Longstreet's soldiers themselves anticipated the word of command by moving forward on the run. In this magnificent charge Lee rode to the front through the storm of shells from the Federal artillery.

Longstreet closed in the Confederate right wing with vigour; across the hills he pushed batteries and brigades against the flank of the flying foe. Far in front of the extreme Confederate right, dashed Stuart with his horse artillery. Warren's Federal brigade left a vast tribute of dead and wounded just east of Groveton; Schenck made gallant defence of the Bald Hill summit, but the Confederates swarmed up in front and flank and the knoll was won. Hood swept the turnpike eastward to the Stone House. Against this tide of Confederate victory, on his left, Pope's reserves made final stand on the Henry Hill. Down-stream for more than a mile Jackson continued to push the Federal rout until darkness fell upon his brigades at the Carter House. Across the Bull Run, between Sudley and Stone Bridge, many Federal regiments had rushed in retreat. Darkness upreared a protecting wall about the demoralized Federal brigades, gathered in a mass on the Bull Run bluffs between the Henry and Robinson houses. Long before sunset, the Stone Bridge began to choke with the rush of fugitives; the coming dark ness saw a turbid stream of defeated soldiers rolling back in rout to find refuge behind Franklin's corps approaching from Alexandria. At dusk, Pope sounded the bugle of general retreat and fled in the night to his fortress at Centreville. The field of Saturday claimed from Pope's army nearly twenty thousand men in dead, wounded, and prisoners. Since the first blow delivered by Jackson upon his rear, the Federal commander had lost thirty thousand men and thirty heavy guns, and stores and small arms innumerable. Lee had paid eight thousand men for the wondrous victory.

Through the rain and mud of the early morning of Sunday (August 31), Lee pushed his horsemen across Bull Run in search of Pope. Frowning upon Stuart from the Centreville heights were the heavy guns of the Federal army. Lee now despatched Jackson by Sudley Ford toward the Little River turnpike with orders to turn the enemy's right and cut off his retreat to Washington. Jackson's men were still eager in spirit, but their feet were battle-weary, and the heavy downpour of rain delayed their progress. Pope was resting in the arms of twenty thousand fresh troops, but when he learned of Jackson's approach he issued orders for a retreat to Fairfax. At the same time he arrayed Reno's corps across the turnpike to fight a rearguard battle; Heintzelman gave support to Reno. In the face of a blinding storm of rain, Jackson's divisions fell upon this Federal force in the afternoon of Monday, September 1. In the midst of the rolling thunder and the lightning, bayonets were freely used in the place of firearms that would not fire. Jackson gave Pope a staggering blow, but the darkness checked his advance. Longstreet did not reach the field of Ox Hill in time to take part in the struggle.

Lee's consideration for the family of a Federal officer was shown the following day when he sent the body of Kearney from the battle-field to Pope under a flag of truce. The night of September 2 found the shattered divisions of Pope's army behind the fortifications at Washington. Lee at Chantilly was giving rest to the hungry veterans, who had out-marched their supply train. The pause gave the Confederates time to discover that they had worn the shoes from their feet in the hot pursuit of Banks, McClellan, and Pope since the days of the previous May and June. In a campaign of about four months, under Lee's guidance, eighty thousand Confederate soldiers had driven two hundred thousand Federal troops beyond the borders of Virginia, with the exception of a small band that still troubled the lower valley.

CHAPTER IX.

THE CAMPAIGN IN MARYLAND—THE CAPTURE OF HARPER'S FERRY—SHARPSBURG.

1862.

ENERAL LEE determined to carry the war at once beyond the Potomac River. To President Davis he made the suggestion, September 3, 1862, that this was " the most propitious time since the commencement of the war for the Confederate army to enter Maryland." Concerning the difficulties of the movement, he said in the same despatch :

" The army is not properly equipped for an invasion of an enemy's territory. It lacks much of the material of war, is feeble in transportation, the animals being much reduced, and the men are poorly provided with clothes, and in thousands of instances are destitute of shoes. Still we cannot afford to be idle, and though weaker than our opponents in men and military equipments, must endeavour to harass if we cannot destroy them. I am aware that the movement is attended with much risk, yet I do not consider success impossible, and shall endeavour to guard it from loss."

On September 4, without awaiting the reply of

Davis, Lee turned the head of his column from Leesburg toward Frederick, Maryland. " The only two subjects that give me any uneasiness," he wrote, " are my supplies of ammunition and subsistence."

The two divisions of D. H. Hill and McLaws with Hampton's cavalry had marched the entire distance from Richmond, and were once again under Lee's banner. This forced journey on foot had left by the way many wearied men. The fare of green apples and green corn, and the continuous bivouac and battle engaged in by the two corps of Jackson and Longstreet left thousands of other stragglers behind. Clad in fluttering rags and with feet either bare or only half-shod, the depleted Confederate army moved forward in high spirit, with shout and song. They looked like a band of scarecrows. Ministers of the Gospel, college professors, lawyers, merchants, physicians, planters, and farm labourers composed the incomparable battalions who followed Lee. They were without tents, and their torn garments were discoloured with battle-stains. But a word from their great leader could change their noisy, irregular column into a steady line of battle in whose valour and skill an equal number of the choicest veterans of the European armies would find metal more than worthy of their steel. Both shores were made to ring with the melody " Maryland, My Maryland " as they waded the Potomac. The groves and green fields of Maryland were made vocal with laughter as the gray-jackets marched toward Frederick. Within six months they had defeated Banks, Milroy, Shields, McClellan, and Pope, and now they were eager for battle in front of Washington.

Lee forbade all depredations upon private property, and ordered his quartermasters to purchase all supplies needed by the army. A general order issued from headquarters announced a Confederate victory in the West, and encouraged the soldiers in the following terms:

"Soldiers, press onward! Let each man feel the responsibility now resting on him to pursue vigorously the success vouchsafed to us by Heaven. Let the armies of the East and the West vie with each other in discipline, bravery and activity, and our brethren of our sister States will soon be released from tyranny, and our independence be established upon a sure and abiding basis."

On September 8, Lee and his brigades were in camp at Frederick, Maryland. Jackson, Longstreet, and Stuart pitched their tents near General Lee in Best's Grove. Lee wrote to President Davis, September 8, suggesting that the Confederate Government should propose to the Federal Government " the recognition of our independence." Concerning this proposal, he added, " The rejection of this offer would prove to the country that the responsibility of the continuance of the war does not rest upon us but that the party in power in the United States elect to prosecute it for purposes of their own." On the same day Lee issued this proclamation:

" To the people of Maryland : It is right that you should know the purpose that brought the army under my command within the limits of your State, so far as that purpose concerns yourselves. The people of the Confederate States have long watched with the deepest sympathy the wrongs and outrages that have been inflicted upon the citizens of a Commonwealth allied to the States of the South by the strongest social, political and commercial ties. They have seen with profound indignation their sister State deprived of every right, and reduced to the condition of a conquered province. Under the pretence of supporting the Constitution, but in violation of its most valuable provisions, your citizens have been arrested and imprisoned upon no charge, and contrary to all forms of law. The faithful and manly protest against this outrage made by the venerable and illustrious Marylander [Taney], to whom in better days no citizen appealed for right in vain, was treated with scorn and contempt; the government of your chief city has been usurped by armed strangers; your legislature has been dissolved by the unlawful arrest of its members; freedom of the press and of speech has been suppressed; words have been declared offences by an arbitrary decree of the Federal Executive, and citizens ordered to be tried by a military commission for what they may dare to speak. Believing that the people of Maryland possessed a spirit too lofty to submit to such a Government, the people of the South have long wished to aid you in throwing off this foreign yoke, to enable you again to enjoy the inalienable rights of freemen, and restore independence and sovereignty to your State. In obedience to this wish our army has come among you, and is prepared to assist you with the power of its arms in regaining the rights of which you have been despoiled.

" This, citizens of Maryland, is our mission, so far as you are concerned. No constraint upon your free will is intended; no intimidation will be allowed within the limits of this army, at least. Marylanders shall once more enjoy their ancient freedom of thought and speech. We know no enemies among you, and will protect all, of every opinion. It is for you to decide your destiny freely and without constraint. This army will respect your choice, whatever it may be; and while the Southern people will rejoice to welcome you to your natural position among them, they will only welcome you when you come of your own free will."

" R. E. LEE, General Commanding."

The section of Maryland near Frederick was hostile to the Confederacy, and time was not given for the men of eastern Maryland to array themselves under Lee's banner. From Washington with a host of nearly ninety thousand men, composed of new and old soldiers, the restored commander McClellan was approaching. In the fortifications about Washington, Banks commanded a garrison of seventy-two thousand five hundred. McClellan rested his left on the Potomac and his right on the Baltimore and Ohio railroad, as he slowly pushed forward his line, in convex form, in search of Lee's army. In order to draw McClellan away from his base of supplies, Lee began to withdraw his forces toward Hagerstown, there to offer battle or to threaten Harrisburg and Baltimore. But the Federal troops had not been altogether removed from the Valley of Virginia. At Martinsburg and at Harper's Ferry, a Federal force of over twelve thousand stood on guard over the stores and munitions of war. Lee had already ordered Loring to clear the Kanawha valley and then to advance upon Martinsburg. Winchester he had designated as a depot for Confederate supplies and as a rendezvous for the great army of stragglers yet south of the Potomac. The Confederate chieftain's plans were now laid for the immediate capture of the forces in and near Harper's Ferry, as preliminary to the massing of his entire army at Hagerstown. Order 191 was issued from the Frederick headquarters, on September 9, giving direction for the movement of the Confederate brigades the following day. The leading position was assigned to Jackson. Across the South Mountain and through Sharpsburg he was ordered to lead his command of fourteen brigades. Beyond the Potomac he was directed to seize the Baltimore and Ohio railway, capture the force in Martinsburg, and cut off the way of escape from Harper's Ferry. This movement was to be completed by the morning of Friday, September 12. Behind Jackson, Lee sent McLaws, reinforced by R. H. Anderson. Ten brigades were combined in this band, which was to move from Middletown toward the left and by Friday morning plant heavy guns on Maryland Heights overlooking Harper's Ferry. J. G. Walker, with two brigades, was sent with orders to establish his guns on the Loudoun Heights. Beleaguered thus on every side, it was expected that Harper's Ferry would yield at once to the Confederate guns, and that Friday, September 12, would see these three detachments in motion again toward the main body of the army at Boonsborough or Hagerstown. This main body was made up, in part, of nine brigades under Longstreet, who was moved across South Mountain toward Boonsborough, there to hold watch over the supply trains; the other part was composed of D. H. Hill's five brigades as a rear-guard. Cavalry was assigned to each of the marching divisions; the main body of the horsemen under Stuart made ready to deliver battle against the heads of McClellan's columns.

The dawning of September 10 marked the beginning of the great game of war. Lee's horse, by a sudden spring, had caused painful injury to his hands, and he rode in an ambulance. The reported advance of a Federal force from Chambersburg in-

duced Lee to move Longstreet as far as Hagerstown. The evening of September 11 found him in
bivouac there, while D. H. Hill at Boonsborough
guarded the upper end of Pleasant Valley. Stuart
was as yet east of the South Mountain, holding in
check the advance of McClellan. The same evening
marked Jackson's bivouac beyond the Potomac; his
infantry held the railroad, and the cavalry had drawn
the toils about Martinsburg. The morning of September 12, the hour appointed by Lee, saw Jackson in position at Martinsburg with all the Federal
troops corralled at Harper's Ferry. Pleasant Valley
was the camping-place of McLaws on the night
of September 11. He had marched behind Longstreet and the ordnance trains as far as Middletown,
hence his progress was retarded. Daybreak of September 12 saw McLaws advancing to attack the
Maryland Heights, but the ledges of rock and dense
undergrowth prevented a vigorous assault. Walker's
brigades were across the river at Point of Rocks on
the morning of the 11th. That entire day, they remained in camp to rest; the morning of the 13th
brought them only to the foot of the Blue Ridge,
and the morning of the 14th saw Walker's guns in
position on the Loudoun Heights.

Lee was engaged in a difficult game on the military chessboard. At Hagerstown on the 12th he
awaited reports concerning Harper's Ferry. In a
letter to President Davis, on that day, he expressed
anxiety concerning food and clothing for his men.
September 13 found him still waiting for news
from Walker and McLaws. To the latter he wrote,

" Jackson will be at Harper's Ferry by noon to-day." The depletion of the army by straggling now began to oppress Lee, and he sent this message to the President: " Our ranks are very much diminished—I fear from a third to one half of the original numbers."

The afternoon of Saturday, September 13, brought news of McClellan's rapid approach toward the Boonsborough mountain-pass. The morning of that day had given to McClellan, in Frederick, a copy of Lee's order (No. 191) outlining the campaign. Two copies had been sent to D. H. Hill, since Hill had been previously made subject to Jackson's commands. The copy of the order received by Hill at Frederick and displayed by him after the close of the war was in Jackson's handwriting. The copy sent to Hill directly from Lee's headquarters was left in the camp by a careless subordinate; a Federal soldier discovered it wrapped about some Confederate cigars. McClellan saw at a glance Lee's entire plan. At once he hastened his main body toward Boonsborough in pursuit of Lee. Franklin's corps was urged toward Crampton's gap to harass McLaws and bring relief to Harper's Ferry. At the close of this day, therefore, Lee was pushing D. H. Hill back again to the defence of his rear, while McLaws was urged to expedite his operations and to join Lee with speed *via* Sharpsburg.

Sunday morning, September 14, as Lee was moving Longstreet's brigades from Hagerstown to Boonsborough, he was greeted with the roaring of heavy guns from the entire eastern and southern

horizon. Upon the mountain's crest near Boonsborough, Hill's five thousand men were wrapped in
the smoke of battle; until the middle of the afternoon they held Fox's Gap against the onset of
Reno's corps.   At three o'clock the corps of
Hooker fell upon Hill's left near Turner's Gap,
north of the National road.   Eight of Longstreet's
brigades, four thousand men, now gave aid to Hill.
The battle raged in both gaps until the coming of
the darkness, and the nine thousand Confederates
continued to hold the mountain-top in the face of
twenty-eight thousand Federal soldiers.

Six miles to the southward from Turner's Gap,
another battle raged that afternoon, in Crampton's
Gap.   Franklin sent his advance column of eight
thousand to drive McLaws's rearguard of twelve hundred men from the summit.   The hour of darkness
brought   complete   success   to   the   Federal force.
Franklin planted his banner on the mountain's crest,
and McLaws now seemed to be imprisoned in Pleasant Valley.   The Sunday afternoon had likewise
borne to Lee's ears the sound of guns from the direction of Harper's Ferry, giving indication that this
fortress had not yet fallen.   So steep and rocky were
the sides of the Maryland Heights, that mid-day of
the 14th came and passed ere the guns of McLaws
were ready to respond to Jackson's signals to begin
the battle.

The outlook was not cheerful as Lee stood on
South Mountain in the gathering darkness of September 14.   Over half his army, in three separate
divisions, was more than a dozen miles away.   The

two divisions under his own direction were not all in line together, and his position was assailed in front and on both flanks by McClellan's main body. At 8 o'clock in the evening, September 14, Lee wrote this order to McLaws: " The day has gone against us, and the army will go by Sharpsburg and cross the river. It is necessary for you to abandon your position to-night. . . . Your troops you must have in hand to unite with this command which will retire by Sharpsburg." But McLaws bravely held his post and began to array his troops in line across the Pleasant Valley to withstand the advance of Franklin. His guns were ready to open on Harper's Ferry with the dawning of the following morning. Lee's forces in the South Mountain passes had won a day's time from McClellan, and had thus secured the sucess of the movement against Harper's Ferry, although Lee, as yet, knew it not.

At daybreak on the morning of the 15th, Lee stood in the roadway on the crest of the ridge at Sharpsburg, directing his forces to positions on the right and left of the turnpike as they retired from Boonsborough. Noonday brought him a note from Jackson, written at an early morning hour : " Through God's blessing, Harper's Ferry and its garrison are to be surrendered." Not until the receipt of this news, with the additional knowledge that " Stonewall " was making all speed to join him, did Lee determine to stand and give battle at Sharpsburg. At 2 P.M. of the 15th, the advanced troopers of McClellan's great host were watering their horses in the Antietam Creek, and Lee was posting his twelve thousand with their batteries on the Sharpsburg hills. In deciding to stand and deliver battle, with his divisions still widely separated, Lee was passing almost beyond precedent in the matter of courageous daring.

With cautious step and slow, McClellan came across the South Mountain into the Antietam valley. Signal flags were waving throughout the day from remote summits; the Federal cavalry snuffed at Lee's banners from afar, and McClellan's long-range guns began to creep into position on the bluffs east of the Antietam, and there exchanged greetings with the Confederate cannon. McClellan was bringing forward in his main column about sixty thousand men. Franklin and Couch, with twenty thousand men, he had left in Pleasant Valley confronting McLaws's line of battle. Franklin spent this beautiful Monday in reconnoitring the position of McLaws and in sending despatches to McClellan to the effect that the Confederate force there, only six thousand in fact, outnumbered his own Federal troops " two to one "! McClellan passed away the morning hours in his rearguard bivouac, sending telegrams to Washington made up of such alliterative phrases as " routed rebels," " perfect panic," and " flying foe!" McClellan's foeman stood defiant all that day at Sharpsburg with his meagre line of troops, only about twelve thousand men of every arm.

Lee well knew that his other divisions were soon to reach him. Already Jackson was in full march from Harper's Ferry. "Stonewall" had not paused to feast his eyes on the captive garrison and the

seventy-three heavy guns and other spoil of war
left in charge of A. P. Hill. His footsore veterans
were on the march before the surrender was completed. A brief respite on the way gave time to
cook and eat, and then a forced march during a part
of the night brought Jackson with six thousand men
to Lee's bivouac at an early hour on September
16. J. G. Walker's thirty-two hundred men came
just behind "Stonewall." Lee stood in the Boonsborough roadway, on the hill-top at Sharpsburg as
Jackson and Walker approached. There was joy in
the face of the Confederate chieftain as he gave
cordial greeting and congratulation to his lieutenants. Complete confidence now marked Lee's words
and actions when Jackson stood with him once
again. Walker thus refers to Lee at this hour:

" Anxious enough no doubt, he was ; but there was nothing in his
look or manner to indicate it. On the contrary, he was calm, dignified and even cheerful. If he had had a well-equipped army of a
hundred thousand veterans at his back, he could not have appeared
more composed and confident. On shaking hands with us, he simply
expressed his satisfaction with the result of our operations at Harper's Ferry, and with our timely arrival at Sharpsburg ; adding that
with our reinforcement, he felt confident of being able to hold his
ground until the arrival of the divisions of R. H. Anderson, McLaws
and A. P. Hill."

To President Davis on the same day, Lee referred
in the following terms to the result of the campaign:
" This victory of the indomitable Jackson and his
troops gives us renewed occasion for gratitude to
Almighty God for His guidance and protection."
September 16 brought McClellan to the front

at Keedysville.   As he peered through the heavy
fog and saw the men in gray jackets on the Sharpsburg ridges, the tone of his despatches was changed
from that of the day before, and he sent messages
concerning Lee's " strong force," and " strong position."   Most of the day he spent in arranging his
troops for the attack.   The afternoon marked the
advance of Hooker's corps across the upper Antietam against the left flank of the Confederate line of
battle.   The corps of Mansfield also moved across
the creek to give support to Hooker.

Lee's army now stood on the defensive along the
ridges between Sharpsburg and the Antietam Creek.
During the battle, the Confederate chieftain took
his station for the most part upon a ledge of rock
near the right-hand side of the Boonsborough road.
This rock, recently demolished by the Federal Government, was within the limits of the present Federal cemetery on the summit of the hill.   At first
he placed his men to defend the direct approaches
from the Boonsborough bridge in front and from
the Burnside bridge to the right.   The entire right
wing of his line of battle under Longstreet extended
from the turnpike about one mile to the southward
where a cluster of heavy guns faced the Antietam
on a bold spur below the Burnside crossing.   The
left wing of the Confederate line, extending northward from this turnpike, consisted of D. H. Hill's
five brigades and Hood's two brigades, on Hill's
left.   Hood was posted in the woods west of the
Dunkard Church to defend the approach offered by
the Hagerstown turnpike.   The advance of Hooker

across the Williamsport bridge, far up the Antietam,
was reported by the cavalry to Lee in Sharpsburg.
He was in council over a map in an old house with
Jackson and Longstreet.   At once Jackson was sent
forward late in the afternoon of the 16th, to rule the
entire battle of the left wing.

When Jackson stood in the roadway at the Dunkard Church, he was in the central field of the approaching conflict.   A broad plateau with rolling
surface was spread out for some distance on every
side.   Behind Jackson to the southward ran the
Hagerstown turnpike along the summit of the ridge;
and just one mile from the Church this road reached
Sharpsburg.   To the northward from the Church,
through the midst of the rolling plateau, ran this
same Hagerstown road.   On the western side of
the roadway stood a forest of oaks, known in this
battle as the West Wood.   At the Church this forest
skirted the turnpike, but two hundred yards northward the woods fell away to leave room for a grass-
field at the roadway's edge.   On the eastern side of
the turnpike, and north of the Church, the central
space was held by a large field of ripening corn,
skirted by broad grass-plots.   These fields had as a
common eastern boundary an irregular forest, known
as the East Wood.   The two tracts of forest, the
West Wood and the East Wood, with the corn and
grass lands lying between them, were to witness
the most formidable blows of McClellan in his vain
attempt to drive Lee from the hills of Sharpsburg.

At 5 P.M., on September 16, Jackson arrayed
his line of muskets facing northward, across the

turnpike, seven hundred yards beyond the Dunkard
Church. In the cornfield on the eastern side of the
turnpike were the brigades of Hood and Law, seventeen hundred muskets. Howitzers were posted in
the open ground, and Law's right was advanced to
the East Wood. Across the open field, behind a
group of stacks on the western side of the turnpike,
with its left in the West Wood, stood the Stonewall
division under J. R. Jones. These sixteen hundred
muskets were arrayed in two lines of battle, with
Poague's battery on a knoll in front. Early's
brigade in the West Wood gave strength to the left
flank, while the brigade of Hays stood behind Early.
The brigades of Lawton and Trimble went into
bivouac in the woods around the Church. A commanding hill, beyond the West Wood to Jackson's
left, was crowned by Stuart's artillery, while the
horsemen hovered about the flank.

The sunset rays were gleaming upon Hooker's
muskets as his corps advanced along the ridge
southward against Jackson. A Federal battery ran
forward and at the distance of five hundred yards
opened fire on Jackson's left; but Poague silenced
the guns in twenty minutes. Hooker's skirmishers
advanced into the East Wood, where Law's veterans grappled with them and drove them back to the
edge of the forest. Darkness fell, and both contest-
ants rested on the field to await the coming of the
dawn. For three days the brigades of Hood and
Law had not tasted bread; they had subsisted on
green corn with only a " half ration of beef for
one day." Under cover of night they were with-

drawn to the West Wood to prepare food; the brigades of Lawton and Trimble took their place.

Lee could now discern McClellan's plan to overwhelm the Confederate left.   Hooker's advance was only the prelude to the assault of the three corps of Hooker, Mansfield, and Sumner, a combined force of forty thousand men.   If an advantage should be gained by these against Jackson's end of the line, McClellan proposed then to throw Burnside across the stream with thirteen thousand men against Longstreet's wing; this blow was to be followed, later, by the attack of Porter and Franklin with twenty-five thousand muskets against the Confederate centre.   Long-range guns were planted on the eastern bluffs of the Antietam to command the entire Confederate line of battle.   McClellan revealed his plan to assault Lee's right by making Burnside's corps approach the lower bridge on the afternoon of the 16th.   The steep, wooded bank at the western end of this bridge was occupied by Toombs with about six hundred Georgian muskets. Lee ordered J. G. Walker to move his thirty-two hundred men at dawn of the 17th to the hill's crest in the rear of Toombs.   At the close of the 16th, Lee had nearly twenty-five thousand men of all arms to withstand McClellan's eighty-seven thousand; he sent urgent messages to McLaws, Anderson, and A. P. Hill to hasten forward their ten thousand.   With mutual confidence in each other and with grim determination, Lee and his hungry band made ready to hold the position.

As early as 3 o'clock on the morning of September 17, skirmishing began in the East Wood. Hooker pushed his corps of twelve thousand five hundred infantrymen against Jackson's front line of thirty-five hundred, and at 5.30 A.M., Shumaker's six Confederate batteries began the harvest of death. Meade commanded Hooker's central division; on his right Doubleday swept down both sides of the Hagerstown turnpike, and Ricketts gave support to Meade's left and rear. This force was supported by a battery of thirty guns posted on the hills near the turnpike in their rear and by the enfilading fire of twenty rifled guns beyond the Antietam. Fierce reply was roared by Jackson's cannon in the centre, by Stuart from the Nicodemus hill, and by S. D. Lee's twenty-six guns near the Church. In the East Wood and the contiguous cornfield, Lawton's men fought long and well in opposition to Meade and Ricketts. West of the turnpike the Stonewall division was forced back into the woods; Jones was wounded, and Starke fell dead as the battle swayed to and fro, but Grigsby rallied the men forward and Doubleday was repulsed. The left of Jackson's line thus remained firm. Against Lawton's right flank came Ricketts through the East Wood facing westward. Into the awful storm of fire that made the eastern cornfield a place of blood, rushed the brigade of Hays, five hundred and fifty muskets. Stubbornly the Confederates fought for every inch of ground; slowly they fell back from the field heaped with dead. With a wild yell, Hood's brigades rushed forward from the Church to stay the tide of Federal advance. Their breakfast was left uncooked by the campfires; in the midst of the corn their weight was thrown against Hooker. The wounded Lawton was borne out as Hood entered. On Hood's right three of D. H. Hill's brigades advanced from the Confederate centre and fell upon the flank of Ricketts near the Mumma house. Little resistance was made by Hooker's broken corps to this fresh onset; his brigades had been torn into fragments, and nearly one fourth of his men lay prostrate on the field. Hooker's shattered regiments found shelter with the Federal guns and with Mansfield's corps in the rear. One-half of Jackson's first line of battle lay in long rows upon the field, but he still stood defiantly awaiting the second Federal assault.

During the night Mansfield had led the old corps of Banks across the Keedysville bridge and encamped near J. Poffenberger's, a mile in Hooker's rear. At 7.30 A.M., three hours after the beginning of Hooker's battle, Mansfield's two divisions came upon the field, resting their right on the turnpike at Miller's, while their left was extended through the East Wood. In the wood and in the cornfield again did carnage reign. Hood's eighteen hundred and the eighteen hundred of Ripley, Colquitt, and Garland stood face to face with the fresh Federal force of seven thousand muskets. Mansfield fell in the beginning of the assault, and Williams took the baton. Hooker's troops had nearly all vanished from the plateau; his captains could not assemble as many as three hundred men of the First corps. The Twelfth corps had to face alone the awful crash of musketry that met them from the Confederate line.   Greene's division began to swing around on the Federal left and advanced in a westward course past the Mumma house toward the Church ; and from thence across the turnpike into the edge of the West Wood Greene forced his troops.   The Stonewall division and Stuart's guns paralysed the forward movement of the Federal right, and it did not cross the roadway.   The Twelfth corps was held in check, for the Federal troops had been fought until they were finished.   The corn in the eastern field was cut as with a knife, and the dead and wounded lay there in long heaps.   Jackson's corps had been forced back with the loss of half its numbers, but it was posted now in a strong fortress.   The ledges of rock, the trees and fences of the West Wood offered shelter to his wearied heroes, and there they still presented an unshaken front.   With seventy-six hundred muskets thus far in action, Jackson had met the successive onslaughts of nineteen thousand five hundred Federal infantry.   He had cut in pieces the two corps of Hooker and Mansfield, and had driven the survivors as stragglers from the field with the exception of Greene's division.   Grigsby and Stafford with only three hundred men of the Stonewall division retired from rock to rock, and still held the northern end of the West Wood, near Miller's house.   Early's brigade of one thousand faced eastward in the central portion of the wood. Stuart brought his guns to a hill-top nearer Jackson's line.

From early dawn Lee had watched the battle

around the Church. At the same time he kept an
eye on Burnside at the lower bridge. Along the
Sharpsburg ridge Lee had eighty heavy guns in
action against McClellan's batteries beyond the Antietam. The sky was obscured by the smoke of
cannon and bursting shells. The shouting of the
captains, the fierce yells of the Confederates, and
the sharp rattle of musketry made a pandemonium
of that Sharpsburg plateau. Lee stood alert on his
rock of observation, and prepared a counterstroke
against McClellan by hastening Walker, McLaws,
and a part of R. H. Anderson's division to the aid
of Jackson. Since early morning McLaws and Anderson had been giving rest, near Sharpsburg, to their
brigades, wearied by the night march from Maryland
Heights.

The hour of 8.30 A.M. brought the head of
Sumner's corps of eighteen thousand men across
the Antietam into the East Wood. Sedgwick's
division followed Sumner himself across the scene
of the morning's carnage. Sumner's spirit was not
cheered by the sight of many unwounded Federal
soldiers assisting wounded comrades to the rear.
This game of generosity was here played by
Mansfield's men in their desire to escape from the
Confederate front. Complete silence reigned on
Jackson's field. Hooker's corps had disappeared;
Greene's men in the edge of the West Wood were
incapable of further effort; Jackson was forming his
line for an advance. In three deployed brigades,
Sumner's division of six thousand soldiers stood in
the East Wood facing the bloody cornfield. The

three lines moved westward toward the Hagerstown road, and then directly across the turnpike into the open field north of the Church. As Sumner moved his brigades toward the West Wood, Stuart's guns poured in a torrent of shells, and Jackson's batteries raked his lines with canister. Immediately in Sumner's front stood the gallant Grigsby and his three hundred. All honour to these noble sons of Virginia. With the courage of lions they fought behind the ledges of rock and kept back the progress of Sumner's division until Lee and Jackson could set the battle in array for his annihilation. Hood's division at the Church was wrecked, and Hood sent S. D. Lee to tell the chief-commander that unless reinforcements were sent at once, the day was lost. S. D. Lee met General Lee approaching on horseback with one orderly, half-way between Sharpsburg and the Dunkard Church. Lee's wounded hand was in a sling, and the orderly was leading his horse, Traveller. Hood's message was delivered. General Lee quietly replied: " Don't be excited about it, Colonel; go tell General Hood to hold his ground; reinforcements are now rapidly approaching between Sharpsburg and the ford. Tell him that I am now coming to his support." A moment later General Lee pointed to McLaws's division then in sight and approaching at a double-quick.

Jackson sent Early's brigade through the West Wood south of the Church, and drove the greater part of Greene's command across the turnpike. As Early turned toward the north at the Church, he found himself on Sumner's left flank. Into the fight against Sumner rushed a new thunderbolt of war. Grigsby and Early were made strong by sixty-five hundred muskets under McLaws, G. T. Anderson, and Walker. A volcano of fire leaped from behind the rocks and oak-trees of the West Wood. Against Sumner's front, left flank, and rear the fierce Confederates, eight thousand strong, poured their volleys. Sumner's six thousand were in the field west of the turnpike. Nearly two thousand Federal soldiers fell where they stood. Sumner attempted to face his third line, the Philadelphia brigade, to meet the fire from the rear, " but the line," says Sumner, " moved off in a body to the right in spite of all the efforts that could be made to stop it." Sumner's biographer declares that this officer became " panic-stricken," and eagerly moved out along the turnpike to the northward with the fragments of his first and second lines to seek refuge with the Federal batteries. McLaws had come too late to swing around against the Federal right, and thus did Sumner escape destruction. The pillar of stone recently erected in this field to the Philadelphia brigade, marks the storm-centre of " Stonewall's " whirlwind of fire that sent panic into the hearts of the brigade, and terrorised their corps-commander.

As this division melted away from Jackson's front, at 9.15 A.M., French's division of Sumner's corps, between five and six thousand strong, was advancing to assault the Confederate left centre. French came up the hill in Sedgwick's rear, but at the East Wood he turned to the left and marched southward against D. H. Hill. The Bloody Lane leaves the

Hagerstown road just south of the Dunkard Church, and pursues a zigzag course in six directions toward the Boonsborough road. From the field near Roulette's house, D. H. Hill had sent the three brigades already mentioned against the left flank of Hooker and Mansfield. When Hill drew back from Sumner's advance he posted Rodes and Colquitt in the lane between the Hagerstown road and the Clipp gateway; to the right of Rodes he arrayed G. B. Anderson in the sunken lane as far as the hill-top at the second turning. Fifteen hundred muskets and a park of artillery made up this defensive band; from Hill's left to the West Wood stood fifteen hundred more from the commands of McLaws and Walker. Hill's wings formed a right angle with each other at the junction of the lane and the turnpike. Into this triangular ambuscade, advancing between the houses of Mumma and Roulette, came French's front brigade. Down upon the right flank of French rushed Hill's left wing from the Hagerstown road; their " sudden and terrible fire " sent French's men reeling backward in flight with heavy loss. French sent his next line to assail Anderson in the second portion of the lane, but the musketry of Rodes and Anderson hurled the entire division of French backward behind the crest of the hill. French's brigades were shattered, and one-third of his men lay prostrate. Richardson's division of Sumner's corps, six thousand strong, approached Hill's right, along the ridge's crest, at the second angle of the lane; at the same hour, eleven o'clock, came thirty-five hun-

dred men of R. H. Anderson's division to Hill's aid.
Lee was keeping watch over his centre, and it was
he who hastened this reinforcement through the
fields near the Piper house.   Richardson secured an
enfilade fire upon the Confederate line in the sunken
road near Clipp's house.   R. H. Anderson's brigades failed to check Richardson and were put to
flight.   Rodes was flanked, and Hill's entire line
was forced back to the Piper house.   The gallant
Hill brought up batteries, rallied his broken line,
and thrust Richardson back again toward the lane.
While Richardson wrestled with Hill at the hour of
noon, Franklin's corps clambered to the plateau.
Franklin thought to try his fortune in Jackson's
field, where an artillery battle was still in progress.
He filled the woods about Miller's house with Hancock's men, and advanced Irwin's brigade in a charge
against the West Wood at the Dunkard Church.
But the crash of Jackson's musketry sent Irwin
scampering back.

Lee from his post on the central summit still kept
watch over the battle of his left and centre.   As
Richardson urged his men against Hill, Lee sent
swift message to Jackson to make assault against
the Federal right flank.   Orders were also sent to
Walker to charge upon the line in front of the Church.
Jackson was ready to move upon the instant; Stuart's
guns were thrown out to test the Federal batteries,
and Stuart attempted to lead his cavalry up the
bank of the Potomac to turn the Federal line.   Mc-
Clellan's guns commanded this entire region as far
as the Potomac, and the movement could not be

made.   But the left wing and centre of Lee's army
at one o'clock stood with defiance ready to defend
the line of the Hagerstown road.   McClellan feared
to assail again the grim gray-jackets, lest he should
lose the entire field.

Since early morning at the lower bridge the six
hundred Georgians under Toombs had inspired caution in Burnside's corps.   Longstreet's guns spent
their fire in support of Toombs.   In a narrow wood
above the margin of the Antietam these riflemen
were stationed.   The steep bluff was like a fortress,
for it commanded the bridge and all its approaches.
With great gallantry, Sturgis led his Federal division
upon the bridge.   A heavy cannonade lent aid to
his bayonet charge.   All in vain.   The storm of
bullets from the sheltered Georgians kept back the
Federal advance during four hours of fierce battle.
Cool and determined were the six hundred, as they
drove back four separate storming parties.   Rod-
man's division sought a ford below the bridge;
Toombs was assailed in flank, and at one o'clock
Burnside's corps crossed the bridge.   Sturgis's
division had spent its strength at the bridge and
dropped behind.   An hour was consumed in arraying the corps for the advance against Lee's right
wing.   In spite of the approach of this formidable
force, Lee was then ordering Jackson to assault the
Federal right.   Couriers brought to Lee news of A.
P. Hill's rapid approach from Harper's Ferry.   Up
the steep ascent Burnside continued to advance.   A
Confederate battery became his spoil, and D. R.
Jones's division was broken and driven back to

Sharpsburg.   Three o'clock marked the full tide of Burnside's success against Longstreet, for Longstreet had only two thousand to set in array against twelve thousand.   But that hour brought A. P. Hill from the Boteler ford against Burnside's left flank. His thirty-four hundred men had marched seventeen miles in seven hours.   Like a clap of thunder they now burst upon the Federal brigades.   A circle of Confederate artillery fire crowned the crest of the hill and poured its storm upon the masses of the Federal troops; one-fifth of the latter were disabled. They could only break in flight to seek the shelter of their guns beyond the Antietam.

Against the actual assaults of about sixty thousand Federal soldiers, courageously and boldly delivered, Lee maintained his position in open, pitched battle with only thirty-five thousand men.   This small band of Confederates was weary from long marches and their only food during the day was plucked from the apple-trees that stood in the field of battle.   More than twenty-five thousand additional Federal soldiers by their presence on the field gave moral support to McClellan's attacks.   McClellan's battle was a failure; he was defeated with heavy loss in every movement.   The Confederate soldiers out-fought the Federal troops in fair conflict. Four of McClellan's corps were shattered, and the fragments deserted the scene of strife; they could not be collected for a renewal of the fight.   Both armies suffered vast losses.   Eight thousand Confederates, one-fourth of Lee's army, lay upon the field; many regiments, and even brigades, had wellnigh disappeared. McClellan's loss was about twelve thousand five hundred. The survivors on both sides sank down to rest where they had fought, amid the after horrors of the bloodiest field of the entire war.

Lee still held the line of the Hagerstown turnpike, and even yet the unconquerable Confederate soldiers were ready for battle. An hour after nightfall, according to the statement of S. D. Lee, General Lee summoned his chief officers to meet him on the roadway leading toward the Potomac. In quiet tone he asked each one as he came up, " General, how is it on your part of the line ? " " As bad as bad can be," said Longstreet. " My division is cut to pieces," replied D. H. Hill. " The greatest odds I have ever met . . . losses terrible," was Jackson's quiet response. Hood displayed great emotion, seemed completely unmanned, and declared that he had no division. General Lee with unwonted excitement exclaimed, " Great God! General Hood, where is your splendid division you had this morning ? " Hood replied, " They are lying on the field where you sent them." All of these officers, says S. D. Lee, suggested that General Lee should cross the Potomac before daylight. After an awful silence, Lee rising more erect in his stirrups, said: " Gentlemen, we will not cross the Potomac to-night. You will go to your respective commands, strengthen your lines; send two officers from each brigade towards the ford to collect your stragglers and get them up. Many others have come up. I have had the proper steps taken to collect all the men who are in the rear. If McClellan wants to fight in the morning, I will give him battle again. Go!" S. D. Lee, watching the group disperse, thought that he read in their countenances, " This is a rash conclusion, and we fear the Army of Northern Virginia is taking a great risk."

The moon came up over the mountains to cast her glow on the field where the dead, the dying, and the wearied were in bivouac in that place of unspeakable suffering. About five thousand Confederate stragglers came up during the night. The morning dawned upon the two lines face to face at short range with shotted guns in readiness. Both stood on the defensive. Silence reigned upon the long ridge. Not a gun was fired. Lee's spirit of combativeness became more and more aroused. He determined to attack the passive McClellan by sending Jackson and Stuart around the Federal right. He ordered Jackson to establish fifty heavy guns under S. D. Lee and crush the Federal batteries north of the Dunkard Church. When Jackson, Stuart, and S. D. Lee reported McClellan's right flank as impregnable, a shade of disappointment passed over General Lee's face, and he gave up the plan of assault.

The afternoon of September 18 brought news to Lee that Humphreys and Couch were advancing to support McClellan, and that the Pennsylvania militia was ready to swarm into Maryland. Under cover of the dense darkness, in good order, Lee crossed the Potomac into Virginia, and left not a waggon nor a gun behind him. He sent Stuart to the northern bank of the Potomac at Williamsport to assail McClellan's rear. McClellan raised not a hand to molest the march of the Confederates, for he did not discover their absence until the morning of September 19. Three Federal brigades crossed the Potomac in pursuit, and laid their hands on four Confederate guns. But they immediately suffered serious disaster from the division of A. P. Hill under the direction of Jackson. McClellan dared not attack Lee in Virginia, for the Federal army was despondent, and was daily growing weaker from straggling and desertion. The Potomac now held the two armies apart for a season of rest. McClellan began to demand more troops, and Lee began to besiege the authorities in Richmond for supplies of shoes for the army. To the anxious wife he sent this message soon after the battle:

"I have not laid eyes on Rob since I saw him in the battle of Sharpsburg going in with a single gun of his battery for the second time after his company had been withdrawn, in consequence of three of its guns having been disabled. Custis has seen him, and says he is very well and apparently happy and content. My hands are improving slowly, and with my left hand I am able to dress and undress myself, which is a great comfort. My right is becoming of some assistance, too, though it is still swollen and sometimes painful. The bandages have been removed. I am now able to sign my name. It has been six weeks to-day since I was injured, and I have at last discarded the sling."

Upon the field of Sharpsburg, Lee had held his position until he forced McClellan to stand on the defensive. As to the campaign of invasion, Lee's fears concerning the lack of equipments had been realised. The movement was not successful because Lee's army was depleted by the failure of barefooted thousands to march with him into Maryland. From his headquarters near Winchester, October 2, 1862, Lee issued the following address to his soldiers:

" In reviewing the achievements of the army during the present campaign, the commanding general cannot withhold the expression of his admiration of the indomitable courage it has displayed in battle and its cheerful endurance of privation and hardship on the march. Since your great victories around Richmond, you have defeated the enemy at Cedar Mountain, expelled him from the Rappahannock, and after a conflict of three days, utterly repulsed him on the plains of Manassas, and forced him to take shelter within the fortifications around his Capital. Without halting for repose you crossed the Potomac, stormed the heights of Harper's Ferry, made prisoners of more than 11,000 men and captured upward of seventy-five pieces of artillery, all their small-arms, and other munitions of war. While one corps of the army was thus engaged, the other insured its success by arresting at Boonsborough the combined armies of the enemy, advancing under their favourite general to the relief of their beleaguered comrades. On the field of Sharpsburg, with less than one-third his numbers, you resisted from daylight until dark the whole army of the enemy, and repulsed every attack along his entire front of more than four miles in extent. The whole of the following day you stood prepared to resume the conflict on the same ground, and retired next morning without molestation across the Potomac. Two attempts subsequently made by the enemy to follow you across the river have resulted in his complete discomfiture and being driven back with loss. Achievements such as these demanded much valour and patriotism. History records few examples of greater fortitude and endurance than this army has exhibited, and I am commissioned by the President to thank you in the name of the Confederate States for the undying fame you have won for their arms. Much as you have done, much more remains to be accomplished. The enemy again threatens with invasion, and to your tried valour and patriotism the country looks with confidence for deliverance and safety. Your past exploits give assurance that this confidence is not misplaced."

On the same day, Lee wrote thus of himself in response to a communication from President Davis:

"I wish I felt that I deserved the confidence you express in me. I am only conscious of an earnest desire to advance the interests of the country and of my inability to accomplish my wishes. The brave men of this army fully deserve your thanks, and I will take pleasure in communicating them."

CHAPTER X.

THE CAMPAIGN AND BATTLE OF FREDERICKS-BURG.

1862.

Y the waters of the Opequon in the lower Shenandoah Valley, the Army of Northern Virginia enkindled its campfires in September, 1862. The mellow autumn days brought rest and health, and the harvest-fields furnished bread. But the marching and fighting of the summer had left the men in rags, and now upon the bare earth they bivouacked, without shelter, awaiting a supply of shoes and blankets. The Commander-in-chief dwelt among his soldiers in a plain pole-tent. So thickly strewn with boulders was the ground about headquarters that horsemen found difficulty in making their approach. A farm-house stood near and offered shelter, but Lee's general orders forbade interference with private property, and this rule he first followed himself by sleeping under the thin canvas. No guard was on duty near his person; everything was arranged with neatness, but with the utmost simplicity. A small army-chest contained his entire private equipment of pewter plates, forks and spoons. A simple suit of plain grey cloth formed the outward apparel of the grave, courtly Virginian. Upon his person were displayed none of the insignia of rank except three stars upon each side of the collar of his coat. The grey slouch hat was in keeping with the unassuming dignity of the man. The hair was silvered; the lines in the brow were becoming deeper, but in the eye there was an intense glow which spake of the fire that slumbered within. The strong temper of a Washington was held under bit and curb. In moments when the patience was tried, the veins in Lee's temples would swell, the neck would twitch nervously, and a deep flush would crimson the forehead, to show that the will to control was stronger than the hidden passion. One of Lee's aides, W. H. Taylor, relates this incident:

" He had a great dislike to reviewing army communications; this was so thoroughly appreciated by me that I would never present a paper for his action unless it was of decided importance and of a nature to demand his judgment and decision. On one occasion, when an audience had not been asked of him for several days, it became necessary to have one. The few papers requiring his action were submitted. He was not in a very pleasant humour; something irritated him, and he manifested his ill humour by a little nervous twist or jerk of the neck and head peculiar to himself, accompanied by some harshness of manner. This was perceived by me, and I hastily concluded that my efforts to save him annoyance were not appreciated. In disposing of some cases of a vexatious character matters reached a climax; he became really worried, and, forgetting what was due to my superior, I petulantly threw the paper down at my side and gave evident signs of anger. Then in a perfectly calm and measured tone of voice, he said, 'Colonel Taylor, when I lose my temper don't you let it make you angry.' "

While encamped near Winchester, Lee received a visit from Colonel Garnet Wolseley and other English officers. One of these has recorded the following account of Lee at this time:

"Every one who approaches him does so with marked respect; although there is none of that bowing and flourishing of forage-caps which occurs in the presence of European generals; and while all honour him and place implicit faith in his courage and ability, those with whom he is most intimate feel for him the affection of sons to a father. Old General Scott was correct in saying that when Lee joined the Southern cause it was worth as much as the accession of twenty thousand men to the 'rebels.' Since then every injury that it was possible to inflict, the Northerners have heaped upon him. Notwithstanding all these personal losses [the pillage of Arlington], however, when speaking of the Yankees he neither evinced any bitterness of feeling nor gave utterance to a single violent expression, but alluded to many of his former friends and companions among them in the kindest terms. He spoke as a man proud of the victories won by his country, and confident of ultimate success under the blessing of the Almighty, whom he glorified for past successes and whose aid he invoked for all future operations."

A half-year's service as Commander in the field had brought Lee face to face with one of the great crises of the war. The prestige of victory was his; inadequate numbers alone prevented him from driving the flag of McClellan from the Maryland Heights and from winning peace beyond the Potomac. The zeal of the Northern people was waning; McClellan's army was growing weaker from desertion and straggling, when Mr. Lincoln boldly threw off the mask by proclaiming the emancipation of

Southern slaves as a military measure. In his Inaugural Mr. Lincoln declared that he had neither the " lawful right " nor the inclination " to interfere with the institution of slavery in the States where it exists." Lee's view of Lincoln's course was thus expressed officially to President Davis:

> " The military Government of the United States has been so perfected by the recent proclamation of President Lincoln, which you have no doubt seen, and civil liberty so completely trodden under foot, that I have strong hopes that the conservative portion of that people, unless dead to the feelings of liberty, will rise and depose the party now in power."

With complete lack of personal resentment toward any individual in the North the above opinion was set forth, for two days later Lee was asking permission of the Confederate Government to return the Federal officer Kearney's sword and horse to his widow " as an evidence of the sympathy felt for her bereavement and as a testimony of the appreciation of a gallant soldier."

All the resources of the South were needed to meet the openly declared war of social reconstruction as well as of conquest announced by the Federal Administration. Lee gave every energy to the task of calling all the forces of the South into the field. In the midst of these manifold labours, the father's heart was wrung with anguish by the death of a beloved daughter. The spirit of the man in personal trial shines forth in the message sent to the mourning home-circle: " But God in this, as in all things, has mingled mercy with the blow in selecting that one best prepared to leave us.   May you be able to join me in saying, ' His will be done.' "

From Winchester Lee besieged the Richmond authorities with letters asking ammunition and supplies of clothing, and urging the Government to recruit the army.   " The number of barefooted men," he wrote, " is daily increasing, and it pains me to see them limping over the rocky roads."   He asked that proper arms be imported from Europe for the cavalry.   The stragglers began to flock to their old regiments.   From Leesburg alone came ten thousand barefooted veterans, and some new soldiers marched to the front.   The Confederacy had begun already to wrestle with that economic problem which was to overwhelm it in the end.   From the army and the country, shoemakers were detailed and set to work that the soldiers might be shod.   It soon transpired that blankets were not to be obtained in all the South; therefore the shivering Confederates all the more sternly resolved to capture them from the enemy.   The financial scheme of a paper currency, issued on the credit of the Confederacy, began also to work ruin.   The inflation of prices foreboded commercial disaster to the Southern commonwealths.   Shoes were rated at fifty dollars per pair, and salt was sold for one dollar and ten cents a pound.   These financial and economic difficulties were greater obstacles in the way of Lee's success than all the Federal armies in the field.

Discipline in the Confederate army was tightened, and incapable officers were removed.   As corps-commanders over the two wings, Longstreet and

Jackson were appointed at Lee's suggestion. To the President he wrote as follows, concerning the latter:

" My opinion of the merits of General Jackson has been greatly enhanced during this expedition. He is true, honest, and brave ; has a single eye to the good of the service, and spares no exertion to accomplish his object."

When Lee's eldest son, G. W. C. Lee, brought messages from Richmond, he sought his father's headquarters near the centre of the camp, but found him in bivouac on the flank of the army, among the boulders near Longstreet's quarters. The latter had pitched his dwelling-place in a beautiful, shaded grass-plot. When asked the reason, General Lee replied: " General Longstreet is so slow. I am compelled to encamp near his headquarters, in order to hasten his movements." This practice Lee continued almost throughout the war. It was, no doubt, his high estimate of Longstreet's ability on the immediate field of battle that led Lee to retain him as permanent commander of the First corps.

The gallant Stuart kept close watch upon McClellan. The saddle seemed to be his constant home, and his eye appeared never to sleep along the forty-mile line of pickets that guarded the mouth of the valley. An humble Christian of joyous temperament was this bold Virginian knight. To the accompaniment of Sweeney's banjo, he sang merry camp-songs as he rode slowly along. Often he would dash at full speed through the bivouac of the infantry, shouting the wild refrain, " Jine the cavalry."

With Stuart on guard at the front, Lee's army was always safe from surprise.

One week after Sharpsburg, Lee was sending the suggestion to Loring to press forward from the Kanawha through Morgantown into Pennsylvania, in the hope that a combined movement might be made in that direction. To Davis he wrote, September 25:

"In a military point of view, the best move, in my opinion, the army could make would be to advance upon Hagerstown and endeavour to defeat the enemy at that point. I would not hesitate to make it even with our diminished numbers, did the army exhibit its former temper and condition."

The former temper of the soldiery was rapidly restored. Military enthusiasm glowed around the brightening campfires, and to this was added a deep and growing religious sentiment. The Confederate chaplains were untiring in their labours. Each night found eager groups of men gathered in wooded glades, lending earnest attention to the appeals of these men of God. Among the men were often seen Lee and Jackson, with heads bowed reverently in prayer. In many brigades, increasing numbers accepted the Christian faith, and thus began that widespread interest in religion that rendered the Army of Northern Virginia more than the equal of Cromwell's Ironsides in piety and in fighting qualities.

The opening days of October marked great increase in the muster-rolls of the two armies that were keeping watch upon each other across the Potomac.

Lee was still more than overmatched in numbers by McClellan, but the Confederate General had the strong desire that the Army of the Potomac should be led into the Valley. McClellan showed no disposition as yet to set his soldiers in battle array. Therefore Lee despatched Stuart with eighteen hundred troopers in quest of information concerning McClellan's plans. Across the river above Williamsport dashed the Confederate cavalry, and October 11 dawned upon them in Chambersburg. Over the mountain to Cashtown marched Stuart; thence he moved southward and passed between the Federal army and Washington. Mid-day of October 12 saw the Confederate horsemen on the southern bank of the Potomac eighty miles distant from Chambersburg, while Pleasanton's troopers were left panting with exhaustion on the Maryland shore at the end of a fruitless chase. This ride of Stuart secured fresh horses for his corps, furnished Lee with information as to McClellan's position, and aroused the Federal Administration. The latter soon stirred McClellan into activity; and he moved the head of his column along the eastern base of the Blue Ridge; a guard being posted in each gap of the ridge as the army passed it, in order to secure the right flank from surprise. Lee guessed McClellan's objective point to be Richmond. Instantly he moved Longstreet's corps eastward across the mountain. November 6, the day of McClellan's arrival in Warrenton, found the Confederate chieftain with Longstreet at Culpeper Court House. McClellan began to reach out from Warrenton toward the upper

Rappahannock, but Jackson yet remained in the valley on the Federal flank at the western outlet of the Manassas Gap. Lee's two wings were sixty miles apart; while McClellan was seeking to strike one of Lee's two lines of communication, Jackson was ready to rush between the Federal army and Washington as in the campaign against Pope.

The defence of Richmond, as the chief requisite in any strategic plan, bound fast the hands of Lee. Jackson was eager to spring through the passes of the ridge and fall upon McClellan's flank and rear. Lee was just as eager that such a blow should be delivered, or that Jackson should move into Maryland and call the Federal force again north of the Potomac. But a strategic manœuvre was out of the question in the face of the political and economic necessity which Lee felt constrained to set before his lieutenant: '' You must keep always in view the probability of an attack upon Richmond from either north or south, when a concentration of forces will become necessary.'' For the defence of his cannon foundry and central commissary, and in behalf of the sentiment that regards the Capital as the country's citadel, the Confederate leader was forced to give up his vantage-ground in the mountains and to stretch out his thin lines as a shield in front of Richmond.

'' As long as General Jackson can operate with safety,'' said Lee, '' and secure his retirement west of the Massanutton Mountains, I think it advantageous that he should be in position to threaten the enemy's flank and rear, and thus prevent his advance southward on the east side of the Blue Ridge. General Jackson has been directed accordingly, and, should the enemy descend into the Valley, General Longstreet will attack his rear and cut off his communications. The enemy, apparently, is so strong in numbers that I think it preferable to attempt to baffle his designs by manœuvring, rather than to resist his advance by main force. To accomplish the latter without too great risk and loss, would require more than double our present numbers."

In order to be able to operate on either side of the Blue Ridge, Lee established two lines for the transmission of supplies—one through Culpeper and the other through Staunton. His antagonist, McClellan, now commanded one hundred and twenty-five thousand men between Manassas and the Rappahannock; eighty thousand were in the defences of Washington, and twenty-two thousand were near Harper's Ferry. Lee's numbers were short of seventy-two thousand.

At Warrenton, McClellan was removed from command, and Burnside entered the military arena with plans for a swift flank movement through Fredericksburg upon Richmond. On November 15 the Federal advance was pushed toward the lower Rappahannock; Stuart's vigilance made known to Lee this movement, and Lee's sagacity was easily equal to the task of divining the Federal plan of campaign. Before Burnside's pontoon bridges could be brought to his army encamped on the Stafford Heights, Lee had thrown Longstreet's corps from Culpeper to Fredericksburg, and on November 22 stood intrenched upon the heights south of the town, ready to dispute the passage of the Rappahannock. Jackson left behind him in the Valley the wreckage of the Baltimore and Ohio railroad, and a wide-spread consternation in the North as to his whereabouts, and in a march of forty-eight hours, pressed through the mountain-passes as far as Orange Court House. Among Lee's last orders at Culpeper was the commander's protest against the vice of gambling in the army. " It was not supposed," ran the order, " that a habit so pernicious and demoralising would be formed among men engaged in a cause, of all others, demanding the highest virtue and purest morality in its supporters." One week later at Fredericksburg the great Christian soldier, unmoved by the danger from Burnside's parks of artillery, was stirred by the conduct of the people of Fredericksburg. Without a murmur they yielded their town as a battle-field, and took up their abode in barns and brush-huts. Lee has left on record the following tribute: " History presents no instance of a purer and more unselfish patriotism, or a higher spirit of fortitude and courage, than was evidenced by the citizens of Fredericksburg." In a letter to his wife, he said: " I tremble for my country when I hear of confidence expressed in me. I know too well my weakness, and that our only hope is in God."

Lee had at first resolved to make a stand behind the North Anna River. This policy was also advocated by Jackson. But the Richmond authorities were anxious to save Virginia's territory from devastation, and Lee acquiesced in the plan of establishing his army on the southern bank of the Rappahannock. Herein we observe the fatal defensive policy pursued by the Confederate Administration.   Hitherto, the Federal armies in Virginia had been defeated so near to their base of supplies on the Potomac and the James, that the Confederates could not reach the flank and rear of the routed enemy to accomplish their destruction.   In December, 1862, the Confederate Government held the corn crops between the Rappahannock and North Anna rivers to be of more importance than the strategic advantage of luring Burnside as far as the Anna, where a Federal defeat, so far from water communication, would most probably result in the destruction of the Army of the Potomac.

Jackson was brought at once from Orange, and D. H. Hill's division was set to watch the lower river at Port Royal; Ewell's division under Early took position at Skinker's Neck; the divisions of A. P. Hill and Taliaferro went into camp near the railroad in readiness to give support to D. H. Hill or Longstreet.   Amid the falling snow of the early December days the Army of Northern Virginia stood ready behind their guns on the hills fringing the plain of Fredericksburg.   Nearly three thousand Confederate soldiers were still barefooted; many were without muskets, and still more destitute of blankets.   Yet Lee wrote of his band of seventy-two thousand, that it " was never in better health or in better condition for battle than now."   Upon the Stafford Heights stood Burnside's host of one hundred and sixteen thousand men and three hundred and fifty heavy guns.   Burnside supposed that all of Jackson's corps was at Port Royal, eighteen miles from Fredericksburg.   He therefore decided to cross the Rappahannock at Fredericksburg, and to move immediately toward Richmond, between the wings of Lee's army.   Provisions for twelve days were assigned to the Federal army as its portion until supplies should be drawn in the Confederate Capital!

Through the dense fog, at the dawning of December 11, two Confederate guns boomed out the signal calling Lee's men to arms.   The Federal bridge-builders were advancing to the river's edge to float their pontoons for the passage of Sumner at Fredericksburg and Franklin near the mouth of Deep Run.   One hundred and forty-three wide-mouthed guns, planted in a line of three and one half miles, began to roar defiance to the Southern soldiers from the Stafford Heights.   Defiance was hurled back by the Mississippi riflemen under Barksdale posted on the southern bank of the Rappahannock.   Behind the river-bluffs, in cellars and behind houses, these marksmen were sheltered.   Their unerring aim brought down the foremost Federal bridge-makers and drove the rest in panic.   Until the middle of the afternoon Barksdale held his dangerous position and thwarted nine different attempts to float the pontoons.   At length the great batteries were turned upon the houses and bluffs that gave shelter to Barksdale's men.   Flame and smoke and battle-yell made the river-bank a pandemonium.   An assaulting party of infantry under cover of the iron storm moved across in boats, but darkness had come at the hour when Burnside won passage into the town of Fredericksburg.   Lee at once sent request to Jackson for aid, and the morning of December 12 saw A. P. Hill and Taliaferro moving into position at Longstreet's right.   D. H. Hill and Early continued to watch the lower river.   Lee supposed that the movement at Fredericksburg was only a feint. The heavy fog of the morning of the 12th veiled the passage at the Deep Run bridges of forty-five thousand five hundred muskets, and one hundred and sixteen guns under Franklin, and of thirty-one thousand under Sumner at Fredericksburg. When the noonday sun shone upon the glittering Federal array, Lee saw Burnside's plan to make direct assault, and at once he called Jackson's remaining divisions to the field and made ready for battle.   During the night D. H. Hill marched eighteen miles and took position at the dawn of the 13th. It was in Burnside's thought to surprise Lee by a quick assault against the Confederate right at Hamilton's Crossing, three miles below Fredericksburg. But Jackson's swift feet brought his entire corps face to face with Franklin on the early morning of December 13.   A. P. Hill's division of ten thousand men was drawn up to form Jackson's first and second lines, twenty-six hundred yards in length. Fourteen heavy guns were planted on his right and thirty-three guns on his left, near Deep Run. Stuart pushed his horsemen in advance of Jackson's right flank.   Behind these two lines stood Early and Taliaferro; D. H. Hill was in reserve to the right rear.   A. P. Hill's front line was two hundred yards in rear of the railroad, along the wooded brow of a slight declivity.   The continuity of this front was broken by a marshy jungle, somewhat triangular in shape, projecting its wooded face into the plain toward the river.

From Deep Run on Jackson's left the divisions of Longstreet held position along the line of hills as far as the Rappahannock above Falmouth. Hood and Pickett held the central field between Deep Run and Hazel Run; R. H. Anderson occupied the extreme left, touching the river, while Ransom and McLaws were posted to defend the salient of Marye's Hill. Like a great fortress this plateau stood in the centre of Lee's left wing, its summit bristling with the guns of the Washington artillery and its flanks guarded by Alexander's guns. The Confederate position was stronger on the left; on the right there was an open field in front of Jackson's corps.

Burnside ordered Franklin to begin the battle against the Confederate right. Federal reinforcements had continued to cross the river. The heavy fog of the morning concealed the deployment of the Federal troops, but the sunshine broke through in the middle of the forenoon and laid bare to the Confederates the mighty panorama of war. In all the pomp and circumstance of spectacular array, with fluttering flags, polished gun-barrels, and bright-coloured uniforms, fifty-five thousand Federal soldiers were marching across the plain to attack the corps of Jackson. Lee took his station on a hill near the left centre of his line, since called Lee's Hill. The deep, luminous glow was in the eye of the chieftain as he gave orders, in quiet tone, for the array of battle. Stretching away to his left he could discern the line of Longstreet, partly fortified, eager for the fight; but Sumner had not yet thrust his head outside of the town. To Lee's right were Jackson's ragged veterans without fortifications, except the woods in which they lay concealed. Jackson's skirmishers were stationed behind the railroad embankment. Lee and Jackson both manifested eager expectancy as they rode toward Hamilton's Crossing, to watch the first exchange of blows.

Meade came bravely onward toward the railroad, leading forty-five hundred men in threefold line of battle. Far to Jackson's front and right Stuart sent Pelham with one Napoleon gun. Fairly upon the Federal left flank he planted his piece. Straight along Meade's front line Pelham began to fire his solid shot. Five Federal batteries ran out to defend the Federal flank and Pelham had to retire, but the advance of Meade's division was checked nearly one hour. During the rest of the day, Doubleday's entire division was kept on guard facing down the Rappahannock to prevent the repetition of the daring gunnery. As Lee watched the effect of the cannon-shot, he is reported to have said to Jackson, "You should have a Pelham on each flank." At the same time, however, he said that Pelham began his fire too soon, and thus halted Meade too far away from the Confederate line of infantry.

Meade moved forward again to the assault after eleven o'clock. Jackson's batteries destroyed his left brigades, and the Federal advance was driven back in dismay before they came within rifle range

of the woodland that concealed the Confederate infantry.   When Lee now saw Jackson's full batteries
paralyse Franklin's initial effort, he turned his personal attention to Longstreet's front.   At 11 A.M.
Sumner was ready to despatch a division across the
open field against Marye's Hill.   At that hour a
great artillery duel began to belch out the flame and
smoke of four hundred guns across the Rappahannock valley.   One and a half hours these cannon
continued to hurl their shell and solid shot while
Hooker was hastening two divisions to the aid of
Franklin for the grand assault upon Jackson at 1
P.M., and while Sumner was offering up a vain sacrifice of blood in front of Longstreet's veterans.
Marye's Hill looks down upon the plain at Fredericksburg that now became a field of blood.   Around
the base of the hill runs the Telegraph road.   This
roadway was sunk below the surface of the earth
to the depth of four feet, and was bordered on
each side by a solid stone wall.   A broad rifle-pit
was thus furnished to the Confederates at the base
of a high plateau crowned with artillery.   From hills
to the right and the left a cross-fire of heavy guns
was directed upon the sloping fields in front.   Two
thousand riflemen from Georgia and North Carolina
under T. R. R. Cobb held the stone wall.   The fire
of these men, assisted by a line on the brow of the
hill and by the artillery, sent havoc into every Federal line of assault.

French's division of Sumner's corps advanced
from the river along two parallel streets of Fredericksburg, and about eleven o'clock looked across

the terraced plain toward the Confederate parapet.
Over the canal bridges they advanced in two
columns. Behind the first embankment near the
canal the two columns were swung around into line
of battle, and onward they came in brigade front
with intervals between the brigades of two hundred
yards. A fierce fire from the long-range guns on
the Stafford Hills lent support to the assault. The
guns from the Marye Hill crest had point-blank
range; from Stansbury's Hill and Lee's Hill, a
cross-fire of shot and shell was poured upon the
brave Federal brigades. Cobb's muskets behind
the wall blazed out in a flame of fire, and the Federal lines went down one after another to redden the
field with their blood; twelve hundred men was the
tribute of dead and wounded rendered up by
French's division. As Hancock's division came on
in gallant form, Ransom sent another regiment into
the sunken road eager to avenge the fall of the
chivalrous Christian, T. R. R. Cobb. With fierce
courage Hancock's brigades, in threefold line of
battle, faced the smoking cannon of the Marye
summit. The riflemen behind the wall reserved
their fire until the Federal line was just one hundred
paces distant; then the muskets spoke while the
Confederates rolled forth their yell of defiance.
Two thousand men left prostrate on the field furnished evidence to the deadly aim of the Confederate riflemen. Howard's division at one o'clock
moved out toward the deadly Confederate guns.
Kershaw took command in the sunken road, and
two regiments of South Carolinians and one from

North Carolina came with him, while the line on the brow of the hill was made stronger. Under their additional fire Howard's lines withered from the field; nearly seven hundred of his soldiers fell, and Sumner's men could fight no longer in this battle. Nine regiments in the sunken road and seven in reserve on the hill's crest had aided the artillery in visiting ruin upon the Second corps.

At one o'clock two great *corps d'armée* of sixty thousand men were advancing against Jackson's thirty thousand. Meade and Gibbon came in advance with bristling bayonets supported by the fire of fifty-one guns. They pressed through the gap made by the projecting tongue of marsh and broke A. P. Hill's first line of battle. The gallant Gregg of the second line gave up his life in the attempt to check the Federal tide. Disaster and bloody repulse fell to the lot of Meade and Gibbon at the hands of Early and Taliaferro. In confusion and dire disorder the Federal divisions were driven back beyond the railroad, with Trimble's brigade in hot pursuit. Their heavy guns were abandoned on the field. The Sixth Federal corps under Smith had kept respectful distance, and only made a noisy artillery battle against the Confederate centre. About two o'clock Lee was looking upon the flight of Franklin's shattered lines from Jackson's front, and at the same time saw Sturgis's division of the Ninth Federal corps set its face against the Marye Hill. A thousand blue uniforms were soon outstretched upon the field to tell the story of Sturgis's defeat.

Two o'clock came and passed. The sounds of strife began to die away on the Confederate right where Jackson had given a quietus to Franklin's grand-parade attack. Burnside was just then ordering Franklin to begin the battle anew, and Franklin was flatly disobeying the command. The latter had lost confidence, he declared, in his soldiers and in Burnside himself. Some of Sumner's men were still crouching under the embankments or hugging the plain in front of Marye's Hill. Lee stood in the midst of his men upon the crest, unmindful of the Federal shells. His presence added inspiration to his gunners, and the fire of enthusiasm leaped from heart to heart as the beloved leader passed in view. Alexander heard him say, " It is well war is so terrible or we would grow too fond of it."

Against Hooker's advice Burnside pushed the Fifth corps into the field already covered with the wreckage of the Second corps. Sheltered behind dead horses and dead men lay the scattered and terrorized Federal musketeers, who could not escape from the presence of the Confederate sharpshooters. Two regiments were brought to the base of the hill and two more to the crest by Ransom to face the advance of Humphreys's division. Alexander's guns now took the place of the Washington artillery on the Marye summit. The spirit of Humphreys was bold, and he pushed his men forward with bayonets fixed. A sheet of flame again enwrapped the base of Marye's heights, and the Federal soldiers fell like leaves. Human valour was not equal to the task laid upon the Federal regiments. One after

another the brigades of Humphreys broke and fled.
A storm of death roared from that hill-slope which
no organised body of men could face and live. Cool
and methodical were the veterans of Kershaw, Ransom, and Alexander as they visited death and wounds
upon one thousand men of this Federal division.
Hooker held Sykes in check to cover the retreat of
Humphreys, while Griffin's division rushed toward
the southern end of the stone wall. Carroll's brigade
was followed by one of Getty's in making this battle
strong. From five to six o'clock the fighting was
terrific; confusion and death reigned in all the Federal lines of assault. Night settled down upon
disaster and disorder in Burnside's right wing.
More than thirty thousand men from three different
corps had been launched against Longstreet's position; seven thousand men of Georgia and the Carolinas had kept them easily at bay. Not a Federal
soldier touched the stone fence, while eight thousand eight hundred lay prostrate on the field in front
of it.

Along the river-bank that night in shelterless
bivouac lay the disheartened Federal regiments.
Burnside made ready to renew the assault against
the Marye heights. But the morning brought the
universal opposition of his subordinate officers, and
he countermanded the order of battle. He waited
quietly until the storm of the night of the 15th gave
the Federal army a way of escape, and without
further harm they sought the northern bank of the
river. Twelve thousand six hundred and fifty-three
men Burnside left behind him, as the victims of

battle.   The Confederate casualties were five thousand three hundred and nine; the larger part of this
loss was in the corps of Jackson.

Into active conflict Burnside had sent more than
fifty thousand men; less than twenty thousand Confederates drew trigger in hurling them back.   No
breastworks offered the Confederates shelter along
Jackson's front.   The fierce valour of " Stonewall's "
men was unconquerable.   Like the grass before the
scythe Franklin's soldiers went down under the Confederate fire.   The ascent was not steep, the field
was open, and the Federal lines had great opportunity to crush Lee's right.   Franklin withheld his
men from slaughter after the grand assault of 1 P.M.
Burnside's attacks against Lee's left were made to
relieve the pressure against Franklin.   The valour
and buoyant spirit of the Confederate privates were
the chief factors that wrought out the great Confederate victory along the entire line.   Burnside
assigned as the reason for his defeat the fact that the
" enemy's fire was too hot "!

Lee was convinced that the attack would be renewed on the 14th.   Silence had just descended
upon the field of strife on the evening of December
13 when Lee sent the order to Jackson to despatch
immediately all the ordnance waggons to bring ammunition from Guinea depot.   To this order Lee
added these words: " I need not remind you to
have the ammunition of your men and batteries re-
plenished to-night and everything ready by daylight
to-morrow.   I am truly grateful to the Giver of all
victory for having blessed us thus far in our terrible

struggle. I pray He may continue it." Longstreet affirms that a Federal courier was captured with Burnside's order for renewed battle; otherwise, Lee might have made a counter assault against the town itself. But the guns on the Stafford hills, and the solid front displayed by Burnside's brigades, admonished him that heavy loss would follow a rash advance. Jackson was given permission to make a counterstroke against Franklin. At sunset he ordered all his batteries forward to shatter Franklin's line on the Richmond road. Stuart made a fierce attack against the Federal flank. But the fire from Franklin's one hundred field-guns, and from the batteries on the Stafford bluffs, compelled Jackson to abandon the movement. Jackson then desired to make a bayonet charge after nightfall, but Lee deemed this plan hazardous, and it was not attempted. Moreover, Lee's ranks were not full enough to justify offensive work; more men were needed, and yet upon the very day of battle there came a call for re-inforcements from his small army to aid in the defence of Wilmington, North Carolina. The different States were continually demanding the defence of all their borders, and thus the Confederacy was handicapped in the presence of the chief invading army. This constant local demand for soldiers from the chief armies to stand at the threshold of nearly every city and State must, to some extent, vindicate the policy of the dispersion of forces adopted by the Confederate Government.

December 16, immediately after Burnside's withdrawal, Lee wrote the following:

" I had supposed they were just preparing for battle, and was saving our men for the conflict. Their hosts crown the hill and plain beyond the river, and their numbers to me are unknown. Still, I felt a confidence we could stand the shock, and was anxious for the blow that is to fall on some point, and was prepared to meet it here. Yesterday evening I had my suspicions that they might return [to the Stafford Heights] during the night, but could not believe they would relinquish their hopes after all their boasting and preparation, and when I say that the latter is equal to the former, you will have some idea of the magnitude. This morning they were all safe on the north side of the Rappahannock. They went as they came—in the night. They suffered heavily as far as the battle went, but it did not go far enough to satisfy me."

Amid the snows and rains of December the two armies sat down to watch each other across the river. Burnside's men were sheltered in tents and had abundance, but Lee's soldiers were forced to build rude log-huts and booths of tree-branches to protect their nakedness from the biting cold. Man and beast in the Confederate service were placed on short allowance; yet the fire of enthusiasm was unquenchable in the bosoms of these heroes. The spirit of earnest religious zeal ran through the camp, and the voice of the chaplain was often heard in preaching and praying. Hundreds were led to accept the Christian faith. The Commander-in-chief thus penned to his wife the reflections brought by Christmas Day, 1862:

" I will commence this holy day by writing to you. My heart is filled with gratitude to Almighty God for the unspeakable mercies with which He has blessed us in this day, for those He has granted us from the beginning of life, and particularly for those He has vouchsafed us during the past year. What should have become of us without His crowning help and protection? Oh! if our people would only recognise it and cease from vain self-boasting and adulation, how strong would be my belief in final success and happiness to our country. But what a cruel thing is war; to separate and destroy families and friends, and mar the purest joys and happiness God has granted us in this world ; to fill our hearts with hatred instead of love for our neighbours, and to devastate the fair face of this beautiful world. I pray that on this day when only peace and good-will are preached to mankind, better thoughts may fill the hearts of our enemies and turn them to peace.

" Our army was never in such good health and condition since I have been attached to it. I believe they share with me my disappointment that the enemy did not renew the combat on the 13th. I was holding back all that day and husbanding our strength and ammunition for the great struggle for which I thought I was preparing. Had I divined what was to have been his only effort, he would have had more of it. My heart bleeds at the death of every one of our gallant men."

Before the year closed, Lee sent his cavalry on raiding expeditions to Burnside's rear as far as Fairfax and Occoquan. In January, the Federal commander entered upon his famous " Mud march." Up the Rappahannock as far as Banks's Ford he marched his men, but a storm began to beat upon him, and then through the deep mire the army plodded its way back to camp. At every crossing the Confederates stood ready for battle. They found amusement in erecting these signs, legible to Burnside's men: " Stuck in the mud!" " This way to Richmond!"

Anxiety for the upbuilding of the Confederate armies filled Lee's thoughts continually. To the Secretary of War, January 10, he wrote concerning " the absolute necessity " of increasing the forces in the field.

" The success with which our efforts have been crowned, under the blessing of God, should not betray our people into the dangerous delusion that the armies now in the field are sufficient to bring this war to a successful and speedy termination. . . . The great increase of the enemy's forces will augment the disparity of numbers to such a degree that victory, if attained, can only be achieved by a terrible expenditure of the most precious blood of the country. This blood will be upon the heads of the thousands of able-bodied men who remain at home in safety and ease, while their fellow-citizens are bravely confronting the enemy in the field, or enduring with noble fortitude the hardships and privations of the march and camp. . . . In view of the vast increase of the forces of the enemy, of the savage and brutal policy he has proclaimed [Emancipation Proclamation of January 1, 1863], which leaves us no alternative but success or degradation worse than death, if we would save the honour of our families from pollution, our social system from destruction, let every effort be made, every means employed, to fill and maintain the ranks of our armies, until God, in His mercy, shall bless us with the establishment of our independence."

When an officer suggested the formation of a battalion of honour, Lee replied:

" The fact is, General, we have now an army of brave men. The formation of a battalion of honour would reward a few and leave many, equally brave and equally faithful, unnoticed and, perhaps, with the feeling that an improper distinction had been made between themselves and their comrades."

During these months of snow and rain, the question of campaign plans filled a place in Lee's mind next to the questions of food and clothing for his army. On the one hand, he sent Longstreet's corps to find subsistence south of the James River. He received frequent reports that the dilapidated railroads could furnish to his men little corn and a daily ration of only one-fourth of a pound of bacon;

when April drew near he ordered his soldiers to gather a daily supply of " sassafras buds, wild onions, garlic, lamb's quarter, and poke sprouts!" On the other hand Lee was waging continual cavalry warfare against the enemy's communications. Imboden and Jones cut the main stem of the Baltimore and Ohio railroad. Stuart and his lieutenants made frequent dashes across the upper Rappahannock. March 3 found him writing as follows:

"Your poor mamma has been a great sufferer this winter. I have not been able to see her and fear I shall not. She talks of coming to Hickory Hill this month, when the weather becomes more fixed. We are up to our eyes in mud now, and have but little comfort. Mr. Hooker looms very large over the river. He has two balloons up in the day and one at night. I hope he is gratified at what he sees. Your cousin, Fitz Lee, beat up his quarters the other day with about four hundred of his cavalry, and advanced within four miles of Falmouth, carrying off one hundred and fifty prisoners with their horses, arms, etc. The day after he recrossed the Rappahannock, they sent all their cavalry after him . . . but the bird had flown. . . . I hope these young Lees will always be too smart for the enemy."

In February, Lee gave his opinion against a flank movement through Culpeper on account of " the liquid state " of the roads. In March, he was mourning the loss of the gallant Pelham, slain in battle against Federal cavalry "before he could receive the promotion he had richly won." In February, he was advising Secretary Seddon to stand ready to meet the foe in South Carolina, because it seemed " the true policy of the enemy now to apply his whole strength to take Charleston, and it is proper for us to expect him to do what he ought to do." In March again he was dealing as follows with the suggestion offered by General Trimble, to bridge the Rappahannock and surprise the enemy:

" I am much obliged to you for your suggestions presented in your letters of February and March. I know the pleasure experienced in shaping campaigns [and] battles, according to our wishes, and have enjoyed the ease with which obstacles to their accomplishment (in effigy) can be overcome. The movements you suggest in both letters have been at various times studied, canvassed with those who would be engaged in their execution, but no practicable solution of the difficulties to be overcome has yet been reasonably reached. The weather, roads, streams, provisions, transportation, etc., are all powerful elements in the calculation, as you know. What the future may do for us, I will still hope, but the present time is unpropitious, in my judgment. The idea of securing the provisions, waggons, guns of the enemy, is truly tempting and the desire has haunted me since December. Personally I would run any kind of risk for their attainment, but I cannot jeopardise this army."

From all the difficulties that beset him, Lee could turn aside to stimulate his army to offer up their prayers on the day set apart by President Davis:

" Soldiers ! no portion of our people have greater cause to be thankful to Almighty God than yourselves. He has preserved your lives amidst countless dangers ; He has been with you in all your trials ; He has given you fortitude under hardships, and courage in the shock of battle ; He has cheered you by the example and by the deeds of your martyred comrades ; He has enabled you to defend your country successfully against the assaults of a powerful oppressor. Devoutly thankful for His signal mercies, let us bow before the Lord of Hosts, and join our hearts with millions in our land in prayer that He will continue His merciful protection over our cause ; that He will scatter our enemies and set at naught their evil designs, and that he will graciously restore to our beloved country the blessings of peace and security."

CHAPTER XI.

THE CAMPAIGN AND BATTLE OF CHANCELLORS-
VILLE.

1863.

 HE year 1863 began with the proclamation of the policy of military emancipation on the part of the Federal
government. President Lincoln announced his purpose to destroy the
institution of slavery by force of arms, and this
purpose was presented to the Northern people as the
chief motive for a more zealous prosecution of the
war against the South. He proposed to change,
through the power of the sword, the entire social
and political basis of the Federal Constitution,
under the guise of alleged military necessity. This
social war was now to be waged by larger armies
than those previously mustered. Joseph Hooker
was placed in charge of the Army of the Potomac,
and in April, with a force of about one hundred and
thirty-four thousand men, he prepared to advance
across the Rappahannock against Lee's army of fifty-

three thousand. From Hamilton's Crossing down-
stream as far as Port Royal, Jackson kept watch
with thirty-three thousand men. From Jackson's
left as far as Banks's Ford stood McLaws with eight
thousand muskets; the fords of the river above were
guarded by Stuart's two thousand, seven hundred
horsemen supported by Anderson's eight thousand
infantrymen. The hill-tops along this extended
line were crowned with artillery. The remaining
brigades of Longstreet's corps were in winter quarters near Suffolk, south of the James River.

Hooker's scheme ran as follows: A great pretence
of crossing the river below the town will be made by
Sedgwick with three *corps d'armée;* at the same
time the other four corps must steal up the river to
Kelly's Ford. Suddenly these will cross and fall
upon the Confederate left flank and rout the Confederate army from the heights in front of Fredericksburg. Two weeks in advance of the infantry
movements, Stoneman was ordered to lead ten
thousand horsemen across the upper Rappahannock
against Gordonsville and the Fredericksburg railroad. On the southern bank of the Pamunkey
River, Stoneman was expected to intrench himself
in order to capture the Army of Northern Virginia
as Hooker should drive it into the toils!

The days that followed April 13 brought the descending rains, and upon the northern bank of the
Rappahannock, Stoneman waited until the river
should flow more gently, and Stuart should cease to
keep close watch. Lee's letter to Jackson, April
23, shows that he already divined Hooker's purpose:

"I think from the account given me by Lieutenant-Colonel Smith of the Engineers, who was at Port Royal yesterday, of the enemy's operations there, the day and night previous, that his present purpose is to draw our troops in that direction while he attempts a passage elsewhere. I would not, then, send down more troops than are actually necessary. I will notify Generals McLaws and Anderson to be on the alert, for I think that if a real attempt is made to cross the river it will be above Fredericksburg."

April 27 saw the abatement of the flood and three Federal corps under Slocum began to move up the stream. The morning of the 29th found this force across the Rappahannock in swift march toward the Ely and Germanna fords of the Rapidan. The same day marked the advance of Stoneman upon Culpeper, where Stuart stood on guard. Hooker's flanking column had thrust itself between Lee and his cavalry.

At the dawn of April 29, Lee was roused from his cot by J. P. Smith, Jackson's aide, with the news that Sedgwick was crossing the river near Hamilton's, below Fredericksburg. Lee playfully said to Smith: "Well, I thought I heard firing and was beginning to think it was time some of you young fellows were coming to tell me what it was all about. Tell your good general that I am sure he knows what to do. I will meet him at the front very soon." Such was Lee's message to Jackson. During the forenoon of the 29th, Stuart's message informed Lee of Hooker's passage at Kelly's Ford. Later in the day Stuart sent news of the two Federal columns approaching the Rapidan. It was evident that Hooker was aiming a blow at Lee's rear. The close of the day, therefore, found Lee sending

Anderson westward to meet Hooker and ordering Stuart to resist the Federal column near the Germanna Ford. At midnight, Anderson found Mahone and Posey at Chancellorsville falling back before Hooker's advance. His head of column had crossed the Rapidan. Anderson made intrenchments at the junction of the mine and plank roads near the Tabernacle Church on the morning of April 30.

On the night of April 29 Stuart was sending W. H. F. Lee with two regiments to oppose Stoneman's movement against Gordonsville, while he led Fitz Lee's brigade southward across the Raccoon Ford to keep in touch with the Confederate infantry. The next morning found him between Hooker and Fredericksburg, skirmishing with the vanguard of the Germanna column. The Fifth Corps under Meade was in bivouac at Chancellorsville. During the night of the 30th Stuart fought his way through the Federal cavalry, and rode *via* Todd's Tavern to join Lee. April 30 closed upon Hooker at Chancellorsville with fifty thousand men ready for battle. Eighteen thousand more were near at hand under Sickles. Over forty thousand under Sedgwick were threatening Lee's right wing on the Rappahannock below Fredericksburg. Hooker's thirteen thousand horsemen at the same time were advancing against Lee's railway communications. When Hooker thus discovered himself occupying the coveted position in the rear of Lee's army, he made proclamation to his soldiers, April 30, that " our enemy must ingloriously fly or come out from behind his defences and give us battle on our own ground, where certain destruction awaits him." Lee acted with despatch. The midnight hour of April 30 found Jackson on the march from Hamilton's Crossing, and eight o'clock the following morning, May 1, brought a part of his corps to Anderson's support in front of Hooker near Chancellorsville. Early's division of Jackson's corps, Barksdale's brigade of McLaws's division, and Pendleton's reserve artillery, remained in front of Fredericksburg to oppose Sedgwick. Lee's army was between Hooker's divided wings, and Hooker's cavalry was swinging off in the distance. Lee faced both ways and prepared to deliver a double battle. He moved the mass of his army within four miles of Chancellorsville and left Early to oppose Sedgwick with eight thousand five hundred muskets and thirty guns. Jackson, Anderson, and McLaws with forty-one thousand men at 11 A.M., May 1, were moving upon Hooker. At that hour, Lee was on Lee's Hill giving orders to Early and Pendleton " not to be deceived by pretended movements of the enemy—and when his real movements came, to meet him with the utmost energy and determination."

At the Tabernacle Church, Jackson ordered Anderson's men to lay aside their spades and at once moved westward to attack the Federal army in the dense jungle of the wilderness. McLaws marched on the turnpike and Anderson on the plank road; Jackson supported Anderson on the left. At the same time, Hooker was pushing out his forces on the same highways toward Fredericksburg. The hostile columns met face to face in the tangled forest,

and the clash of arms began.   Alexander's battalion
of artillery accompanied the Confederate advance.
One battery moved in front with the infantry on the
turnpike, and fourteen guns at the head of the infantry column on the plank road—one howitzer
with the line of skirmishers.   The Confederate line
marched steadily forward through the unfenced
fields and woodlands.   Cheer after cheer rolled up
from the grey jackets as Lee and Jackson both rode
abreast of the line on the Confederate left.   McLaws
repulsed Sykes on the turnpike, after the latter was
flanked by Jackson.   Anderson turned the right
flank of Slocum and both of Hooker's columns retreated to Chancellorsville.   There they were com-
forted by the presence of eighteen thousand under
Sickles.   The Confederates advanced until they discovered Hooker in " a position " says Lee, " of
great natural strength, surrounded on all sides by
a dense forest filled with a tangled undergrowth, in
the midst of which breastworks of logs had been constructed, with trees felled in front, so as to form an
almost impenetrable abatis.   His artillery swept the
few narrow roads, by which his position could be
approached from the front, and commanded the
adjacent woods."

Hooker's position was the following: The Fifth
Corps (Meade) looked eastward from strong intrenchments two miles in length, extending from the Rappahannock to the White House near Chancellorsville.
The Second Corps (Couch) lay behind fortifications
that ran southward from the White House to Chancellorsville and thence eastward along the turnpike

to Mott's Run. The Twelfth Corps (Slocum) dwelt
in a fortress that looked southward between Fairview
and Hazel Grove; the divisions of Berry and Whipple lay just north of Chancellorsville; Birney's division of the Third Corps (Sickles) supported by
Williams and his log-works defended the woods
north of Hazel Grove. The Eleventh Corps (Howard), forming Hooker's right wing, was extended
for more than a mile along the turnpike west of
Dowdall's Tavern. On the road leading to the Ely
Ford, Hooker's rear was guarded by Sykes's division
of the Fifth Corps. More than seventy-five thousand men with many heavy guns were thus mustered
under Hooker's banner in his lair of strength at
Chancellorsville.

In the forest of scrub-oak and pine, east and
south of Hooker's fortifications, Lee drew up his
forty-one thousand men in a line across the two
roadways, extending as far to the left as the Wellford furnace where Stuart held the flank. Wilcox
stationed his brigade on Lee's extreme right to guard
Banks's Ford. After sunset, Lee and Jackson met
at the edge of the plank road, where another road
turned south-westward to the furnace. The slight
elevation upon which they stood was carpeted with
dry pine-needles from the trees that towered above
them. Talcott and Boswell were despatched from
this point to make a moonlight reconnaissance of
Hooker's fortress where it faced eastward. At 10
P.M. these officers returned to report the Federal
line as presenting no favourable point for attack
in front. Lee then said to Jackson, " We must

attack on our left as soon as practicable," and he bade Jackson prepare to execute this movement. Afterwards the two chieftains made ready their bivouac for the night.   At the foot of a pine tree, wrapped in army blankets, with the head pillowed on a saddle, they stretched themselves upon the ground.   Later in the night, J. P. Smith returned from an errand and aroused General Lee. " Come here and tell me what you have learned on the right," said Lee.   " Laying his hand on me," writes Smith, " he drew me down by his side, and, passing his arm around my shoulder, drew me near to him in a fatherly way that told of his warm and kindly heart,"   After expressing his thanks for the service rendered, Lee began to jest with the young officer about an incident of the advance during the afternoon.   As the latter broke away, he was followed by General Lee's hearty laugh that broke again and again upon the stillness of the night.

Meanwhile the cavalry had brought news of the extended position of Hooker's right wing.   Before the dawn of May 2, Jackson sent Jed. Hotchkiss and Rev. B. T. Lacy to search for a roadway leading westward from the furnace.   In the early morning twilight Hotchkiss returned from the reconnaissance to find Lee and Jackson seated on cracker-boxes over a fire of twigs.   He indicated on a map the position of the desired pathway.   The general plan of a flank movement under Jackson had been already ordered by Lee.   When the aide reported a feasible route across Hooker's front, Jackson pointed out the possibility of leading a force in circuit around Hooker's flank against the rear of the Federal right wing. After some discussion, Lee gave Jackson permission to lead his entire corps around the Federal right, while Lee held the two divisions of McLaws and Anderson between Hooker and Fredericksburg.

On January 25, 1866, in a letter to the wife of General Jackson, General Lee thus described the origin of the great flank march:

" . . . I decided against it [an attack upon Hooker's central works] and stated to General Jackson, we must attack on our left as soon as practicable, and the necessary movement of the troops began immediately. In consequence of a report received about that time from General Fitz Lee, describing the position of the Federal army, and the roads which he held with his cavalry leading to its rear, General Jackson, after some inquiry concerning the roads leading to the furnace, undertook to throw his command entirely in Hooker's rear, which he accomplished with equal skill and boldness ; the rest of the army being moved to the left flank to connect with him as he advanced."

With the rising of the sun, Rodes began to lead D. H. Hill's old division past the furnace in the advance westward through the dense forest. Colston and A. P. Hill followed next in order in the march made by the twenty-six thousand ragged and sturdy infantrymen, flanked by four regiments of horsemen under Stuart and Fitz Lee. When Jackson was in full progress directly across Hooker's front, General Lee inaugurated fierce demonstrations against the Federal left and centre. Artillery was moved forward against Meade, and strong bands of skirmishers assailed Couch and Slocum. Sickles caught sight of the column moving past the Wellford furnace, and his rifled cannon induced Jackson's veterans to seek another course farther south. Sickles then hastened a force beyond the furnace to the unfinished railroad where he made prey of a part of the 23d Georgia regiment, Jackson's rearguard. When this news ran through the Federal camp, most of the Federal officers were seized with the idea that Lee's entire army was in retreat toward Richmond. Sickles organised a strong pursuing column. At first, Birney, and then Whipple, of his own corps, and then Williams of the Twelfth Corps, led their divisions southward from the furnace in pursuit of Jackson! Lee turned the guns of Anderson upon Sickles, and the latter called for reinforcements. After 4 P.M., Barlow's brigade of Howard's corps was sent to the furnace. Twenty thousand men from Hooker's centre were thus astray in the wilderness seeking Jackson at the very hour when the latter was preparing to launch a thunderbolt of war against Hooker's right flank.

Noonday marked Jackson's arrival at a point upon the plank road two miles south-west of Howard's position. He left the "Stonewall" brigade with Fitz Lee's horsemen on this road, and pushed the main column to the Orange turnpike. At 3 P.M. Jackson was sending from a point in Hooker's rear this last message to Lee: " I hope as soon as practicable to attack. I trust that an ever-kind Providence will bless us with great success." He was then arraying Rodes in line of battle across the turnpike at the Luckett Farm, two miles west of Dowdall's Tavern. Jackson's left wing was directly in Howard's rear. Colston formed the second line; A. P. Hill followed in column. At 5.15 P.M., Jackson's bugles rang out, and the fierce Confederate yell startled the deer from their lair into Howard's camp, and sent terror throughout the Eleventh Corps, composed chiefly of Germans. Six guns of Stuart's horse artillery under Beckham moved at a gallop along the turnpike, with the riflemen, in sections of two guns each, and poured canister into Howard's regiments. A concentric fire was directed against every band of Federal soldiers that dared to stand, and multitudes were made prisoners. The roadway was soon blocked with the dense mass of fugitives that fled in panic and wild rout toward the Chancellor House two miles away. Jackson's men dashed forward with fierce eagerness. Colquitt, commanding Rodes's right brigade supposed that he saw a Federal force on his flank; he halted, faced southward, and retarded the advance of Jackson's right wing for one hour. This delay allowed Schurz's division to escape. But Howard's corps was an utter wreck and the fragments were carrying dismay and terror into the very heart of Hooker's army. The lines of Rodes and Colston became mingled in the pursuit, and all together leaped over the Federal works at Dowdall's Tavern. Still onward Jackson pressed the routed corps until he captured the log-works north of Hazel Grove, and drove Howard's battered regiments behind the divisions of Berry and Williams. Darkness had descended upon the field. Rodes and Colston declared that their lines had lost formation in the forest, and Jackson reluctantly ordered a halt and prepared for a night attack by bringing A. P. Hill to the front. He had reached a point within one mile of Hooker's headquarters, and held control of the Bullock road leading to the White House directly in rear of the Federal army and only two thousand yards distant. The entire Federal army was just within his grasp. At 9 P.M. Jackson rode forward to reconnoitre, remaining behind his own pickets. He had just given Hill the order: " Press them; cut them off from the United States Ford, Hill; press them!" As he listened to the ringing of axes that told of the construction of Federal defences the pickets began firing, and Jackson rode back with his staff toward Hill's line of battle. Hill's 18th North Carolina regiment fired upon the party, supposing them to be Federal cavalry. Two fell dead and Jackson was severely wounded and borne from the field. Soon afterward, Hill was stricken down, and Jackson sent for Stuart to take command of his corps. Stuart spent the hours after midnight in arranging the artillery for the assault.

At midnight Sickles reached Hazel Grove on the return march from the furnace. Neither Sickles nor Anderson, nor McLaws, had heard, at first, the sound of Jackson's battle. This was due to the peculiar condition of the atmosphere. The attack ordered by Lee was, therefore, not made until Jackson's pyrotechnic display after nightfall brought McLaws into a heavy skirmish against Hooker's left. Anderson suffered Sickles to march back again to Hazel Grove. That point had witnessed a tragic comedy about the time when Jackson was ordering his front divisions to halt. Two hundred Georgians from Rodes's line found their way as far as Hazel Grove, one mile to the right of Jackson's position and there met the fire of some Federal guns under the eye of Pleasanton, leader of Hooker's cavalry. Pleasanton reported that Keenan led four hundred Federal horsemen into the midst of the Confederate line of battle, and that the Federal artillery at Hazel Grove swept back the advance of five thousand riflemen and checked Jackson's assault! At midnight, came Sickles from the furnace to repeat the drama. Some of his skirmishers entered the forest north of Hazel Grove and were easily repulsed by the pickets of Hill's regiments. The larger part of Sickles's force then moved against the flank of Hooker's Twelfth Corps and entered into conflict with Slocum's men. Out of this battle against his Federal associates, Sickles manufactured the report that his men recaptured the plank road and inflicted the fatal wound upon Jackson! *

During the night Wilbourne and Hotchkiss made a wide détour around the corps of Sickles and brought the news of Jackson's success to General Lee. They found him beneath the same pine-trees whence he had despatched Jackson to assault Hooker's rear. By the light of a candle, these officers saw the shadow of deep grief pass over Lee's countenance when they told of Jackson's injury in the hour of victory. After a pause occasioned by the struggle to suppress his emotion, Lee

* *The Battle of Chancellorsville*, by Augustus Choate Hamlin, Historian, Eleventh Army Corps.

said, " Any victory is dearly bought which deprives
us of the services of General Jackson, even for a
short time."

Lee at once sent orders to Stuart to drive Hooker
from the Chancellor House by direct assault; at the
same time he bade Stuart to press toward his right
in order to unite his force with the division under
Anderson.   He then dictated the following letter to
Jackson :

> " I have just received your note informing me that you were
> wounded.   I cannot express my regret at the occurrence.   Could I
> have directed events, I should have chosen for the good of the coun-
> try to be disabled in your stead.
> "I congratulate you upon the victory which is due to your skill
> and energy.
> " Very respectfully, your obedient servant,
> " R. E. LEE, General."

This message was read to Jackson while the battle
of May 3 was in progress.   The suffering hero turned
away his face and said, " General Lee is very kind,
but he should give the praise to God."   At an
earlier time during the war, Jackson said of Lee :
" General Lee is a phenomenon.   He is the only
man whom I would be willing to follow blindfold."

The fall of his lieutenant aroused all the fierceness
of Lee's combative ardour.   " Those people shall
be pressed immediately," he said to his staff-officers,
and the early dawn of May 3 found him in the saddle
making ready his divisions for the battle.   The sun
arose upon Lee's two wings advancing against the
central part of Hooker's position at Chancellorsville.
Between Stuart and Anderson there was at first a

gap of one mile. Stuart moved eastward, for the most part south of the plank road, with Hill's division led by Heth in the front line. From his position Lee moved McLaws westward along the plank road and Anderson northward over the space between that road and the furnace.

Hooker had been strengthened by Reynolds's First Corps of seventeen thousand men. Exclusive of losses, he had now a force of nearly eighty thousand. These were arranged in the form of the letter V; the sharp angle on the high ground at Fairview, south of Chancellor's house, was defended by a park of forty-three guns. In the line facing westward were Sickles and Williams with twenty-three thousand men. Opposed to these were Stuart's twenty thousand. In the Federal line facing eastward stood Geary, Hancock, and a fragment of Howard's corps, twenty thousand effectives. McLaws and Anderson were directing fourteen thousand against them. Meade, Reynolds, and Couch with thirty-seven thousand, stood within ready call of both these Federal lines.

Stuart began the battle by sending Jackson's corps against Hooker's westward ramparts. An abatis of sharpened stakes and brushwood defended the approach to the heavy works constructed of felled trees. Over the entire defence rushed Stuart's left wing, north of the plank road. Stuart himself rode behind the line like another Henry of Navarre, his black hat-plume waving and his merry voice singing at the highest pitch, " Old Joe Hooker, come out of the wilderness! " Stuart's right wing captured four Federal guns at Hazel Grove and held that plateau. As the sun lifted the mist that enshrouded the field, Stuart saw the advantage of this elevation on his right, and he there concentrated thirty guns under Walker. These secured an enfilade fire northward along the two Federal lines. A similar enfilade was poured in from the direction of the furnace by Hardaway's guns of Anderson's division. This fierce cross-fire of artillery in little more than one hour rendered Hooker's entire position untenable.

McLaws was assailing Hooker's left from the direction of Fredericksburg; Anderson was pressing his centre from the furnace road, and Stuart was sending line after line against the Federal right. Eight o'clock marked the junction of Lee's two wings. The fighting on both sides was stubborn and desperate. Over tremendous barriers the Confederate infantrymen rushed, only to be driven back by the Federal reserves. Three times the Federal defences were captured and lost again. But the guns of Walker and Hardaway gradually broke the strength of the Federal artillery. A shell rendered Hooker himself unfit to direct the battle, and Couch was left in command without a plan of defence. At 10 A.M. Hooker's key-point, Fairview, was in the hands of the Confederates, and his troops were retreating past the flames of Chancellor's house. Hooker was literally driven from strong intrenchments into new fortifications nearer the Rappahannock.

Lee rode with his troops as they pressed forward

in pursuit. The air was filled with Confederate shells passing over the infantry in search of Hooker's rear. The surrounding forest was in flames. Charles Marshall, Lee's aide, thus describes the scene when Lee spurred Traveller up to the burning house from which Hooker had fled :

" His presence was the signal for one of those uncontrollable outbursts of enthusiasm which none can appreciate who have not witnessed them. The fierce soldiers, with their faces blackened with the smoke of battle, the wounded crawling with feeble limbs from the fury of the devouring flames, all seemed possessed with a common impulse. One long unbroken cheer, in which the feeble cry of those who lay helpless on the earth blended with the strong voices of those who still fought, rose high above the roar of battle and hailed the presence of the victorious chief. He sat in the full realisation of all that soldiers dream of—triumph ; and as I looked on him in the complete fruition of the success which his genius, courage, and confidence in his army had won, I thought that it must have been from some such scene that men in ancient days ascended to the dignity of the gods."

This witness affirms that Lee's first thought was in behalf of the wounded who were endangered by the fire that raged around them. At the same time a message was brought from Jackson congratulating Lee upon the great victory. " I shall never forget the look of pain and anguish that passed over his face as he listened," says Marshall. " With a voice broken with emotion he bade me say to General Jackson that the victory was his and that the congratulations were due to him. . . . I forgot the genius that won the day in my reverence for the generosity that refused its glory."

While Lee was urging forward the preparations

for a renewed attack against Hooker, a courier
turned his attention toward Fredericksburg. On
the previous day, a member of Lee's staff misinter-
preted his commands and ordered Early to march
from Hamilton's crossing to Chancellorsville.
Early's withdrawal permitted Sedgwick, then on
the southern bank of the Rappahannock, to move
up the river against Barksdale on the Marye Heights.
On Sunday morning, May 3, Early returned to his
former position, only in time to see twenty thousand
Federal troops assailing Barksdale's front and right
flank. Sedgwick's success against Barksdale's artillery and his one thousand muskets was won with
difficulty and at a great cost; but it enabled the
corps of thirty thousand Federal soldiers to move
past Early's left flank to the westward, and to
threaten Lee's rear on the plank road. Wilcox
marched at once from Banks's ford, threw his brigade across the path of Sedgwick at the Salem
Church and sent news of the situation to General
Lee. With the same quiet courage that always
marked him, Lee immediately despatched McLaws
with four brigades to assist Wilcox in the battle
against Sedgwick. The remaining Confederate brigades were retained in front of Hooker. Thus for
the second time Lee took measures to withstand the
advance of a numerous foe against the rear of his
main army. He then wrote to President Davis as
follows: "We have again to thank Almighty God
for a great victory."

McLaws moved toward Fredericksburg with all
speed, arrayed his regiments across the roadway at

the Salem Church, and at once began the fierce conflict which forced Sedgwick backward one mile toward
Fredericksburg.   On the morning of May 4, Early
marched along the Telegraph road and recaptured
the heights near the town.   He now stood in Sedgwick's rear.   Noonday brought Lee with Anderson's
brigades to the Salem Church.   By 6 P.M. Anderson
had extended his line eastward until he joined hands
with Early.   Their advance forced Sedgwick northward across the plank road as far as the Rappahannock, but McLaws was slow to perceive his retreat
and did not attack.   A pontoon bridge near Banks's
ford enabled Sedgwick to save his entire force from
capture.

Lee returned at once to Chancellorsville to assail
Hooker with his entire army.   But the early dawn
of May 6 revealed to Lee the deserted Federal
trenches, and the rising sun found Hooker on the
northern bank of the Rappahannock issuing the
order, " General headquarters to-night will be at
the old camp near Falmouth."   Before night,
Hooker himself was in camp at Falmouth tendering
" congratulations " to his army!   He had abandoned beyond the Rappahannock more than seventeen thousand of his men killed, wounded, and
captured, fourteen heavy guns, twenty thousand
stand of arms, and thirty-one thousand knapsacks,
and yet in the order of May 6 he said, " The events
of the last week may swell with pride the heart of
every officer and soldier of this army "!   Moreover,
he made this declaration: " Profoundly loyal and
conscious of its strength, the Army of the Potomac

will give or decline battle whenever its interest or honour may demand "!

Lee's casualties numbered thirteen thousand. Many of his brigadiers were wounded, and the brave Paxton was slain at the head of the " Stonewall " brigade. The flower of Lee's matchless army was, in part, destroyed at Chancellorsville, and the South was unable to send others to fill the vacancies. In his official report Lee spoke of

" the dangers and difficulties which under God's blessing, were surmounted by the fortitude and valour of our army. The conduct of the troops cannot be too highly praised. Attacking largely superior numbers in strongly intrenched positions, their heroic courage overcame every obstacle of nature and art and achieved a triumph most honourable to our arms."

In mentioning individual instances of gallantry, he wrote:

" Among them will be found some who have passed by a glorious death beyond the reach of praise, but the memory of whose virtues and devoted patriotism will ever be cherished by their grateful countrymen. . . . To the skilful and efficient management of the artillery the successful issue of the contest is in great measure due."

On May 7, the commander summoned his soldiers to return " grateful thanks to the only Giver of victory for the signal deliverance He has wrought."

Lee's personal affection for Jackson was exceedingly strong. Immediately after the battle, sanguine hopes were entertained that Jackson would recover from his wounds. Lee's messages to his lieutenant were many, and they all indicated the tender love and sincere generosity of the Southern chieftain.

" Give him my affectionate regards," said Lee to a messenger, " and tell him to make haste and get well, and come back to me as soon as he can. He has lost his left arm, but I have lost my right." When it was announced that Jackson's wounds were serious and might prove fatal, Lee manifested strong emotion and said : " Surely, General Jackson must recover. God will not take him from us, now that we need him so much. Surely he will be spared to us, in answer to the many prayers which are offered for him." Then, after a moment's silence, spent in evident anguish of spirit, Lee sent this message : " When you return I trust you will find him better. When a suitable occasion offers, give him my love, and tell him that I wrestled in prayer for him last night, as I never prayed, I believe, for myself."

The death of his great colleague and beloved friend brought to Lee the keenest personal sorrow and a sense of irreparable loss to his country. General Order No. 61, issued on May 11, ran as follows :

" With deep grief, the Commanding-General announces to the army the death of Lieutenant-General T. J. Jackson, who expired on the 10th instant, at 3.15 P.M. The daring, skill and energy of this great and good soldier, by the decree of an all-wise Providence, are now lost to us. But while we mourn his death, we feel that his spirit still lives, and will inspire the whole army with his indomitable courage and unshaken confidence in God as our hope and our strength. Let his name be a watchword to his corps, who have followed him to victory on so many fields. Let officers and soldiers emulate his invincible determination to do everything in the defence of our beloved country.   R. E. LEE, General."

Lee's right arm was removed when the noble Christian hero passed beyond the river. From this time onward Lee's mind dwelt almost continually upon the sore calamity of Jackson's departure. After the experiences of the summer of 1863, Lee wrote in September his official report of the Chancellorsville campaign, wherein he made the following reference to Jackson:

" The movement by which the enemy's position was turned and the fortune of the day decided, was conducted by the lamented Lieutenant-General Jackson, who, as has already been stated, was severely wounded near the close of the engagement on Saturday evening. I do not propose here to speak of the character of this illustrious man, since removed from the scene of his eminent usefulness by the hand of an inscrutable but all-wise Providence. I nevertheless desire to pay the tribute of my admiration to the matchless energy and skill that marked this last act of his life, forming as it did a worthy conclusion of that long series of splendid achievements which won for him the lasting love and gratitude of his country."

As Lee turned to face the new situation, on May 11 he wrote to his wife concerning " the loss of the good and great Jackson." To this he added: "Any victory would be dear at such a price. His remains go to Richmond to-day. I know not how to replace him, but God's will be done. I trust He will raise some one in his place."

GENERAL THOMAS JONATHAN JACKSON.
(STONEWALL JACKSON.)

CHAPTER XII.

THE CAMPAIGNS OF GETTYSBURG AND MINE RUN.

1863.

ENERAL LEE was eager to follow up the victory of Chancellorsville by an aggressive movement against the Federal army. The lack of subsistence had restrained him, early in the spring, from driving Milroy out of the valley. Lee declared, on April 16, that such a movement would recall Hooker north of the Potomac, and that " greater relief would in this way be afforded to the armies in middle Tennessee and on the Carolina coast than by any other method." He urged Davis to recruit the strength of the army by bringing northward the troops stationed in South Carolina, Georgia, and Florida. " I know there will be difficulties raised to their withdrawal," wrote Lee, " but it will be better to order General Beauregard in with all the forces which can be spared, and to put him in command here, than to keep them there inactive and this army inefficient from paucity of numbers."

When Longstreet returned from the regions beyond the James River, Lee divided his army into
three corps under Longstreet, Ewell, and A. P. Hill.
Of Ewell and Hill he expressed the following opinion: " The former is an honest, brave soldier, who
has always done his duty well.   The latter, I think
upon the whole, is the best soldier of his grade with
me."   Lee had used these identical words just
after the battle of Sharpsburg to set forth his opinion
of Hill.   This estimate of A. P. Hill must be placed
in the balance against Longstreet's charge that Lee
showed partiality in behalf of Hill as a Virginian, by
not assigning to the Third Corps either D. H. Hill
the Carolinian, or McLaws the Georgian.

The last days of May found Lee still " endeavouring to get this army in a condition to move—to
anticipate an expected blow from the enemy."   He
was not in favour of sending Pickett's division to assist Pemberton on the Mississippi, and expressed the
hope that J. E. Johnston would at once assail Grant.
To the cry of alarm raised about the safety of Wilmington he paid little heed, and continued to advocate the ordering of all Confederate soldiers into the
two arenas of Virginia and Mississippi, leaving the
Atlantic coast to be defended by local troops.   He
urged aggression, lest the weight of Hooker's numbers should finally force the Confederate army back to
the trenches in front of Richmond.   Since the battle
of Fredericksburg, Lee had not abated his urgency in
asking for an army of sufficient strength to destroy
the Army of the Potomac.   He recognised the latter
as his true objective.   The Confederate administra-

tion, however, seemed never to recognise the wisdom
of concentration in order to strike a decisive blow.
Lee's government left him vastly outnumbered on
every battle-field; he always gave the enemy a staggering blow and sent him bleeding from the field,
but the latter soon presented himself with undimin-
ished numbers. In June, 1863, as in December,
1862, and in May, 1863, Lee was moving forward to
deliver battle with an army that was matchless in
everything except in numbers. Thirty thousand
additional soldiers at any of the above dates would
have enabled him to destroy or capture the Army of
the Potomac.

Lee's plan of campaign was laid before A. L.
Long in the camp near Fredericksburg. When
Long entered Lee's tent, he found that the latter
" had a map spread on the table before him." Lee
" traced on the map the proposed route of the army
and its destination in Pennsylvania." " In his
quietly effective manner " Lee outlined his plan to
manœuvre Hooker out of his position on the Rappahannock, and bring him to battle at Chambersburg, York, or Gettysburg. Lee's design was to
transfer hostilities to Northern soil and there subsist
his army, cause the evacuation of Washington by a
victory in Pennsylvania, and at the same time force
the recall of Federal troops from the siege of Vicksburg. Hampton, Robertson, and Jones increased the
number of Stuart's horsemen a little beyond six
thousand. The artillery organised in battalions
under General W. N. Pendleton made a park of
more than two hundred guns. With a total force

of about sixty thousand enthusiastic veterans Lee made ready to move northward. On May 31, he wrote this: " I pray that our merciful Father in Heaven may protect and direct us. In that case I fear no odds and no numbers."

On June 2, Lee sent this parting message to Davis: " If I am able to move, I propose to do so cautiously, watching the result, and not to get beyond recall until I find it safe." On June 3, he began to push Longstreet toward Culpeper; Ewell followed, and A. P. Hill was left in front of Fredericksburg to restrain Hooker from advancing against Richmond. June 8 witnessed the concentration of the two advanced Confederate corps and Stuart's cavalry near Culpeper. Of the cavalry review held the same day, Lee wrote thus to his wife:

" It was a splendid sight. The men and horses looked well. They had recuperated since last fall. Stuart was in all his glory. Your sons and nephews are well and flourishing. The country here looks very green and pretty, notwithstanding the ravages of war. What a beautiful world God in His loving kindness to His creatures has given us ! What a shame that men endowed with reason and knowledge of right should mar His gifts ! "

The Federal cavalry crossed the Rappahannock to engage in battle with Stuart near Brandy Station, on the ninth of June. Confederate infantry assisted to drive the enemy across the river, leaving large spoil in Stuart's possession. As Lee rode upon the field he met his second son, Brigadier-General W. H. F. Lee, borne wounded from the battle, " more concerned," as the father wrote, " about his brave men and officers who had fallen in the battle than himself."

At this juncture a growing party in the North was making itself heard in denunciation of the Federal President's arbitrary assumptions of power. This party's suggestions of peace were treated with scorn by some of the Southern newspapers. Lee rebuked the latter as acting unwisely and blindly:

"We should not, therefore, conceal from ourselves that our re-sources in men are constantly diminishing, and the disproportion in this respect between us and our enemies, if they continue united in their efforts to subjugate us, is steadily augmenting. . . . Under these circumstances, we should neglect no honourable means of divid-ing and weakening our enemies, that they may feel some of the diffi-culties experienced by ourselves. It seems to me that the most effectual mode of accomplishing this object now within our reach, is to give all the encouragement we can, consistently with truth, to the rising peace party of the North."

But these reflections were interrupted by reports of the incursions of Federal cavalry, and Lee's wrath was roused to say:

"I grieve over the desolation of the country and the distress to innocent women and children, occasioned by spiteful excursions of the enemy, unworthy of a civilised nation."

He called upon the citizens at home to organise themselves for defence "against outrages of our barbarous enemy." On June 10, Lee despatched Ewell from Culpeper toward the valley to capture Milroy. The cavalry of Jenkins at the same time moved down upon Winchester, and Imboden was ordered to lead his horsemen as far as Romney Three days passed, and Ewell stood before the defences of Winchester, with his advance holding Martinsburg; Jenkins was pressing northward to Williamsport, and Imboden held control of the Baltimore and Ohio railway. On this thirteenth day of June, Longstreet was encamped at Culpeper, and A. P. Hill still remained before Fredericksburg. Hooker had folded his tents and was marching toward Washington. At the same time Lee was calling upon the Confederate authorities for a larger force of cavalry.

June 15 saw Ewell scattering Milroy's ten thousand from Winchester, driving the Federal garrison from Harper's Ferry, and asking his soldiers to unite with him " in returning thanks to our Heavenly Father for the signal success " evidenced by the capture of four thousand prisoners and twenty-nine guns. The evening of this eventful day marked the advance of Jenkins toward Chambersburg, and the passage of Ewell's vanguard across the Potomac. Longstreet was moving out of Culpeper to seize the passes of the Blue Ridge, while Hill, who had watched the muskets of Hooker's rearguard disappear behind the Stafford Hills, was now drawing nigh unto Culpeper.

The Army of Northern Virginia was pressing steadily northward. Lee's plan now was to advance Ewell into Pennsylvania to seek supplies. If Ewell should meet with success, Lee intended to march his entire army into the Cumberland valley. June 17 saw the Confederates outstretched from Culpeper to Chambersburg. The latter place was held by Jenkins's horsemen; one of Ewell's divisions was encamped near Hagerstown, another occupied Sharpsburg, and the third was approaching the Potomac. Longstreet was guarding the passes of the Blue Ridge, and Hill remained at Culpeper. Stuart kept watch at the gaps of the Bull Run Mountains to repress the curiosity of Hooker, whose camp-fires were ablaze from Manassas to Leesburg.

During five successive days Stuart was engaged with Hooker's cavalry in the game of advance and retreat, until at length he stood at bay in the Ashby Gap of the Blue Ridge. While Stuart thus veiled the Confederate manœuvres, Longstreet stood on the Ridge's summit, and A. P. Hill passed behind his line through Chester Gap into the valley. The next movement in the game is thus described by Lee:

"As these demonstrations did not have the effect of causing the Federal army to leave Virginia, and as it did not seem disposed to advance upon the position held by Longstreet, the latter was withdrawn to the west side of the Shenandoah."

On June 18, Lee drew nigh unto Millwood, and gave orders to throw his entire army across the Potomac, since Stuart's reports indicated the advance of Hooker's main body northward from Manassas. Hill set forth through Shepherdstown in search of Ewell; Longstreet began to follow Hill, while Stuart, assisted by the division of McLaws, remained to defend the passes of the Blue Ridge. Lee directed Imboden to enter Pennsylvania, suggested to Sam Jones to advance into Western Virginia, and called for some of the brigades left at Richmond. The men of all arms under Lee's immediate command were in number about sixty thousand. As the heads of columns pressed toward northern territory, Lee issued an order that began with the injunction, " No private property shall be injured or destroyed."

Lee now took final measures to guard his right flank and rear; his left was made safe by Jones and Imboden. The morning of June 22 found this message on the way to Stuart:

> " Do you know where he [Hooker] is and what he is doing? I fear he will steal a march on us and get across the Potomac before we are aware. If you find that he is moving northward, and that two brigades can guard the Blue Ridge and take care of your rear, you can move with the other three into Maryland and take position on General Ewell's right, place yourself in communication with him, guard his flank, keep him informed of the enemy's movements and collect all the supplies you can for the use of the army."

On the same day, Lee's commands to Ewell were these : " Toward the Susquehanna. . . . If Harrisburg comes within your means, capture it."

June 23 was a day of momentous events. Ewell was sweeping up the Cumberland valley toward Carlisle. Lee was preparing to lead the First and Third corps northward across the Potomac. To Stuart he made the suggestion that two brigades of cavalry should keep watch upon Hooker while the other three should cross the Potomac. Shepherdstown and some point east of the Ridge were suggested as alternative places for this passage. Stuart must select one ford or the other, just as Hooker's own movements should permit, but Lee laid this injunction upon Stuart: " In either case, after crossing the river, you must move on and feel the right of Ewell's troops." H. B. McClellan tells us of Lee's later message, received during the night of June 23, giving Stuart discretion to pass around Hooker's rear and to cross the Potomac to the eastward of Hooker's army, at the same time placing Stuart under bond to bring his cavalry " as speedily as possible " into touch with Ewell's advance (under Early) at York, Pennsylvania. The same day, Lee urged President Davis to withdraw the troops from the Southern Atlantic coast and to concentrate them at Culpeper Court-House under Beauregard as a menace to Washington. Lee asserted that this movement " would not only effect a diversion most favourable for this army, but would, I think, relieve us of any apprehension of an attack upon Richmond during our absence."

The Federal government called for one hundred thousand troops to defend Pennsylvania against Lee's advance; they also concentrated a force in Maryland, and Hooker moved to the northern bank of the Potomac. Consternation reigned in the North, and Mr. Lincoln, at Washington, as he himself said, was making this prayer: " Oh Lord, this is your fight; but we your humble followers and supporters here can't stand another Fredericksburg or Chancellorsville." From Williamsport, June 25, Lee sent this message:

" It is plain that if all the Federal army is concentrated upon this, it will result in our accomplishing nothing and being compelled to return to Virginia. If the plan . . . of organising an army, even in effigy, under General Beauregard at Culpeper Court-House,

can be carried into effect, much relief will be afforded. . . . I
have not sufficient troops to maintain my communications, and therefore, have to abandon them.   I think I can throw General Hooker's
army across the Potomac and draw [Federal] troops from the South,
embarrassing their plan of campaign in a measure, if I can do nothing
more and have to return."

So urgent was Lee concerning the advance of another Confederate force upon Washington from the
direction of Culpeper, that he pressed the matter at
great length upon the attention of President Davis
in a second letter this same day.

June 27 found Longstreet and Hill in Chambersburg, Ewell in Carlisle, and Early approaching York.
Hooker had commenced the passage of the Potomac
the very day (June 25) on which Lee turned his back
upon that river.   Two days later, Lee in Chambersburg was unaware of Hooker's advance, for Stuart
was just then (June 27) crossing the Potomac at
Seneca, near Washington.   On the 28th, four Federal
corps were in bivouac at Frederick and three near
Middletown, Maryland.   Hooker's demand that the
ten thousand men at Harper's Ferry should take the
field under his orders brought to a climax the Federal administration's lack of confidence in their
commander.   He was relieved from duty, and General George G. Meade was promoted to the command of the Army of the Potomac.

Lee at Chambersburg issued an address to his
troops (June 27) commending their spirit and fortitude, and forbidding injury to private property.   He
reminded them that " civilisation and Christianity "
forbade retaliation againt their foes :

" It must be remembered that we make war only upon armed men, and that we cannot take vengeance for the wrongs our people have suffered, without lowering ourselves in the eyes of all whose abhorrence has been excited by the atrocities of our enemies, and offending against Him to whom vengeance belongeth, without whose favour and support our efforts must all prove in vain."

On the night of June 28, the scout Harrison brought to Lee at Chambersburg the first intelligence that Hooker had crossed the Potomac and was approaching the South Mountain. Lee feared that the Federal army would cross the mountain and secure his line of communication with Virginia. He therefore sent couriers to recall Ewell's divisions from the Susquehanna and ordered the entire army to concentrate east of the mountains at Cashtown. The morning of June 29 witnessed the advance toward Cashtown of Heth's division from Hill's corps. Longstreet remained near Chambersburg. Near the close of the day Ewell at Carlisle received Lee's order just as he was moving forward to attack Harrisburg. The 29th also marked Meade's advance northward from Frederick in search of Lee. At sunset, two Federal corps were near Emmittsburg, one was at Taneytown, and four at varying distances behind Pipe Creek. Buford's cavalry patrolled the Federal front at Fairfield. The heads of the hostile columns were not far removed from each other, yet each leader was ignorant of his foe's proximity.

The morning of June 29 was utilised by Stuart in the work of tearing up the railway between Meade and Washington. Westminster was his place of bivouac. From this point he set forth northward at the dawning of the 30th, still retarding his own progress by driving a captured train of two hundred mule teams. As he fought his way into Hanover through the squadrons of Kilpatrick, Stuart was not aware of the opening scenes of the great drama little more than a dozen miles to the westward from his line of march. That last day of June saw Pettigrew's brigade of Heth's division marching over the eight-mile course from Cashtown to Gettysburg in search of shoes to cover their naked feet. In the town they found Buford's cavalry. The heads of the converging columns had collided; the news was flashed to both armies, but as yet the significance of the meeting was unknown to both Lee and Meade.

Pettigrew returned in haste to Cashtown, Lee's appointed rendezvous. The night of June 30 saw the camp-fires of the larger part of Hill's corps kindled on the eastern slopes of South Mountain. Longstreet was still west of the Mountain at Greenwood, with Pickett guarding the trains at Chambersburg. Of Ewell's corps, Johnson's division was near Longstreet; the divisions of Rodes and Early were near Heidlersburg on the return march from the Susquehanna to Cashtown. As Stuart moved all night with weary pace from Hanover toward York, he passed within seven miles of Early's bivouac. The fatal waggon train had delayed his march. Stuart afterwards asserted that Early failed to follow Lee's order to warn the approaching cavalry of the return march southward. The horsemen moved on to York and thence to Carlisle, while Lee in the distance on the eve of battle was anxiously awaiting their aid. Perhaps Stuart's presence on the Federal right flank, on June 30, caused Meade to disperse his seven corps from Westminster to a point north of Emmittsburg, a dispersion that proved advantageous to Lee on the following day. But it is more probable that a speedier march of the cavalry would have permitted Lee to capture Harrisburg and then to offer defensive battle at the eastern base of the South Mountain, either at Cashtown or at some point farther northward.

Lee spent June 30 in Longstreet's camp at Greenwood. July 1 found him riding with the latter through the mountain-pass eastward. The Confederate forces were pressing toward Cashtown. At 5 A.M., however, Hill had sent the divisions of Heth and Pender from Cashtown toward Gettysburg, " to discover what was in my [Hill's] front." Hill supposed that naught but Federal cavalry was in the town. His advance precipitated a battle with two of Meade's *corps d'armée* whom Buford had summoned to his aid. The movement was contrary to the spirit of Lee's orders. He intended to fight a defensive battle at Cashtown. Hill's advance compelled Lee to deliver offensive battle at Gettysburg.

At sunrise, Heth's scouts confronted Buford's pickets at Willoughby Run, west of Gettysburg on the Chambersburg road. The Run flows along the western edge of a broad swell of ground called McPherson's Ridge. Heth's men forced Buford backward from the stream and from 8 until 10 o'clock

the roar of fierce battle resounded northward over
the level plains calling Ewell to the field, and westward across the ridges to bring Lee down the moun-
tain-slope in great haste to Cashtown.   Meade, far
away to the eastward, caught the sound of the
guns and quickened the pace of his legions.   Lee
found R. H. Anderson holding his division at Cashtown awaiting orders from Hill.   Anderson reports
Lee as listening there intently to the guns and then
saying :

> " I cannot think what has become of Stuart : I ought to have
> heard from him long before now.   He may have met with disaster,
> but I hope not.   In the absence of reports from him, I am in ignor-
> ance as to what we have in front of us here.   It may be the whole
> Federal army or it may be only a detachment.   If it is the whole
> Federal force we must fight a battle here ; if we do not gain a vic-
> tory those defiles and gorges through which we were passing this
> morning will shelter us from disaster."

Lee seemed much disturbed by the sounds of increasing battle, for his order had already been imposed upon both Hill and Ewell that they should
not bring on a general engagement before the concentration of the Army of Northern Virginia.   Contrary to Lee's plan, Hill was delivering heavy battle
against the advanced corps of the Army of the
Potomac, eight miles farther from the mountains
than the field selected by Lee himself at Cashtown.
While Lee waited thus in anxiety at Cashtown, at
10 o'clock, Reynolds was deploying the Federal First
Corps along the slight elevation half a mile west of
Gettysburg known as Seminary Ridge.   As Reynolds
looked down the gradual slope five hundred yards

to the westward, he saw Heth and Buford in deadly battle upon the parallel elevation, McPherson's Ridge. Reynolds advanced a division to Buford's support; he forced Archer's brigade over Willoughby Run and captured Archer, but Reynolds himself was slain. Pender gave ready aid to Heth, and the two divisions held the First Corps at bay. Noonday saw the Eleventh Corps approach and now Howard ruled the Federal field. Howard arrayed two divisions of the Eleventh on Seminary Ridge to hold his right flank; the other division he held in reserve on Cemetery Hill south of Gettysburg. At this juncture Ewell's storm of war burst upon Howard from the direction of Heidlersburg. In line of battle across Seminary Ridge, at 2.30 P.M., Rodes came sweeping southward from Oak Hill against Howard's right flank. Through the open country east of Rock Creek, at 3.30 P.M., Early advanced like a thunderbolt against the right and rear of Howard's line. At 4 P.M., Ewell's divisions began to drive the Eleventh Corps southward through the streets; at the same hour Hill advanced his entire line against the front and flanks of the First Corps and broke it into fragments. The hour of half-past four witnessed the flight of Howard's shattered brigades through Gettysburg with Ewell pressing them in close pursuit. The Federal fugitives found refuge with the division and the batteries left in reserve on Cemetery Hill.

Among Hill's yelling veterans on the Ridge near the Seminary, Lee stood watching the retreat of the disorganised Federal soldiers. More than five thousand Federal prisoners remained in Lee's hands, and the field of Howard's defeat was covered with multitudes of Federal dead and wounded. Four Confederate divisions had wrought out this victory over five Federal divisions; the latter had held their ground tenaciously and the Confederate brigades had met severe losses. Lee's veterans were jubilant and eager to continue the pursuit. Ewell led the advance, and while Lee continued his observation the bayonets of Hays's brigade began to gleam along the eastern boundary of Gettysburg near the foot of the Cemetery Hill.

Not many Federal soldiers were visible to the Confederate commander, for only about six thousand armed men out of more than twenty thousand engaged had escaped to the refuge of the stone walls and boulders on Cemetery Hill. Lee at once sent Taylor with the order to Ewell: " Press those people and secure the hill, if possible." At this moment Early was arraying two brigades in the field east of the town and sending a request to Hill to order forward a division from Seminary Ridge to assist in assailing the Cemetery. But "Extra-Billy" Smith, one of Early's brigadiers, sent him a sensational report that a Federal force was approaching the Confederate left from the direction of York. Gordon was countermarched to the left rear to meet the imaginary foe. Early and Rodes urged upon Ewell the necessity of immediate assault. But Ewell looked toward the rock-covered hill and the blazing guns and declared the Cemetery unassailable in front with the brigades at hand. Gordon had not yet returned from the vain march to the left. Ewell determined to await Johnson's division, and to send the latter to scale the wooded hill east of Gettysburg known as Culp's Hill; from that position he expected to fall upon the Federal right flank. At the same time Ewell sent J. P. Smith to Lee near the Seminary, to ask support for the proposed attack of Early and Rodes against the Federal force in the Cemetery. The time was about 5 P.M. Lee and Longstreet were scanning the Cemetery with field-glasses. When Ewell's request came, Hill was loath to send forward the two divisions recently engaged; Anderson was behind Johnson and had not yet reached the field, and Longstreet's men were held far in the rear by Ewell's waggon train. Lee urged Longstreet to hasten McLaws and Hood to the front and sent this reply to his lieutenant in Gettysburg: "Tell General Ewell that I will support him by an advance on his right as soon as I can. I wish him to use whatever opportunity he has to advance and to hold the ground in his front."

The first reinforcement upon the field was Johnson's division, but the sun had disappeared when his column halted near the college building. At that hour Lee was in conference with Ewell, Early, and Rodes near the Carlisle road north of Gettysburg. The plan of immediate attack had then been abandoned by all these officers. They could look southward in the twilight and see the two Round Tops looming up above the hill's crest. Reconnaissance had discovered the arrival of fresh Federal troops, for Hancock now was in command and Slocum's eight thousand six hundred men were in line, partly on Culp's Hill and partly on Cemetery Hill. It was now Lee's purpose, says Early, " to attack the enemy as early as possible next day—at daylight, if practicable." To the three officers jointly Lee presented the question: " Can't you, with your corps, attack on this flank at daylight to-morrow ? " The officers pointed to the rugged hill in their front and the Federal brigades on the hill-tops; they mentioned the gradual ascent to the Cemetery from the direction of the Seminary Ridge as affording favourable approach against the enemy's left flank. Lee's next interrogation was this: " Perhaps I had better draw you around towards my right, as the line will be very long and thin if you remain here, and the enemy may come down and break through it ? " But the leaders of the Confederate Second Corps declared their ability not only to hold the ground already won, but Ewell asserted his ability to capture Culp's Hill at once and threaten the Federal right. Thereupon Lee said: " Well, if I attack from my right, Longstreet will have to make the attack." Then for a moment he paused, says Early, his head bowed in deep thought; he looked up and added, " Longstreet is a very good fighter when he gets in position and gets everything ready, but he is *so slow.*" The decision reached in the conference was that the main assault should be delivered from the Confederate right at daylight the following morning, "or as soon thereafter as practicable," and that Ewell should stand ready to attack from the Confederate left. Lee returned to the Seminary to find Longstreet and Hill. Longstreet urged Lee to move to the Confederate right and place his army between Meade and Washington, and thus force Meade to make assault. This suggestion was only an extension of Lee's proposal to move Ewell around to the Emmittsburg road. Ewell's assurance that he could occupy Culp's Hill induced Lee to plan a double assault against the flanks of the force in the Cemetery before the arrival of Meade's rearguard and thus defeat the Army of the Potomac in detail. In the presence of his staff Lee said to Longstreet and Hill, " Gentlemen, we will attack the enemy in the morning as early as practicable." He directed Longstreet to lead forward McLaws and Hood to deliver the chief attack from the Confederate right. Hill was to demonstrate against the Federal centre, and a message was sent to Ewell to caution him against assailing Culp's Hill until he should hear Longstreet's guns.

Longstreet's two divisions moved from Fayetteville on the morning of July 1. Pickett's division remained on guard at Chambersburg and Law's brigade of Hood's division held New Guilford. The advance of Longstreet was retarded until the afternoon by Ewell's waggon train, but midnight saw his central camp-fires ablaze near Willoughby Run. The bivouac of his leading brigade under Kershaw was only two miles from Gettysburg. During the night Longstreet's order went to McLaws bidding him advance at 4 A.M. July 2; but this order was afterwards countermanded, and McLaws was directed to march " early in the morning." At the early dawn of July 2, Longstreet's orders started Law and Pickett across the South Mountain toward the battle-field.   Lee's report thus describes the general situation at this juncture:

" It had not been intended to deliver a general battle so far from our base unless attacked, but coming unexpectedly upon the whole Federal army, to withdraw through the mountains with our extensive trains would have been difficult and dangerous. At the same time we were unable to await an attack, as the country was unfavourable for collecting supplies in the presence of the enemy, who could re-strain our foraging parties by holding the mountain-passes with local and other troops. A battle had, therefore, become in a measure unavoidable, and the success already gained gave hope of a favourable issue."

The hour of sunrise on July 2 saw Meade's divisions widely scattered.   Less than ten thousand men of the First and Eleventh Corps held the Cemetery.   To their right and to their left were Slocum's eight thousand six hundred in line of battle.   Four thousand under Birney and four thousand under Humphreys, both of the Third Corps, were near at hand.   Lee's proposed assault against both Federal flanks would have found less than twenty-seven thousand men ready to receive him at any hour before seven o'clock.   At that hour the Federal Second Corps reached the field with two divisions of the Fifth.   Eight o'clock saw the arrival of another brigade of the Fifth; the hour of nine marked the coming of two brigades of the Third, and the Federal artillery reserve was on Cemetery Ridge at half-past ten.   At noon came another division of the Fifth. Along the thirty-four-mile route from Manchester, and yet far from the field, Sedgwick was pressing the fifteen thousand of the Federal Sixth Corps. The hour of sunrise, therefore, furnished an admirable opportunity for Lee to strike the Federal army before it was concentrated, and unto this task the Confederate commander was urging forward his lieutenants.

Lee had breakfast and was in the saddle before the coming of the dawn. At four o'clock he was despatching an officer to reconnoitre across the Emmittsburg road toward Round Top. He scanned Meade's line in the early light, as the latter stood on Culp's Hill and in the Cemetery. Lee looked eagerly for the coming of Anderson's division of Hill's corps, and for Longstreet's two divisions, that he might send them against Meade's left. But it was seven o'clock when Anderson began to move; eight o'clock brought the rattle of musketry from the woods south of the Seminary, where Anderson's advance under Wilcox was driving the Federal skirmishers. Nine o'clock had struck when Hill's line was arrayed along the Seminary Ridge, with his right near the Emmittsburg road.

If Hill was slow, Longstreet's men were still more tardy in reaching the field. They had not received orders to hasten their steps. It was after sunrise when his divisions began the march from Willoughby Run. Ewell's trains caused some delay. Eight o'clock was about the hour that saw the first of Longstreet's brigades under Kershaw of McLaws's division arrive at Seminary Ridge where Lee was waiting. McLaws saw Lee seated on the trunk of a fallen tree with a map before him; he saw Longstreet " walking up and down a little way off, apparently in an impatient humour."

Hood's division was behind that of McLaws, but Hood himself had sought Lee's point of observation shortly after daybreak. Hood bears this witness: " General Lee, with coat buttoned to the throat, sabre-belt around his waist, and field-glass pending at his side, walked up and down in the shade of large trees near us, halting now and then to observe the enemy. He seemed full of hope, yet at times buried in deep thought." Lee was anxious for Longstreet to attack, but at seven o'clock, with the sun already two and a half hours above the horizon, Longstreet's corps had not reached the field. Lee's words to Hood were these: " The enemy is here and if we do not whip him, he will whip us." Longstreet had been with Lee since daybreak, urging a movement around Meade's left. Lee rejected this plan and then Longstreet asked him to await the arrival of Pickett's division; with persistence he suggested this policy, but Lee was determined to begin the battle with the two divisions of McLaws and Hood as soon as they should arrive. As they continued to await the arrival of these troops, Longstreet sat apart with Hood, and Lee kept up his anxious watch upon the enemy. Then Longstreet said to Hood : "The General is a little nervous this morning; he wishes me to attack; I do not wish to do so without Pickett. I never like to go into battle with one boot off."

When McLaws drew nigh at eight o'clock he found Longstreet in the impatient humour and Lee

bending over the map.* Kershaw's brigade led the
column and Hood's men brought up the rear.
Longstreet's men had consumed more than three
hours of sunlight in making a journey of from two
to four miles. Kershaw's head of column was
turned southward along Seminary Ridge behind
Hill's corps and halted opposite the Black Horse
Tavern; this building stood where the Hagerstown
road passes over Marsh Creek. The hour was about
nine; Hill was just getting into position west of the
Emmittsburg road. The most favourable moment
for attack had passed, but even yet there was time
to crush Meade's left wing.

Lee was ready to aim straight at his mark. The
officer sent to reconnoitre had reached the slope of
Round Top without finding any Federal force in
that vicinity. He reported Meade's troops as arrayed within and near the Cemetery. Seated on the
tree, Lee pointed to the map and said, " General
McLaws, I wish you to place your command across
this road," pointing to a position on the map near the
Peach Orchard, perpendicular to the Emmittsburg
turnpike. Lee said, further, " I wish you to get
there, if possible, without being seen by the enemy."
Longstreet thrust himself between Lee and McLaws
and ordered the latter to arrange his division in a
line *parallel* to the turnpike. But Lee's decision

---

* Hood writes that he rode forward with his staff to Lee's position
"shortly after daybreak, July 2." He says further : " My division
soon commenced filing into an open field near me." The more defin-
ite statements of McLaws and Kershaw settle the hour of the arrival
of Longstreet's troops as eight o'clock. With this agrees also Longstreet's letter to W. H. Taylor (1875).

was prompt and positive: " No, General, I want his division *perpendicular* to the Emmittsburg road." Lee's orders were positive and explicit—that Longstreet should *partially envelope* the Federal left on the Emmittsburg road and drive it in. This movement he expected Longstreet to make immediately. Shortly after nine o'clock, Lee informed Hill and Anderson that Longstreet would occupy the territory south of Hill; that Longstreet's " line would be in a direction nearly at right angles " with the line of Hill's corps, and that Longstreet " would assault the extreme left of the enemy and drive him towards Gettysburg." At the same time Hill was ordered to move into battle in conjunction with Longstreet's left. McLaws affirms that Longstreet seemed " irritated and annoyed " when Lee turned away and left him under orders to lead his corps into immediate battle along the Emmittsburg road.* After giving orders to Longstreet and Hill, Lee rode into Gettysburg to examine Ewell's position. At sunrise he had despatched Venable to learn Ewell's opinion about bringing the entire Confederate army around to the right to make the attack from the westward against the Cemetery. When Lee came in person he found Ewell still confident of sending Johnson without difficulty to the sum-

---

* McLaws glanced across the terrain of forest and field and mentally decided that he could lead his troops unobserved from the Seminary Ridge to the enemy's position on the turnpike within half an hour. But Longstreet, later, directed him to follow a more circuitous route. The responsibility for choosing this winding course is laid by Longstreet upon Lee's engineer officer who made the early morning journey to Round Top.

mit of Culp's Hill, while Early, since two o'clock in the morning, had his men arrayed in line at the foot of the slope ready to scale Cemetery Hill from the direction of Gettysburg.*

At Ewell's headquarters, Lee anxiously awaited the sound of Longstreet's guns. He then made a close personal examination of the Federal position near the Cemetery, and watched the approach of Federal reinforcements. He saw the necessity of immediate attack. He manifested impatience at Longstreet's delay. He rode back to seek the cause of the silence that reigned at noonday along the Seminary Ridge, saying, " What *can* detain Longstreet ? He ought to be in position now." That cause is thus recorded in Longstreet's report:

" I received instructions from the Commanding-General to move, with the portion of my command that was up, around to gain the Emmittsburg road. . . . Fearing that my force was too weak to venture to make an attack, I delayed until General Law's brigade joined its division [Hood's]."

At noonday Law's men arrived after a march of twenty-four miles since the dawn. At one o'clock Longstreet set his column in motion. Three golden hours and more had been given to inactivity during

---

* Lee saw the danger involved in the extension of his left wing. Ewell's left brigades were beyond Rock Creek, under orders to wade the stream and move a little south of westward against the steep rock-covered fortress of Culp's Hill. It seems to have been Ewell's persistent confidence in his ability to capture the stronghold that led Lee to give up his original view which favoured the transfer of Ewell's corps to the Seminary Ridge and the Emmittsburg road.

Lee's absence with Ewell, through the stark obstinacy of Longstreet. Two more hours were consumed in bringing the corps to the field of action;
two countermarches were made, one a long circuit
as far as Black Horse Tavern, in the effort to find a
route concealed from the signal station on Round
Top. At four in the afternoon, the slow march
brought the corps into line of battle in front of Little
Round Top.

Early on July 2, Meade commanded Butterfield
to prepare a detailed order for the retreat of the
Federal army. He called a council of his corps-
commanders to consider this order, but Longstreet's
guns at 4 P.M. broke up the conference and called
the Federal officers to the defence of their left.
Just before this, Sickles had pushed his corps as far
as the Emmittsburg road without informing Meade,
and occupied the salient angle formed by that road
and the ridge extending from the Peach Orchard to
Little Round Top. McLaws faced the Peach
Orchard, and Hood was drawn out to the right
across the turnpike. Hood was expected to sweep
down the Federal line parallel to the turnpike and
roll it toward Gettysburg.

General Meade's position at 4 P.M. was as follows:
The right wing under Slocum, consisting of the
Twelfth Corps and the fragments of the First and
Eleventh, was bent around like a fishhook from the
Cemetery to Culp's Hill. Hancock, with the Second
Corps, occupied the central position along Cemetery
Ridge, thus forming the shank of the fishhook.
The Third Corps on Hancock's left, was holding the

Peach Orchard on the Emmittsburg turnpike.* The Fifth Corps was resting along Rock Creek on the Baltimore road. Longstreet's force of less than thirteen thousand now confronted the twelve thousand under Sickles. The latter were arrayed behind stone walls and partly in the forest and among heavy boulders, and their position bristled with artillery.

E. M. Law was in command of Hood's right brigade opposite Round Top. Law sent couriers to the crest of this high peak and they found the entire Federal left flank unprotected. Law and Hood sent to Longstreet formal protest against advancing up the turnpike, and urged the occupation of Round Top by extending Hood's division toward the Confederate right. Three times was this protest made to Longstreet. The latter returned each time the peremptory answer, " General Lee's orders are to attack up the Emmittsburg road." †

It was after the hour of four when Hood advanced across the valley toward the Round Tops under the fire from the Federal guns. Among the boulders of

---

* Meade would have withdrawn the Third from this advanced position, but Longstreet's assault prevented him.

† Law expresses the opinion, in the *Century Magazine*, that this protest did not reach General Lee, and adds the view that the battle of Gettysburg was lost to the Confederates by this failure to capture Round Top from the south, and thence extending the Confederate line toward the Federal rear on the Baltimore road. Law seems to forget, however, that Lee's line was already a half-circle, and that the suggested movement would have required the immediate withdrawal of Ewell toward the Confederate right. Otherwise it would have been an attempt to *surround* Meade's army with little more than half his numbers.

20

Devil's Den he found the left wing of Sickles's line
of battle. Law took the place of the wounded Hood
and pressed the grey-jackets steadily forward against
the blazing fortress. The Federal brigades were
broken and driven back by sheer courage and
tenacity, and three cannon were seized. The Alabamians under Oates passed completely over the
northern slope of Round Top and then advanced
directly toward Little Round Top. Law's centre
made a dash to gain this keypoint of the entire
field. But Warren led a battery and a brigade from
the Fifth Corps to the mountain-top just as Law's
shouting riflemen were climbing the slope, and the
entire Confederate division was forced back to the
boulders of Devil's Den.

Meanwhile the veterans of McLaws were fairly
aflame with enthusiasm. Alexander's guns were
taming the fire of the Federal artillery in the Peach
Orchard angle. Kershaw's Carolinians and Barksdale's Mississippians formed the front line. Barksdale stood before his eager brigade sword in hand
and with uncovered head and pleaded with McLaws:
" General, let me go; General, let me charge."
Amid the roar of Law's battle Barksdale, Wofford,
and Kershaw crashed against the angle at the
Orchard with wild cheers. Backward over stone
fences they literally drove the shattered brigades of
Sickles. Longstreet's men fought like demons.
Alexander's six batteries advanced in the charge
with the infantry. Nothing seemed able to withstand their terrific onslaught. The gallant Barksdale fell but his heroic men pressed forward. Barnes

from the Fifth Corps, Caldwell from the Second, and Ayres from the Fifth successively led three Federal divisions, thirteen thousand men, to give aid to Sickles. They were all forced back with the loss of half their numbers in the face of Longstreet's gallant charge. About six o'clock Hill's right brigades pressed up to the Emmittsburg road and sent the right wing of Sickles's corps in retreat toward Cemetery Ridge. The hour of 7 P.M. witnessed the complete defeat of Meade's left wing. Longstreet's victorious divisions were rushing forward to deliver battle at the base of the Round Tops. Wilcox, Perry, and Wright, of Hill's corps, were advancing against Meade's centre on Cemetery Ridge. Hill failed to send supporting brigades. Wilcox advanced to the base of Cemetery Ridge and captured eight guns, but there he paused. Wright's Georgians marched steadily up the long slope, leaped the stone fences and took possession of the crest of the Ridge, a short distance south of the Cemetery. Wright laid his hand on twenty Federal cannon. Meade's line was cut in twain. But Wright was alone. Perry had not kept pace with him; Posey remained behind the turnpike. Hill's other divisions stood motionless one mile away. Longstreet's gallant attack had practically won the field if Hill had pushed forward his brigades to hold it. Meade was hastening troops from Culp's Hill and the Cemetery toward his imperilled left and centre. Sedgwick's Sixth Corps was arriving upon the field. More than half of the Army of the Potomac was massed along the Cemetery Ridge behind a multitude of guns. Wright was surrounded and driven back, and the tide of Federal defeat was checked at the summit of the Ridge. Hundreds of Confederate heroes, however, lay disabled upon that field of carnage.

The crisis of battle came just before sunset, when Lee's right wing was making Meade's entire position to tremble. The hour for action had long before come to Ewell and to Hill. Ewell was tardy. Johnson's batteries were shattered by the Federal guns. When his division advanced to assault Culp's Hill, Longstreet's battle was almost concluded.

Although Meade had withdrawn an entire division from Culp's Hill to withstand Wright's assault, yet the darkness prevented Johnson from attaining complete success. With great gallantry his men marched up the side of the fortress and fought their way into the first line of Federal intrenchments. The night restrained them from a further advance. To the sound of Johnson's muskets, at sunset, Early led his two brigades against Cemetery Hill. Over stone walls, up the steep face of the slope, rushed the gallant men of North Carolina and Louisiana. They tarried not under the withering fire from musket and cannon until they overran the Eleventh Corps and established themselves in the Federal works on the summit. Rodes, on Early's right, was slow in getting into position, and did not advance at all to the aid of Early. The inactivity of Rodes kept Hill's left wing stationary. Hancock sent reinforcements to the Cemetery and the Federal troops in front of Rodes and Hill turned upon Early's right flank, and the gallant hero was forced to withdraw.

As night fell upon the field of blood, Lee was still sanguine of success. His losses in men were heavy but he knew that Meade's loss was yet heavier. The Confederate soldiers were eager for the continuance of the battle. Southern valour never shone more resplendently than on that field of July 2. In most cases Lee's brigades visited slaughter and defeat upon superior numbers posted behind walls of stone. At the close of the day Law held Devil's Den and the bases of the Round Tops. Johnson held the crest of Culp's Hill, almost in reach of the Baltimore road. Wright and Early had broken through the Federal line in two places and failed to hold Cemetery Ridge itself only from lack of support. Stuart had reached the field and Lee's artillery was all ready for service.

Consternation reigned in Meade's camp. He called his twelve principal officers about him to discuss the advisability of retreating.* Meade himself was in favour of retreating, according to the statement of Slocum, though other Federal officers deny the truth of this opinion. Three of his corps were completely shattered. Twenty thousand men were missing from the Federal divisions that had marched to Gettysburg. F. A. Walker says, " It was indeed a gloomy hour." Only Meade's Sixth and Twelfth corps remained unshaken by the storm of war. He

---

* Meade's questions brought out these opinions : "Slocum, stay and fight it out. Newton thinks it a bad position. Hancock puzzled about practicability of retiring. . . . Howard favour of not retiring. Birney don't know. Third Corps used up and not in good condition to fight. Sedgwick doubtful whether we ought to attack."

still had in readiness the order of retreat prepared by Butterfield. After long and anxious conference it was decided to remain one day and await Lee's assault. During the night the scout Dahlgren brought to Meade two captured despatches, the replies of Cooper and President Davis to Lee's request for an army under Beauregard to menace Washington. They spoke of the Federal force threatening Richmond, and the impossibility of gathering a Confederate army at Culpeper. These despatches relieved Meade's apprehensions about Washington and gave him nerve to hold his ground and abide the result of Lee's onslaught.*

In his official report, Lee thus describes the plan which he adopted at the close of July 2:

" The result of this day's operations induced the belief that, with proper concert of action, and with the increased support that the positions gained on the right would enable the artillery to render the assaulting columns, we should ultimately succeed, and it was accordingly determined to continue the attack. The general plan was unchanged. Longstreet, reinforced by Pickett's three brigades, which arrived near the battle-field during the afternoon of the 2d, was ordered to attack the next morning, and General Ewell was directed to assail the enemy's right at the same time. The latter, during the night, reinforced General Johnson with two brigades from Rodes's and one from Early's division."

Lee's purpose, therefore, was to renew the attack against both flanks of the Federal army. Longstreet

---

* William L. Royall, Esq., of Richmond, Virginia, has secured letters and papers from the family of Dahlgren, showing that, in the opinion of Lincoln, Stanton, and other officials, the captured despatches served to change Meade's plan, as he was upon the point of withdrawing his army to Pipe Creek during the night of July 2.

instructed Law to be ready to assail the enemy in front of Devil's Den. But the morning of July 3 revealed the Federal Fifth Corps, supported by the Sixth Corps, in complete possession of both Round Tops, with their riflemen behind strong works and supported by heavy artillery. Moreover, Kilpatrick's cavalry was threatening Longstreet's right flank. When Lee stood before Round Top, on the morning of July 3, and saw the strength of Meade's left, he immediately changed his general plan. Ewell's battle on Culp's Hill was every moment roaring out a call for aid. Lee, therefore, ordered Longstreet to organise a column of attack against the Federal centre on Cemetery Ridge and, after that, in conjunction with Ewell, to assail from opposite directions the curved position held by the Federal right wing. Hood and McLaws were to keep the Federal left wing engaged and to make an advance when the opportunity came.* The two lines of the column of attack against Hancock's position were composed of Pickett's division of Longstreet's corps on the right, and Pettigrew's (Heth's) division of Hill's corps. Wilcox's brigade and Perry's brigade of Anderson's division were ordered to guard Pickett's right flank, while Trimble was to lead the brigades of Lane and Scales to the support of Pettigrew. " General Hill was

---

* Some of Lee's staff-officers state that Longstreet was ordered to support Pickett with the divisions of McLaws and Hood. It was impossible, however, to withdraw these divisions in order to move them against Meade's centre. Lee evidently expected them to attack Meade's left wing as soon as Pickett should seize the Federal centre.

directed," says Lee, " to hold his line with the rest of his command, afford General Longstreet further assistance, if required, and avail himself of any success that might be gained." Ewell's battle was still raging on Culp's Hill when Lee gave the order to attack. He was confident that this column could break through Meade's line at the point where Wright's brigade had cut it in twain on the previous evening, and then assist Ewell in crushing the Federal right wing. Lee pointed out to Longstreet as the objective point of attack, the famous " clump of trees " near the middle part of Hancock's line, occupied by the Federal Second Corps and two divisions of the First Corps. As Lee stood upon the field won the previous day, and looked eastward from the Emmittsburg road toward Cemetery Ridge, the country seemed almost level. With the exception of the stone walls behind which his men protected themselves, Hancock's position, in itself, was not of great strength. Lee proposed to protect the flanks of his attacking column by advancing his cannon. First, however, he gave orders to neutralise the power of the Federal guns in his front by the concentrated fire of his own artillery.

At 10 A.M. E. P. Alexander had in readiness for action along the Emmittsburg road a battery of seventy-five guns. To his left, on Seminary Ridge, R. L. Walker's park of sixty-three cannon was prepared for battle. It was expected that their fire would silence the Federal batteries, and then was Longstreet's column to " advance under cover of the combined fire " of the Confederate guns. Lee says: "The batteries were directed to be pushed forward as the infantry progressed, protect their flanks, and support their attacks closely." He wished to repeat the artillery tactics that had brought success on the first day's battle against Hooker at Chancellorsville. At nine o'clock Pickett and Pettigrew were in line on the Ridge. Longstreet was not in favour of making the assault; and three hours passed away in unnecessary delay before the battle was opened. These three hours brought to a close Ewell's desperate fight on the slope of Culp's Hill. With his repulse Lee's chances for success against Meade's centre and right were less favourable. At twelve o'clock the nine brigades intended for the assault were moved forward to the edge of the woods; in their front, skirting the open fields were the Confederate guns. Longstreet states that he was so opposed to the movement that he asked Alexander to order Pickett into the charge when the favourable moment should arrive. At one o'clock the artillery duel began; Lee's guns drew upon them the fire of eighty Federal cannon. The crash and the roar of that fearful cannonade from more than two hundred guns was of surpassing grandeur. The two ridges, fourteen hundred yards apart, were like blazing volcanoes. Their crests were wreathed in flame and smoke. Upon the intervening fields there settled down a dense, dark battle-cloud. The heavens seemed full of screaming, bursting shells. Both sides suffered. The Confederate aim was accurate and swept the Cemetery Ridge; no infantry dared move along that elevation, and the Federal line of battle lay crouching behind the stone fence near the summit.   Francis A. Walker states that

"the whole space behind Cemetery Ridge was in a moment rendered uninhabitable.   General headquarters were broken up; the supply and reserve ammunition trains were driven out; motley hordes of camp followers poured down the Baltimore pike, or spread over the fields to the rear.   Upon every side caissons exploded; horses were struck down by hundreds; the air was filled with flying missiles; shells tore up the ground and then bounded for another and perhaps more deadly flight, or burst above the crouching troops and sent their ragged fragments down in deadly showers.   Never had a storm so dreadful burst upon mortal men."

After thirty minutes the Federal fire began to slacken and the eighteen guns in the Cemetery limbered up and withdrew.*   Alexander wrote to Pickett, "If you are coming at all you must come at once."   Pickett sought Longstreet and said, "General, shall I advance?" but Longstreet was silent.   Pickett saluted and cried out, "Sir, I shall lead my division forward," and ordered his men into the charge.   Pickett's three brigades of Virginians and Heth's four brigades of North Carolinians, Tennesseans, Alabamians, Mississippians, and Virginians under Pettigrew moved out of the woods and advanced slowly toward the Emmittsburg road.   The two lines of glittering bayonets were in strong contrast with the dull grey garments of the

---

* This was due in part to the accuracy of the Confederate fire, and in part to Meade's order to husband the ammunition for the anticipated charge.

ragged heroes. Behind Pettigrew's right flank marched Trimble with two brigades of North Carolinians. Wilcox was expected to strengthen Pickett's right flank with his brigade of Alabamians. Twelve thousand riflemen were now moving across the open plain, fourteen hundred yards in width. After passing the Confederate batteries, Pickett's division changed direction to the left, and pressed toward the salient in Hancock's line. At first, a deep silence reigned upon the entire field. Half the distance was completed before the fire became serious from the Federal guns in the Cemetery and on the Round Tops. The Confederates gallantly advanced over the post-and-rail fences at the Emmittsburg road, to meet the canister and musketry fire directly in their front.

At this crisis in the battle, the artillery failed to play the part which General Lee expected. The Federal guns reopened their fire, but the Confederate batteries had nearly exhausted their ammunition in the hour's cannonade and " were unable to reply," says Lee, " or render the necessary support to the attacking party. Owing to this fact, which was unknown to me when the assault took place, the enemy was enabled to throw a strong force of infantry against our left, already wavering under a concentrated fire of artillery."

Lee expected his guns to move forward as a part of the attacking column. Alexander held nine howitzers in reserve, intending to " take them ahead of Pickett up nearly to musket range " but they were removed without his sanction and he failed to find them. When Pickett advanced, Alexander selected the guns that still possessed ammunition, about fifteen in number, and moved them forward behind Pickett's division. But the failure to keep the chests filled from the reserve train left the Confederate guns practically silent at the moment when Pickett and Pettigrew stood face to face with Hancock at the stone wall on Cemetery Ridge.

The Federal guns in the Cemetery began to wear away the left end of Pettigrew's line, and Trimble advanced to mingle his two brigades with Pettigrew's right. Pickett's right was thrown in toward the centre of the column by the flank attack of Stannard's Vermont brigade. The Round Top guns enfiladed his line. But the casualties were not yet very great. When the column was within one hundred yards of the wall, the Federal line began to flee to the rear. The Confederate muskets flamed forth in a fierce volley, and with a far-resounding yell the left of Pickett's division and the right of Pettigrew and Trimble rushed upon the stone wall, and took possession. Prisoners were captured, and the Federal guns on the crest were silenced. Pettigrew's left pressed up against the Federal works, and Kemper on Pickett's right fought hand to hand with Stannard. Carnage and death reigned upon both flanks. Nearly every Federal and Confederate officer above the grade of captain lay bleeding among the hundreds of fallen soldiers.

Armistead's brigade, forming Pickett's second line, rushed up to the stone wall, almost at the same moment with the front line. For several minutes

there were no enemies immediately before them.
Norman J. Hall, commanding a Federal brigade,
thus makes report:

> "A portion of the line of General Webb on my right had given
> way, and many men were making to the rear as fast as possible.
> . . . I was forced to order my own brigade back from the line
> and move it by the flank under a heavy fire. The enemy was rapidly
> gaining a foothold ; organisation was mostly lost ; in the confusion,
> commands were useless, while a disposition on the part of the men
> to fall back a pace or two each time to load gave the line a retiring
> direction."

A long space in Meade's centre acknowledged the
supremacy of the Stars and Bars. The presence of
Confederate artillery would undoubtedly have held
the captured works.

A fresh line of Federal troops advanced to the
crest and opened fire, but the Confederates drove
them back with repeated volleys. Then Armistead
placed his hat on the point of his sword and sprang
over the stone wall with the cry, " Boys, we must
use the cold steel; who will follow me ? " The Virginians followed the grim hero as he rushed beyond
the stone wall to the crest of the Ridge to seize the
Federal guns. There Armistead fell, and his men
retired to the wall to await reinforcements. Com-
parative quiet again prevailed. Lieutenant G. W.
Finley had time to cast a careful look backward
over the field of Pickett's advance and was " surprised to see comparatively so few men lying dead
or wounded on the field." A voice from the ranks,
without authority, ordered a retreat, and many
turned to flee. Fearful slaughter was visited upon

them as they sought to escape. The Federal troops from the flanks then swarmed around the men at the wall and led away four thousand prisoners.

A full half-hour after the advance of the main column, Longstreet sent Wilcox forward to support Pickett's right. Perry lent aid to Wilcox. They met the fragments of Pickett's right regiments returning from the assault, and Wilcox himself was driven back with loss. Anderson's division of Hill's corps stood ready to advance on Pettigrew's left, but Longstreet kept him out of the battle. McLaws stood at Wilcox's right hand, but received no order to deliver battle. An earlier advance of Wilcox and Perry on Pickett's right and of Anderson's remaining brigades on Pettigrew's left, even without the artillery, would most probably have given a great victory to Lee.

Lee sat upon his horse near E. P. Alexander's guns to watch the return of his brave column. His bearing was calm and self-possessed. Alexander makes the remark that Lee

"had the instincts of a soldier within him as strongly as any man. . . . No soldier could have looked on at Pickett's charge and not burned to be in it. To have a personal part in a close and desperate fight at that moment would, I believe, have been at heart a great pleasure to General Lee, and possibly he was looking for one."

Colonel Fremantle of the English army, an eyewitness, thus describes the Confederate leader:

"General Lee was perfectly sublime. He was engaged in rallying and encouraging the broken troops and was riding about, a little in front of the wood, quite alone—the whole of his staff being engaged in a similar manner farther to the rear. His face, which is always placid and cheerful, did not show signs of the slightest disappointment, care or annoyance, and he was addressing to every soldier he met a few words of encouragement ; such as : ' All this will come right in the end ; we 'll talk it over afterward ; but in the meantime all good men must rally.' . . . He spoke to all the wounded men that passed him, and the slightly wounded he exhorted to bind up their hurts and ' take a musket ' in this emergency. Very few failed to answer his appeal, and I saw badly wounded men take off their hats and cheer him.

" General Wilcox now came up to him and in very depressed tones of annoyance and vexation, explained the state of his brigade. But General Lee immediately shook hands with him and said, in a cheerful mannner : ' Never mind, General ; all this has been my fault. It is I that have lost this fight, and you must help me out of it the best way you can.' In this manner did General Lee, wholly ignoring self and position, encourage and reanimate his somewhat dispirited troops, and magnanimously take upon his own shoulders the whole weight of the repulse. It was impossible to look at him, or to listen to him, without feeling the strongest admiration."

During the battle of the afternoon, Farnsworth led a cavalry charge against the Confederate right and rear, only to reap disaster. On the Confederate left, Stuart arrayed his horsemen and attempted to get possession of the Baltimore turnpike in the Federal rear. Gregg's cavalry confronted him. A series of charges and counter-charges took place in which Hampton was wounded. Stuart fought a gallant battle, but Gregg maintained his position.

Lee stood with guns in position on Seminary Ridge ready to receive Meade's assault. But the Federal army was not in condition to deliver offensive battle. Only through the most desperate fighting had it been able to maintain itself behind strong works. The loss in killed, wounded, and prisoners on both sides was terrific. The armies had torn each other almost to fragments and neither was capable of making another assault. Over twenty-three thousand names were erased from the list of ninety-five thousand who followed Meade into the battle. Lee's loss was a little over twenty thousand out of a total of about fifty-eight thousand men engaged in the fight, including the cavalry. This estimate included a number of stragglers who afterwards returned to the Confederate ranks. Among the brave dead were Armistead, Garnett, Pender, Barksdale, and Semmes. Kemper, Pettigrew, Hood, Trimble, Heth, Scales, G. T. Anderson, Jenkins, and Hampton were seriously wounded, and Archer was left a prisoner. Concerning the result of the conflict, Lee says: " The severe loss sustained by the army, and the reduction of its ammunition, rendered another attempt to dislodge the enemy inadvisable, and it was, therefore, determined to withdraw."

On July 4, Lee stood the entire day in defiant attitude, awaiting Meade's advance. The latter was wise enough to know that disaster would follow an assault. Lee started all his *impedimenta* toward the Potomac, and during the night of the 4th withdrew his entire army in good order *via* Fairfield. Ewell's corps, as Lee's rearguard, did not leave Gettysburg until the forenoon of July 5. He thus compelled Meade to follow him by circuitous routes through the passes to the southward. The *morale* of the Confederate army was unimpaired. The men were ready for battle at any hour. They ascribed their repulse on the third day solely to the advantageous position of the Federal army. Upon the field of Gettysburg their honour had remained untarnished. In nearly every part of the struggle they had contended against superior numbers. Even in Pennsylvania, as upon all other fields, the Army of Northern Virginia, man for man, greatly out-fought the Army of the Potomac.

July 6 found Lee's army at Hagerstown; his trains stood at Williamsport, checked in their progress by the swollen Potomac. The Confederates established themselves behind intrenchments covering the ford at Williamsport and the bridge at Falling Waters. Stuart was indefatigable in guarding both flanks. With great caution, Meade marched through Frederick and Middletown. The battle of Gettysburg had left him about forty-seven thousand effective men out of his original ninety-five thousand. The authorities at Washington grew bolder with the lapse of time and urged Meade to destroy Lee's army at once. French brought forward eleven thousand Federal veterans, while Couch and Smith led to Meade's aid a swarm of militia. July 11 saw Meade carefully bridging the Antietam, and the 12th brought him within view of Lee's position near the Potomac. There he speedily placed fortifications in front of the Federal army. Meade called a council of war, but his subordinates were almost unanimous against the policy of attacking Lee's thin line. They knew well enough the unconquerable spirit of the Confederates, who were eagerly awaiting an opportunity to defend their position. Lee himself said of his soldiers at this juncture, " Our noble men are cheerful and confident." He wrote to President Davis again urging the assembling of an army from the Southern coast, and its advance under Beauregard to "make a demonstration upon Washington."

> "I hope your Excellency will understand," he continued, "that I am not in the least discouraged, or that my faith in the protection of an all-merciful Providence, or in the fortitude of this army, is at all shaken. But, though conscious that the enemy has been much shattered in the recent battle, I am aware that he can be easily reinforced, while no addition can be made to our numbers."

On July 11, while Meade drew nigh, Lee issued the following address to his soldiers:

> "After long and trying marches, endured with the fortitude that has ever characterised the soldiers of the Army of Northern Virginia, you have penetrated the country of our enemies, and recalled to the defence of their own soil those who were engaged in the invasion of ours. You have fought a fierce and sanguinary battle, which, if not attended with the success that has hitherto crowned your efforts, was marked by the same heroic spirit that has commanded the respect of your enemies, the gratitude of your country, and the admiration of mankind.
>
> "Once more you are called upon to meet the army from which you have won on so many fields a name that will never die. . . . Let every soldier remember that on his courage and fidelity depends all that makes life worth having—the freedom of his country, the honour of his people, and the security of his home. . . ."

On July 13, the river-flood was within its banks again and during the night Ewell's corps waded the Potomac at Williamsport. Longstreet and Hill began to cross the pontoon bridge at Falling Waters. Stuart defended the rear with such success that Meade did not discover the Confederate movement until it was practically completed. The Federal cavalry pressed forward against Hill's rear only to feel the strength of Heth's division; the brave Pettigrew was slain in this rearguard skirmish. Noonday saw the three Confederate corps on the Virginia side of the river, and Meade was left astonished at the consummate skill shown in the method of Lee's withdrawal. The spirit of aggressiveness had been hammered out of the Army of the Potomac at Gettysburg, and Meade was henceforth held carefully between Lee and the city of Washington.

From the lower valley, on July 15, Lee wrote as follows:

" The army has returned to Virginia. Its return is rather sooner than I had originally contemplated, but, having accomplished much of what I proposed on leaving the Rappahannock—namely, relieving the valley of the presence of the enemy and drawing his army north of the Potomac—I determined to recross the latter river. The enemy, after centring his forces in our front [at Williamsport], began to fortify himself in his position and bring up his troops, militia, etc., and those around Washington and Alexandria. This gave him enormous odds. It also circumscribed our limits for procuring subsistence for men and animals, which, with the uncertain state of the river, rendered it hazardous for us to continue on the north side. . . . I hope we will yet be able to damage our adversaries when they meet us, and that all will go right with us. That it should be so we must implore the forgiveness of God for our sins and the continuance of His blessings. There is nothing but His Almighty power can sustain us. God bless you all."

Meade followed McClellan's plan of the previous autumn, and crossed the Potomac into the regions east of the Blue Ridge. The Federal Third Corps looked cautiously through the passes of the Ridge as Lee moved up the valley, to throw his army across Meade's path at Culpeper on July 24. Operations upon a wider field now claimed the attention of both armies. Meade sent troops to assist in beleaguering Charleston and also to suppress the riots in New York due to the enforced enlistment of Federal recruits. Lee was called upon to face the results of the fall of Vicksburg and the depletion in strength of the Confederate armies.

Perhaps the most serious obstacle to the ultimate success of the Southern Confederacy was the Federal control of ocean and rivers. Water routes of communication enabled the North to attack salient points on the Atlantic coast. The Confederacy was cut in twain by the fall of Vicksburg and the consequent loss of the Mississippi River. The stronghold of the Confederates was now limited to the southern Appalachian Mountains and their slopes. The Southern people were isolated from the rest of the world by a ring of fire. Rosecrans was advancing into Tennessee, and Charleston was fiercely assailed. Wilmington remained as the only port of entry for the blockade-runners from foreign ports. Men, horses, cloth, and provisions were becoming every day more scarce. The railroads were out of order, and every State was besieging President Davis with demands for the defence of its borders. Under the stress of complaints from the public press, General Lee, on August 8, wrote, in part, as follows to President Davis:

". . . Everything points to the advantages to be derived from a new commander, and I the more anxiously urge the matter upon your Excellency from my belief that a younger and abler man than myself can readily be obtained. I know that he will have as gallant and brave an army as ever existed to second his efforts, and it would be the happiest day of my life to see at its head a worthy leader—one that would accomplish more than I can perform and all that I have wished. I hope your Excellency will attribute my request to the true reason—the desire to serve my country and to do all in my power to insure the success of her righteous cause."

To this letter, Davis replied, in part, in these words:

". . . I am truly sorry to know that you still feel the effects of the illness you suffered last spring, and can readily understand the embarrassments you experience in using the eyes of others, having been so much accustomed to make your own reconnaissances. . . . But suppose, my dear friend, that I were to admit, with all their implications, the points which you present, where am I to find that new commander who is to possess the greater ability which you believe to be required. . . . To ask me to substitute you by some one in my judgment more fit to command, or who would possess more of the confidence of the army, or of the reflecting men of the country, is to demand an impossibility."

Lee's appeals for men were heard and his roll of August 10 numbered fifty-eight thousand six hundred " present for duty." Early in September, Longstreet led away two divisions to assist Bragg in holding Tennessee against Rosecrans, and Pickett's division was moved to Petersburg. This left Lee in command of about forty-six thousand men. Upon his departure Longstreet wrote this to Lee: " Our affections for you are stronger, if it is possible for them to be stronger, than our admiration for you."

Meade advanced in force to Culpeper, and Lee stood on the defensive behind the Rapidan. Lee sought to quiet jealousies among his own soldiers from different States, called for more troops, and then, on September 25, wrote as follows to Longstreet concerning the battle of Chickamauga:

" My whole heart and soul have been with you and your brave corps in your late battle. It was natural to hear of Longstreet and [D. H.] Hill charging side by side, and pleasing to find the armies of the east and west vying with each other in valour and devotion to their country. . . . Finish the work before you, my dear General, and return to me. I want you badly, and you cannot get back too soon."

On October 9, Lee advanced his army across the Rapidan to seek battle with Meade. By concealed and circuitous routes, he passed around Meade's right flank and threatened his rear *via* Madison Court-House. Meade had marched all the way from Gettysburg to find a battle with Lee, but during the night of October 10, he moved backward rapidly until the Rappahannock rolled between the two armies.

Lee then crossed the river at the Warrenton Springs and again moved around Meade's right flank to Warrenton. A halt was made to apportion food to the troops. The delay gave Meade the opportunity to hasten eastward along the railroad and thus to reach Bristoe Station before Lee could cut off his retreat. Hill led Lee's advance-guard. As Hill drew nigh to Bristoe Station, the Fifth Federal Corps was just crossing Broad Run in front of the Confederates. Without a reconnaisance, Hill pushed parts of two divisions over the Run to attack the rear of the Fifth. Suddenly the fire of Warren's (Second) corps was poured into Hill's flank from behind the railroad embankment. Nearly fourteen hundred Confederates were disabled or captured. The tardiness of both Hill and Ewell had permitted the escape of Meade, but the greater tardiness of Ewell allowed Warren thus to assail Hill's flank. Lee listened to the latter's words of excuse for the mortifying disaster, and then with grave sadness replied, " Well, well, General, bury these poor men and let us say no more about it." Even yet, however, Meade's situation " was singularly precarious," says one of his own officers, for his waggon trains were massed in the fields away from the roads. At length the Federal army was on the northern side of Bull Run and fortified itself at Centreville. Lee then decided to withdraw, and assigned the following reasons:

" Nothing prevented my continuing in his front but the destitute condition of the men, thousands of whom are barefooted, a greater number partially shod, and nearly all without overcoats, blankets or warm clothing. I think the sublimest sight of the war was the cheerfulness and alacrity exhibited by this army in the pursuit of the enemy under all the trials and privations to which it was exposed."

While the Confederates were returning toward the Rapidan, Stuart gave Meade's cavalry a staggering blow as they advanced in pursuit. The horsemen wrought heroic deeds during the entire campaign both in the pursuit and in the withdrawal. Lee moved the main body of his troops across the Rappahannock and left two of Early's brigades on the northern bank in the redoubts near the site of the former railroad bridge. A sudden onset of the advanced Federal brigades in the late evening of November 7, secured possession of the redoubts before aid could be sent to Early's troops. Sixteen hundred prisoners, eight colours, and several guns became Federal spoil. Just before this disaster Lee wrote as follows to his wife:

" I moved yesterday into a nice pine thicket, and Perry is to-day engaged in constructing a chimney in front of my tent which will make it warm and comfortable. I have no idea when Fitzhugh [General W. H. F. Lee] will be exchanged. The Federal authorities still resist all exchanges, because they think it is to our interest to make them. Any desire expressed on our part for the exchange of any individual magnifies the difficulty, as they at once think some great benefit is to result to us from it. His detention is very grievous to me, and, besides, I want his services. I am glad you have some socks for the army. Send them to me. They will come safely Tell the girls to send all they can. I wish they could make some shoes, too. We have thousands of barefooted men. There is no news. General Meade, I believe, is repairing the railroad, and I presume will come on again. If I could only get some shoes and clothes for the men I would save him the trouble."

After Lee returned to the southern bank of the Rapidan, Meade essayed a movement of the Napoleonic sort. At the dawn of November 26 he ordered the Fifth and First Corps to cross the Rapidan at Culpeper Mine ford; the Second Corps was expected to cross at the Germanna ford, while the Third and Sixth were to seek passage higher up the stream. This host in five bands was expected to seize the Orange turnpike and the plank road, which run parallel to the Rapidan, and to follow these highways up-stream against Lee's right flank. The Rapidan banks were difficult; other causes assisted *in* delaying Meade an entire day. The Third Corps moved too far to the right on the 27th, and ran against Edward Johnson's division of Ewell's corps. Stuart's vigilance had brought Lee the news, and the swift marching of Hill united his corps with Ewell in the intrenchments hastily constructed by the troops on the western border of Mine Run. This forest stream seeks the Rapidan in a northward course and formed the right flank of Lee's position. On its rugged banks Lee arrayed his eager veterans.

The gallant Johnson held the Federal Third Corps engaged, and thus the rest of the Federal army was delayed. When Meade advanced on the morning of the 28th to run riot in Lee's camp, he was confronted in the Wilderness with one hundred and fifty guns behind heavy works. Meade paused to devise further strategic movements. Warren led the Federal Second Corps and a part of the Sixth to turn Lee's right flank. Sedgwick found what seemed to be a vulnerable point in the defences of Lee's left wing. Warren's force was increased to twenty-six thousand, and Meade gave his two lieutenants the order to crush the Confederate flanks. The signal guns sounded early on the morning of November 30. Sedgwick on the Federal right was ready to move. Warren on the left was ready but unwilling to assault. During the night Lee's heroes had thrown up heavy breastworks and adorned them with cannon for the defence of their right flank. Naught but wounds and death did the Federal officers anticipate in advancing against the grim Confederate heroes. With chagrin, Meade withdrew his troops to the fields of

Culpeper. Though greatly outnumbering them, he dared not attack the defiant Confederate veterans of Gettysburg.

Ten days before this movement, on November 19, President Lincoln delivered his celebrated speech upon the Gettysburg battle-ground. He said, in part:

> " Fourscore and seven years ago our fathers brought forth on this continent a new nation, conceived in liberty, and dedicated to the proposition that all men are created equal. Now we are engaged in a great civil war, testing whether that nation, *or any nation so conceived and so dedicated, can long endure.*"

The address was a masterpiece of rhetorical beauty and also of the art of shifting great issues. The words italicised were shrewdly interpolated as expressing a proposition synonymous with the testing of the experiment of nearly a century. That experiment had culminated in the attempt of the Federal administration to invade and subdue by force of arms some of the States " conceived in liberty." Mr. Lincoln's dialectical skill imposed upon his audience the belief that they were struggling for the perpetuity of any government by the people. He thus added fresh impetus to the waning energies of those who had accepted his legal fiction of 1861 that the Federal administration was striving to "save the Union." The Confederate soldiers were striving for the principles involved in the italicised words of the address. The Southern heroes who died upon the field of Gettysburg, and those who lived to drive back the Army of the Potomac from Mine Run were dedicated to the maintenance of the principles set forth in Lee's address to his army at Hagerstown on July 11,—" all that makes life worth having— the freedom of his country, the honour of his people, and the security of his home."

CHAPTER XIII.

THE CAMPAIGN IN THE WILDERNESS.

1864.

HE Army of Northern Virginia spent the dreary months from December, 1863, until May, 1864, upon the bluffs that skirt the southern bank of the Rapidan River. Behind the army to the southward were outspread the tangled forests of the Piedmont and Tidewater sections of central Virginia. The flight of the bee toward the rear from the position of the Confederate intrenchments would pass across the network of streams that feed the York and the James rivers and at the distance of sixty-five miles would find Richmond, the capital of the Southern Confederacy. The Confederate line of defence behind the Rapidan was twenty miles in length. The left wing under A. P. Hill lay around Orange Court-House. The right wing was commanded by Ewell, and its flank was made strong by the works that followed the windings of Mine Run. From this stronghold the Confederate guns frowned upon every avenue of approach from the direction of Culpeper Court-House. The latter was the adopted home of the Army of the Potomac, ten miles due northward from the central point of Lee's encampment. The worst-clad and the worst-fed army, perhaps, ever mustered into service was the band of Confederate heroes who shivered and starved together on the banks of the Rapidan. Rude huts of pine and oaken logs, furnished inside with beds of straw, formed the habitations of both officers and men. The soldiers were clad in garments made up of patches and fluttering strings. Very few possessed comfortable shoes. Thousands were absolutely destitute of covering for head or foot. The only complete outfits were the products of hand-looms, woven by wives, mothers, and daughters who kept brave watch and prosecuted unmurmuring labours in the old plantation-homes.

Hunger was the most inveterate enemy of the Confederates in the Rapidan bivouac. One quarter of a pound of fat pork, with a little meal or a little flour, was the portion of food assigned daily to each man. Very frequently the pork only was dealt out, or perhaps the meal, or a bundle of crackers. This winter of 1863 saw the climax of high prices due to the inflated paper currency of the Confederacy. When bacon was selling for eight dollars and sugar for twenty dollars a pound, beans for sixty dollars and corn-meal for fifty dollars a bushel, the result was famine in the army. The negro servants were still faithful; very few, except along the border, had been enticed into the North. They were manifesting strong affection for their masters by cultivating the plantations to feed the Southern armies in the field, and the old men, women, and children at home. But the railways were dilapidated, and the rolling-stock was worn out, and the meat and corn and flour produced in the far South could not be swiftly borne to the starving men who were defending the northern threshold of the Confederacy.

General Lee's winter home was pitched in the midst of the camp. His small tent stood on a steep hillside, about two miles northeast of Orange Court-House. Two or three additional tents furnished accommodations for his staff. Only the man himself was there to indicate the presence of one in authority. General Lee shared the sufferings and privations of his men. He allowed himself a small ration of meat only twice a week and sometimes declined even that. He lived on corn-bread or crackers or a bit of cabbage as each or all came with convenience. All luxuries sent him by friends went invariably to the sick and wounded in the hospitals. In reply to remonstrances he would always say, " I am content to share the rations of my men" *

* We are told that on one occasion Lee received through the mail from an anonymous private soldier a very small slice of salt pork carefully packed between two oaken chips, with the statement in a letter that this was the daily ration of meat ; the writer claimed to be unable to live on this allowance and, although a gentleman, had been compelled to steal. But the Commander himself fared no more sumptuously. It is stated that some officers once came to dine in General Lee's tent. The fare set before them was only a plate of boiled cabbage : in the centre of the dish rested a diminutive slice of bacon. With knife well poised above this morsel, General Lee invited each guest in turn to receive a portion. But the small size of the piece of bacon led them all to decline. The meat remained on

Lee's humility of spirit seemed to increase, if possible, day by day. His devout trust in God grew stronger and more childlike. His great heart was full of solicitude for the welfare of his men, and for the upbuilding of the strength of his army. Upon himself he laid the lowliest duties in order to relieve the sufferings of his soldiers. The man who always sat upon the most uncomfortable seat in his tent lest some one else might secure it, could also bring to the army for distribution the socks knit by his wife and daughters and other devoted women of Virginia.

After a visit from his soldier-nephews, Fitz, John, and Henry Lee, in the autumn of 1863, General Lee wrote this: " As soon as I was left alone, I committed them in a fervent prayer to the care and guidance of our Heavenly Father." When the City Council of Richmond made him the gift of a house, Lee expressed his appreciation of the kind generosity of the Council, and added these words:

" The house is not necessary for the use of my family, and my own duties will prevent my residence in Richmond. I shall, therefore, be compelled to decline the generous offer, and trust that whatever means the City Council may have to spare for this purpose may be devoted to the relief of the families of our soldiers in the field who are now in need of assistance, and more deserving of it than myself."

To his wife he wrote the following:

the plate untouched ; hunger was appeased with cabbage. On the following day, General Lee called again for the bit of swine-flesh, but his coloured servant, with many bows, gave the information that the bacon had been borrowed to grace the official board of the day before and had been already returned to the owner.

" The kindness exhibited toward you as well as myself by our people, in addition to exciting my gratitude, causes me to reflect how little I have done to merit it, and humbles me in my own eyes to a painful degree."

The midwinter days brought increase of suffering to the soldiers and greater anxiety to Lee. He wrote this letter on January 24, 1864:

" I have had to disperse the cavalry as much as possible to obtain forage for their horses, and it is that which causes trouble. Provisions for the men, too, are very scarce, and with very light diet and light clothing I fear they suffer ; but still they are cheerful and uncomplaining. I received a report from one division the other day in which it was stated that over four hundred men were barefooted and over a thousand without blankets."

On February 6, he sent this message:

" . . . It is so long since we have had the foreign bean [coffee] that we no longer desire it. We have a domestic article which we procure by the bushel, that answers very well. . . . We have had to reduce our allowance of meat one-half, and some days we have none. . . . The soldiers are much in need. We have received some shoes lately, and the socks will be a great addition. Tell ' Life ' [his daughter Mildred] I think I hear her needles rattle as they fly through the meshes."

The eighteenth day of March found him writing this:

" There were sixty-seven pairs of socks in the bag I brought up instead of sixty-four, as you supposed, and I found here three dozen pairs of beautiful white-yarn socks, sent over by our kind cousin Julia and sweet little Carrie, making one hundred and three pairs, all of which I sent to the Stonewall brigade. One dozen of the Stuart socks had double heels. Can you not teach Mildred that stitch. They sent me also some hams, which I had rather they had eaten. I pray that you may be preserved and relieved from all your troubles, and that we may all be again united here on earth and forever in heaven."

The following message was sent by General Lee on April 2:

"Your note with the socks arrived last evening. I have sent them to the Stonewall brigade; the number all right—thirty pairs. Including this last parcel of thirty pairs, I have sent to that brigade two hundred and sixty-three pairs. Still, there are about one hundred and forty whose homes are within the enemy's lines and who are without socks. I shall continue to furnish them till all are supplied. Tell the young women to work hard for the brave Stonewallers."

This letter to his wife bears the date, April 21, 1864:

"Your note with bag of socks reached me last evening. The number was correct—thirty-one pairs. I sent them to the Stonewall brigade, which is not yet supplied. Sixty-one pairs from the ladies in Fauquier have reached Charlottesville, and I hope will be distributed soon. Now that Miss Bettie Brander has come to the aid of my daughters, the supply will soon be increased."

General Lee's second son, W. H. F. Lee, the spirited leader of cavalry, was disabled in the battle of Brandy Station, June 10, 1863, and was afterwards carried off as a prisoner of war. In Fortress Monroe and Fort Lafayette, with Capt. R. H. Taylor, he was held under sentence of death, as hostage for Federal officers who were threatened with execution in Richmond on account of some retaliatory measure. While the younger Lee was thus wounded and in prison, his wife and children were stricken with sickness even unto death. The elder brother,

G. W. Custis Lee, through the agency of a flag of truce, asked permission of the Federal authorities to take his brother's place and to die, if needs be, in his stead. But the rules of warfare would not permit the exchange. When the wife and children died, the sorrowful event drew from General Lee this letter, dated December 27:

" Custis's despatch which I received last night demolished all the hopes in which I had been indulging, during the day, of dear Charlotte's recovery. It has pleased God to take from us one exceedingly dear to us, and we must be resigned to His holy will. She, I trust, will enjoy peace and happiness forever, while we must patiently struggle on under all the ills that may be in store for us. What a glorious thought it is that she has joined her little cherubs and our angel Annie in heaven ! Thus is link by link of the strong chain broken that binds us to earth, and smooths our passage to another world. Oh, that we may be at last united in that haven of rest, where trouble and sorrow never enter, to join in an everlasting chorus of praise and glory to our Lord and Saviour. I grieve for our lost darling as a father only can grieve for a daughter, and my sorrow is heightened by the thought of the anguish her death will cause our dear son, and the poignancy it will give to the bars of his prison. May God in His mercy enable him to bear the blow He has so suddenly dealt, and sanctify it to his everlasting happiness." *

When General Lee received the suggestion that he should give to his youngest son a position on his staff, he thus replied :

" . . . His company would be a great pleasure and comfort to me, and he would be extremely useful in various ways, but I am opposed to officers surrounding themselves with their sons and rela-

* In March, 1864, General W. H. F. Lee was exchanged and returned to his cavalry brigade in time to take part in the Wilderness campaign.

tives. It is wrong in principle, and in that case selections would be made from private and social relations rather than for the public good. There is the same objection to going with Fitz Lee. I should prefer Rob's being in the line in an independent position, where he could rise by his own merit and not through the recommendation of his relatives. I expect him here soon, when I can better see what he himself thinks. The young men have no fondness for the society of the old general. He is too heavy and sombre for them."

A month prior to the writing of the above-quoted letter, General Lee sent the following to his son Robert, then at Charlottesville:

". . . Tell Fitz [General Lee's nephew] I grieve over the hardships and sufferings of his men in their late expedition. I would have preferred his waiting for more favourable weather. He accomplished much under the circumstances, but would have done more in better weather. I am afraid he was anxious to get back to the ball. This is a bad time for such things. We have too grave subjects on hand to engage in such trivial amusements. I would rather his officers should entertain themselves in fattening their horses, healing their men, and recruiting their regiments. There are too many Lees on the committee. I like them all to be present at battles, but can excuse them at balls. But the saying is, 'Children will be children.' I think he had better move his camp farther from Charlottesville, and perhaps he will get more work and less play. He and I are too old for such assemblies. I want him to write me how his men are, [and] his horses, and what I can do to fill up his ranks."

On the sixth day of February, Meade marched down to Morton's Ford to test the mettle of Lee's half-fed veterans. With eager impetuosity the latter fell upon the division of Hays and sent it back across the Rapidan with loss. In the opening days of the month of March, Kilpatrick and Dahlgren were leading a troop of Federal horsemen across the Ely Ford and through Spotsylvania toward Richmond. Dahlgren had great expectation of burning and sacking the Confederate Capital and of capturing all the executive officers of the Confederacy. Instead of this, he lost his own life, and the entire expedition was another Federal disaster.

The second day of May, 1864, brought General Lee to the signal-station, on the summit of Clark's Mountain, just behind the advanced guns of his own right wing. The frosts of three winters spent in camp had added an additional silvery tinge to his hair and had made deeper the lines in the brow, but they had also set a more intense glow in the eye whose flashing spake of eagerness for battle. Unabated was Lee's natural vigour as he stood in the beauty of perfect manhood, and with field-glass swept the plains of Culpeper to discern the future movements of the Army of the Potomac.

Along the Orange and Alexandria railway from the Rapidan far northward toward the Rappahannock, Lee could look upon a great city of tents and above the city he saw banners unfurled in multitude to declare the presence of a vast host of Federal soldiery. Long time did Lee scan the warlike horizon. Carefully he noted the location and arrangement of the Federal encampment, to see if Grant's intent was favourable to early battle. Early battle the Federal commander seemed to desire. There was much riding to and fro; there was great commotion in Culpeper that May day, and it was evident to Lee that the Army of the Potomac would soon strike tent and advance southward.

Again Lee scans the horizon of the field of war. What route will the new commander choose? Recent cavalry movements along the borders of the upper Rapidan beyond the left flank of the Army of Northern Virginia indicate a possible advance of the Federal army in that direction. But eastward from the Confederate position lies the region of previous Federal assaults. In the distance to Lee's right is Fredericksburg, the field of Burnside; half-way between Lee's mount of observation and the Marye Heights lies Hooker's battle-ground at Chancellorsville. Immediately on his right Lee's glass may discern the course of Mine Run, from whose intrenched banks General Meade withdrew his army the previous November. Only two months old in May is the memory of the Kilpatrick-Dahlgren raid around the Confederate right flank. While Lee thus seeks to discern the future through his field-glass, and weighs the chances of approaching battle, his corps and division commanders stand near their leader and assist him to scan the field. Longstreet has recently returned from Tennessee, and holds his corps in bivouac on the Central railroad. Field leads Hood's old division while Kershaw directs the division once commanded by McLaws. Pickett's division is standing on guard near the coast of North Carolina. Ewell's division leaders are Early, Edward Johnson, and Rodes; those of A. P. Hill are R. H. Anderson, Heth, and Wilcox. To this company of councillors General Lee turns himself after long-continued searching of the Rapidan valley-slopes. With quiet dignity he points down-stream toward Chancellorsville, and gives his opinion that the Army of the Potomac will advance across the Rapidan at the Germanna or Ely Ford. He bids his officers hold the Confederate divisions in readiness to take up the line of march at the waving of the signal-flag.

On that same second day of May, perhaps at the very hour when Lee's field-glass caught glimpses of the city of tents, General Meade was writing an important military order. Lee possibly could not discern the solferino colour of Meade's headquarters' flag, nor could he see the golden eagle in a silver wreath wrought into the banner's folds, but he had already divined the intent of the commands now issued by the Federal commander. Meade was directing the Army of the Potomac to set itself in motion across the Germanna and the Ely fords at the midnight hour, which should usher in the fourth day of May. This order of General Meade was written in obedience to the instructions of Lieutenant-General Grant, then commanding all the Federal forces in the field. This spring of 1864 saw only two Confederate armies yet abiding in strength. Both of these bands were facing northward, under J. E. Johnston, in northern Georgia, and R. E. Lee in northern Virginia. Against these armies General Grant ordered an advance "all along the line." Sherman was directed to press forward from Chattanooga to crush Johnston. Crook had orders to move south-eastward from the mountains of western Virginia. Sigel was sent up the Valley of Virginia to threaten the Central railroad; Butler was placed in charge of an armament intended to plough the waters of the James River and usher its commander within the portals of Richmond. At the same time Grant came eastward wearing the laurels of Vicksburg and Chattanooga, and pitched his tent with the Army of the Potomac. Across the Rapidan he proposed to send Meade with the duty laid upon him of destroying the Army of Northern Virginia. Grant's instructions to Meade were these: "Lee's army will be your objective point. Wherever Lee goes, there you will go also." The system inaugurated by Grant was "to *hammer continuously* against the armed force of the enemy and his resources, until by *mere attrition*, if by nothing else, there should be nothing left for him but . . . submission." The purpose of Grant was set forth in other terms as the intention "to fight Lee between the Rapidan and Richmond *if he will stand.*"

The fourth day of May was the date assigned for the simultaneous advance of all the Federal hosts against Johnston, Lee, and Richmond. Under his own immediate direction near Culpeper, Grant could count about one hundred and forty-seven thousand men. Meade's Army of the Potomac was arrayed in three grand *corps d'armée.* The Second Corps was commanded by Hancock, the Fifth was under Warren, and the Sixth followed Sedgwick. Burnside held the Ninth Corps apart from Meade's forces, on the northern bank of the Rappahannock. Of this great Federal host about twenty thousand had charge of the waggon trains. More than one hundred and twenty thousand soldiers with arms were ready to obey Grant's orders. General Sheridan controlled nearly thirteen thousand cavalry, and a park of two hundred and seventy-four heavy guns accompanied the army. " The best-clothed and best-fed army " that ever took the field was Grant's invading host, according to the judgment of one of his officers. For the furnishing and comfort of this multitude Grant possessed a supply train that would have extended in a continuous line from the Rapidan to Richmond. This tremendous engine of war was about to hurl itself across Lee's right flank in the effort to accomplish the destruction of the ragged Confederate heroes of the Rapidan. The total effective force under Lee's command at the end of the month of April, 1864, fell short of sixty-two thousand men.*

---

* In the Third Corps, under A. P. Hill at Orange Court-House, about twenty-two thousand officers and men were ready for duty. The Second Corps on the Rapidan under Ewell was reckoned at a little over seventeen thousand. Two divisions of the First Corps, commanded by Longsteet, lay in camp at Gordonsville, and numbered ten thousand effectives. Four batteries of four guns each were assigned to Lee's eight infantry divisions. Seventy-two cannon were in the Reserve and twenty-four guns constituted Stuart's horse-artillery. Four thousand eight hundred men served this park of two hundred and twenty-four guns. Eight thousand three hundred troopers followed the black plume of " Jeb " Stuart. The corps of horsemen was organised in two divisions of three brigades each. Wade Hampton, the Carolinian, rode at the head of the first division and Fitz Lee, the Virginian, led the second. In Hampton's division, the brigade of Gordon came entirely from the mountains of North Carolina, the brigade of Young was made up of South Carolinians and Georgians, and Rosser's brigade was gathered from Virginia. From Virginia also were mustered the three brigades of Fitz Lee's division, and they were commanded by W. H. F. Lee, Lomax, and

When Grant made ready to advance, Stuart's couriers bore swift messages to Lee that the Federal cavalry were swarming on the northern bank of the Rapidan, opposite Chancellorsville. Lee knew that the hour of battle was at hand, and he stood ready to spring upon the flank of his adversary as soon as the latter entangled himself in the toils of the Wilderness.

The third day of May saw much burnishing of muskets in the Confederate camp. Letters were written and final farewells sent to the circles where love and tenderness kept watch at home. No busy cookery scattered its noisy din among the houses of the soldiers, for the supply of meal was short. But the hungry began to talk of Federal provision trains as the possible spoil of battle, and comrade bade good-bye to comrade and looked upon faces in other brigades which he might not see again.

General Lee began the duties of May 4 by issuing general order No. 38, repeating his previous commands to " prevent injury to fencing, crops, and other private property " during the approaching campaign. The war-horse was already snuffing the battle from afar. At 9 A.M. the signal-flag on Clark's Mountain was waving the news to Lee's headquarters that Grant's tents were folded and his column in motion around the Confederate right flank across the Rapidan. At once the order was given to advance. On parallel roads leading a little

Wickham.   In the opening days of May, Stuart held most of these swordsmen along the lower Rapidan and on the Rappahannock guarding the Confederate right.

east of a due southward course from the Rapidan,
Grant was moving his army in two columns. He
was thrusting himself into the thickets of the Wilderness at a right angle to Lee's front line. Lee
wheeled instantly toward his own right flank and
turned his face eastward along two other parallel
roads that led him with the course of the Rapidan
in perpendicular line against the right flank of
Grant's long columns. At noontide on the 4th,
Ewell moved from the Palmyra Ford by the right
flank eastward along the Orange turnpike. At the
same hour two of Hill's divisions marched from
Orange Court-House eastward toward Chancellorsville along the plank road two or three miles southward from Hill's advance on the turnpike.

As early as 11 A.M. Longstreet was ordering Field
and Kershaw to follow a cross-country road that
runs eastward from Gordonsville. But it was 4 P.M.
when the two divisions fell into the line of march.

Lee left Anderson's division of Hill's corps to
guard his rear and with twenty-eight thousand
muskets under Hill and Ewell was making all speed
to strike a blow at the side of Grant's columns. The
Confederate artillery moved to the front with the
infantry. Stuart was already making obstinate
battle far in advance. Lee rode with Hill's column
on the plank roadway and sent urgent messages to
Longstreet to speed forward and support the Confederate right wing.

As the three columns of bronzed veterans press
onward to deliver battle, we mark their eagerness
for the coming strife. Confidence in their leader

and in themselves reigns supreme. The starving-
time in the Confederate " Valley Forge " has
whetted their appetite for the field of war. The
men of Virginia and Maryland are here whose
fathers suffered cold and hunger with Washington
at the first Valley Forge. Here march the sons of
the Virginian riflemen who made a " bee-line for
Boston " under Daniel Morgan in 1775, stood with
Washington at Trenton and Princeton, broke the
strength of Burgoyne by their unerring aim at Saratoga, assisted in driving Cornwallis from the Carolinas, and in forcing his surrender at Yorktown.
Under Lee's command are assembled the sons of
North Carolina, whose fathers trailed muskets after
Wayne at Stony Point, and followed both Washington and Greene into battle. South Carolina, Georgia,
and the Mississippi Valley States have sent the sons
and grandsons of Revolutionary veterans. In Lee's
camp, multitudes never weary of telling how their
sires won the day at King's Mountain, Cowpens,
New Orleans, Buena Vista, and Chapultepec. The
gaudium certaminis which glows in the soul of almost
every individual soldier of Lee's army is a direct
heritage from his fathers. Moreover, most of these
Southern soldiers are descended from warlike races
beyond the sea. The majority of the Army of
Northern Virginia is made up of Ulstermen, who
are, for the most part, non-slaveholders. Their
fathers in Scotland suffered persecution in the days
of Charles II., fought at Bothwell Bridge, passed
over to Ireland to stand with William of Orange in
the battle of the Boyne, and endured the pangs of

hunger in Londonderry. From the province of Ulster, Ireland, they came to plant themselves in the fortress formed by the ridges and foot-hills of the Alleghany Mountains. These belligerent Calvinists held the front line in battle from the time of the old French and Indian War down to this struggle between the States; their days of peace they filled up with disputations in theology.

From the tidewater section of Virginia and South Carolina, Lee has summoned a small band of English Cavaliers whose ancestors followed Marlborough and Prince Rupert; whose love of good cheer and whose courtly bearing make them the centre of jovial comradeship in the starving-time in camp, and whose unquenchable courage sends them to the very cannon's mouth in the hour of battle. From the same regions also come the Huguenots, whose patient endurance under sufferings in France, and whose gallantry in the days of partisan warfare under Francis Marion in the Carolina swamps, have ripened into that brave steadiness that wins the battle or dies upon the field.

Nearly all these sons of fighting sires were brought up in the quietude of plantation-life. Nearly all have used the rifle, nearly all from childhood upward have spent hours on horseback in the mountains and the fields; nearly all have strength and skill to make the woodland ring with the hunter's wild echoing shout. When all these regiments of country-bred soldiers advance in line of battle until they catch sight of the men in blue uniform, it is only the old view-halloo upon the hunting-field that has become the battle-slogan to greet the ears of the Federal soldiers as the terror-producing " rebel yell.'' The yell and the chase are linked by long associa- tion. Scarcely a day has passed during the sojourn of the Confederate army in camp that has not seen a full regiment of soldiers in full chase across the fields after the swift-footed rabbit, every leap accom- panied by wild shouts. It was a frequent remark in bivouac throughout the war, when the notes of this far-resounding enthusiasm were borne along on the breeze, " There goes Marse Robert or an old hare.''*

---

* Two characteristics are stamped upon this army that follows Lee —the deep religious faith of many and the buoyant good temper of all. In the ranks march ministers of the Gospel and laymen who from youth have been devotees of the religious teachings handed down through pious ancestors from Knox, Cranmer, Wesley, and Bun- yan. The labours of the chaplains during the winter on the Rapidan have been followed by a heightened religious devotion throughout the army. A veritable parallel to Cromwell's Ironsides is the Army of Northern Virginia in this Wilderness campaign, when it wards off weariness by keeping step to the vocal music of psalms and hymns. The piety of General Lee himself has reached as full a measure of religious devotion as that manifested by Havelock and Stonewall Jackson. Often is Lee found engaged in earnest prayer. With bowed head he is frequently beheld standing in the assemblies for prayer held by the soldiers. He constantly asks for the prayers of his friends, and always ascribes to Providence the successes of his army.

The unfailing good humour of the men on the march is often their only panacea for thirst, hunger, and weariness. Privations furnish material for the spirit of innocent mirth. A lively fellow whistles an air, another chirps the fragment of a song, and all join in the chorus. Then a slip in the mud, a peculiar cry or quaint jest sets an entire regiment into a roar of laughter. After that follows the hum and the

The evening of the 4th of May found one hundred and twenty-seven thousand men under Grant's
banner south of the Rapidan. Hancock's corps
crossed at Ely's Ford, and pitched camp for the
night amid the wreckage of the field of Chancellorsville. He was three miles eastward from the Brock
road, and threw out Gregg's cavalry in advance. Warren's corps made passage at Germanna, and moved
on the Germanna road to the Wilderness Tavern.
Sedgwick led the Sixth Corps behind the Fifth, and
his camp-fires were kindled along the Germanna highway just south of the Rapidan. Cavalry vedettes
kept watch at every path that looked westward toward Lee's position. Burnside's corps remained as
yet on the northern bank of the river. Like a huge
serpent, Grant's army was outstretched in the Wilderness from the Rapidan as far as Jackson's last
battle-ground. In the very heart of the dense
forest-land between Orange Court-House and Fredericksburg, Grant thus wedged the Army of the

---

buzz of a bewildering medley of merriment and song that makes light
the burden of the journey.

This lightness of spirit is the most significant fact connected with
Lee's army in the Wilderness. It indicates the superb morale of the
Confederate troops. It is the sign of that cheerful endurance that
carries them through the marching and starving and fighting of the
fiercest campaign of the entire war. It follows them into battle. It
marks them as they fight in the trenches. The men scarcely ever
cease to talk and yell as they load and fire their muskets. We see
the merriment and well-attempered buoyancy changed into the earnest enthusiasm of a devoted soldiery when Lee gallops forward along
Hill's column on the afternoon of May 4. Affection for their great
leader breaks out in the tumult of wild cheers and the rolling of the
battle-yell as the soldiers catch sight of their hero in the plain slouch
hat and the suit of grey.

Potomac, and, unfortunately for himself, paused to wait for another day.

This part of the Wilderness is a deserted mining region, the home of the whippoorwill, the bat, and the owl. Between the numerous rivulets are oak-covered ridges. The sweet-gum, the cedar, and the low pine lift their tops just above the dense undergrowth. Numerous ravines bar the way, and the tangled thickets can be traversed only with extreme difficulty. A few cleared fields offer space for the deployment of a regiment or a brigade.

As the night of May 4 drew nigh, Grant called the passage of the river "a great success," and declared that all his apprehensions had vanished. He had as yet met no opposition. He therefore telegraphed this message to Halleck in Washington: "Forty-eight hours will now demonstrate whether the enemy intends giving battle this side of Richmond." At the same time with the sending of this despatch Ewell's corps of Confederates was about to bivouac within one hour's march of Grant's right flank, ready to leap to battle in the jungle.

Through this dense forest two roads seek passage from Orange Court-House to Fredericksburg. The Orange turnpike runs parallel to the Rapidan; the Orange plank road follows the same course, farther away from that stream. Upon these same highways Jackson delivered his rear attack against Hooker; in the same direction Lee was now hastening eastward to deliver a flank attack against Grant. Lee also declared that his apprehensions had taken wings, and that he had the Federal army in the position which he himself would select.

Lee was advancing with three columns *en échelon* against Grant's central and advanced corps. Ewell was foremost on the turnpike as he rushed across the intrenchments at Mine Run and pitched camp at Locust Grove and Robertson's Tavern; his advanced pickets stood on guard only three miles from the bivouac of Warren's corps. Lee set up his tent with Hill near Verdiersville in a roadside grove. He dwelt thus with his central column on the plank road. Farther to Hill's right and rear was Longstreet. Twelve miles he marched from Gordonsville on May 4, and darkness found him at Brock's Bridge on the Catharpin road. Lee's troops were well in hand for the tiger-spring of the morrow. At eight o'clock in the evening he sent a courier to Ewell with orders to move forward at the dawning of May 5, and expressed the strong desire " to bring him [the enemy] to battle now as soon as possible."

A great chorus of forest birds greets the coming of the dawn of the fifth day of May as Lee sits to eat the scanty morning meal. His face beams with cheerfulness; he is communicative beyond his wont. He passes pleasant jests at the expense of the staff. He openly gives expression to surprise that Grant has pushed himself into the same position occupied by Hooker just a year before, and he breathes the hope that the result may prove even more disastrous to Grant. In such an issue to the combat he declares his perfect confidence. He then mounts horse and gallops to the head of Hill's column on the plank road. Just behind his own advanced pickets he rides when the skirmish opens with Grant's cavalry at Parker's store. Far to the right front he can hear the carbines of his own troopers, and across the woods from the left comes the brisk rattle of Ewell's sharpshooters. An occasional heavy gun sends its deep echo rolling backward from the line of Confederate advance. Lee is ready to strike with his centre and left,—but his own right wing is yet far afield. Ewell leads the advance on the morning of May 5 along the turnpike. But Longstreet has not yet reported his presence on the right, and at 8 A.M. Lee instructs Ewell (left wing) to regulate his march by Hill (centre), whose progress along the plank road may be marked by the firing at the head of Hill's column. At the same time Lee prefers not " to bring on a general engagement " before the arrival of Longstreet. A general battle he means to have, but his plan now contemplates brisk skirmishing to hold the Federal army in its present position until he can swing his centre and right wing against Grant's advanced corps.

Ewell advances slowly in readiness for action. Johnson's division leads the column and Jones's brigade marches to the front. The Federal pickets fall back before the vigour of Jones until the latter, at 11 A.M., catches sight of Warren's column crossing the turnpike and pressing southward on the Germanna road. Jones is greatly in advance of Hill, and his attack has brought him face to face with Grant's regular line of battle. At the same hour to Ewell comes Lee's repetition of the order " no general engagement " until Longstreet shall reach the field. From his central position with

Hill, Lee holds his two columns in check, waiting for the First Corps. The Confederate soldiers are like war-dogs straining at the leash, eager for battle with their old antagonists.

In advance of the main column on the plank road, Lee, Hill, and Stuart ride forward beyond Parker's store and pause under the trees in the edge of an old field. Grant's skirmishers break like a blue cloud from the grove of pines to the eastward; but the line of grey-jackets leaps forward to the charge. In the very forefront along the plank road Poague pushes his guns. The yells of the Confederates and the roll of their musketry tell Lee that a stronger line must press forward, and now he sends Heth's division to hold the crest of the ridge in the edge of the forest. Just as Heth moves to the front, the music of regular battle comes from the left; the crash of rifle-volleys, the deep roar of a few scattered batteries, the occasional report of a Parrott gun, and the stirring cadence of the Confederate yell, warn Lee that Ewell has found Grant's full line of battle. The sun is already sloping his course toward the west—and still Longstreet tarries.

If we recall the hour of noon on Ewell's front, we find him ordering the adventurous Jones to " fall back slowly if pressed." This is Ewell's obedience to Lee's injunctions against general battle. Therefore Jones withdraws the heavy guns which stand in front with his skirmishers. This retirement of artillery in the turnpike invites Griffin's division of Warren's corps into strong attack upon the Confederate brigade. The line of Jones is broken and

driven back over the dead body of the brave brigadier. But Ewell will retire no farther. He gives
the word and the brigades of Daniel and Gordon
rush forward to pour a musketry fire into Griffin's
front and flanks. Griffin's column is crushed; still
onward press the Confederates through the undergrowth until they catch the flank of the two Federal
divisions of Crawford and Wadsworth. These have
become entangled in the forest and speedily go down
before the Southern woodsmen. Four Federal guns
and several hundred Federal prisoners become
Ewell's spoil. At close range each line of battle
begins to make its position strong with breastworks
of logs and earth. Sedgwick has brought his corps
into touch with Warren's right. Ewell stands block-
ing the advance of both the Fifth and Sixth Federal Corps. The entire Confederate left wing is
deployed in line across the turnpike facing Warren
and Sedgwick, who hold the Germanna road. In
Ewell's centre stands Johnson; the left is held by
Early, while the right division under Rodes extends
itself southward through the tangled forest to touch
elbows with the left of Hill's corps.

From the plank road where Lee's eye keeps
watch, arises the roar of desperate battle about the
hour when Ewell is counting his prisoners and making stronger his line. Heth has led the attack from
Lee's centre; he has struck Warren's head of column under Crawford and has driven it back; as
Crawford recoiled toward the turnpike his line was
caught in flank by Ewell's charge. But Getty of
Sedgwick's corps reaches the junction of the plank

and Brock roads, and against Getty rushes Heth's line of battle.   It would seem that Grant has not expected battle in the Wilderness.   His order of march for the morning of the fifth of May has bidden Hancock advance to Shady Grove Church, has ordered Warren to bring the Fifth Corps as far as Parker's store, and Sedgwick must lead the Sixth to Wilderness Tavern.   The huge serpent thus seeks to crawl forward and thrust its head outside of the Wilderness.   At 11 A.M. Hancock finds himself at Todd's Tavern, southward from the plank road; a gap of ten miles he has left between the Second Corps and the Fifth and Sixth which are now compelled to halt and face the thunderbolts of war moving eastward on the parallel roadways.   At 11 A.M. Hancock turns his face back over his morning pathway, and hastens to aid Getty in the defence of the Brock road.   But it is 2 P.M. before Hancock's head of column begins to assist Getty in the work of erecting fortifications along the Brock road, facing Lee on the plank road.

That space of three hours from eleven until two o'clock marks the passing of a rare opportunity. "What can delay General Longstreet?" The crimson flush is on Lee's brow and every vein is swollen with the hot blood of battle.   The Confederate commander rides up and down his line, his quiet dignity scarce conceals the anxious eagerness of the moment as he longs for the First Corps.   With those ten thousand men he might rush between the divided wings of Grant's army and in this tangle of narrow pathways hold one portion at bay while he makes assault upon the other.   But Longstreet comes not.   Far to Lee's right, beyond the plank road he plods along, misses the way and retraces his steps, and reaches not the field of war.

On the Brock road Hancock makes ready his corps for battle.   Behind the first line of breastworks he piles up logs to form a second intrenchment, and behind the left centre of this second defence he erects a third.   In front of Hancock's threefold fortress, Heth's men build at first only a slight defence across the turnpike.   The Confederate line is in horseshoe shape behind the crest of a slight elevation in the midst of a dense growth of young trees.   Beyond this line a strong body of skirmishers advance, and in the open forest, three hundred yards from the Brock road, they await the approach of Hancock.   Wilcox has sent brigades to strengthen Heth's flanks, and to keep in touch with the right of Ewell's corps. Poague's battalion of heavy guns is planted in the front on the roadway.   The other cannon of the corps cannot reach the scene and are silent in the rear.

At 4.30 P.M. Hancock advances two divisions to strengthen the attack of Getty's division in the centre.   Two-thirds of Gibbon's division and one-half of Owen's division also lend their aid.   On Hancock's right, Wadsworth's division seeks Hill's flank. More than four Federal divisions engage in actual conflict with Hill's two divisions, and other Federal troops threaten an advance.   The forest is at once ablaze with the flame of musketry.   The roar of deadly combat resounds through the dark woods where the two lines of riflemen, less than one hundred feet apart, fire into each other's faces. Hill's men, behind the crest of the slight elevation, can hear the moaning of the leaden hail that cuts off the forest of saplings four and five feet above their heads. They lie flat upon the ground and with deliberate aim scatter havoc among the men in blue. As the night falls upon the grim wrestlers in this *inferno*, they can aim only at the flashing of the opposing muskets. The fierce yells and the business-like cheerfulness of the Confederates tell of the bravery and grim battle-ardour of these ragged and hungry heroes.*

While nearly one-half of Grant's army thus vainly strives to break through Hill's two little divisions, Lee sends swift message to Ewell to move forward and capture the Wilderness Tavern ridge and thus cut off Grant from the Rapidan. Ewell assumes the aggressive and sends two brigades against the centre of Sedgwick's corps and stands ready to follow up the charge. But Sedgwick has made himself impregnable behind a fortress of logs, and Ewell withholds his men. In Hill's centre a counter-charge by

---

* Frank Wilkeson, a private Federal soldier, discovered a line of sentinels in the rear of Grant's troops, charged with the duty of keeping the Federal soldiers in the fight. It seems that many of the men who were serving under Grant for bounty-money had strong desire to escape from the battle. Wilkeson states that the sentinels, or guards, "seemed to be posted in the rear of the battle-lines for the express purpose of intercepting the flight of cowards. At the time it struck me as a quaint idea to picket the rear of an army which was fighting a desperate battle."—*Recollections of a Private Soldier in the Army of the Potomac.* Published by G. P. Putnam's Sons.

Heth makes capture of Rickett's battery, but the guns are lost again. Hill's right is pushed by Wilcox around Hancock's left flank, and two Federal brigades are routed from their position. Hancock makes " repeated and desperate assaults," writes Lee, but Hill's line is unyielding, while the Confederate cavalry on the right drives back Sheridan's advanced horsemen. A heavy tribute in blood has Lee exacted from Grant and as deep darkness covers the weird and dismal field of wounds and death Lee can send despatch to Richmond that all is yet well: " By the blessing of God we maintained our position against every effort until night, when the contest closed."

The tardy Longstreet has made only a twelve-mile advance eastward during the entire day of May 5, and halts at Richard's shop on the Catharpin road, miles away from Lee's field of action. At 8 P.M. Lee sends a courier to bid Longstreet make a night-march, and at the same time promises Hill that his men shall be relieved at the coming of the dawn, and he sends Ewell the order to make early assault on May 6 with the left wing of the Confederate army. Lee seeks rest upon the bare ground among his weary, hungry veterans. His plans are laid to push Ewell, Longstreet, and Anderson's division of Hill's corps in full offensive battle against both flanks of Grant's army. Hill's soldiers sleep on the ground where they have fought; little food passes their lips. They take no care to strengthen the slight irregular breastworks, for Longstreet's men are under orders to march and take Hill's position. One hour after

midnight, Longstreet's corps breaks camp and follows the special guide toward the battle-ground.
As the forest birds again announce the dawn, Ewell
opens fierce fire along the Confederate left wing before 5 A.M.   Lee has taken up again the part of the
aggressor.   Warren and Sedgwick make reply to
Ewell, and then from left to right along the entire
Confederate line the musketry battle begins its
deadly work.

During the night Burnside has led his twenty
thousand across the Rapidan and Grant orders his
entire army to make assault "along the whole line"
at five o'clock in the morning.   Hancock leads
one-half the Federal army against Lee's right, and
Burnside moves forward to pierce the Confederate
centre.

Before the dawn is the hour set by Lee for Longstreet's arrival.   Hill expects to be withdrawn, and
is not prepared for battle; but Hancock's assault
upon Hill's front is met with obstinate courage;
Hill's centre does not yield.   Wadsworth's fresh
division strikes Hill's left flank; Hancock's brigades swarm around to Hill's right and the Confederate line is rolled up and driven backward.
Desperately the men of Hill contend for their field,
delivering a fierce fire as they retreat.   Close and
savage is the fight, but Lee's right wing is broken.
One hour after the first shot, Hill has been forced
upon Poague's battalion of artillery, that stands defiant near the roadway.   Hancock dares not pass
Poague's grape and canister.   Just behind the guns
is Lee on horseback.   " Why does not Longstreet

come ? '' he continually says to his staff as he rides
to and fro to rally the brigades of Hill's corps.

From the Confederate left wing come the sounds
of heavy battle. Ewell has made his log-works to
bristle with cannon and heaps disaster upon every
assault by Warren and Sedgwick. But at last Lee's
counter-stroke against Hancock's assault is prepared.
In closed ranks and in double column, advancing
in a long trot down the plank road rushes Longstreet's corps, Field's division on the left, side by
side with Kershaw's division on the right.

Already is the sun beaming upon the awful game
of death; the forest wears the smile of the spring-
tide; the birds in the tree-tops are singing while the
tempest of wrath breaks below. The thunder of
Poague's guns shakes the very earth. Lee rides
forward to meet the head of Field's division.
'' What boys are these ? '' he asks. '' Texas boys,''
is the quick reply from the brigade that once followed Hood but is now led by Gregg. The light of
battle is shining in his deep, luminous eyes as he
calls out, '' My Texas boys, you must charge.'' The
Confederates go fairly wild when they see before
them the grey-bearded man with the grey slouch
hat. The voices of the eight hundred Texans are
hoarse with joy, and their blood catches fire as they
hear Lee himself give the order to charge. Ragged
caps fly into the air as the veterans rend the sky
with their wild yell. Then the line of battle is
formed, they advance beyond the batteries against
Hancock. Immediately behind the line rides Lee to
direct the charge in person. '' Charge, boys,'' is

Lee's deep, thrilling call as he advances into the thickest of the fight. Suddenly the men divine his desperate purpose and they begin to shout, " Go back, General Lee—Marse Robert go back.'' Then the artillerymen whom Lee has passed respond with the answering call, " Come back, come back, General Lee.'' Lee rides onward, waving his old grey hat, but the very heavens are rent with the cry, " Lee to the rear! Lee to the rear!'' A tall, lanky ragged Texas sergeant moves from the ranks, seizes the bridle-rein and turns Traveller's head to the rear. A look of disappointment crosses the face of General Lee, but he yields. A last earthly salute the entire line wave to their leader and forward they sweep to meet the advancing foe. At the same time a part of Poague's battalion moves forward with cannon. " Good-bye, boys!'' cry the advancing gunners to the comrades left behind. At the head of the return-charge dash the Texans. They are the heroes of Cold Harbor, Second Manassas, Sharpsburg, and Round Top. At the very head of the Federal column massed in the plank road the brigade flings itself. The ceaseless fury of the Federal fire is pouring into front and flanks. To right of them, to left of them, in front of them, muskets and cannon volley and thunder, but into the jaws of death charge the eight hundred. A circle of fire envelops the band, but already the Federal column staggers. Benning and Anderson with their Georgians, and Law leading his Alabamians, crash forward against the encircling host. The forest rings with yells; the roar of battle becomes terrific. Half of the Texas brigade fall within ten minutes. But the tide of Federal success has been turned backward by the gallant men who have shown their willingness to meet death and to spare their beloved leader.

Lee's counter-stroke is continued. Three guns are thrown forward with the infantry on the highway. Field deploys to the left and Kershaw to the right of the road. The conflict sweeps to and fro in the tangled woods and marshes. The crisis in the battle of the Wilderness has come.*

Now Anderson comes to give strength to Lee's onset. Hill's men return to the front. At 10 A.M. Longstreet moves four brigades under Mahone by the right flank. They find a covered way in an unfinished railroad that brings them against the left end of Hancock's line. They fall upon his flank and rear and roll up his regiments " like a wet blanket," as Hancock himself declared. At 11 A.M. Lee pushes his entire force against Hancock's front and flank in impetuous charge. Hancock's brigades

---

* Lee waits behind his field-battery for the arrival of Anderson's division of Hill's corps. The fight is raging in his front ; the guns of Ewell are calling across from the turnpike that all is well on the left wing. An engineer is sent to find an opening for a flank attack against Hancock's left. At this moment of anxiety a courier—a mere lad—dashes up to General Lee with a message from Anderson. The courier's small pony is panting like a hunted deer. Lee reads the message and turns to look upon the tired pony. " Young man," he says, " you should have some feeling for your horse ; dismount and rest him." Lee thereupon draws forth from the bag attached to his saddle a buttered biscuit, and half of this with his own hand he gives to the courier's pony.

are forced backward and broken into fragments.
Wadsworth's division, on Hancock's right, is scattered in dire disorder. Twelve o'clock finds Grant's
entire left wing defeated and disorganised. "Down
the plank road from Hancock's centre," says General Francis A. Walker, " a stream of broken men
was pouring to the rear, giving the onlooker the impression that everything had gone to pieces."

Like a lion of war, Longstreet is closing in upon
Grant's routed host. Not even the attack of the
tardy Burnside can retrieve the Federal disaster.

The blaze of muskets has ignited the dried leaves
and the smoke obscures the noonday glow. Longstreet's regiments are ablaze with the ardour of battle. The gallant Georgian places himself at the
head of Kershaw's division and arrays it in line
across the plank road. In hot pursuit of Hancock
he moves rapidly toward the eastward, nor does he
note the fact that his four flanking brigades have
made pause in line, facing the plank roadway.
Their loaded muskets are pointing northward to
command the very avenue upon which Longstreet
rides. They mistake the latter for a Federal officer
and in full volley they fire upon the general and his
staff. The brave brigadier Jenkins falls dead and
Longstreet is disabled. The Confederate advance
is checked. Another Bull Run rout is averted from
the Federal army only by the fall of Longstreet in
the moment of victory. Lee hastens to the front
and seeks to straighten out his line of battle. The
hour of four o'clock has struck when the order is
given to charge through forest, flame, and smoke

upon the Brock road. Before this hour Burnside has raised a storm against the Confederate centre but Hill's troops already have tamed the fury of the Ninth Corps. As Burnside becomes quiet in the centre, Lee makes ready to deliver assault against both flanks of the Federal army. Ewell sends Early and Gordon to envelop Sedgwick's right flank at the very hour when Lee urges his right wing to the charge against Hancock's triple wall of defence. The forest has communicated its fire to the front line of Federal logs. Forward rush the divisions of Field and Anderson. They pour in a hot musketry fire, but Hancock's second line is bristling with heavy guns and their canister sweeps the field. Up to the very breastwork on Hancock's left the Confederates advance; a gap is made and disorder reigns among the Federal defenders, who turn in flight. The Confederate flag is planted in triumph on Hancock's first intrenchment. But his second and third walls are impregnable. The Federal artillery compels the Confederates to loosen their grasp on Hancock's fortress.

The sun is yet above the horizon, and Gordon is ready for the charge against Grant's extreme right. Two Confederate brigades beyond the turnpike are facing southward; their bayonets are pointing directly along Grant's line of battle. They advance to the music of the far-resounding yell. Sedgwick's right brigade is engaged in the busy work of piling log upon log, but the men lay down the axe and the spade, and join their brigadier as prisoners of war. The second brigade is likewise rolled up and broken

and a second brigadier is captured.   Darkness falls
upon Gordon in possession of a mile of Grant's rifle-
pits, six hundred prisoners, and Generals Shaler and
Seymour.   The dense thickets have disordered the
Confederate line and Gordon halts.   The Sixth
Corps spends the night in drawing back its front
and right to a line of defence entirely new along the
Germanna road.   " Had there been daylight,"
writes Grant, " the enemy could have injured us
very much in the confusion that prevailed."

The awful struggle in the tangled forest has closed
with Lee pressing the attack against Grant's right
and left.   As this second day fades into darkness
the Army of the Potomac is struggling in a purely
defensive contest, and holds its position behind
three heavy walls of log-work on the left and draws
back its right wing behind a second freshly constructed intrenchment.   At the same time Grant is
urging Burnside to place himself behind strong
works in the Federal centre.

When Grant looks through the thickets on the
morning of the seventh of May he beholds Lee's
breastworks crowned with heavy guns and has no
desire to renew the battle.   Likewise, Lee sees the
strength of Grant's intrenchments, and does not
attack.   A cavalry battle is in progress this day to
the southward, where Fitz Lee on the Brock road,
and Hampton on the Catharpin road, oppose the
troopers of Sheridan.

If the casualties suffered in battle are an indication of success or failure, we may place the seventeen thousand disabled Federal soldiers in contrast

with the probable Confederate loss of less than half that number.

Grant's early order of May 7 commanded Meade to make ready for a night-march to Spotsylvania Court-House.   Hancock was to hold his ground while Warren led the Fifth Corps southward along the Brock road, and Sedgwick moved eastward to Chancellorsville and thence to Piney Branch Church. Burnside was sent eastward to Chancellorsville and thence southward.   Two Federal corps thus drew back from before the face of Lee toward the east, while two remained in his front.

All day long both Grant and Meade were troubled with anxious fear of an attack from the Confederate army.   The new purpose formed in Grant's mind found expression the following day in a despatch to Washington: " My efforts will be to form a junction with General Butler as early as possible, and be prepared to meet any enemy interposing. . . . My exact route to the James River I have not yet definitely marked out."   We hear no longer the command to Meade to seek Lee's army as his objective point!   Grant had enough of Lee's army.   He now turned toward Butler on the distant James.   Early on the morning of May 7, Lee ordered a roadway cut through the forest directly southward from the plank road.   He anticipated Grant's movement from the latter's failure to renew the battle.   The cavalry soon brought word that Grant's trains were moving.   Ewell sent a force to reconnoitre the Federal right and found the Germanna road deserted.   Grant was withdrawing from his defences, and behind him he left his dead and some of his wounded to care for themselves.

At the coming of darkness Lee issued the order to Anderson to lead Longstreet's corps along the new forest roadway toward Spotsylvania Court-House. Ewell was next ordered to begin the night-march while Hill remained to guard the Confederate rear. Anderson's corps began to march at 11 P.M. of May 7. The Wilderness was illuminated by the blaze of the burning leaves. Rapidly the Confederate column moved southward, and an hour before the dawn they lay down to rest in a grove near Spotsylvania Court-House. Lee held Ewell's corps at Parker's store, and early on the morning of May 8 advanced to support Anderson.*

During the previous night Fitz Lee held his dismounted men on the Brock road to resist the advance of Warren. Trees were felled, attacks were delivered, and obstinate resistance was offered to the Federal advance. The sun of May 8 arose upon Warren still distant from the goal, while Anderson,

---

* Grant's withdrawal eastward led Lee to suppose that the Federal army was retiring to Fredericksburg. Lee therefore left Early with Hill's corps near Todd's Tavern to hold the attention of Grant's rear until he could swing Anderson and Ewell around to strike Grant's flank or his head of column. Lee's movement was executed with skill and vigour. Grant himself remained behind with Hancock's corps to watch Early. Until noonday and afterwards he was sending to the front detailed specifications for the advance of his army beyond Spotsylvania to the James River! At 1 P. M. he learned that Warren's corps had received a disastrous check at the Court-House, and that he must halt to deliver battle against Confederate intrenchments. Lee's advanced corps had won the race for position and held the coveted field of defensive battle on Spotsylvania Ridge.

after a more circuitous journey, was arrayed across
the Federal pathway.   After sunrise, Anderson
marched one mile northward from the Court-House
to assist the cavalry in stemming the Federal tide of
war.   Upon a pine-covered ridge, Anderson threw
up hasty works composed of logs and rails.   The
Confederates wore a grim smile behind their defences as they saw Warren's corps advancing to the
assault to meet disaster in front of their unerring
rifles.*   Lee's First Corps held the Court-House
cross-road and the onset of Grant's advance corps
failed to take the position.

The two armies were shaping their course south-
eastward across the swamps and sluggish streams
that feed the upper York River.   Between the
Po and the Ny rivers lies the Spotsylvania Ridge.
Lee's swifter marching during the night enabled him
to array his line of battle across this peninsular ridge,
with his guns pointing northward face to face with
Grant's head of column.   In ignorance of this fact,
Grant remained in dalliance with Early at Todd's
Tavern, and permitted Lee to make a more speedy
concentration of his entire army at Spotsylvania.
At 5 P.M. on May 8, Lee arrived with Ewell's corps,
after a double passage of the Po, and at sunset the
First and Second Confederate corps were in po-

---

* Stuart was there.   For the last time the ascending sun glanced
upon that plumed hat in the presence of the Army of Northern
Virginia.   Amid the storm of bullets, Stuart wore his old, sweet
smile, and cheered the riflemen by commending the accuracy of their
aim and the rapidity of their fire.   His shout of gratification was
mingled with theirs when they beheld Warren's corps recoiling from
the deadly fire that blazed along the ridge's crest.

sition across the Brock road ready to receive the
assault of the Fifth and Sixth Federal corps under
Sedgwick.   As darkness fell, the second Federal
attack was repulsed and Ewell advanced northward
a half-mile in a counter-charge on the right of the
roadway. In the darkness, the Confederates began
to throw up intrenchments in front of Sedgwick's
breastworks.*

The works erected during the night were slight and
irregular. Lee thought the position untenable, but
Ewell called attention to the high open point on the
ridge defended by Johnson's salient. From that
elevation hostile cannon might sweep the entire
region between the rivers. Lee, therefore, ordered
his heavy guns into position behind the defences
and commanded the chief engineer to mark off a

---

* On the evening of May 8, Ewell's corps formed Lee's right
wing and Anderson's corps his left. The division of Rodes rested
its left on the Brock road, while Edward Johnson's division was
drawn out to the right of Rodes. Gordon held his division in reserve. The half-mile advance brought Ewell's corps northward
beyond Anderson's corps. Lee's entire right wing faced westward
while his left wing faced northward, both guarding the approach of
the Brock road from the north-west.

The early morning of May 9, saw Lee riding along Ewell's line.
Through the pine-tree groves it wound its way almost northward toward Sedgwick's flank. Johnson's division on the extreme right was
extended through the forest, across ravines and marshes, beyond the
Harrison and McCool farm-houses, to command the open ground that
slopes eastward to the Ny River. At Rodes's right brigade the
line bent outward in a salient, and near the centre of Johnson's position an acute angle in the line was formed by bending back his right
brigade to face the Ny. This was the apex of the famous salient of
the battle of May 12.

second line behind the advanced right wing, to be held by Gordon's division.

Far behind at Todd's Tavern on the Brock road, most of Hancock's corps tarried throughout the eighth day of May. Early and Hampton thus held the tail of the serpent, while Anderson and Ewell were hammering his head. On the morning of the 9th, Grant sent Sheridan on a raid toward Richmond, and thus gave Lee longer time to concentrate his entire army at Spotsylvania. On this same day the head of Early's corps reached the Court-House just in time to check the advance of Burnside across the Ny from the eastward. The latter had marched far afield and was moving on the Fredericksburg road to strike Lee's right and rear. Early established his guns in a north and south line along the ridge and visited confusion upon Burnside. The left of the Third Confederate Corps was then extended to unite with Ewell's right, and the great salient was thus completed. The western face was held by Ewell and the eastern face by Ewell and Early. Lee's right wing formed nearly a right angle with his centre and left. At the angle, the Confederate line was pushed out northward in the shape of an acorn, one mile in length and a half-mile in width. The Confederate soldiers called this excrescence "The Mule Shoe." The gallant Confederate artillerymen were ready to sweep with canister every approach toward the elevation where Johnson's division held the apex of the salient.

Hancock followed the Brock road on May 9 to take position on Grant's extreme right. He sent three divisions across the Po to press against Lee's left and rear. Grant proposed to assail Lee's peninsula from the north and from the east and from the west.

Under cover of darkness Lee made ready his counter-stroke. Across the Po below the Court-House he moved Heth's division. At the dawn of the 10th, Heth fell upon the flank and rear of Hancock's force, just as Hancock was seeking to obey Grant's order to withdraw his men to the northern bank of the Po. Grant seems to have become nervous in attempting the mild manœuvre of an assault against Lee's left flank, for he hastily recalled the column in order to mass his forces in front of the Confederate intrenchments. Amid the thick-grown pines, Heth visited fearful loss upon Barlow's division. Through an *inferno* of burning woods he hastened Hancock's retreat across the Po and rejoiced over the capture of one of Hancock's heavy guns.

On May 10, Grant began to storm the Confederate works. At 11 A.M., a strong force rushed against Lee's left wing. Field's division wrapped their defences in the flame of musketry and cannon fire, and the Federal soldiers poured out their blood in vain. At three in the afternoon the men in blue uniform made a second dash against the wooded crest where the guns and muskets of Lee's First Corps were hurling a tornado of death through the wilderness of stunted cedars. After the repulse, the Confederates leaped over their works to collect the muskets and ammunition of Grant's defeated and fallen men. These were distributed along the line until each Con-

federate soldier was armed with more than one loaded
rifle. The sun drew near the hour of setting. Hancock was united with Warren and in long heavy lines
the two corps dashed themselves against Lee's thin
left wing. But Hancock's front line went down before the multiplied fire of Field's division. Gallantly
onward rushed the second Federal line over the
breastwork of the Texas brigade. Like tigers
fought the fragment of the eight hundred. With
bayonets and with clubbed muskets they struggled
hand to hand and yielded not. The adjoining brigade turned upon the flank of the foe and Grant's
assault was rendered fruitless.

At the same hour another assault was raging
against the western face of the salient. Sedgwick
sent Upton's brigade to charge Ewell's centre. In
four lines Upton advanced. He broke through
Doles's brigade and swept him from the Confederate
works. Daniel and Steuart unleashed their brigades
against Upton's flanks. Battle and Johnson assailed him in front; and still the gallant Upton continued the struggle. Gordon and Walker struck
heavy blows against the Federal flanks and Upton
was forced back with heavy loss. Ewell's terrific
firing had meanwhile repulsed the reinforcements
pressing forward to the aid of Upton.

The Confederate right wing facing eastward under
Early did not escape attack on this day of general
assault.* Several lines from Burnside's corps essayed

---

* "To assault 'all along the line,' as was so often done in the
summer of 1864, is the very abdication of leadership."—FRANCIS A.
WALKER.

to seize the roadway at the Court-House. But the guns of Cutts and Pegram speedily drove Burnside to seek shelter.

This day of Federal sacrifice was followed by a day of rain and skirmishing. On May 10, Grant wired thus to Halleck: "Send to Belle Plain all the infantry you can rake and scrape." On May 11, he despatched to Washington the well-known boast that he would "fight it out on this line if it takes all summer" and added to this the following: "The arrival of reinforcements here will be very encouraging to the men, and I hope they will be sent as fast as possible and in as great numbers." *

On May 11, Lee marked great commotion in the Federal army. Burnside turned his head of column northward across the Ny, and then marched back again to sit down before the Court-House. Far up the Po opposite Lee's left marched a Federal brigade. Hancock withdrew a division from the Federal right. Lee interpreted this restlessness as the sign of a withdrawal from the field. He ordered all artillery "difficult of access" on the Confederate line to be withdrawn and held in readiness for the march. In obedience to this command Long drew back through the narrow winding roadway the guns from the Mule Shoe salient. Johnson's division was left to guard the apex with muskets alone and two pieces of artillery. At midnight Johnson reported the massing of

---

* Francis A. Walker says in connection with this crisis in the Federal movement: "The partition of authority between Grant and Meade had worked badly from the first, as it was destined to do through the remainder of the campaign."

troops in his front and asked for the return of the guns.*

Through the heavy mist at the dawn of May 12, Hancock's corps rushed forward to envelop the apex of the salient. Johnson's division was alert, but musketry fire alone could not shake the masses of the Second Corps.† Over the log-works they swarmed. Johnson's division of twenty-eight hundred was made captive. The Confederate batteries rushed forward at a gallop, and reached the salient just in time to become Federal spoil. Twenty cannon and a troop of banners fell into Hancock's hands, along with Generals Johnson and Steuart. Hancock's corps filled up the inner angle of the salient, and his line began to sweep down within the Mule Shoe from point to heel. Lane's Confederate brigade poured in a galling fire from the eastern face and Hancock's left wing recoiled. Across the base of the salient Gordon formed his line; so dense was the fog and smoke of battle that Hancock's position was defined only by the sound of his muskets and the direction of the bullets. Lee spurred his horse toward the place of strife and found Gordon arraying his men for the charge. Lee quietly took his position to lead the division. " This is no place for General Lee," said Gordon in stage-whisper. The soldiers heard the words and began to shout, "General Lee to the rear." " These men are Georgians

---

*Lee was not informed. Ewell ordered the guns to return at daybreak.

†On account of the dampness many of the Confederate rifles refused to fire ; this fact imparted greater courage to the assailants.

and Virginians; they have never failed you; they
will not fail you now," cried the impetuous Gordon
to his commander.   A ragged soldier stepped from
the ranks and turned Traveller's head toward the
rear.   The cry of " Lee to the rear " rang out again
and again, and then it changed to the battle-slogan
as the line advanced.   Like a primitive bee-hunter,
Gordon followed the course of the leaden messengers
back to their origin.   The din of battle swelled into
a roar when Gordon met Hancock amid the dense
growth of pines.   The Federal left was thrust backward and Gordon set his flag above the eastern
face of the salient.

Ewell urged Ramseur's brigade against Hancock's
right flank.   From Early's corps came two brigades
under Harris and McGowan.   Lee rode forward to
lead Harris's Mississippians into the deadly breach,
but again was heard the protest " General Lee, go to
the rear."   " Lee to the rear " was the battle-cry of
this line that repulsed Hancock's right wing.   Severe
losses had befallen Hancock and he was driven out
side the salient.   The Federal troops now held the
outer trenches at the apex and along the western face
of the Mule Shoe.   Two Federal divisions from the
Sixth Corps advanced to support Hancock's line
along this western portion of the angle.   Three
Confederate brigades occupied the corresponding
inner trenches.*   Across the pile of logs for twenty

---

* Mississippi under Harris held the place of honour in this conflict.   In close support stood South Carolina, led by McGowan, and
North Carolina under Ramseur.   These three brigades held the inner
trenches of the western face of the salient.   From the apex at their

hours the murderous struggle continued hand-to-hand, until this place of battle was baptized in the life-current from the veins of heroes as the Bloody Angle.

right, an enfilading Federal fire swept along their line. Just across the heap of logs in the outer trenches stood the Federal divisions, four lines deep.

The three brigades must hold this key-point in the Confederate archway. Lee had not another man to place in the imperilled centre, for Grant was hurling the whole Army of the Potomac against him "all along the line." The Fifth and a part of the Sixth Corps were charging Lee's left, and Burnside was storming the right. But cannon crowned the Confederate lines, and the story of Grant's assaults was again written in the blood of his own soldiers. A division of the Fifth Corps was sent to aid Hancock. Ravines and forests outside the salient were filled up with Federal regiments; batteries were planted to fire over the works; mortars dropped their shot among the beleaguered Confederates. Cannon were dragged up to thrust their muzzles across the top of the intrenchments. And yet the three brigades stood bravely to their work.

On each side of the fortification, men climbed to the top and fired into the faces of the foe. They grappled and dragged one another across the logs. Over the works and through the crevices were bayonets thrust. A cold, drenching rain fell upon the wrestlers; both trenches were partly filled with water and seemed to run with blood. The heaps of dead and dying were more than once removed to leave fighting room for the living. Large standing trees behind the lines were cut off by musket-balls.

Throughout the day the roar of battle was continuous in this field of blood. The brigades ordered forward by Grant to support the assault suffered more, perhaps, than the Federal force in the trenches. The Confederate fire was so keen that it split the blades of grass around the approaching foe. (A Federal officer speaks of the "Miniés moaning in a furious concert as they picked out victims by the score.")

Under the cover of darkness Hancock's line of toilers in the ditch was relieved by men who took their place. (All were relieved except the 37th Mass. regiment.) As these Federal soldiers withdrew they dropped to the ground from exhaustion. But the three Confed-

Gordon's men were toiling to erect a breastwork across the base of the salient. At the early dawn of May 13, the wearied Confederates were withdrawn from the angle. Lee's wings were bound together by this stronger second line. In spite of Confederate losses by capture on this fearful day, Grant's disabled men were so numerous that the casualties on both sides stood in number about the same,—seven thousand. Twenty-two brigades in all were thrown against Lee's centre at the salient, only to meet disaster.

From May 13 to May 18, Grant " manœuvred and waited for reinforcements," notwithstanding his previous words to Meade, " I never manœuvre." About twenty-five thousand men came to his aid. The Confederates rested and satisfied their hunger from the captured Federal haversacks. Real coffee boiled in new Federal tin cups, with foreign sugar, gave additional vigour to Lee's veterans. The evening of May 12 brought the news of J. E. B. Stuart's heroic death the previous day in front of Richmond. On May 20, Lee made this official announcement of the sad event:

" Among the gallant soldiers who have fallen in this war, General Stuart was second to none in valour, in zeal, and in unflinching devotion to his country. His achievements form a conspicuous part of the history of this army, with which his name and services will be forever associated. To military capacity of a high order, and to the nobler virtues of the soldier, he added the brighter graces of a pure

erate brigades were not relieved. Lee could not spare the men. Without food, or drink, or rest, or covering, beneath the falling rain, they stood in the bloody trenches and loaded and fired throughout the watches of the night.

life, guided and sustained by the Christian's faith and hope. The mysterious hand of an all-wise God has removed him from the scene of his usefulness and fame. His grateful countrymen will mourn his loss and cherish his memory. To his comrades in arms he has left the proud recollections of his deeds and the inspiring influence of his example."

May 17 brought unwelcome messages to Grant. Halleck telegraphed the following: " Sigel is in full retreat on Strasburg. He will do nothing but run. Never did anything else." At New Market, in the Valley of Virginia, on May 15, Sigel had suffered defeat at the hand of John C. Breckinridge with the loss of six Federal guns and nearly nine hundred men.* The information also came to Grant that May 16 had closed on Butler fast in the huge bottle formed by the James and Appomattox rivers. Beauregard held the cork of the bottle and Butler could neither advance nor retreat.

On the morning of May 18, Grant massed his Second and Sixth Corps and sent them to storm the salient. Lee's heavy guns were ready along the new base-line. Spherical case and canister from twenty-nine guns broke the Federal host of twelve thousand before they came within rifle-range. At

---

* Sigel's force numbered six thousand five hundred men and twenty-eight guns. Breckinridge had about four thousand five hundred men, including the artillery under William McLaughlin and the horsemen of J. D. Imboden. McLaughlin's eight guns with the horse-artillery tamed the spirit of the Federal soldiery ; Imboden placed his cavalry on Sigel's flank and the Confederate infantry advanced to drive Sigel down the valley. The corps of cadets from the Virginia Military Institute, mere boys in age, advanced with the steadiness of veterans side by side with the 62d Virginia regiment, and captured a blazing battery from the centre of Sigel's line.

the same hour Burnside fell back from his attack against Lee's right wing. The Army of the Potomac was slowly drifting toward its own left. Grant was looking for weak points in Lee's line, but at every assault the Confederate breastworks fairly bristled with cannon and Grant drew back. On May 19, Ewell was sent around the Federal right to ascertain Grant's position. He found severe battle, and was repulsed with the loss of nine hundred men. But Grant was held back one entire day from his march southward. The night of May 20 found Hancock leading Grant's advance south-eastward to the Fredericksburg railroad. The chapter of Federal losses on the Spotsylvania field recounts the fall and capture of nearly eighteen thousand men. Over thirty-seven thousand was the total number of disabled in the Army of the Potomac from the Rapidan to Spotsylvania. About one-third of that number measured the reduction in Lee's effective strength.

At noonday, May 21, Ewell led the advance towards Hanover Junction beyond the North Anna River. The forenoon of the 22d brought Ewell's head of column to the Junction. Noonday marked the passage of Anderson's column across the Anna bridge while the morning of May 23 found the Third Corps, again under Hill, on the southern bank of the stream. Lee did not possess the strength to strike Grant's flank in the latter's circuitous march. He preferred to follow the shorter pathway and to block Grant's journey southward.* Pickett

---

* Lee remarked to Jed Hotchkiss on the journey to Hanover: " We wish no more salients."

and Breckinridge with nine thousand muskets awaited Lee's approach at the Junction. Noonday of May 23 found the Army of Northern Virginia looking out northward from rude intrenchments to mark the approach of Grant's columns beyond the river.

In the centre, commanding the telegraph road stood the First Corps behind heavy guns. Lee's right was held by the Second Corps, and his left by the Third. Farther up the stream the corps of Warren found passage and threatened the Confederate left flank. Hill sent Wilcox at 6 P.M. to drive Warren back, but Warren manifested much strength, and as darkness fell both sides began to build fortifications.

Sunrise of the 24th brought Lee to his left wing, to mark the advantage gained by Warren. His wrath was aroused. The crimson flush mounted high on neck and forehead. The eyes were as a flame of fire. The courtly manner was stiffened into reserve. The words of questioning fell like a scathing rebuke: " General Hill, why did you let these people cross the river ? Why did you not drive them back as General Jackson would have done ? "

Since Hill had already drawn back the left wing, Lee retired his right from the river, and allowed his centre to rest on the North Anna at Ox Ford. The Confederate army was drawn up in form like a wedge with the point thrust against the river. Grant pushed his Fifth and Sixth Corps over-stream to face southward and Hancock's corps crossed below and faced northward. Burnside sought passage in the

Federal centre, but suffered loss from Lee's guns on the river's edge. Grant's army was cut in twain on the point of the Confederate wedge. If either Federal wing should bring assistance to the other, the Federal force must make a double passage of the river.*

The morning of May 27 dawned upon the vacant Federal encampment. Grant had again sought the northern bank of the river and was heading his columns south-eastward. He had received a complete checkmate and had failed to cut the Central railroad. Lee was disappointed that greater results did not follow the separation of Grant's two wings. But his combative spirit never wavered, and at a swift pace the Confederates started on the home-stretch. Directly southward between the Central and Fredericksburg railways, Lee moved the Second Corps now under Early. The First Corps marched around to Lee's right *via* Ashland. A journey of twenty-four miles in thirty hours brought the Confederates into line of battle facing north-eastward on the central ridge between the Totopotomoy and Beaver Dam creeks. Grant kept close to the northern bank of the Pamunkey and sought to cross that stream and seize Richmond. Fitz

---

* At this juncture Lee was seized with sickness. During the previous twenty days he rested little. Not until ten or eleven at night did he seek his blanket, and three o'clock each morning found him at breakfast by candle-light, and then to the front to spend eighteen hours along the line of battle. His iron frame yielded at last, but he still retained his command. As he lay in his tent he cried out in impatience : " We must strike them ! We must never let them pass us again ! We must strike them ! "

Lee's cavalry retarded Grant's progress until the entire Confederate army stood athwart Grant's pathway on May 28. Grant moved his army south of the Pamunkey, but Lee's front was formidable, and Grant halted to await reinforcements from Butler. On May 30, W. F. Smith's corps reached the White House on the lower Pamunkey and marched to give strength to Grant's left wing.*

From Beauregard's army, south of Richmond, Lee asked reinforcements. Since May 20, Beauregard had beset the Richmond officials with proposals for a game in grand strategy. Grant and Butler occupied outside lines, while Beauregard and Lee held the inner defensive lines. Let Lee fall back to the Chickahominy and draw Grant after him, was Beauregard's suggestion. A portion of Lee's force might hold Grant at bay while the other portion brought aid to Beauregard. After the capture of Butler, Beauregard would move northward and stand by the side of Lee to receive the capitulation of Grant in the swamps of the Chickahominy. Whatever the merits of the scheme, Lee steadfastly maintained that continual battle must be offered to Grant. When at length he reached the immediate vicinity of the Capital, he asked Beauregard to lend assistance. But Beauregard seemed unwilling now to play at strategy. He telegraphed to Richmond: " War Dept. must determine when and what troops

---

* Lee's sickness continued during these critical days. For the first time in the campaign he spent the night under the roof of a house near Atlee's Station. His determined will kept him at the front each day.

to order from here.'' Lee's reply to Beauregard is
this: ''If you cannot determine what troops you can
spare, the Department cannot. The result of your
delay will be disaster. Butler's troops will be with
Grant to-morrow.''

Grant withdrew from Lee's front and once again
moved by the left flank towards Cold Harbor. On
May 31, Hoke's division from Beauregard confronted
the Federal advance on the old battle-ground of 1862.
Lee extended his right to give support, and the
afternoon of June 1 witnessed severe battle on the
roadway between Old and New Cold Harbor. A
Federal charge broke through Lee's right wing and
carried away five hundred captives. But Grant paid
the tribute of twelve hundred men.

During the hot sultry night of June 1, Grant withdrew his own right wing and moved it by the left
beyond the Cold Harbor road. Lee met this
change of position by sending Hill and Breckinridge
to defend his own right flank. Lee's right wing on
Turkey Hill now defended the passage of the Chickahominy at Grapevine Bridge. The heat of the second
day of June brought weariness and thirst to the men
of both armies. The dust from marching columns
hovered over the field in dense clouds. The pangs
of hunger oppressed the Confederates as they took
their places behind the earthworks.* In Lee's cen-

---

* Many of the Confederate troops, according to George C. Eggles-
ton of the artillery, had received only two issues of rations since
leaving the Junction. One issue contained three hard biscuits and a
meagre slice of pork to each man. Two days after this issue, one
cracker was apportioned to each soldier. Upon this allowance the
Confederates entered the battle of Cold Harbor.

tre, Anderson's (Longstreet's) corps and Hoke's division were arrayed across the roadway between New and Old Cold Harbor, facing eastward. Beyond Hoke's right, to the southward, Breckinridge and Hill extended the Confederate line to the Chickahominy. Fitz Lee patrolled the region between that stream and the James River. Looking northward from Lee's centre, one might see Ewell's corps under Early standing at Anderson's left hand. Heth's division of Hill's corps defended the extreme Confederate left.

In the afternoon of June 2, Lee assumed the offensive. He ordered Early to assail Grant's right flank and sweep down in front of the Confederate line of battle. Early found Grant's right wing intrenched behind impregnable works. The opportunity was offered to Grant to fight in open ground For such an opportunity he expressed a great desire in his despatches to Washington. But he came not forth from his fortress to deliver battle against Early. The latter built strong breastworks in front of Grant's right and awaited the coming of the morning.

At 4.30 on the morning of June 3, Grant sent his army to the assault all along the line, six miles in length. The Confederate works were full of salient angles, and Lee's heavy guns secured a cross-fire at short range against nearly every one of the attacking brigades. The Confederate riflemen took deliberate aim. Hunger had maddened Lee's veterans and they multiplied their shots with fearful swiftness. The rifle-pits seemed to speak with tongues of flame. No man and no body of men could stand in front of that fire and live.   Grant's vast host could only rush forward to die before the Confederate marksmen.

Hancock's corps assailed Lee's right in double line of attack with supports in rear.   A salient in front became Federal prey.   A fierce counter-stroke by Breckinridge drove the assailants in flight, and the enfilading fire of the Confederate artillery stretched three thousand of Hancock's men upon the field.   A like tragic fate met the Federal corps which attacked Lee's centre and left.   The front lines of Grant's assault were almost destroyed within ten minutes, and the rest sought shelter.

At nine o'clock Meade sent Grant's order to his subordinates to renew the attack.   Hancock refused to give the order to his men.   W. F. Smith, commanding the Eighteenth Corps, writes this sentence: '' That order I refused to obey.''   Major-General M. T. McMahon, Chief-of-staff, Sixth Federal Corps, states that a second and a third command to attack came from Grant.   The order, says McMahon,

"came to the corps headquarters, was transmitted to the division headquarters, and to the brigades and the regiments without comment.   To move that army farther, except by regular approaches, was a simple and absolute impossibility, known to be such by every officer and man of the three corps engaged.   The order was obeyed by simply renewing the fire from the men as they lay in position."

In the battles of June 1 and June 3, Grant's loss was about ten thousand men.   Most of these fell in the grand assault of the last day.   From the time of crossing the Pamunkey to June 12, Grant's casualties numbered over fourteen thousand men; three thousand sick soldiers sent North makes a ghastly

aggregate of over seventeen thousand. Lee's loss
was small.*

Grant ordered his army to approach Lee's lines by
constructing regular approaches as in a siege. His
professed object was to restrain Lee from sending
troops against Hunter who was prosecuting a campaign with the torch in the Valley of Virginia. In
this purpose Grant did not succeed. Lee assumed
the offensive on a wider field than the Wilderness.
Two attacks were delivered by Early against Grant's
right and rear on June 6 and 7, but strong fortifications held him in check. June 10 found Lee
despatching Breckinridge toward the Valley. On
June 12, Hampton crossed the path of Sheridan at
Trevilian's and checked his advance against Lynch-

---

*The wounded left upon the field after the assault of June 3
were all Federal soldiers. Unspeakable suffering abounded. Not
until June 5 did Grant seek to relieve his men, and then only by
making the strange proposition to Lee " that, hereafter, when no
battle is raging, either party be authorised to send to any point between the pickets or skirmish-lines unarmed men bearing litters to
pick up their dead or wounded, without being fired upon by the
other party." Lee suggested that Grant should follow the regular
method of asking a truce. When Grant finally determined to act in
accordance with the usual mode his wounded men were dead. He
then sought to lay upon Lee the blame for the delay. General
Francis A. Walker writes on this point as follows : " If it be asked
why so simple a duty of humanity as the rescue of the wounded and
burial of the dead had been thus neglected, it is answered that it was
due to an unnecessary scruple on the part of the Union Commander-
in-chief. Grant delayed sending a flag of truce to General Lee for
this purpose because it would amount to an admission that he had
been beaten on the 3d of June. It now seems incredible that he
should for a moment have supposed that any other view could be
taken of that action."

burg. The evening of June 12 marked Lee's order to Early to lead the Second Corps in search of Hunter. He commanded Early to march afterwards across the Potomac to threaten Washington. Not long did Lee wait to hear of the swift-footed march of Early to Lynchburg. There he confronted Hunter who came fresh from the burning and pillage of collegiate buildings and private dwelling-houses in the Valley. In dismay, Hunter turned himself westward through the mountains while Early sought the Federal Capital.

Under cover of the night of June 12, Grant moved his army across the Chickahominy toward the James. His campaign had been a disastrous failure. He had sought to reach Richmond from the northward. He was compelled to unite his army with Butler's shattered force, and to assail Petersburg in order to secure a way of advance from the southward. Moreover, the Federal army was broken in spirit. Its morale was gone. The next few days brought Grant's men nerveless and cautious into the presence of Confederate intrenchments.*

---

* General F. A. Walker thus writes of the bravest and strongest body of troops in Grant's army, the Second Corps: " As the corps turned southward from Cold Harbor to take its part in the second act of the great campaign of 1864, the historian is bound to confess that something of its pristine virtue had departed under the terrific blows that had been showered upon it in the series of fierce encounters which have been recited. Its casualties had averaged more than four hundred a day for the whole period since it crossed the Rapidan. . . . Moreover, the confidence of the troops in their leaders had been severely shaken. They had again and again been ordered to attacks which the very privates in the ranks knew to be hopeless from the start ; they had seen the fatal policy of 'assaults

Lee met Grant's movement by sending Hoke's division to Petersburg on the morning of June 13. Anderson and Hill were moved to the right and covered the approaches toward Richmond by establishing a line of battle from White Oak Swamp to Malvern Hill. Lee had less than thirty thousand men north of the James. Grant veiled his passage of the river behind a cloud of cavalry supported by his Fifth Corps. Smith's corps was hastened forward to aid Butler in the capture of Petersburg. Hancock followed in the track of Smith.

On the morning of June 16, Lee transferred the divisions of Field and Pickett to the southern bank of the James. On the 17th, they drove Butler from a part of Beauregard's old line near Bermuda. The spirit of Lee's entire army is set forth in the following despatch from Lee: "We tried very hard to stop Pickett's men from capturing the breastworks of the enemy, but could n't do it."

As soon as Lee made himself certain that Grant would not assail Richmond from the northern bank of the James, he threw his columns across the river. The evening of June 18 found Lee conjoined with Beauregard, ready to visit slaughter upon the armies of Grant and Butler. Between the 15th and the 18th of June, ten thousand additional names disappeared from the Federal rolls as the result of daily assaults against Beauregard's intrenchments. Dur-

---

all along the line' persisted in even after the most ghastly failures; and *they had almost ceased to expect victory when they went into battle.* The lamentable story of Petersburg can not be understood without reference to facts like these."—*Life of Hancock*, pp. 228, 229.

ing these four days, Beauregard made a gallant defence against more than half of Grant's army, with a
Confederate force of only about ten thousand men.
Between the Rapidan and the James, Grant's losses
reached the number of fifty-four thousand nine
hundred and twenty-six.   This ghastly aggregate
of sixty-five thousand disabled men between the
Rapidan and Petersburg was counterbalanced by
Federal reinforcements to the number of fifty-five
thousand men.

The Army of Northern Virginia still retained its
old elasticity and vigour.   Lee's losses amounted
to about twenty thousand.   The spirit of the soldiers
was yet buoyant.   The old yell had gathered additional fierceness; the men went into battle with all
their former dash and impetuosity.   Perhaps not
one in Lee's heroic band held a doubt as to the
ultimate success of the Confederacy.   After the
bloody repulse which these heroes visited upon the
Federal assault of June 18, Grant wrote thus to
Meade: '' Now we will rest the men and use the
spade for their protection until a new vein can be
struck.''

CHAPTER XIV.

PETERSBURG AND APPOMATTOX.

1864–1865.

HE Confederate administration, in the summer of 1864, decided to continue the fatal policy of defending Richmond. For more than a year Lee had persisted in pointing out the certainty of defeat, if his small band should be compelled to withstand the Federal hosts in the trenches around the Capital of the Confederacy. Lee's withdrawal to the base of the Blue Ridge in July, 1864, would very probably have enabled him to destroy Grant's army. The bravest men of that army were destroyed and its spirit was completely broken by the campaign in the Wilderness. Grant himself suffered a reaction, and began the policy of playing around the ends of Lee's fortifications.* His flank attacks during the autumn and winter were costly failures. His own intrenchments were impregnable against Confederate assaults and he drew his re-

---

* On July 27, Grant sent this despatch to **Meade**: "I do not want Hancock to attack intrenched lines."

sources from sea-going vessels near the head of tide-
water.   Lee could not get at him.   Grant had the
patience to wait three-fourths of a year, until starv-
ation forced Lee's heroes to submit.   General
Francis A. Walker bears this testimony concerning
Grant's new policy and the lack of spirit in the
Federal army:

> " Unfortunately, this change of purpose did not take place until
> the numbers, and even more the *morale*, of the troops had been so far
> reduced that the flanking movements became, in the main, ineffectual
> from the want of vigour in attack at critical moments, when a little of
> the fire which had been exhibited in the great assaults of May would
> have crowned a well-conceived enterprise with victory. *That fire for
> the time had burned itself out ;* and on more than one occasion dur-
> ing the months of July and August the troops of the Army of the
> Potomac, after an all-day or all-night march, which placed them in a
> position of advantage, failed to show a trace of that enthusiasm and
> *élan* which had characterised the earlier days of the campaign."—
> *Life of Hancock*, pp. 246–7.

A growing party in the North seemed to echo the
sentiment of the chief Federal army, that the war of
invasion had proved a failure.   When Mr. Lincoln
sought to secure half a million additional soldiers to
throw into the breach, a great clamour of protest
was sent up by the Northern press.   Just after the
battle of Cold Harbor, gold in New York went up
to 2.52, and the hopes of the war-advocates, according to Horace Greeley, went down to the depths of a
most profound despair.   The Republican party, on
June 7, renominated Mr. Lincoln for the Presidency, but the unrest of the succeeding weeks led
the Democratic party to conceive the sanguine hope
of defeating him.   On August 29, the latter brought

forward as standard-bearer, General George B. Mc-
Clellan.   The second plank in the Democratic platform declared,

> "that after four years of failure to restore the Union by the experi-
> ment of war, during which, under the pretence of a military necessity
> of a war power higher than the Constitution, the Constitution itself
> has been disregarded in every part, and public liberty and private
> right alike trodden down, and the material prosperity of the country
> essentially impaired ; justice, humanity, liberty, and the public wel-
> fare demand that immediate efforts be made for a cessation of
> hostilities."

The third plank denounced as revolutionary " the
direct interference of the military authority of the
United States in the recent elections held in Kentucky, Maryland, Missouri, and Delaware." The
fifth ran as follows:

> " Resolved, That the shameful disregard of the administration to
> its duty in respect to our fellow-citizens who now are, and long have
> been, prisoners of war, in a suffering condition, deserves the severest
> reprobation, on the score alike of public policy and common human-
> ity."

Under the stress of failure in the field, Lincoln
and Grant had been driven to the desperate expedient of refusing to exchange prisoners of war.   They
desired to retain all Confederate captives in order to
make permanent reductions in the Southern armies.
In consequence there was great suffering among the
overcrowded   prison-pens   in   the   South.   Federal
prisoners had to share the meagre food of the Confederates in the field, and since this was often only a
daily handful of cornmeal, the Federal captives very
naturally complained of hunger.   In order to con-

ceal from the Northern public their policy of non-
exchange, the Federal authorities refused to receive
captive Federal soldiers when the Confederate com-
missioner, Judge Ould, offered to hand them over
without equivalent.   Moreover, the Federal administration inflicted upon Confederate soldiers in
Northern prison-pens the direful pangs of hunger
and cold in a land of plenty.   This plan of retaliation resulted in the death of a far higher percentage
of Confederates held in bonds than was the case
among Federal prisoners in the South.

The Army of Northern Virginia had virtually won
peace and perhaps independence in the Wilderness
campaign, when Confederate reverses in Alabama
and Georgia changed the despair of the North into
a determination to continue the war of aggression.
In the early days of July, 1864, J. E. Johnston was
withdrawing his army across the Chattahoochee
River from the presence of Sherman's forces.   From
July 20 until September, Hood was losing the game
of war in front of Atlanta.   On August 23, Farragut
had complete possession of the bay and fort of Mo-
bile.   In the autumn, Hood was breaking his army
to pieces in Tennessee while Sherman was making
an unopposed march, torch in hand, from Atlanta
to Savannah.   The early winter found the Federal
fleet closing in upon Fort Fisher, on the Carolina
coast, the last seaport connecting the Confederacy
with foreign countries.   During all these reverses,
wherein the control of rivers and sea permitted the
Federal forces gradually to reduce the territorial
limits of the Confederacy, Lee and his grim veterans

stood before Richmond and Petersburg with courage steadfast and unmoveable. Grant's army was the real garrison; his strong works alone prevented Lee from driving him into the sea. The Southern sentiment which demanded the defence of the Capital, kept the Army of Northern Virginia away from the mountain slopes and ridges where the only chance for victory still remained.

Beauregard's heroic defence of Petersburg during four days of assault was succeeded by the Sunday quietude of June 19. Lee spent the morning in prayer at church, while his men were throwing up earthworks. Both armies were intrenching. Lee faced eastward on the southern side of the Appomattox. He was ready to hold Petersburg, the key to the Richmond defences. Beauregard stood with his left resting on the Appomattox; to his right was the First Corps under Anderson, while beyond Anderson to the southward A. P. Hill's corps formed the Confederate right wing. Pickett's division occupied the line across the angle between the Appomattox and the James rivers. The fortifications on the northern bank of the James were manned by batteries and local troops under Ewell. More than thirty miles in length was this line of frowning redoubts, connected by extended breastworks, strengthened by mortar batteries and field-works of every description. Abatis and bushy entanglements were constructed in front of these defences. Even stronger were Grant's fortifications. Bomb-proofs and parapets manifested his intention to dwell under the earth until regular siege operations should reduce the beleaguered city. Near the close of the month of June, 1864, when these siege operations began, Grant's force aggregated more than one hundred and seven thousand men. The Confederate defenders of Petersburg and Richmond were about fifty-four thousand in number.

Confederate supplies were drawn from the South over three railroads. The Weldon road on Lee's right flank was exposed to the first Federal assaults. The Southside (Lynchburg) and the Danville roads were in the rear of the Confederate works. Grant's first movement in the new game was to send forth from his long fortress three *corps d'armée* against the Weldon railway.

On the morning of June 21, the Second Corps, followed by the Sixth, moved across the Jerusalem plank road and took position on the left of the Federal Fifth Corps. Grant was seeking to execute a great wheeling movement to envelop Lee's right wing, south of Petersburg. Birney's corps (Second) formed the centre of the wheeling column; the Sixth was on Birney's left. On the same day Wilson's six thousand horsemen were sent southward to strike the railroad still farther away from Lee's lines.

The morning of June 22 found Lee on his extreme right in the midst of the tangled wilderness. He was soon able to discern the approach of Grant's forces. A. P. Hill was ordered to bring three brigades southward as far as the Johnson House. The Sixth Corps on the Federal left was tardy in its advance, and the gap was growing wider between the Sixth and the Second. Hill's brigades under Mahone rushed into this gap. They dashed through the pine forests with a fierce yell to assail the left flank of the Second Corps. The Federal line was thrown into confusion and driven back, and Mahone carried off four guns and seventeen hundred prisoners. The Second Corps then hid itself behind heavy works. The attempt to push the Sixth Corps forward to the railroad on June 23 resulted in the loss of five hundred Federal prisoners.

June 22 found Wilson's cavalry tearing up the railroad track at Reams's Station. From that point they marched westward to the Southside road to meet W. H. F. Lee's division of horsemen. On the 23d, Wilson attacked Lee with vigour only to be repulsed. The 24th dawned upon Wilson in retreat. At Staunton River bridge, the local militia turned him backward to seek Petersburg. Lee's troopers were in close pursuit. Hampton came from his victory over Sheridan at Trevilian's to render aid to Lee. At Reams's Station, Mahone with two brigades of infantry stood across Wilson's route, while Fitz Lee's horsemen assailed his rear. Wilson's troops were scattered in wild flight; they left behind them a long supply-train, thirteen guns, and one thousand captured negroes.*

Lee now sought to break Grant's grasp by sending Early to threaten Washington. On July 5, Early

---

* In the *Richmond Examiner*, June 27 and July 5, 1864, were printed official lists, sent by Generals Lomax and F. Lee, of various items of private property and personal effects which had been taken from Virginian homes by the Federal cavalry and which were found in the waggon-trains captured by the Confederates at Trevilian's and at Reams's Station.

led ten thousand men across the Potomac at Shepherdstown.   Three days later he was moving eastward over South Mountain.   Consternation reigned
among the twenty thousand troops in the Washington defences.   Exaggerated reports of Early's
numbers were sent broadcast throughout the North.
Federal troops were hastened southward from Baltimore.   The Nineteenth Corps, *en route* from New
Orleans to Grant's army, was turned aside to Washington.   Grant was ordered to withdraw his Sixth
Corps from his left on the Jerusalem plank road to
man the forts in front of the Federal Capital.   On
July 9, Early visited utter defeat upon Lew Wallace's
six thousand on the eastern bank of the Monocacy
near Frederick.   The intrepid Confederates continued
their bold advance.   July 11 brought Early to the
very gates of the city.   During the entire day of July
12, his little band stood in threatening attitude before
the frowning guns of Washington.   The two Federal
corps from the field were just at hand.   It was not
possible for Early's small force to capture and hold
the city.   He withdrew across the Potomac to Leesburg, and July 22 found him in the lower valley at
Strasburg.   His expedition led to the organisation
of a large army under Sheridan for the defence of
Washington.   The immense numbers of men furnished to the Federal administration by the bounty
system enabled them to give Sheridan a distinct
force, while Grant was left in his bomb-proofs on the
James.*

* On July 20, Grant sent the following to Stanton : " I must enter
my protest against States sending recruiting agents into the Southern

Throughout the month of July, Grant was preparing to make a direct advance upon Petersburg beneath the surface of the earth. In front of the Cemetery, the Confederate works on the crest of the hill were known as the Elliott Salient. The rifle-pits of Burnside's corps (Ninth) were only one hundred yards distant from this salient. In Burnside's rear the ground made a rapid descent to a deep ravine. The Pennsylvania miners under Burnside began to dig a tunnel at the base of the slope. They completed a passageway, about five hundred and ten feet in length, and then excavated lateral

States for the purpose of filling their quotas. The negroes brought within our lines are rightfully recruits for the U. S. Service, and should not go to benefit any particular State. It is simply allowing Massachusetts (I mention Massachusetts because I see the order of the Governor of that State for establishing recruiting agencies in the South, and see no such order from any other State authority) to fill her quota by paying an amount of money to recruits the United States have already got."

In the same connection, S. S. Cox made this statement : " Delaware . . . had in 1860, eighteen hundred slaves, and the enlisting agents have mostly sold them out to this humanitarian government for soldiers, costing $150 apiece in Delaware and selling for $1000 in New York. Surely Delaware will soon be free !"

On July 22, Brigadier-General Cutler, from his outlook on the Jerusalem road, sent the following to Mr. Lincoln :

" . . . For the first time since the war commenced I confess that I am seriously apprehensive for the result, not from any lack of confidence in the army or its commanders, but because I am almost certain that you will not get the necessary number of men of the right sort, and in season, under the late call, and if you do not, and the struggle goes on through the autumn without decisive results, it requires no prophet to fortell the consequences. I take it for granted that a large proportion of the new men are to be substitutes furnished by those able to do so. They will get the cheapest they can. . . ."

galleries. July 28 saw eight thousand pounds of powder, ready for the match, placed directly beneath some of Pegram's guns and Elliott's Carolinians. Through the ghastly avenue to be produced by the explosion of the mine, Grant expected to send three corps, composing more than one-half of his army, with orders to seize Petersburg.

To assist Burnside in the proposed assault, Grant attempted a little game of strategy. On July 27, he sent Sheridan's cavalry and the Second Corps, once again commanded by Hancock, across the James River to assail the Confederate defences at Chaffin's, and to capture Richmond by a sudden onset of the Federal horsemen. If this plan should fail, Grant expected that the expedition would at least call Lee's forces to the northern bank of the James, and leave Petersburg exposed to Burnside's attack. Hancock advanced from Deep Bottom, drove back Kershaw's division, and captured four Parrott guns, only to find a strong Confederate line of battle behind Bailey's Creek. July 29 found five of Lee's divisions with his cavalry, after swift marching, between Hancock and Richmond. Pickett remained between the James and the Appomattox, and only three divisions were left to defend Petersburg. Thirteen thousand infantrymen and artillerymen were ready to receive Burnside on the morning of July 30, while the bulk of Lee's army was twenty miles away on the northern bank of the James.

Meade feared to order Burnside forward without the assistance of Hancock. Grant therefore withdrew one-half of the Second Corps, and gave up the

direct assault against Richmond. At the dawn of
July 30, the mine was fired and Elliott's brigade was
partially destroyed. A broad gateway was opened
into Petersburg, and not a Confederate soldier stood
directly between Burnside and the city. Eighty-
one heavy guns and mortars, and more than eighty
field guns began to concentrate their fire on the adjacent portions of the Confederate works.

The explosion itself sent terror into the Federal
column of assault, and they recoiled in confusion.
Twenty minutes sufficed to shake off the initial
fright, and then the Second brigade of the First
division slowly ascended the slope and sheltered
themselves in the yawning crater, which was one
hundred and thirty-five feet in length and thirty feet
deep. The Cemetery was just before them on the
hill undefended; but the attacking column lingered
in the chasm. The brigade ordered to support the
assault advanced and likewise sought shelter in the
pit. The entire assaulting division remained here in
a confused mass; their officers could not move them
forward in the face of the scattering Confederate
musketry fire that grew louder and louder on both
flanks. Haskell, the Carolinian, hastened forward
his light battery and from the plank road and its
vicinity poured in the fire of his guns. Hampden
Chamberlayne, sick with fever, rushed from the
hospital to render gallant service with his cannon.
Wright and Langhorne, under cover of the pines to
the Confederate left, raked with canister the ground
between the crater and Burnside's corps.

The Confederate gunners stood gallantly to their
26

work under the fierce fire from Grant's artillery. Two additional Federal divisions were led to the hill's crest, but most of the men crept into the crater, which now presented the appearance of an overturned bee-hive. "Do you mean to say your officers and men will not obey your orders to advance?" wrote Meade to Burnside. "I mean to say that it is very hard to advance to the crest," was Burnside's reply. At eight o'clock Burnside's negro division was pushed forward over the white men in the crater, but they at once sought shelter in the adjacent rifle-pits. A division of the Tenth Corps followed. The timid assailants were gradually gathering courage from the presence of numbers to make an advance on Cemetery Hill.

In this crisis Lee arrived from beyond the Appomattox. He had withdrawn two of Hill's brigades from the extreme Confederate right, and Mahone was now throwing them into the breach. Pegram's guns were rolling rapidly to the place of danger. The Confederates moved along the covered way from the plank road to the ravine in front of the crater. Weisiger's Virginians made a gallant dash toward the chasm. The negro division fled in terror, and leaped into the pit; most of the other Federal troops were forced into the same deep abyss. Wright's Georgians came to Weisiger's aid. The Confederate works were recaptured shortly after noonday. The crater became a place of indescribable suffering and death for the entrapped Federal soldiers, until the survivors surrendered at discretion. Grant had massed sixty-five thousand men for the grand assault, but the lack of vigour, and even the timidity of his officers and men, resulted in a failure and the loss of nearly five thousand men.*

In the opening days of August, Sheridan took control of Federal operations in the valley of Virginia; the Sixth Corps and the cavalry of Torbert and Wilson were sent to strengthen his army. Lee sent Kershaw's division and Fitz Lee's horsemen to render support to General Early. Grant therefore conceived the plan of again assaulting the Confederate works on the northern bank of the James. On August 14, Hancock led the Second and the Tenth Corps and Gregg's cavalry against Lee's line, only to suffer defeat. General Francis A. Walker speaks thus of Hancock's movement:

" It should frankly be confessed that the troops on our side engaged behaved with little spirit. . . . When it is added that the two brigades most in fault were the Irish brigade and that which had been so long and gloriously commanded by Brooke, it will appear to what a condition the army had been reduced by three months of desperate fighting."

With the loss of one thousand men Hancock withdrew to Petersburg in order to take part in another disastrous assault against the Weldon railroad.

While Hancock was wasting his strength at Deep Bottom, the Fifth Corps was exchanging the monotony of trench-life for the excitement of a move-

---

* A great despairing outcry arose in the North. Gold went up to 2.90. The *New York Herald* called for the sending of an embassy to the Confederate Government " to see if this dreadful war cannot be ended in a mutually satisfactory treaty of peace."

ment against Lee's right flank.   On August 18, Warren led this corps from the Jerusalem plank road as far as the Globe Tavern on the Weldon railroad.   He then moved along the railway toward Petersburg until Heth with two brigades struck him on the left flank, and killed and captured nearly a thousand Federal soldiers.   On the 19th, A. P. Hill confronted Warren with two divisions.   Heth assailed the left of the Federal corps while Mahone thrust his brigades against Warren's right flank. The Federal loss was two thousand nine hundred men.   Warren threw up strong works near the Gurley House, and on the 21st Hill assaulted him but was repulsed with loss.

On the same day Hancock led two divisions beyond Warren to the southward and began to tear up the railway track.   August 24 found him in bivouac with Gregg's cavalry within some old intrenchments at Reams's Station.   A. P. Hill made a swift movement, with eight brigades aided by Hampton's cavalry, against Hancock's isolated works.   Pegram secured an enfilade and reverse fire with his eight guns at half-musket range.   His terrific hail of iron was followed by Heth's charge.   Most of Hancock's men were seized with panic and broke away in flight; their works were taken and nine guns, twelve colours, more than three thousand stand of small arms, and twenty-one hundred and fifty prisoners, became Confederate spoil.   Hill's loss was seven hundred and twenty men.   It was only the desperate fighting of Hancock himself at the head of a small band of courageous men that prevented the rout and capt-

ure of his entire corps.   Francis A. Walker, of
Hancock's staff, ascribes this Federal defeat chiefly
to " The weakened spirit of our [Hancock's]
men." *

Grant's losses in the month of August reached
the total of about eight thousand men; Lee's casualties during the same time numbered about two
thousand.   Nevertheless, Grant continued his blows
at both Confederate flanks, his chief effort being
directed toward the extension of the Federal left in
order to seize Lee's lines of communication with the
South.

The closing days of September saw the Federal
Tenth and Eighteenth corps advancing to assail the
Confederate defences north of the James, only to
offer in sacrifice about two thousand three hundred
men.   Lee's loss was likewise heavy.   In connection with this movement, Grant sent four divisions
to seize the Confederate right flank.   Hill threw two
divisions against the flank of the assaulting column;
the Federal loss was more than two thousand.   Gen-

---

* Walker states further that Hancock " had seen his troops fail in
their attempts to carry the intrenched positions of the enemy, but he
had never before had the mortification of seeing them driven, and his
lines and guns taken, as on this occasion ; and never before had he
seen his men fail to respond to the utmost when he called upon them
personally for a supreme effort ; nor had he ever before ridden toward
the enemy, followed by a beggarly array of a few hundred stragglers
who had been gathered together and pushed toward the enemy.   He
could no longer conceal from himself that his once mighty corps retained but the shadow of its former strength and vigour. . . . 'I
do not care to die [cried Hancock], but I pray God I may never
leave this field.'   The agony of that day never passed away from the
proud soldier."

eral Parke, commander of the Federal Ninth Corps, explains the disaster as follows: " The large amount of raw material in the ranks has greatly diminished the efficiency of the corps."

When the month of October was nearly past, Grant made one last desperate effort to win a success in order to strengthen Lincoln in the approaching election. He sent a column of thirty-two thousand infantry and three thousand cavalry to turn Lee's right at Hatcher's Run, fourteen miles southwest of Petersburg. Hancock was ordered to lead his corps westward along the Vaughan road across Hatcher's Run, until he should seize the Boydton plank road. He was then to move eastward again, recross Hatcher's Run and seize the Southside railroad in the rear of Lee's right wing. The Fifth and the Ninth corps with Gregg's cavalry were moved to the Federal left to support Hancock. On the morning of October 27, the great host began the march. The Ninth Corps advanced against the right extremity of Lee's intrenchments, only to find the grey-clad riflemen alert and still possessed of an accurate aim. The Ninth Corps, therefore, halted and placed itself behind earthworks.

Hancock passed across Hatcher's Run and secured the Boydton plank road. Hill's grim veterans under Heth stood ready on the eastern bank of the Run and Hancock paused. A division of the Fifth Corps crossed the stream to lend aid to Hancock, but many of the Federal regiments lost their way and went astray in the wilderness. The entire Federal force was now astride Hatcher's Run, with its left wing separated into detached bands and entangled in the dense forest. Heth followed the usual tactical method. He sent Mahone's division westward across the Run and thrust them into the gap between the Second and the Fifth corps and made a fierce attack against Hancock's right flank. Hampton fell upon Hancock's left. Hancock's numbers speedily regained their lost ground. During the night Grant withdrew the entire Federal force and left as Hill's spoil six guns and seven hundred prisoners. Hancock left part of his wounded on the field. Although Grant's entire loss amounted to seventeen hundred and sixty-one men, yet he telegraphed to Stanton at the close of the day (October 27): '' . . . Our casualties have been light— probably less than two hundred. . . . We lost no prisoners except the usual stragglers, who are always picked up.''

On the same day, Longstreet celebrated his return to the field by visiting a loss of more than one thousand upon Butler's brigades who were attempting to creep through the White Oak Swamp into the Richmond defences.

While Grant was thus pouring out the blood of the new bounty-paid recruits on the banks of the James and the Appomattox, he was at the same time attempting to incite Sheridan up the Valley of Virginia in order to seize Lee's lines of communication at Lynchburg. On August 7 the Federal cavalry leader was placed in charge of a large force, and sent against Early at Winchester. Since his advance against Washington that Confederate officer had been the source of much apprehension in Maryland and Pennsylvania. He had sent a detachment of horsemen to set fire to Chambersburg * in retaliation for Hunter's bonfires in the Valley of Virginia. The latter retired to Harper's Ferry, and there maintained his position for more than a month.

During these August days, Early checked the traffic on the canal and on the Baltimore and Ohio railroad, and constantly threatened to cross the Potomac beyond Martinsburg. On September 1, Sheridan had about fifty-six thousand six hundred men. Sheridan finally led forward about forty-eight thousand foot and horse to assail Early's band of little more than thirteen thousand. At Winchester on September 19, Early was forced from the field, and eventually compelled to retire up the valley. Sheridan used the torch even more recklessly than Hunter; houses, mills, barns, and farming implements were reduced to ashes, with the gathered harvests of corn, grass, and wheat. Early followed Sheridan again to Cedar Creek, where the latter was contemplating a removal of his force to Petersburg. Early could count under his banner only eight thousand five hundred muskets, and less than four thousand cavalry and artillery. In the early morning of October 19, this small band dashed upon the flank and the rear of the city of tents occupied by the Federal soldiery outnumbering them four to one. Sheridan's army was driven in rout. Early

---

* The burning of Chambersburg did not receive Lee's approving sanction.

hesitated and the vigour of the pursuit was abated. The Federal regiments paused and formed line of battle. Afterward Sheridan himself reached the field and his men drove Early up the valley. But Early's purpose was largely accomplished. He restrained Sheridan from sending reinforcements to Grant, and continued to show a bold front in the upper valley.

In the opening days of December, Grant recalled the Sixth Corps from the valley to the James. Lee met this movement by summoning the Second Corps away from Early's field to man the trenches before Petersburg. Sheridan's great flanking force of fifty-six thousand had failed to cut the Central railway or to seize Lee's depot of supplies at Lynchburg. The Federal losses in Sheridan's Valley campaign reached the ghastly aggregate of seventeen thousand!

The defeat of Hood on December 16, left Lee's army as the only force of any magnitude in the Southern Confederacy. Sherman's seizure of Savannah on December 21 placed Lee between two great Federal hosts whose base of supply was the Atlantic Ocean. The spirit of the Confederate commander and of his men seemed to rise higher as the terrors of war were thickening about them. There was great lack of harmony in the councils of the Confederate government. A party in the Congress, hostile to President Davis, led by Wigfall and Foote, grew more bitter in their denunciations of the administration. The friends and the critics of Beauregard, Bragg, and J. E. Johnston were prosecuting

a great war of recrimination.   Some of the Cotton
States were threatening to make terms with the
Federal administration, unless President Davis
should send troops to defend their thresholds.. Governor Vance asked for a corps from Lee's army to
resist the assaults against Wilmington, on the
ground that this seaport was of as great value to the
Confederacy as was Richmond.

The Conscription Act, calling into the field all
males between the ages of eighteen and fifty,
was denounced as unconstitutional.   Governor
Brown of Georgia refused to obey the statute.
President Davis was termed a despot because he
sought to enforce the law.   Property-holders in
large numbers succeeded in evading the call and remained at home.   Moreover, Vice-President Stephens began to loom up as the leader of a peace
party, which increased the clamour against Davis.
From the beginning the Confederate President was
too sanguine of success.   He played his cards as
the head of a perfected system of statesmanship.
He never seemed to recognise his imperative duty
to secure every possible advantage in order to win
the game.   A man of lofty patriotism, of unfailing
integrity and of spotless purity, Mr. Davis supposed
that the Confederacy would attain a position of permanency through the ordinary and regular operations of his system of administration.   He never
recognised the military necessity of destroying the
Army of the Potomac by mobilising the forces of the
South, and now that army was about to destroy him.

It must be remembered, however, that strong

State jealousies stood in the way of mobilising a great Confederate army in Virginia or in Tennessee. This same cause was strongly operative in the winter of 1864 in weakening Lee's army. Nearly all the men who left his ranks went back to the Cotton States. To the honour of Virginia be it said, that as she did not in the outset seek war, so at the close she did not seek peace while war was possible. Her General Assembly expressed confidence in the administration of President Davis, and pledged him unto the very end all the men and resources of the Commonwealth.

With unconquerable spirit, Lee stood like the strong man he was in the midst of all these difficulties. He kept the peace with all the warring factions. None of them dared to assail him who was the personal friend and idol of the grim grey-jackets who manned the Petersburg trenches. The newspapers would perhaps have subjected Lee to criticism if they had not feared his popularity. To the Hon. B. H. Hill of Georgia, Lee made these remarks:

" We made a great mistake, Mr. Hill, in the beginning of our struggle, and I fear, in spite of all we can do, it will prove to be a fatal mistake. . . . In the beginning we appointed all our worst generals to command the armies and all our best generals to edit the newspapers. As you know, I have planned some campaigns and quite a number of battles. I have given the work all the care and thought I could, and sometimes, when my plans were completed, as far as I could see they seemed to be perfect. But when I have fought them through I have discovered defects, and occasionally wondered I did not see some of the defects in advance. When it was all over I found by reading a newspaper that these best editor-generals saw all the defects plainly from the start. Unfortunately, they did not communicate their knowledge to me until it was too late.

" I have no ambition but to serve the Confederacy, and do all I can to win our independence. I am willing to serve in any capacity to which the authorities may assign me. I have done the best I could in the field, and have not succeeded as I should wish. I am willing to yield my place to these best generals, and I will do my best for the cause in editing a newspaper."

On August 23, Lee wrote as follows:

" . . . Without some increase of strength, I cannot see how we are to escape the natural military consequences of the enemy's numerical superiority."

September 2 found him making an urgent call for all the able-bodied white men in the South, and on September 20 he asked for negro recruits to manage all the waggon trains and to throw up fortifications. In reply to his wife's remonstrance concerning his own unceasing toil and watchfulness, on September 18, he wrote these words:

" . . . What care can a man give to himself in time of war? It is from no desire of exposure or hazard that I live in a tent, but from necessity. I must be where I can speedily at all times attend to the duties of my position, and be near or accessible to the officers with whom I have to act. I have been offered rooms in the houses of our citizens, but I could not turn the dwellings of my kind hosts into a barrack, where officers, couriers, distressed women, etc., would be entering day and night."

Lee's energies were directed toward the solution of the problems created by the attempted conscription, by the commissariat, and by the enemy. Throughout September and October he was asking for more troops. He called attention to the scarcity of horses. He spoke of " the discouragement of our people and the great material loss that would follow the fall of Richmond " as outweighing every possible sacrifice. He lived on sweet potatoes, corn-bread, and buttermilk, while he pressed every agency to secure food for his starving veterans. When he crossed to the southern bank of the Appomattox early in November, he sent his aide, W. H. Taylor, to select a dwelling-place.

" I, of course, selected a place," says Taylor, " where I thought he would be comfortable, although I firmly believe he concluded that I was thinking more of myself than of him. I took possession of a vacant house, and had his room prepared with a cheerful fire, and everything made as cosy as possible. It was entirely too pleasant for him, for he is never so uncomfortable as when comfortable."

Winter poured down its snows and its sleet upon Lee's shelterless men in the trenches. Some of them burrowed into the earth. Most of them shivered over the feeble fires kept burning along the lines. Scanty and thin were the garments of these heroes. Most of them were clad in mere rags. Gaunt famine oppressed them every hour. One quarter of a pound of rancid bacon and a little meal was the daily portion assigned to each man by the rules of the War Department. But even this allowance failed when the railroads broke down and left the bacon and the flour and the meal piled up beside the track in Georgia and the Carolinas. One-sixth of this daily ration was the allotment for a considerable time, and very often the supply of bacon failed entirely. At the close of the year, Grant had one hundred and ten thousand men. Lee had sixty-six thousand on his rolls, but this included men on detached duty, leaving him barely forty

thousand soldiers to defend the trenches that were
then stretched out forty miles in length from the
Chickahominy to Hatcher's Run.

With dauntless hearts these gaunt-faced men endured the almost ceaseless roar of Grant's mortar-
batteries.   The frozen fingers of Lee's army of
sharpshooters clutched the musket-barrel with an
aim so steady that Grant's men scarcely ever lifted
their heads from their bomb-proofs.   An eye-witness
thus describes Lee himself :

> " His cheeks were ruddy, and his eye had that clear light which
> indicates the presence of the calm, self-poised will.   But his hair had
> grown grey, like his beard and mustache, which were worn short and
> well trimmed.   His dress, as always, was a plain and serviceable
> grey uniform, with no indications of rank save the stars on the collar.
> Cavalry boots reached nearly to his knees, and he seldom wore any
> weapon.   A broad-brimmed, grey-felt hat rested low upon the fore-
> head ; and the movements of this soldierly figure were as firm, meas-
> ured, and imposing as ever.   It was impossible to discern in General
> Lee any evidences of impaired strength, or any trace of the wearing
> hardships through which he had passed.   He seemed made of iron,
> and would remain in his saddle all day, and then at his desk half the
> night, without apparently feeling any fatigue."

On November 30, Lee wrote thus to his wife:
"I   .   .   .   am glad to learn your supply of socks
is so large.   If two or three hundred would send an
equal number we should have a sufficiency.   I will
endeavour to have them distributed to the most
needy."   December 17 found him thanking her for
a box with hat, gloves, and socks, and also for a
barrel of apples.   On January 10 he was able to bestow some apples on three little girls who brought
him their donation of eggs, pickles, and pop-corn.

On the next day he wrote Secretary Seddon that his army possessed supplies for only two days. At that time meal was rated at eighty dollars a bushel, and flour at one thousand dollars a barrel in Confederate currency!

In February, Lee was appointed generalissimo of all the Confederate forces in the field. Sherman was just then starting northward through the Carolinas to effect a junction with Grant. Fort Fisher had fallen on January 18. The failure of A. H. Stephens's vain dream of peace in the Hampton Roads conference with Lincoln on February 3 nerved the Confederacy to greater efforts than before. A fair supply of meat and meal was brought to the army. Lee devised the plan of withdrawing behind the Staunton (Roanoke) River within reach of the Confederate troops in the Carolinas. But the policy of defending Richmond to the last was forced upon him, and without a murmur his men faced Grant for the final struggle.

On February 5, 6, and 7, Grant sent a large force to seize the Confederate works at Hatcher's Run. Three Confederate divisions drove them back. Evans's division made a charge with the old Confederate spirit and broke the line formed by the Federal Fifth Corps. In these operations the gallant John Pegram was slain. Lee's heroes were still ready for obstinate battle and a continued watch of three days and nights in the midst of the severest weather of the winter.

" Under these circumstances," wrote Lee, " heightened by assaults and fire of the enemy, some of the men had been without meat for three days, and all were suffering from reduced rations and scant clothing, exposed to battle, cold, hail, and sleet. . . . The physical strength of the men, if their courage survives, must fail under this treatment."

On February 9, Lee issued his first general order as Commander-in-chief. The substance of the order ran as follows:

" Deeply impressed with the difficulties and responsibilities of the position, and humbly invoking the guidance of Almighty God, I rely for success upon the courage and fortitude of the army, sustained by the patriotism and firmness of the people, confident that their united efforts, under the blessing of Heaven, will secure peace and independence."

February 14 marked Lee's publication of a second order in which he said of his soldiers:

" The choice between war and abject submission is before them.
" To such a proposal, brave men with arms in their hands can have but one answer. They cannot barter manhood for peace, nor the right of self-government for life or property.
" But justice to them requires a sterner admonition to those who have abandoned their comrades in the hour of peril."

He offered pardon to returning deserters and then said:

" Our resources, wisely and vigorously employed, are ample ; and with a brave army, sustained by a determined and united people, success with God's assistance cannot be doubtful."

With reference to the scheme brought before the Confederate Congress to employ negroes as soldiers, Lee wrote thus, on February 18:

" I think the measure not only expedient but necessary. The enemy will certainly use them against us if he can get possession of them. . . . I do not think that our white population can supply the necessities of a long war without overtaxing its capacity, and imposing great suffering upon our people ; and I believe we should provide resources for a protracted struggle—not merely for a battle or campaign. . . . In my opinion, the negroes, under proper circumstances, will make efficient soldiers. . . . I think those who are employed should be freed. It would be neither just nor wise, in my opinion, to require them to serve as slaves."

On February 19, while Sherman was approaching Charlotte, North Carolina, Lee wrote this:

" It is necessary to bring out all our strength, and, I fear, to unite our armies, as separately they do not seem able to make head against the enemy. . . . Provisions must be accumulated in Virginia, and every man in all the States must be brought off. I fear it may be necessary to abandon all our cities, and preparation should be made for this contingency."

February 24 found this letter on its way from Lee to Governor Vance of North Carolina:

" The state of despondency that now prevails among our people is producing a bad effect upon the troops. Desertions are becoming very frequent, and there is good reason to believe that they are occasioned to a considerable extent by letters written to the soldiers by their friends at home. In the last two weeks several hundred have deserted from Hill's corps, and as the divisions from which the greatest number of desertions have taken place are composed chiefly of troops from North Carolina, they furnish a corresponding proportion of deserters. I think some good can be accomplished by the efforts of influential citizens to change public sentiment, and cheer the spirits of the people. It has been discovered that despondent persons represent to their friends in the army that our cause is hopeless, and that they had better provide for themselves. They state that the number of deserters is so large in the several counties that there is no danger to be apprehended from the home-guard. The deserters generally take their arms with them. The greater number are from regiments from the western part of the State. So far as the despondency of the people occasions this sad condition of affairs, I know of no other means of removing it than by the counsel and exhortation of prominent citizens. If they would explain to the people that the cause is not hopeless, that the situation of affairs, though critical, is so to the enemy as well as ourselves, that he has drawn his troops from every other quarter to accomplish his designs against Richmond, and that his defeat now would result in leaving nearly our whole territory open to us ; that this great result can be accomplished if all will work diligently, and that his successes are far less valuable in fact than in appearance,—I think our sorely tried people would be induced to make one more effort to bear their sufferings a little longer, and regain some of the spirit that marked the first two years of the war."

On March 9, Lee sent these words of commendation to the gallant Vance :

" I   .   .   . return you my sincere thanks for your zealous efforts in behalf of the army and the cause. I have read with pleasure and attention your proclamation and appeal to the people, as also extracts from your addresses. I trust you will infuse into your fellow-citizens the spirit of resolution and patriotism which inspires your own action.   .   .   ."

Early in March, Lee and Davis decided that the former should lead his army to Danville and unite with J. E. Johnston's eighteen thousand in battle against Sherman's ninety thousand men before Grant could reach North Carolina. In order to check the extension of Grant's left wing toward the Southside and Danville railroads, Lee proposed to assault the central works in the Federal line near the Appomattox. Gordon arrayed the Second Corps in front of Petersburg with his left resting on the river. Other troops stood ready to lend their aid. One-half of Lee's army was thus massed against a Federal redoubt on the southern side of the Appomattox, known as Fort Stedman. Just before the dawn of

March 25, Gordon's storming party rushed from the Confederate intrenchments across the intervening space of one hundred and fifty yards, and captured the fort with three adjacent batteries. The attack had been delayed by the tardiness of the supporting detachment from Longstreet's corps, and the approach of daylight found the plan only half executed. Gordon made vain attempts to lay his hands on the forts to the right and to the left of Stedman. But the supporting Confederate forces did not advance. The Federal artillery, from a more commanding position, raked his lines, and the Federal infantry swarmed in to overwhelm the attacking column. Lee's loss amounted to three thousand men. Two thousand men was the measure of the injury inflicted upon Grant.

On March 27, with Sherman at Goldsborough, Grant began to make slow advances with his host of one hundred and twenty-four thousand seven hundred men. Thirteen thousand of these formed his cavalry. Lee's total force of all three arms was reduced in size to about forty-five thousand men. Fitz Lee's corps of cavalry numbered less than five thousand, and the failure of forage had reduced the horses to the condition of walking phantoms.

Grant first sent Butler's old army under Ord toward his own left flank. On the 29th, Sheridan's troopers were despatched to Dinwiddie Court-House, and the Federal Second and Fifth corps moved across Hatcher's Run and advanced north-eastward against Lee's right flank along the Boydton and Quaker roads. Hill's line looked dangerous, and

Grant's forces did not attack the Confederate works. Lee swiftly moved his cavalry and Pickett's division from his left to his right. The evening of March 30 closed upon ten thousand infantry and cavalry arrayed under Pickett at Five Forks, four miles west of the extremity of Lee's intrenchments. In connection with Pickett's movement against Sheridan, Lee in person moved three brigades out of his works on the morning of the 31st, and the fierce rush of his men drove Warren's corps in confusion behind Gravelly Run. Pickett pressed Sheridan backward to the Court-House, but found himself near the Federal infantry, and withdrew to Five Forks. There, in his isolated position, Pickett was outflanked and defeated by Sheridan's cavalry and Warren's corps on April 1. On the morning of April 2, the Federal Sixth Corps broke Lee's thin line at a point about four miles southwest of Petersburg, and the brave A. P. Hill was numbered with the Confederate dead. The Confederate soldiers in isolated bands continued to fight with desperate valour, and Grant lost heavily; but Federal numbers won their way through Lee's line. Lee himself looked upon the disaster with the utmost composure in his demeanour. He raised his grey hat with the same old courteous salute to every approaching officer. As he rode back toward Petersburg, he quietly remarked to an aide, "This is a bad business, Colonel." Soon again he spoke to this effect: "It has happened as I told them at Richmond it would happen. The line has been stretched until it has broken."

As Lee continued his slow return, the shells from the advancing Federal batteries began to burst about him.

" He turned his head over his right shoulder," says an eye-witness, " his cheeks became flushed and a sudden flash of the eye showed with what reluctance he retired before the fire directed upon him. No other course was left him, however, and he continued to ride slowly toward his inner line—a low earthwork in the suburbs of the city—where a small force was drawn up, ardent, hopeful, defiant, and saluting the shells now bursting above them with cheers and laughter. It was plain that the fighting spirit of the ragged troops remained unbroken ; and the shout of welcome with which they received Lee indicated their unwavering confidence in him, despite the untoward condition of affairs."

Under cover of the gathering darkness, on April 2, Lee turned the head of his army toward Amelia Court House along the banks of the Appomattox. The Confederate government officials passed over the railroad to Danville, and thence to Charlotte. The soldiers on the march regained the buoyancy of the early days of the war. They were

" in excellent spirits," says a participant in the retreat, " probably from the highly agreeable contrast of the budding April woods with the squalid trenches, and the long-unfelt joy of an unfettered march through the fields of spring. General Lee shared this hopeful feeling in a very remarkable degree. His expression was animated and buoyant, his seat in the saddle erect and commanding, and he seemed to look forward to assured success in the critical movement which he had undertaken."

On April 5, most of the Confederate troops reached Amelia. Contrary to Lee's expectation, the supply of food found here was insufficient for his

army.* Sheridan was between Lee and Danville
and his caution was so great that he placed his
eighteen thousand Federal troops behind strong
intrenchments.   If they had possessed food, Lee's
veterans would probably have pushed their way
through Sheridan's line to Danville.   Lee's estimate of the situation was thus recorded:

" Not finding the supplies ordered to be placed at Amelia Court
House, nearly twenty-four hours were lost in endeavouring to collect
in the country subsistence for men and horses.   The delay was fatal
and could not be retrieved."

The night of April 5 marked Lee's advance toward
Farmville.   On the following day Sheridan's cavalry
and the Federal Sixth Corps, marching on Lee's
left flank, thrust themselves into gaps left open in
the Confederate columns by the passage of the
stream called Sailor's Creek.   The Confederate
artillery was not available and the flank assaults resulted in disaster to Lee.   The Federal Second
Corps fell upon Gordon's rearguard and captured
many prisoners.   Lee's losses reached the aggregate
of nearly eight thousand men with Generals Ewell,
G. W. Custis Lee, Kershaw, Dubose, Corse, and
Hunton.   Bread and meat were found at Farmville.
Since leaving Petersburg the chief article of food was
parched corn!   Four miles beyond Farmville, Lee
formed line of battle on April 7, and visited disaster
on the Federal Second Corps and Crook's cavalry.

* The officials of the commissary department have stated that no
order was received by them with reference to the concentration of
supplies at Amelia Court House.   See *Southern Historical Papers.*

The evening of April 8 saw Sheridan in control of
Appomattox Station between Lee and Lynchburg.
Large masses of the Federal infantry added strength
to Sheridan's position, and Lee's little band of
wearied and half-starved heroes was between the
two wings of Grant's great host. " On the morning of the 9th," Lee wrote, " according to the
reports of the ordnance officers, there were 7892
organised infantry with arms, . . . the artillery
reduced to 63 pieces . . . [and] the cavalry
. . . did not exceed 2100 effective men. The
enemy was more than five times our numbers." *
Two days before, Lee had received from his corps-
commanders the suggestion that he should surrender. With a flash of the eye he cried, " Surrender! I have too many good fighting men for that."
On the morning of the 9th when he found Grant's
infantry in his front, a great sadness fell upon Lee
as he said: " There is nothing left but to go to
General Grant, and I would rather die a thousand
deaths." The soldier-spirit within him longed for
the soldier's death. " How easily I could get rid
of this, and be at rest," he said. " I have only to
ride along the line and all will be over. *But it is our
duty to live.* What will become of the women and
children of the South, if we are not here to protect
them." His sadness was lighted up with a faint
touch of humour at his own personal display when
he arrayed himself in a new Confederate uniform and
rode to the McLean house to hand over his army

---

* After the surrender, stragglers came up until the number of
prisoners paroled reached the aggregate of twenty-eight thousand.

to Grant. The latter manifested no spirit of exulta-
tion; he courteously yielded the horses to the Confederate privates who owned them, and apportioned
provisions to Lee's army from the captured Confederate railway train.

Among the Confederate soldiers themselves there
had been scarcely a thought of surrender. When
they saw their beloved leader riding back from the
place of negotiation, their grief was wellnigh unspeakable. They halted his horse and gathered in
clusters about him. Tears were running down every
cheek as the grim, ragged veterans came up to wring
his hand. Only sobs were heard or prayers uttered
in broken words calling down the benedictions of
heaven upon Lee. The tears in his own eyes
formed his answer to the agony of his men. He
could only say in a tone that trembled with sorrow,
'' Men, we have fought through the war together.
I have done the best I could for you. My heart is
too full to say more.'' On April 10, 1865, he issued
to his immortal band the following address:

"After four years of arduous service, marked by unsurpassed
courage and fortitude, the Army of Northern Virginia has been compelled to yield to overwhelming numbers and resources.

" I need not tell the survivors of so many hard-fought battles, who
have remained steadfast to the last, that I have consented to this
result from no distrust of them ; but, feeling that valour and devotion
could accomplish nothing that could compensate for the loss that
would have attended the continuation of the contest, I have determined to avoid the useless sacrifice of those whose past services have
endeared them to their countrymen.

" By the terms of agreement, officers and men can return to their
homes and remain there until exchanged.

" You will take with you the satisfaction that proceeds from the consciousness of duty faithfully performed ; and I earnestly pray that a merciful God will extend to you His blessing and protection.

" With an unceasing admiration of your constancy and devotion to your country, and a grateful remembrance of your kind and generous consideration of myself, I bid you an affectionate farewell.

" R. E. LEE, General."

CHAPTER XV.

LEE AS PRESIDENT OF THE WASHINGTON
COLLEGE.

1865–1870.

HE disbanding of the Army of Northern Virginia marked the virtual down-
fall of the Southern Confederacy.
The surrender of the remaining Confederate troops in the South and
Southwest in the month of May, 1865, inevitably
followed the capitulation of Lee at Appomattox.
The soldiers of the Confederacy laid aside their arms,
and turned from the bivouac to find desolate homes
in a land laid waste. They uttered not a regret for
the past nor a murmur concerning the present. They
retained their former dauntless courage. They set
themselves to work to restore their broken country.
It was well that they were not broken in spirit, for
the multiplied humiliations imposed upon the people
of the South by the successful political party in the
process called Reconstruction, were far more galling
than the burdens laid upon them by a state of public
warfare. When Lee returned from Appomattox he
found Richmond partially in ashes. He sought

426

privacy and rest in a rented house. He denounced
the assassination of President Lincoln as a grievous
crime, and deplored the intensified animosity toward
the South on the part of the dominant political faction at Washington. On April 25, Lee wrote to
Grant asking for the liberation from prison of all
Confederate captives, at the same time remonstrating
against the Federal practice of " requiring oaths of
paroled soldiers before permitting them to proceed
on their journey. Officers and men on parole are
bound in honour to conform to the obligations they
have assumed. This obligation cannot be strengthened by any additional form or oath, nor is it cus-
tomary to exact them."

On May 29, President Andrew Johnson issued a
proclamation, offering amnesty and pardon to all
participants in " the rebellion," with the exception
of certain classes who had obtained prominence as
leaders. It was announced, however, that special
application for pardon might be made to the President by any person belonging to the excepted classes.
General Lee, therefore, on June 13, sent the following letter to President Johnson:

" Being excluded from the provisions of amnesty and pardon contained in the proclamation of the 29th ult., I hereby apply for the
benefits, and full restoration of all rights and privileges, extended to
those included in its terms.

" I [was] graduated at the Military Academy at West Point in
June, 1829 ; resigned from the U. S. Army, April, 1861 ; was a Gen-
eral in the Confederate Army, and included in the surrender of the
Army of N. Va., April 9, 1865."

It was the sense of duty toward his comrades in
arms that led Lee thus to ask a pardon that was never

granted.   At that time President Davis was held as
a prisoner in a damp, stone casemate in Fortress
Monroe.   This man of noble mould, this upright
Christian, was accused of complicity in the murder
of President Lincoln, and was subjected to treatment
of the most severe type.   Lee said to his eldest son,
in connection with the letter to Johnson, " that
it was right for him to set an example of making
formal submission to the civil authorities, and that
he thought, by so doing, he might possibly be in a
better position to be of use to the Confederates who
were not protected by military paroles, especially
Mr. Davis."   After Lee's indictment for treason, in
accordance with the orders of a Federal judge, he
withdrew this application for amnesty.   Grant himself urged the sacredness of Lee's military parole,
and the indictment was not pressed to a trial.

Arlington, the home of Lee, was held by the
Federal officials.   The White House on the Pamunkey River was in ashes.   Lee's desire for privacy
was thus expressed to General A. L. Long: " I am
looking for some little quiet house in the woods
where I can procure shelter and my daily bread if
permitted by the victor.   I wish to get Mrs. Lee
out of the city as soon as practicable."   In the latter part of the month of June, 1865, he led his family
to a quiet country-home in Powhatan County, on
the James River, in Virginia.   There he busied himself in vain efforts to collect material for a history of
his military campaigns.

" I am desirous," he wrote, " that the bravery and devotion of the
Army of Northern Virginia be correctly transmitted to posterity.

This is the only tribute that can be paid to the worth of its noble officers and soldiers. And I am anxious to collect the necessary information for the history of its campaigns, including the operations in the Valley of Western Virginia, from its organisation to its final surrender."

To Colonel R. L. Maury he sent this message concerning a scheme for the emigration of Southern planters to Mexico :

" .   .   . I do not know how far their emigration to another land will conduce to their prosperity. Although prospects may not now be cheering, I have entertained the opinion that, unless prevented by circumstances or necessity, it would be better for them and the country to remain at their homes and share the fate of their respective States.   .   .   ."

To his second son, General W. H. F. Lee, then dwelling on the White House plantation, the father wrote thus, on July 29 :

" .   .   . It is very cheering to me to hear of your good prospects for corn, and your cheerful prospects for the future. God grant that they may be realised, which I am sure they will be, if you will unite sound judgment to your usual energy in your operations.

" As to the indictments : I hope you, at least, may not be prosecuted. I see no more reason for it than for prosecuting *all* who ever engaged in the war. I think, however, we may expect procrastination in measures of relief, denunciatory threats, etc. We must be patient and let them take their course. As soon as I can ascertain their intention toward me, if not prevented, I shall endeavour to procure some humble but quiet abode for your mother and sisters, where I hope they can be happy. As I before said, I want to get in some grass country, where the natural product of the land will do much for my subsistence.   .   .   ."

On August 4, 1865, General Lee was elected President of the Washington College in Virginia. His letter of acceptance runs as follows:

"POWHATAN COUNTY, 24th August, 1865.

"*Gentlemen :*—I have delayed for some days replying to your letter of the 5th inst., informing me of my election by the Board of Trustees to the Presidency of Washington College, from a desire to give the subject due consideration. Fully impressed with the responsibilities of the office, I have feared that I should be unable to discharge its duties to the satisfaction of the Trustees or to the benefit of the country. The proper education of youth requires not only great ability, but I fear more strength than I now possess, for I do not feel able to undergo the labour of conducting classes in regular courses of instruction. I could not, therefore, undertake more than the general administration and supervision of the institution. There is another subject which has caused me serious reflection, and is, I think, worthy of the consideration of the Board. Being excluded from the terms of amnesty in the proclamation of the President of the United States of the 29th of May last, and an object of censure to a portion of the country, I have thought it probable that my occupation of the position of President might draw upon the College a feeling of hostility, and I should therefore cause injury to an institution which it would be my highest desire to advance. I think it the duty of every citizen, in the present condition of the country, to do all in his power to aid in the restoration of peace and harmony, and in no way to oppose the policy of the State or General Governments directed to that object. It is particularly incumbent upon those charged with the instruction of the young to set them an example of submission to authority, and I could not consent to be the cause of animadversion upon the College.

Should you, however, take a different view, and think that my services in the position tendered me by the Board will be advantageous to the College and country, I will yield to your judgment and accept it. Otherwise I must most respectfully decline the office.

Begging you to express to the Trustees of the College my heartfelt gratitude for the honour conferred upon me, and requesting you to accept my cordial thanks for the kind manner in which you have communicated its decision, I am, gentlemen, with great respect,

"Your most obedient servant,

"R. E. LEE."

August 28 found him writing these words to Governor Letcher:

" . . . The questions which for years were in dispute between the State and General Government, and which unhappily were not decided by the dictates of reason, but referred to the decision of war, having been decided against us, it is the part of wisdom to acquiesce in the result, and of candour to recognise the fact.

" The interests of the State are, therefore, the same as those of the United States. Its prosperity will rise or fall with the welfare of the country. The duty of its citizens, then, appears to me too plain to admit of doubt. All should unite in honest efforts to obliterate the effects of war, and to restore the blessings of peace. They should remain, if possible, in the country ; promote harmony and good feeling ; qualify themselves to vote, and elect to the State and General Legislatures wise and patriotic men who will devote their abilities to the interests of the country, and the healing of all dissensions. I have invariably recommended this course since the cessation of hostilities, and have endeavoured to practise it myself. I am much obliged to you for the interest you have expressed in my acceptance of the presidency of Washington College. If I believed I could be of advantage to the youth of the country, I should not hesitate. . . ."

September 4 marked his refusal to take part in the management of a public journal. In connection with this he said :

" It should be the object of all to avoid controversy, to allay passion, [and] give full scope to reason and every kindly feeling. By doing this, and encouraging our citizens to engage in the duties of life with all their heart and mind, with a determination not to be turned aside by thoughts of the past and fears of the future, our country will not only be restored in material prosperity, but will be advanced in science, in virtue, and in religion."

On the same day he wrote thus to the Count Joannes :

" In your letter to me you do the people of the South but simple justice in believing that they heartily concur with you in opinion in regard to the assassination of the late President Lincoln. It is a crime previously unknown to this country, and one that must be deprecated by every American."

On September 7 he expressed himself in these terms:

" . . .   I believe it to be the duty of everyone to unite in the restoration of the country, and the re-establishment of peace and harmony. . . .   It appears to me that the allayment of passion, the dissipation of prejudice, and the restoration of reason, will alone enable the people of the country to acquire a true knowledge and form a correct judgment of the events of the past four years. It will, I think, be admitted that Mr. Davis has done nothing more than all the citizens of the Southern States, and should not be held accountable for acts performed by them in the exercise of what had been considered by them unquestionable right."

With reference to the plan of migration beyond the Rio Grande, Lee wrote thus to Matthew F. Maury, on September 8:

" . . .   As long as virtue was dominant in the republic, so long was the happiness of the people secure. I cannot, however, despair of it yet. I look forward to better days, and trust that time and experience, the great teachers of men, under the guidance of an ever-merciful God, may save us from destruction, and restore to us the bright hopes and prospects of the past. The thought of abandoning the country and all that must be left in it is abhorrent to my feelings, and I prefer to struggle for its restoration and share its fate, rather than to give up all as lost. I have a great admiration for Mexico; the salubrity of its climate, the fertility of its soil, and the magnificence of its scenery possess for me great charms ; but I still look with delight upon the mountains of my native State. . . ."

In the closing days of September, General Lee was borne by his war-horse Traveller through the country to Lexington, Virginia. On October 2, 1865, the Confederate chieftain was inaugurated as President of the Washington College.

This school was the outgrowth of a " log-college " erected under the shadow of the Blue

Ridge, in the valley of Virginia, in the year 1749. The founder of the colonial seat of learning was Robert Alexander, whose nephew, Archibald Alexander, afterwards became the first teacher in the Princeton Theological Seminary. Robert Alexander was an Ulsterman who had received mathematical and classical training in Edinburgh. His school, called the Augusta Academy, stood in the midst of a portion of those immigrants of Scotch descent who came immediately from the province of Ulster, Ireland, to take possession of the Appalachian Country, and to form the basis of the Revolutionary party that led the way to the separation of the colonies from England.

In 1776, the new baptismal name of Liberty Hall Academy was bestowed upon the young seminary, as it passed under the ecclesiastical control of the Hanover Presbytery. In 1782 Liberty Hall received the earliest charter granted to a school of learning by the Commonwealth of Virginia. This charter bestowed upon the trustees all the powers and privileges usually conferred upon the directors of a completely equipped college. In 1865, General Lee's oath of office bound him to the performance of duties required in accordance with " an act for incorporating the Rector and Trustees of Liberty Hall Academy."

The head master of Liberty Hall during a term of twenty years was the Rev. William Graham, a classmate of " Light-Horse Harry " Lee, in Princeton College. Many theologians, statesmen, lawyers, and teachers were trained at the feet of Graham for large service in the rising commonwealths of the trans-Alleghany regions. In the last decade of the eighteenth century, the endowment of the academy reached the sum of ten thousand dollars. In the year 1796 a larger fund was bestowed through the generosity of General George Washington.

As a testimonial to his character and public services, the General Assembly of Virginia, in 1785, tendered to General Washington certain shares in two canal companies. He accepted the gift only on the condition of being permitted, as he himself stated, "to turn the destination of the fund vested in me from my private emoluments to objects of a public nature." The claims of Liberty Hall were presented to him. He saw the school standing in the very centre of that colony of Ulstermen whose riflemen under Daniel Morgan and William Campbell had turned the tide of battle at Saratoga and at King's Mountain. Washington at once transferred to the academy the stock in one of the canal companies. In gratitude to him the school was given the name of Washington Academy. To an address by the board of trustees, he made the following response:

" MOUNT VERNON, 17th June, 1798.

" *Gentlemen :*—Unaccountable as it may seem, it is nevertheless true that the address with which you were pleased to honour me, dated the 12th of April, never came into my hands until the 14th instant.

" To promote literature in this rising empire and to encourage the arts have ever been amongst the warmest wishes of my heart, and if the donation which the generosity of the Legislature of the Commonwealth of Virginia has enabled me to bestow on Liberty Hall—now by your politeness called Washington Academy—is likely to prove a means to accomplishing these ends, it will contribute to the gratification of my desires.

"Sentiments like those which have flowed from your pen excite my gratitude, whilst I offer my best vows for the prosperity of the Academy and for the honour and happiness of those under whose auspices it is conducted.

"Go. Washington.

"Trustees of Washington Academy."

Through this gift of Washington, the treasury of the academy was enriched by the sum of fifty thousand dollars. In the year 1802 the Virginian branch of the Society of the Cincinnati donated their funds to the Washington Academy as a mark of deference to their "late illustrious leader and hero." The year 1813 marked the change in title to "The College of Washington in Virginia," but the governmental powers conferred upon the trustees remained the same as under the former academic administration. In 1826, John Robinson, a soldier of the Revolution, added his handsome estate as an offering upon the shrine made sacred by the gift of his venerated leader.

Prior to the year 1861, the Washington College was, for the most part, under the direction of three Presbyterian clergymen, George A. Baxter, Henry Ruffner, and George Junkin. There were two brief administrations under the presidency of laymen, Louis Marshall and Henry Vethake. During this *ante-bellum* period the influence of the Washington College was spread abroad into the regions of the West, South, and Southwest. Her sons were foremost among those engaged in the work of carving

new commonwealths for the Federal Union. Twelve
presidents of colleges she equipped for the work of
education. Some States received their Governors
and United States Senators from her halls; among
these were Crittenden, Breckinridge, and the Browns
of Kentucky, McDowell and Letcher of Virginia,
Ellis, McNutt, and Foote of Mississippi, and Pres-
ton of South Carolina. As founders of theological
schools and teachers therein, she sent Archibald
Alexander to the Princeton Seminary, John Holt
Rice and George A. Baxter to the Union Seminary
in Virginia, and William S. Plumer to the Alleghany
and Columbia seminaries. Judges and lawyers and
State legislators not a few were trained in her halls.
For the armies of the Southern Confederacy the
College of Washington made ready a gallant band
of officers and private soldiers.

From 1861 until 1865 the actual banner of the college was in the field of war. The academic class of
1861 went forth to battle under the captaincy of
their instructor in the Greek language, James J.
White. They styled the organisation "Liberty
Hall Volunteers" and upon their flag was the
motto, *Pro aris et focis*. These beardless youths
formed a part of the 4th Virginia regiment; they
stood in the central part of that line of five regiments under Thomas J. Jackson at Manassas, July
21, 1861, which received in baptism of fire the immortal name of the "Stonewall Brigade." That
dauntless brigade itself was drawn almost entirely
from the constituency of the Washington College.

The storm of war left the old college a wreck.

General Hunter, in 1864, permitted his soldiery to destroy her apparatus and to scatter her library. The endowment fund, invested in Virginia State securities, was temporarily unproductive. But individual trustees pledged their private credit to secure a loan, and in the autumn of 1865 the school resumed work under the direction of her soldier-president.

General Lee brought his wife and three daughters to the new home in Lexington. His eldest son was invited to a chair in the Virginia Military Institute, located in the same town. Lee entered with zeal into the laborious routine of his executive functions. The wearisome task of examining the detailed reports of instructors, and of looking after the individual deportment of the body of students, he performed with unstinted faithfulness. He began his labours with this declaration:

"I have a self-imposed task which I must accomplish. I have led the young men of the South in battle; I have seen many of them fall under my standard. I shall devote my life now to training young men to do their duty in life."

As the ideal hero of his people, General Lee at once drew about him the young men of the South and Southwest. Many of his former soldiers came to complete under his eye the intellectual training interrupted by four years of warfare. Strong was the reverence manifested toward him by the growing band of students. The force of his own personal character was the most potent agency in the system of discipline maintained by General Lee. His ability in organisation secured enlarged courses of instruction, and his name and fame brought increasing patronage and financial donations to the college. In 1871 a new charter changed the name of the college to the Washington and Lee University, under the presidency of his eldest son, General G. W. Custis Lee.

Upon a wider field, however, General Lee continued to play a noble part during the performance of these humble academic duties. The day of dire misfortune came upon the South to find Lee's great heart bleeding on account of her woes; but he showed himself the noble leader still, and from his place of retirement taught his countrymen how to practise the sublime duties of patience and submission under oppression.

On October 3, he wrote thus to Beauregard:

" I hope both you and Johnston will write the history of your campaigns. Everyone should do all in his power to collect and disseminate the truth, in the hope that it may find a place in history, and descend to posterity. I am glad to see no indication in your letter of an intention to leave the country. I think the South requires the aid of her sons now more than at any period of her history. As you ask my purpose, I will state that I have no thought of abandoning her unless compelled to do so. . . ."

To his son, on October 30, he wrote thus:

". . . I accepted the presidency of the College in the hope that I might be of some service to the country and the rising generation, and not from any preference of my own. I should have selected a more quiet life, and a more retired abode than Lexington, and should have preferred a small farm where I could have earned my daily bread. If I find I can accomplish no good here, I will then endeavour to pursue the course to which my inclinations point."

After the assembling of the Federal Congress in December, 1865, Lee wrote these words to General Wilcox:

" I fear the South has yet to suffer many evils, and it will require time, patience, and fortitude to heal her afflictions."

Lee's fears were more than realised. The Congress of 1865 soon made flotsam and jetsam of the already shattered Federal Constitution. Its actions were based upon the assumption that the dominant political organisation was exactly synonymous with the Federal Union itself. The war of aggression against the Southern States had been prosecuted upon Lincoln's theory that these States were still *in* the Union, and could not possibly get out. Congress dealt with them upon the theory that the war had left them *out* of the Union and they could not enter within, except through the mercy of the conquerors, who held them as subjugated provinces! * The Southern States were not regarded as a part of the Union that had been " saved " by the war-party.

---

* Howe of Wisconsin declared that " A State is a manufacture as much as a waggon is," and then added that the States of the Southern Confederacy had all committed suicide ! Stevens of Pennsylvania extended the theory by alleging that the Southern States were " only dead carcasses lying within the Union " ! Howe's reason for regarding the States as dead, and for desiring them to remain dead, was the argument called *ab inconvenienti*, thus expressed : " Do Senators comprehend what consequences result necessarily from restoring the functions of those States ? It will add fifty-eight members to the House of Representatives, more than one-fourth of its present number. It will add twenty-two members to the Senate, nearly one-half its present number." No assertion was necessary to express the conviction that these Southern votes would all be cast in the wrong way !

Stevens fell back upon this same argument when he declared that the old-time quota of Southern representatives " with the Democrats that will in the best times be elected from the North, will always give them a majority in Congress and in the Electoral College. They will at the very first election take possession of the White House and

Under the guise of guaranteeing to each of these States " a republican form of government," Congress placed them under a strict military rule. Military commanders under orders from Washington could depose from office the highest judicial or executive functionaries in any of these commonwealths. The legislation of Congress was a virtual bill of attainder against millions of people, and the despotism inaugurated in the South was the most severe that the nineteenth century has witnessed. At the point of the bayonet these commonwealths, the founders

---

the Halls of Congress. I need not depict the ruin that would follow."

The theory of these two advocates of a government by the people was adopted as the ground-principle of our republic in 1865–'70. Before a committee of this Congress General Lee was summoned to appear in March, 1866, to answer certain questions concerning the condition of the Southern States. Among the questions, all of them answered with quiet dignity, were these :

Q. Is there not a general dislike of Northern men among secessionists ?

A. I suppose they would prefer not to associate with them ; I do not know that they would select them as associates.

Q. Suppose a jury was impannelled in your own neighbourhood, taken by lot, would it be possible to convict, for instance, Jefferson Davis, for having levied war upon the United States, and thus having committed the crime of treason ?

A. I think it is very probable that they would not consider he had committed treason.

In answer to the question as to whether he considered himself guilty of treason, Lee expressed the view " that the act of Virginia in withdrawing herself from the United States carried me along as a citizen of Virginia, and that her laws and her acts were binding on me." He said further that he and his people considered " the act of the State as legitimate " and that the seceding States " were merely using the reserved rights which they had a right to do."

of the Federal Union, were compelled to acquiesce
in the bestowal of unlimited voting privileges upon
the emancipated race of Africans. Universal suf-
frage, not even yet attained in England after more
than a thousand years of training in self-government,
was thrust upon many individuals actually born as
African savages, and upon thousands who were the
sons and grandsons of the denizens of the dark con-
tinent.

The Southern people had then the same anxious
desire which they have always manifested to advance
the welfare of the coloured race. The latter were,
and are still, incapable of self-government, and
emancipation simply left them as sheep wandering
without a shepherd. The " carpet baggers " who
came from the North in search of the spoils of office
only incited the new generation of negroes into
groundless animosity against the white race in the
South. The fearful race-problem, thus made more
difficult, was set before the South while she was yet
in the grasp of an irresponsible faction. It may be
said, in brief, that while no other people were ever
yet called upon to pass beneath greater governmental
humiliation, no other people have ever manifested a
superior racial dignity and strength of endurance.
The great-hearted Lee must receive praise for setting
before his countrymen a personal demeanour that
remains unsurpassed in quiet dignity and forbearance. He suffered with his people and taught them
how to suffer and be strong. Not a murmur escaped
his lips. Not a word of recrimination against the
North did he utter. By reason of the example

which he set before them, his countrymen likewise
laboured in silence to restore prosperity to their
beloved land.

" All that the South has ever desired [wrote Lee on January 5,
1866] was that the Union, as established by our forefathers should be
preserved ; and that the Government, as originally organised, should
be administered in purity and truth. If such is the desire of the
North, there can be no contention between the two sections ; and all
true patriots will unite in advocating that policy which will soonest
restore the country to tranquility and order, and serve to perpetuate
true republicanism."

"I am not in a position [he wrote on January 23] to make it
proper for me to take a public part in the affairs of the country. I
have done and continue to do, in my private capacity, all in my
power to encourage our people to set manfully to work to restore the
country, to rebuild their homes and churches, to educate their
children, and to remain with their States, their friends, and countrymen. But, as a prisoner on parole, I cannot with propriety do
more."

With reference to the test-oath, he thus wrote to
Reverdy Johnson, on January 27 :

" . . . I have hoped that Congress would have thought proper
to have repealed the acts imposing it and all similar tests. To pursue a policy which will continue the prostration of one-half the country, alienate the affections of its inhabitants from the Government,
and which must eventually result in injury to the country and the
American people, appears to me so manifestly injudicious that I do
not see how those responsible can tolerate it.* I sincerely thank you
for the repetition of your kind offer to aid me in any way in your
power. I have been awaiting the action of President Johnson upon
my application to be embraced in his proclamation of May 29, and

* The Supreme Court of the United States (*Ex parte* Garland 4
Wall. 333) has decided that the test-oath which forbade a Confederate to appear as barrister in the courts of the United States, came
within the constitutional inhibition against *bills of attainder*.

for my restoration to civil rights, before attempting to close the estate of Mr. G. W. P. Custis, of which I am sole administrator. His servants were all liberated [in 1862], agreeably to the terms of his will; but I have been unable to place his grandchildren in possession of the property bequeathed them. A portion of his landed property has been sold by the Government, in the belief, I presume, that it belonged to me ; whereas I owned no part of it, nor had any other charge than as administrator. His will, in his own handwriting, is on file in the court of Alexandria county. Arlington, and the tract on ' Four-Mile Run,' given him by General Washington, he left to his only child, Mrs. Lee, during her life, and at her death, to his eldest grandson. Both of these tracts have been sold by Government. It has also sold Smith's Island (off Cape Charles), which Mr. Custis directed to be sold to aid in paying certain legacies to his granddaughters. . . ." *

To P. S. Worsley he sent this word of thanks for a copy of his translation of the *Iliad* :

---

* On June 7, 1862, the Federal Congress passed an " Act for the collection of direct taxes in insurrectionary districts within the United States." The Commissioners assessed on Arlington in the name of Mrs. Lee, a tax of $207.17, and on the Custis Mill Tract, a tax of $46.77. It was afterwards shown by sworn testimony that these Commissioners refused to receive the taxes from anyone but " the owner *in person*, or a party in interest in person." On January 11, 1863, these lands were sold for the taxes. Arlington was bought by the United States upon the order of President Lincoln, at two-thirds of its assessed value, and turned over to the War Department. The latter hastened to make its title permanent by immediately converting the Arlington lawn, up to the very walls of the house, into a burial-ground for Federal soldiers. Lee's only reference to the assessment of the tax was this : " I should have thought that the use of the grounds, the large amount of wood on the place, the teams, etc., and the sale of the furniture of the house, would have been sufficient to have paid the taxes."

Several years after the death of General Lee and his wife, the Supreme Court of the United States reversed the statute of attainder against the estate by ordering payment of its full value to the lawful owner, G. W. Custis Lee.

". . . Its perusal has been my evening's recreation, and I have never enjoyed the beauty and grandeur of the poem more than as recited by you. The translation is as truthful as powerful, and faithfully reproduces the imagery and rhythm of the bold original.

" The undeserved compliment to myself in prose and verse on the first leaves of the volume, I receive as your tribute to the merit of my countrymen who struggled for constitutional government."

To Mrs. Jefferson Davis he wrote the following words, on February 23:

". . . I have thought, from the time of the cessation of hostilities, that silence and patience on the part of the South was the true course, and I think so still. Controversy of all kinds will, in my opinion, only serve to continue excitement and passion, and will prevent the public mind from the acknowledgment and acceptance of the truth. These considerations have kept me from replying to accusations made against myself, and induced me to recommend the same to others.

" As regards the treatment of the Andersonville prisoners, to which you allude, I know nothing and could say nothing of my own knowledge. I never had anything to do with any prisoners, except to send those taken on the fields where I was engaged, to the provost-master-general at Richmond. *

* On April 17 Lee wrote further concerning this matter : ". . . Sufficient information has been officially published, I think, to show that whatever sufferings the Federal prisoners at the South underwent, were incident to their position as prisoners and produced by the destitute condition of the country, arising from the operations of war. . . . It was the desire of the Confederate authorities to effect a continuous and speedy exchange of prisoners of war. . . . [Judge Ould] offered, when all hopes of effecting the exchange had ceased, to deliver all the Federal sick and wounded, to the amount of fifteen thousand, without an equivalent, provided transportation was furnished. Previously to this, I think, I offered to General Grant to send into his lines all the prisoners within my department . . . provided he would return me man for man ; and when I informed the Confederate authorities of my proposition, I was told that, if it was accepted, they would place all the prisoners at the South at my disposal. . . . But my proposition was not accepted."

" I have felt most keenly the sufferings and imprisonment of your husband, and have earnestly consulted with friends as to any possible mode of affording him relief and consolation. He enjoys the sympathy and respect of all good men ; and if, as you state, his trial is now near, the exhibition of the whole truth in his case will, I trust, prove his defence and justification. With sincere prayers for his health and speedy restoration to liberty, and earnest supplication to God that He may take you and yours under His guidance and protection. . . ."

On March 15, he wrote to General Early, then in Mexico, as follows:

". . . I have been much pained to see the attempts made to cast odium upon Mr. Davis [in connection with the Andersonville prison], but do not think they will be successful with the reflecting or informed portion of the country. The accusations against myself I have not thought proper to notice, or even to correct misrepresentations of my words and acts. We shall have to be patient and suffer, for a while at least ; and all controversy, I think, will only serve to prolong angry and bitter feelings, and postpone the period when reason and charity may resume their sway. At present, the public mind is not prepared to receive the truth. . . ."

With reference to the erection of a monument to one of his soldiers, he thus wrote on March 31 :

" I yield to no one in admiration of the noble qualities, or in appreciation of the Christian virtues, of him whom you propose to commemorate. He will live in my affections when my eyes become too dim to distinguish the monument raised by the esteem of his comrades."

June 8 found him sending this message to an absent friend :

" I am sorry you have felt called on to reside in Europe ; though you will have the satisfaction of being removed from the vexations which those here have to endure."

To James May, of Illinois, Lee wrote thus on
July 9:

". . . I must give you my special thanks for doing me the
justice to believe that my conduct during the last five eventful years
has been governed by my sense of duty.   I had no other guide, nor
had I any other object than the defence of those principles of American liberty upon which the constitutions of the several States were
originally founded ; and unless they are strictly observed, I fear there
will be an end to Republican government in this country.   .   .   ."

December 15, 1866, saw the following letter on its
way to Sir John Dalberg-Acton, in Rome:

" While I have considered the preservation of the constitutional
power of the General Government to be the foundation of our peace
and safety at home and abroad, I yet believe that the maintenance of
the rights and authority reserved to the States, and to the people, not
only essential to the adjustment and balance of the general system,
but the safeguard of the continuance of a free government.   I consider it as the chief source of stability to our political system ; whereas
the consolidation of the States into one vast republic, sure to be aggressive abroad and despotic at home, will be the certain precursor of
that ruin which has overwhelmed all those that have preceded it."

The letter continues with references to New England's early advocacy of the principle of secession,
pauses to say that " the judgment of reason has been
displaced by the arbitrament of war," and then declares that

" The South has contended only for the supremacy of the Constitution and the just administration of the laws made in pursuance of it."

He charges the Republican party with originating
the war and concludes:

" Although the South would have preferred any honourable compromise to the fratricidal war which has taken place, she now accepts

in good faith its constitutional results, and agrees without reserve to the amendment which has already been made to the Constitution for the extinction of slavery. That is an event which has been long sought, though in a different way, and by none has it been more earnestly desired than by citizens of Virginia."

On February 4, 1867, he wrote as follows to Judge Ould, declining to run for the governorship of Virginia:

". . . You will agree with me, I am sure, in the opinion that this is no time for the indulgence of personal or political considerations in selecting a person to fill that office ; nor should it be regarded as a means of rewarding individuals for supposed former services. The welfare of the State, and the interests of her citizens should be the only principle of selection. Believing that there are many men in the State more capable than I am to fill the position, and who could do more to promote the interests of the people, I most respectfully decline to be considered a candidate for the office."

He said further that his governorship would be injurious to the State by exciting the hostility of the dominant party, and added these words:

" If *my* disfranchisement and privation of civil rights would secure to the citizens of the State the enjoyment of civil liberty and equal rights under the Constitution, I would willingly accept them in their stead. . . ."

On January 17, he wrote as follows concerning education:

" In its broad and comprehensive sense, education embraces the physical, moral and intellectual instruction of a child from infancy to manhood."

He affirms that system to be the best which

" abases the coarse animal emotions of human nature and exalts the higher faculties and feelings."

He laid stress upon obedience, the love of truth, and the development of " sentiments, of religion." He urged the value of self-control and self-denial united with diligence and integrity. In May, 1867, he declared that the matter of first importance in any system of education was the selection of proper teachers. The instruction imparted by the latter should

" embrace morals and religion as well as the intellect. The teacher should be the example to the pupil. He should aim at the highest attainable proficiency, and not at a pleasing mediocrity."

On April 3 he thus referred to public affairs : " I think there can be no doubt in the minds of those who reflect, that conventions must be held in the Southern States under the Sherman bill, that the people are placed in a position where no choice in the matter is left them, and that it is the duty of all who may be entitled to vote to attend the polls and endeavour to elect the best available men to represent them and to act for the interest of their States."

He urged " good faith and kind feeling " toward the existing government, at the same time expressing " great reluctance to obtrude my opinions on the public."

April 11 found him sending this message to Mrs. George W. Randolph concerning the death of her husband :

" For what purpose can a righteous man be summoned to the presence of a merciful God [other] than to receive his reward. . . . His worth and truth, his unselfish devotion to right, and exalted patriotism, will cause all good men to mourn the country's loss in his death, while his gentle, manly courtesy, dignified conduct, and Christian charity must intensely endear him to those who knew him."

He wrote as follows on May 21 : " I know that in pursuing the path dictated by prudence and wisdom, and in endeavouring honestly to accomplish only what is right, the darkness which overshadows our political horizon will be dissipated, and the true course to pursue will, as we advance, become visible and clear."

He therefore advised all who were not disfranchised to cast their votes and wait and pray for better things.

The following letter was written to General D. H. Maury, on May 23 :

" . . . A Convention will be called and a State Constitution formed. The question then is, shall the members of the Convention be selected from the best available men in the State, or from the worst ; and shall the machinery of the State government be arranged and set in motion by the former or by the latter ? "

He urged the duty of all good men to take part in the election and thus concluded :

" Judge Underwood, Messrs. Botts, Hunnicutt, etc., would be well pleased, I presume, if the business were left to them and the negroes. . . ."

" . . . I look upon the Southern people as acting under compulsion, not of their free choice, and that it is their duty to consult the best interests of their States as far as it may be in their power to do so. . . . Every man must now look to his own affairs and depend upon his good sense and judgment to push them onward. We have but little to do with general politics. We cannot control them ; but by united efforts, harmony, prudence and wisdom, we may shape and regulate our domestic policy."

In the early part of 1867, the dominant party discovered that they had no legal ground upon which to prosecute Jefferson Davis for the alleged crime of treason. Mr. Davis was therefore released from imprisonment. On June 1, Lee wrote him the following letter :

" You can conceive better than I can express the misery which your friends have suffered from your long imprisonment and the
29

other afflictions incident thereto. To none has this been more painful than to me ; and the impossibility of affording relief has added to
my distress. Your release has lifted a load from my heart which I
have not words to tell, and my daily prayer to the great Ruler of the
world is that He may shield you from all future harm, guard you
from all evil, and give you that peace which the world cannot take
away.

" That the rest of your days may be triumphantly happy, is the
sincere and earnest wish of your most obedient faithful friend and
servant."

October 29 found him giving expression to this
view in a letter to Longstreet :

" While I think we should act under the law, and according to the
law imposed upon us, I cannot think the course pursued by the
dominant political party the best for the interests of the country, and
therefore cannot say so, or give them my approval."

At the White Sulphur Springs in West Virginia, in
the summer of 1868, General W. S. Rosecrans sought
the opinion of Lee and others with reference to existing social and political conditions in the South.
On August 26, Lee wrote out for Rosecrans the following expression of his views :

" . . . Whatever opinions may have prevailed in the past with
regard to African slavery or the right of a State to secede from the
Union, we believe we express the almost unanimous judgment of the
Southern people when we declare that they consider that these questions were decided by the war, and that it is their intention, in good
faith, to abide by that decision. At the close of the war, the Southern people laid down their arms and sought to resume their former
relations to the government of the United States. Through their
State conventions they abolished slavery and annulled their ordinances of secession ; and they returned to their peaceful pursuits with
a sincere purpose to fulfil all their duties under the Constitution of
the United States which they had sworn to support. If their action
in these particulars had been met in a spirit of frankness and cordial-

ROBERT E. LEE
AS PRESIDENT OF WASHINGTON COLLEGE, VIRGINIA.

ity, we believe that, ere this, old irritations would have passed away, and the wounds inflicted by the war would have been, in a great measure, healed.   As far as we are advised, the people of the South entertain no unfriendly feeling towards the government of the United States, but they complain that their rights under the Constitution are withheld from them in the administration thereof.   The idea that the Southern people are hostile to the negroes, and would oppress them, if it were in their power to do so, is entirely unfounded.   They have grown up in our midst, and we have been accustomed from child-hood to look upon them with kindness.   The change in the relations of the two races has wrought no change in our feelings towards them. They still constitute an important part of our labouring population. Without their labour, the lands of the South would be comparatively unproductive ; without the employment which Southern agriculture affords, they would be destitute of the means of subsistence, and be-come paupers dependent upon public bounty.   Self-interest, if there were no higher motive, would therefore prompt the whites of the South to extend to the negroes care and protection.

" The important fact that the two races are, under existing circum-stances, necessary to each other, is gradually becoming apparent to both, and we believe that but for influences exerted to stir up the passions of the negroes, the relations of the two races would soon adjust themselves on a basis of mutual kindness and advantage.

" It is true that the people of the South, in common with a large majority of the people of the North and West, are, for obvious rea-sons, inflexibly opposed to any system of laws which would place the political power of the country in the hands of the negro race.   But this opposition springs from no feeling of enmity, but from a deep-seated conviction that, at present, the negroes have neither the intelli-gence nor the other qualifications which are necessary to make them safe depositories of political power.   They would inevitably become the victims of demagogues who, for selfish purposes, would mislead them to the serious injury of the public.

" The great want of the South is peace.   The people earnestly desire tranquillity and a restoration of the Union.   They deprecate disorder and excitement as the most serious obstacle to their pros-perity.   They ask a restoration of their rights under the Constitution. They desire relief from oppressive misrule.   Above all, they would appeal to their countrymen for the re-establishment, in the Southern States, of that which has justly been regarded as the birthright of every American, the right of self-government. Establish these on a firm basis, and we can safely promise, on behalf of the Southern people, that they will faithfully obey the Constitution and laws of the United States, treat the negro population with kindness and humanity, and fulfil every duty incumbent on peaceful citizens, loyal to the Constitution of their country."

This paper was signed by General Lee and thirty-one other representative men from nine of the Southern States.

When Mrs. Lee fled from Arlington in 1861, she left in the house, with her furniture, nearly all the heirlooms in silver-plate, china, and ornaments brought from Mount Vernon. The Federal administration sold the furniture for direct taxes, and confiscated the Washington relics. The latter were deposited in the Patent Office in the Capital. President Johnson gave an order for their return, but Congress vetoed this order. When Mrs. Lee petitioned Congress for the restoration of her property, her request was termed by the Committee on Public Buildings " an insult to the loyal people of the United States." They still remain in the possession of the United States, under the sanction of a virtual bill of attainder ! The following letters were written by General Lee with reference to this matter:

" I am sorry [he wrote to James May, on March 12, 1869] to learn from your letters, the trouble you have incurred by your kind endeavours to have restored to Mrs. Lee certain articles taken from Arlington, and I particularly regret the inconvenience occasioned to yourself and Mr. Browning in having been summoned before the investigating committee of Congress. I had not supposed that the subject would have been considered of such importance, and had I conceived the view taken of it by Congress, I should have dissuaded Mrs. Lee from making the application. But I thought that there would not only have been no objection to restoring to her family relics bequeathed her by her father, now that the occasion for their seizure had passed, but that the government would thus be relieved of their disposition. As Congress has, however, forbidden their restoration, she must submit, and I beg that you will give yourself no further concern about the matter. . . ."

" . . . I do not see what my character had to do with their restoration, for whatever fault may be attributed to me, Mrs. Lee is in no way to blame for it ; and if by your indorsation of me, you meant that I am not antagonistic to the government, or hostile to the Union, you were certainly correct."

" In reference [letter to Geo. W. Jones, March 22] to certain articles which were taken from Arlington, Mrs. Lee is indebted to our old friend, Capt. James May for the order from the late administration for their restoration to her. Congress, however, passed a resolution forbidding their return. They were valuable to her as having belonged to her great-grandmother [Mrs. George Washington] and having been bequeathed to her by her father. But as the country desires them she must give them up. I hope their presence at the Capital will keep in the remembrance of all Americans the principles and virtues of Washington."

In the same letter he spoke of other affairs in the following terms :

" I was not in favour of secession and was opposed to war. In fact I was for the Constitution and the Union established by our forefathers. No one now is more in favour of that Union and that Constitution, and as far as I know, it is that for which the South has all along contended ; and if restored, as I trust they will be, I am sure there will be no truer supporters of that Union and that Constitution than the Southern people. . . . Present my kindest regards to your brave sons who aided in our struggle for State rights and Constitutional government. We failed, but in the good providence of God, apparent failure often proves a blessing. I trust it may eventuate so in this instance."

General Lee's modest salary of three thousand dollars was sufficient for a man with habits of such simplicity. When an effort was made to increase his remuneration, his refusal to accept was thus expressed: " I already receive a larger amount from the college than my services are worth." When the trustees settled upon him and his family the president's house and a liberal annuity, he declined them; after his death, his wife ratified for herself this action of her husband. Several times the offer was made him of large remuneration to serve as president of different commercial organisations, but all these offers he declined. When certain eulogistic verses were pressed upon him, he answered thus:

" I feel that I have no claim to such oblation, and have a general disinclination to be brought before the public without good and sufficient reason."

To an ambitious female author he sent this message:

" I am sensible of the implied compliment in your proposal to write a history of my life. I should be happy to see you in Lexington, but not on the errand you propose, for I know of nothing good I could tell of myself, and I fear I should not like to say any evil."

Now and then General Lee's quiet humour would manifest itself, and his love for children seemed to grow more intense. The following letter to his daughter gives us a glimpse of him in the winter of 1867:

". . . We are getting on in the usual way. Agnes takes good care of us, and is always thoughtful and attentive. It is very cold. The ground is covered with six inches of snow, and the mountains, as far as the eye can reach, elevate their white crests as monuments of winter. I must leave to your sisters a description of all the gayeties, and also an account of the ' Reading Club.' As far as I can judge, it is a great institution for the discussion of apples and chestnuts, but is quite innocent of the pleasures of literature.

" Our feline companions are flourishing. Young Baxter is growing in gracefulness and favour, and gives cat-like evidences of future worth. He indulges in the fashionable colour of ' moonlight on the lake '—apparently a dingy hue of the kitchen—and is strictly aristocratic in appearance and conduct. Tom, surnamed the ' Nipper,' from the manner in which he slaughters our enemies the rats and mice, is admired for his gravity and sobriety, as well as his strict attention to the pursuits of his race. They both feel your absence sorely. Traveller and Custis are both well, and pursue their usual dignified gait and habits. . . ."

Lee gave much anxious thought to the moral and religious training of the students in the college. His devout personal piety increased with his years, and his prayers were continually offered in behalf of those committed to his charge. He said with much emotion :

"I shall be disappointed,—I shall fail in the leading object that brought me here, unless these young men all become consistent Christians."

At length the end drew nigh. Since the campaign of 1863, Lee had been troubled with rheumatism in the region of the heart. In September, 1868, he wrote to his son, " My life is very uncertain." In October, 1869, the rheumatic trouble became more acute, and in March, 1870, he wrote as follows :

" My health has been so feeble this winter that I am only waiting to see the effect of the opening spring before relinquishing my present position. I am admonished by my feelings that my years of labour are nearly over and my inclinations point to private life."

In this same month, accompanied by his daughter
Agnes, he sought the mild climate of Georgia.   On
the trip southward he paid a visit to the grave of his
daughter Annie, at Warrenton, in North Carolina.
Of this visit he wrote:

> " I have always promised myself to go, and I think if I am to
> accomplish it I have no time to lose.   I wish to witness her quiet
> sleep, with her dear hands crossed over her breast, as it were, in mute
> prayer, undisturbed by her distance from us, and to feel that her
> pure spirit is roaming in bliss in the land of the blessed."

From the city of Savannah he wrote as follows,
on April 18:

> " We visited Cumberland Island, and Agnes decorated my father's
> grave with beautiful fresh flowers.   I presume it is the last time I
> shall be able to pay it my tribute of respect.   The cemetery is un-
> harmed and the graves are in good order, though the house of
> ' Dungeness' has been burned and the island devastated.   I hope I
> am better.   I know that I am stronger, but I still have the pain in
> my chest whenever I walk.   I have felt it, too, occasionally recently
> when quiescent."

September 28, 1870, after a day of arduous
labours, he stood at his table to ask God's blessing
upon the evening meal.   Not a syllable fell from his
lips and he sank into a chair.   The pain in the chest
had wellnigh completed its fatal work.   The family
continued to watch at his bedside with tender min-
istrations; from day to day they indulged the hope
that the beloved husband and father would yet be
spared.   The heart of the entire people of the South
ascended to Heaven with the petition that his days
might be prolonged.   But he knew that the end
was at hand.   His mind was clear and the look of

peace was upon his face. In the closing hours
the great spirit, like that of the dying Jackson,
seemed to visit again the field of battle. His last
words were these: " Tell Hill he must come up ! "
At half-past nine o'clock on the morning of October
12, 1870, Robert E. Lee entered into glory everlasting. His body lies in the mausoleum erected
at the rear of the college chapel, and beside him
are laid his wife and his daughter Agnes. Above
the tomb, and visible from the chapel hall, is Valen-
tine's recumbent marble figure of Lee the soldier
taking his rest, with his sword sheathed at his side
and his martial cloak around him. Beneath the
creeping ivy in this quiet abode reposes all that is
mortal of him who abides in the hearts of his countrymen as ideal soldier and as perfect man.

INDEX.

459